DICTIONARY BUYING GUIDE

Dictionary Buying Guide

*A Consumer Guide to General
English-Language Wordbooks in Print*

Kenneth F. Kister

R.R. Bowker Company
NEW YORK & LONDON, 1977

"The question is," said Alice, "whether you can make words mean so many different things."

"The question is," said Humpty Dumpty, "which is to be master—that's all."

LEWIS CARROLL, *Through the Looking Glass*

Published by R.R. Bowker Company
1180 Avenue of the Americas, New York, N.Y. 10036
Copyright © 1977 by Xerox Corporation
All rights reserved
Printed and bound in the United States of America

Library of Congress Cataloging in Publication Data

Kister, Kenneth F   1935–
  Dictionary buying guide.

  Bibliography: p.
  Includes index.
  1. English language—Dictionaries—Biography.
2. English language—Lexicography. I. Title.
Z2015.D6K57 [PE1611]   016.423   77-15010
ISBN 0-8352-1038-3

CONTENTS

ADULT DICTIONARIES (Cont.)

SCHOOL AND CHILDREN'S DICTIONARIES

SCHOOL AND CHILDREN'S DICTIONARIES (Cont.)

SPECIAL-PURPOSE DICTIONARIES AND WORDBOOKS (Cont.)

SPECIAL-PURPOSE DICTIONARIES AND WORDBOOKS (Cont.)

SPECIAL-PURPOSE DICTIONARIES AND WORDBOOKS (Cont.)

SYNONYMS, ANTONYMS, AND HOMONYMS (Cont.)

CROSSWORD PUZZLES AND WORD GAMES

RHYMES — 280

SPECIAL-PURPOSE DICTIONARIES AND WORDBOOKS (Cont.)

SPECIAL-PURPOSE DICTIONARIES AND WORDBOOKS (Cont.)

APPFNDIXES

PREFACE

Dictionary Buying Guide is for consumers in the market for a reliable dictionary. The guide is especially designed to assist individuals—parents, students, educators, word buffs, gift givers, secretaries, professional people of all kinds— who want authoritative information about the numerous and sometimes indistinguishable dictionaries currently available from American publishers and distributors. The guide should also prove useful to librarians and teachers as a reference and selection aid.

The *Buying Guide* reviews 58 general adult English-language dictionaries, ranging from the largest unabridged works (e.g., *Webster's Third New International Dictionary*) to very small pocket items (e.g., the *Langenscheidt Lilliput Webster English Dictionary*). The guide also evaluates approximately 60 school and children's dictionaries, from those especially prepared for high school students (e.g., the *Thorndike-Barnhart Advanced Dictionary*) to picture dictionaries for preschoolers (e.g., *The Strawberry Picture Dictionary*).

Some 225 special-purpose dictionaries and wordbooks which complement or supplement general dictionaries (such as etymological, usage, slang, synonym, and pronunciation dictionaries) are likewise covered, though much more concisely.

All dictionaries and wordbooks included in the *Buying Guide* are currently in print (as of August 1977), unless otherwise indicated, as in the case of the discontinued titles described in Appendix A. In-print titles can ordinarily be acquired through local bookstores or, where libraries and schools are concerned, through book jobbers or publisher representatives. Pertinent bibliographic and order information is provided for each title.

The author of *Dictionary Buying Guide* is ultimately responsible for the opinions and data in the book. Critical input derived from several sources, including published reviews and commentaries in such standard reference guides as Katz' *Basic Information Sources*, Cheney's *Fundamental Reference Sources*, and Sheehy's *Guide to Reference Books*. A list of the significant publications consulted appears in Appendix B under "Additional Sources for Dictionary Evaluations." Five academic and library subject consultants, commissioned by the R. R. Bowker Company, comparatively analyzed entries in the major dictionaries. The author gratefully acknowledges the contribution of these consultants: Dr. Anthony Llewellyn (Professor, College of Engineering, University of South Florida, Tampa); Dr. Richard L. Mansell (Professor, College of Natural Sciences, University of South Florida, Tampa); Jess Mullen (Head, Humanities-History Department, Tampa-Hillsborough Public Library, Florida); Elliot I. Ravetz (formerly Readex

Microprint Corporation, New York, N.Y.); and Clarice M. Ruder (Assistant Head, Special Collections Department, Tampa-Hillsborough Public Library, Florida).

A three-member *Dictionary Buying Guide* Advisory Board offered professional advice and counsel throughout the project. Although not responsible for the guide's critical content, board members provided invaluable suggestions on the book's scope, organization, and overall development. The author cannot sufficiently thank the following librarians who served on the Advisory Board: Dr. Jack A. Clarke (Professor, Library School, University of Wisconsin at Madison); Allan J. Dyson (Director, Moffitt Undergraduate Library, University of California, Berkeley); and Eleanor Radwan (Head of General Reference Services, Mid-Manhattan Library, New York Public Library).

With only a few exceptions, dictionary publishers and distributors graciously cooperated with the *Buying Guide* project. All of the major publishers promptly sent review copies and often went out of their way to provide information about individual titles or their lexicographical operations. Everyone associated with the guide sincerely thanks the publishers for their cooperation.

Dictionary Buying Guide continues *English Language Dictionaries in Print,* published by Bowker in 1965 and again in 1969 as part of *Home Reference Books in Print.* The *Buying Guide,* however, is a completely new publication. Its scope and critical range are significantly broader than *English Language Dictionaries in Print* which covered less than 100 titles. Bowker editors naturally contributed suggestions about the guide's coverage and format, but by general agreement Bowker personnel had no role in the process of evaluating individual titles. For their editorial support, knowledge, and understanding, the author is particularly indebted to Nancy Volkman, Bowker Sponsoring Editor; Judy S. Garodnick, Bowker Acquisitions Editor; and Desmond F. Reaney, Manager, Bowker Book Editorial Department.

Kenneth F. Kister

HOW TO USE THIS BOOK

There are an enormous number of dictionaries available for home, office, and school use. Obviously they vary widely in size, quality, depth of information, intended user suitability, recency, price, and so on. No one dictionary is "best" for everyone's needs. The main function of this book is to find that dictionary which best meets *your* individual needs.

Arrangement

The book provides information about dictionaries from the general to the specific. Part I begins with a discussion not of specific titles but dictionaries as a type of reference work. Part I concludes with two charts which offer a quick statistical overview of the general dictionaries covered in the guide. Finally, the profiles in Part II evaluate specific titles.

The serious prospective dictionary buyer is advised to read Part I before consulting the charts or the individual profiles. The chapter "A Word about Dictionaries" briefly discusses the purpose and contents of dictionaries, notes the kinds of dictionaries on the market, traces the historical development of English-language dictionaries, points up the main principles and techniques of modern lexicography, attempts to throw some light on possibly confusing terminology (what does *unabridged* mean?), and explains how dictionaries are sold. "Choosing the Right Dictionary" offers specific consumer advice on shopping for dictionaries, including how to examine a dictionary critically using the evaluative criteria established by the *Buying Guide*.

The comparative statistical charts which follow should be consulted next. These charts include quantitative information in convenient tabular form about comparable dictionaries in the general adult category and then the school and children's category. By studying the appropriate chart, the prospective purchaser can readily identify those titles which meet the simple requirements of size and price. In this manner, the consumer can zero in on those dictionaries which, at least at first glance, appear to be potentially good buys. The charts will also be useful to librarians and publishers as a source of comparative data.

After consulting Part I of the *Buying Guide*, dictionary consumers will have some fundamental understanding of what dictionaries are about and which of the many titles on the market might best serve their particular needs. The next step is to study the appropriate profiles in Part II.

The profiles are arranged in three broad categories: Adult Dictionaries; School and Children's Dictionaries; and Special-Purpose Dictionaries and

Wordbooks. As shown in the table of contents, these categories are subdivided by dictionary function or size. The category Adult Dictionaries, for instance, is divided into four dictionary types based on size: *unabridged* (dictionaries containing 250,000 or more entries); *semi-unabridged* (130,000–250,000 entries); *abridged* (55,000–130,000 entries); and *pocket* (under 55,000 entries). Profiles are arranged alphabetically by title within each subdivision. For example, profiles in the semi-unabridged section of Adult Dictionaries begin with *The American College Dictionary* and end with *The World Book Dictionary*. NOTE: The index at the back of the guide should always be consulted for specific titles not readily found in the text.

Profiles of the major general dictionaries consist of analyses based on such standard evaluative criteria as purpose and scope, authority, use of graphics, quality of physical format, and, most important, treatment of vocabulary. Are the definitions current? Clear? Accurate? Comprehensive? Are illustrative quotations or examples provided? Are etymologies included and are they understandable to the layperson? Does the dictionary provide references to synonyms and antonyms when appropriate? Are they discriminated—that is, are shades of meaning explained? A summary statement which provides an overall assessment of the dictionary being evaluated—along with brief comparative comments on dictionaries of like size, scope, usership, and cost—concludes each profile. Citations to recent reviews are attached for the convenience of those users of the *Buying Guide* who want additional critical opinions.

Profiles of the smaller adult dictionaries, school and children's dictionaries, and special-purpose wordbooks are less detailed. They include standard descriptive information, concise evaluative comments, and, when possible, references to other recent critical opinions. In some instances, a "Consumer Note" follows the descriptive information. Such notes concern works which are evaluated more fully elsewhere in the *Buying Guide*, often under a different title.

The guide has three appendixes. Appendix A identifies recently discontinued dictionaries. Such dictionaries are no longer available from the original publisher but might be encountered in secondhand bookstores or in discount stores as remainder stock. Appendix B, "Dictionary Bibliography," includes a selected reading list of books and articles about dictionaries, as well as an annotated listing of additional sources for critical information about dictionaries. Appendix C is a directory of publishers and distributors of general dictionaries and special-purpose wordbooks in the United States. The directory includes both addresses and telephone numbers.

A title-author-subject index completes the book. The index should always be checked for individual authors or editors and for specific titles. Detailed subjects can also be located through the index. For example, there is a discussion of word frequency lists in the introduction to school and children's dictionaries. Access to this topic is found under such index entries as *Semantic counts*, *Word frequency studies*, and *Frequency (word) studies*.

Methodology

Practically all the general dictionaries evaluated in the *Buying Guide* were analyzed from review copies provided by the publishers. Opinions found in other published reviews and standard reference guides were taken into account, but the final assessment of each title is based largely on a detailed analysis of approximately 100 entries in the larger dictionaries and at least 25 entries in the smaller ones. The sample entries were preselected by the author of the *Buying Guide* and analyzed by him or one of the subject consultants. In the case of the consultants, sample entries were identified by code rather than dictionary title to insure unbiased analysis.

The sample entries, which were used to evaluate both vocabulary coverage and treatment, represent a broad cross section of standard and nonstandard English, new and old words and phrases, and some technical nomenclature encountered in popular reading matter or textbooks at the high school level. Terms checked and analyzed include aesthetic, bunco, burthen, busing (or bussing), buttress, capable, cell, certiorari, cholestasis, conceit, creek, crude, data bank, decoupage, deep-six, deep space, derisible, détente, dicey, discernible/discernable, ekistics, Existentialism, facetious, fast, flat-out, formalism, fuck, funky, futile, gay, gene, going to the dogs, groupie, happening, hard-core, hoagie (or hoagy), holism, honcho, impressionist, inalienable/unalienable, irregardless, jaw, jawbone (or jawboning), kerogen, laetrile, launder, leverage, lift, mace, macrame, mad, medicaid, mensch, meridan, minibike, misandry, mix, mixed drink, mob, modulus, motor home, New Left, nitrofurantoin, Orwellian, oscillation, oxygen cycle, Pap smear, pathetic, patrifocal, photovoltaic, plea bargaining, radiation, recision, redneck, renovascular, reprography, residual, revanchism, self-destruct, shtick (or schtick), sic, sizable/sizeable, spaced-out, stare decisis, timesharing, tour de force, ultrafiche, upfront, visualization, Wankel engine, and yesterday.

Price and Other Data

Price information is provided at the beginning of each profile under "Descriptive Information" and, in the case of general adult and school and children's dictionaries, in the charts in Part I. The figure given represents the price quoted at the time the *Buying Guide* went to press in late 1977. Prices are subject to change by the publishers at any time.

In most instances, statistics like the number of total entries or visual illustrations are data provided by the publishers and verified by the *Buying Guide* via sample counts. Some statistics, however, are derived from counts initiated and conducted by the *Buying Guide*, most notably those figures which indicate the average number of words per entry in a given dictionary.

Exclusions

Dictionary Buying Guide attempts to evaluate all in-print general English-language dictionaries and related special-purpose wordbooks. Excluded from the guide are nonlexical works such as biographical, genealogical, and geographical dictionaries. Reprints of eighteenth-, nineteenth-, and early twentieth-century dictionaries, which are of historical interest to lexicographers but of limited contemporary usefulness, are not included. Likewise, research dictionaries which cover specific historical periods and nationalities (such as the *Middle English Dictionary* and *The Scottish National Dictionary*) are excluded. Also excluded are quotation dictionaries (such as Bartlett's *Familiar Quotations*), subject dictionaries (e.g., the *McGraw-Hill Dictionary of Modern Economics*), and encyclopedic works which call themselves dictionaries (e.g., *The Dictionary of American History*). These latter types of reference works will be evaluated in Bowker's forthcoming *Encyclopedias & Dictionaries for Specialists*.

Cross-References

The *Buying Guide* contains numerous references comparing one dictionary with another. Unless otherwise noted, all dictionaries referred to in a comparative manner are evaluated in Part II of the guide. Comparative references, therefore, may also be used as cross-references.

Other Critical Opinions

Reviews cited at the end of the dictionary profiles are ordinarily limited to those published in the 1970s. In most cases, reviews published prior to that time are so dated as to be of little value to present-day consumers. Major reviews are noted, however, no matter what the date. Review sources consistently cited are *American Reference Books Annual*, The Reference and Subscription Books Review Committee in *Booklist*, *Library Journal*, *RQ*, Charles A. Bunge in *Wilson Library Bulletin*, and Bill Katz's *Basic Information Sources* (2nd ed., 1974).

DICTIONARY BUYING GUIDE

I

GENERAL INFORMATION

A WORD ABOUT DICTIONARIES

Everyday our world seems to move faster and faster, propelled by the relentless force of new technical, political, and social developments. Americans have been to the moon and back. The "pill" has altered our sexual attitudes. We stand on the brink of a genetic revolution. Race and sex barriers to equal opportunity are under vigorous attack on many fronts. Television, drugs, crime, Vietnam, Watergate, the energy crisis, rock music, inflation, and interstate highways are phenomena which have had a startling impact on the way we as a society live and think. And write and speak.

For good or for ill, our language reflects the volatile world in which we live. Vogue words are here today and gone tomorrow, like miniskirts and maxicoats. Word meanings change overnight. Consider the term *chauvinism*, which ordinarily meant blind patriotism until the women's movement came along. Yesterday's noun is today's verb. Not long ago, for instance, the noun *parent* produced the verb *to parent*. Now *priority* has spawned *to prioritize*. New words are coined faster than you can say *bloviation*. In a recent book about Edward Kennedy, the senator is said to have been *Chappaquiddickized*—that is, stripped of his political prestige by a fateful accident. *Chappaquiddickized* is a coinage not likely to get into the dictionaries, unless of course enough people begin using it. The word *gerrymander*, for instance, entered the American vocabulary in a similar manner and it is still used today. Ours is a living and therefore constantly changing language. Moreover, perhaps because we are a pluralistic and democratic people, Americans feel free to ignore or flout the established rules of language with more gusto than practically any other nationality.

Verbal and written communication, however, requires some agreement among users of the language about the generally accepted meaning, spelling, hyphenation, pronunciation, and usage of the words and phrases which make up the language. Dictionaries serve this function. They record established facts and attitudes about our vocabulary, thus to some degree standardizing the language based on current usage. In a quality dictionary, for example, such similar sounding but dissimilar words as *egoism* and *egotism* will be clearly and accurately differentiated. Dictionaries also assist with vocabulary building (what does *egoism* mean?) and aid language study through the provision of etymologies (what is the origin of *egoism*?), synonyms and antonyms, parts of speech, and the like. On the most elementary level, dictionaries provide quick, basic reference information about words, word elements (such as prefixes and affixes), abbreviations, compound words (e.g., *mixed drink*), and idiomatic phrases (e.g., *kettle of fish*).

Small wonder, then, that general dictionaries are found in practically every home, office, school, and library. Or that between eight and ten million dictionaries are sold each year in the United States alone. Indeed, dictionaries outnumber television sets in this country. But, like television, dictionaries are sometimes either misused or not utilized to their fullest potential. In some cases a person may simply be using the wrong type of dictionary. You cannot expect a small pocket dictionary, for example, to do the work of an unabridged edition. Or the user may be uncertain about how the dictionary—a book of many complicated space-saving devices—actually works. Perhaps the user has not taken the time to discover, for instance, that etymologies are included in the dictionary, or if so, where they are located, or how to interpret them. It is important at the outset to know what types of general dictionaries are available and how to utilize their contents most effectively.

TYPES OF DICTIONARIES

Dictionaries can be grouped into five broad types based on function. These are: (1) general English-language dictionaries which serve the vocabulary needs of most adults and students; (2) special-purpose dictionaries and wordbooks which complement or supplement general dictionaries, such as slang and pronunciation dictionaries, thesauri, and usage manuals; (3) research dictionaries which cover the historical periods of English, such as Anglo-Saxon, as well as regional dialects and archaic and obsolete words; (4) foreign-language or translating dictionaries which provide definitions or equivalent words in two or more languages; and (5) subject dictionaries which treat the specialized vocabulary of a particular field of study, for instance, physics or economics. There are also numerous reference works dealing with people, places, and things which, because of their alphabetical or "dictionary" arrangement, are called dictionaries. Examples are the *Dictionary of American Biography, Webster's New Geographical Dictionary,* and the *Dictionary of Inventions and Discoveries.* As previously noted, the *Buying Guide* is concerned with the first two types of dictionaries.

General English-language dictionaries are divided into those compiled for adults and those designed especially for use in schools and by children. Adult dictionaries, which range from the huge *Webster's Third New International Dictionary* (12 pounds; 460,000 entries) to the tiny *Langenscheidt Lilliput Webster English Dictionary* (½ ounce; 7,000 entries), are further divided into four categories based on size. These are: unabridged; semi-unabridged; abridged; and pocket.

The term *unabridged* popularly refers to the largest general adult dictionaries available. Most (though not all) authorities include dictionaries of 250,000 or more entries in the unabridged category. *Unabridged* also implies that the dictionary has been prepared from scratch and not based on a larger work. Unabridged dictionaries are also physically large, requiring a stand or special library shelf. In yet another sense, *unabridged* suggests completeness—that is, a dictionary which includes all words and word elements in the language. No single dictionary can possibly provide an exhaustive record of our rich and varied vocabulary. Indeed, English contains far more words than any other language in the world—millions of them if all technical, informal, and rare terms are counted. Unabridged dictionaries do attempt, however, to include all standard "live"—or currently active—words. Estimates say that at any given time there are about 340,000 live words in the English language. Why is it, then, that *Webster's Third New International Dictionary* contains 460,000 entries? Or that its illustrious predecessor, *Webster's New International Dictionary* (Second Edition, 1934), boasted 600,000 entries? Can *The Random House Dictionary of the English Language* (Unabridged Edition), with *only* 260,000+ entries, properly be considered "unabridged"? In the final analysis, the term *unabridged*, when applied to dictionaries, is ambiguous and relative. Even lexicographers are unable to agree on a firm definition of the term.

Semi-unabridged, another less than satisfactory term for classifying adult dictionaries, denotes those in the 130,000–250,000 entry class. Dictionaries in this category are usually desk-size and normally contain between 150,000 and 175,000 entries. They are often designed explicitly with the college community in mind, as representative titles of semi-unabridged dictionaries indicate: *The American College Dictionary; Funk & Wagnalls Standard College Dictionary; New Webster's Dictionary* (College Edition); *The Random House College Dictionary; Webster's New Collegiate Dictionary;* and *Webster's New World Dictionary* (Second College Edition). Such dictionaries make a particular effort to include vocabulary likely to be encountered in the college curriculum, such as literary terms, historical movements, and scientific theories. Sometimes semi-unabridged dictionaries are simply called "college" dictionaries.

Abridged signifies adult dictionaries containing between 55,000 and 130,000 entries. Designed principally for use in the home or office, abridged dictionaries usually contain 60,000–80,000 words, representing the hardcore live vocabulary of the language. Frequently, abridged dictionaries are scaled-down versions of unabridged or semi-unabridged editions. For example, *The Concise Heritage Dictionary* (55,000 entries) is based on the 155,000-entry *American Heritage Dictionary*. However, the two newest titles in the abridged class—*The Doubleday Dictionary* and *The Scribner-Bantam English Dictionary*—are unrelated to any larger dictionary. It should also be noted that, with the exception of the Second College Edition of *Webster's New World Dictionary* (158,000 entries), all general adult dictionaries currently available in paperbound editions fall into the abridged or pocket category. Abridged dictionaries are sometimes referred to as "concise" or "desk" dictionaries. The fourth and final category of adult dictionaries is *pocket*, which signifies quite small and usually insignificant works under 55,000 entries. Frequently pocket dictionaries are published in paperback.

The other broad group of general English-language dictionaries—those for school and children's use—are categorized by educational levels. School dictionaries usually range in size from 25,000 to 95,000 entries, depending on the level of intended use. The Merriam-Webster school series illustrates the typical spread: *Webster's New Elementary Dictionary* (32,000 entries); *Webster's Intermediate Dictionary* (57,000 entries); and *Webster's New Students Dictionary* (81,000 entries). With the possible exception of *The World Book Dictionary* (225,000 entries), which combines features of both the semi-unabridged and school dictionary, all school dictionaries are abridged. School dictionaries of substance, however, base their vocabulary entries on scientifically prepared word frequency counts which show how often a particular word appears in various types of literature, and at what grade level. There are also a number of smaller, less sophisticated dictionaries prepared for young children. Such dictionaries ordinarily contain from 500 to 5,000 words and are heavily illustrated with colorful drawings.

Special-purpose dictionaries and wordbooks are logically divided by function, such as etymology, slang, usage, synonyms, pronunciation, spelling, and abbreviations. These wordbooks cover the lexical waterfront and serve as indispensable adjuncts to general dictionaries.

INSIDE THE DICTIONARY

Dictionaries are complicated reference tools. The large unabridged dictionary has been called "a masterpiece of condensation" and indeed all dictionaries, no matter what their size, offer an enormous amount of information compressed into a relatively small space. Although the quality and quantity of information will vary from dictionary to dictionary, the dictionary format (or makeup) is well established and adhered to by practically all lexicographers. Almost without exception, general dictionaries include the following information:

1. *Main Entries.* Main (or vocabulary) entries are printed in boldface type. The entry may be a common word, a proper name (person, place, event, idea, etc.), a word element (e.g., a suffix like *-ness*), an abbreviation or acronym, a compound word (e.g., *doggie bag*), or an idiomatic phrase (e.g., *go to the dogs*). In most dictionaries, idiomatic phrases like *go to the dogs* will be treated as subentries of the main word, i.e., *dog.* Main entries are almost always arranged alphabetically, letter-by-letter (e.g., *firearm* precedes *fire escape*).

2. *Spelling and Syllabication.* How do you spell *sizable?* Or is it *sizeable?* Preferred and variant spellings are given when appropriate. Syllabication (or word division) is shown for all entries and variants.

3. *Pronunciation.* Pronunciation information varies in complexity and ease of understanding from dictionary to dictionary. Nearly all lexicographers use a method which entails phonetic respelling, diacritical marks, and accent marks. The phonetic respelling utilizes symbols which more closely approximate speech sounds than does our alphabet, which is quite limited as a guide to pronunciation. Diacritical marks indicate specific vowel sounds, and accent marks note which syllables are stressed in pronunciation. Variant or regional pronunciations may be provided. A pronunciation key is always included, usually at the very front of the dictionary with a condensed version at the bottom of each page spread.

4. *Parts of Speech.* The grammatical classification of each entry (noun, pronoun, verb, adjective, adverb, etc.) is indicated, usually following the pronunciation.

5. *Definitions.* Dictionaries are most frequently consulted for spelling, pronunciation, and the meaning of words; probably the most important of these is the meaning of words. Definitions account for the bulk of a dictionary's contents. How thoroughly vocabulary entries are defined depends on the size and quality of the dictionary involved. Larger dictionaries include both general and specialized meanings, each definition (or word sense) being

numbered and presented in some logical order. The order might be historical, with the earliest meaning given first and so on to the most recent. Or the order might be based on frequency of use, with the most common meaning first. Good dictionaries will provide both denotative (exact or literal) and connotative (implied or suggested) meanings. The word *home*, for example, literally means where a person lives but the word also implies a warm, congenial environment. Homographs—words spelled the same way but different in meaning—are usually treated as separate entries. For instance, the word *cow* will be a main entry as a noun (the animal) and as a verb (to intimidate).

    6. *Etymology.* Abbreviated notations indicating word origin and development either precede the definitions or follow immediately thereafter. Etymologies can provide a better understanding of a word's core meaning. For example, the word *fraternal* originated from the Latin *frater*, meaning "brother."

    7. *Inflected Forms.* Verbs, nouns, pronouns, adjectives, and adverbs change their forms depending on how they are used grammatically. Nouns and pronouns, for example, can be singular or plural (e.g., *goose/geese; I/we*). Pronouns have different cases to indicate who is acting and who is receiving (*we/us*). Verbs express time change by forming different tenses (*run/ran/run*). Adjectives have comparative and superlative forms (*warm/warmer/warmest*). In most cases, dictionaries do not enter inflected forms when the formation is regular. An example of a regular formation is the noun *dog* which forms its plural by adding -*s* (*dogs*) or the verb *walk* which forms its past tense and past participle by adding -*ed* (*walk/walked/walked*). But when, as frequently happens in the English language, the inflected form is irregular, as in the case of the noun *goose* (the plural is *geese*, not *gooses*) or the verb *throw* (*throw/threw/thrown*), the dictionary will most likely enter inflected forms as subentries under the main entry.

    8. *Run-on Entries.* Words created by adding or dropping suffixes such as -*ity*, -*ment*, and -*ous* are called run-on entries (or run-on derivatives or simply run-ons). An example is *cancer/cancerous*. Except in the largest dictionaries, run-ons are not entered separately but, like inflected forms, as subentries of the main entry.

    9. *Usage Labels.* Lexicographers use a variety of labels to indicate restrictive or special usage of certain words and phrases. Usage labels may show that a word is used chiefly in a particular country or geographical locality (e.g., New England). They may show that a word is no longer used with the same currency as it once was (and is thus labeled "archaic" or "obsolete"). Finally, such labels may indicate that a word has limited social or cultural status (denoted by labels like "slang," "colloquial," "illiterate," "vulgar," "informal," "substandard," and "nonstandard"). This latter category of usage labels has generated strident controversy in recent years. How lexicographers employ such tags as "slang" and "nonstandard" goes to the heart of a long-standing dispute about the dictionary's cultural role. Should the dictionary provide ironclad rules about "correct" usage or should its function be to describe, as objectively as possible, how the language is used at a given time—not how it should be used? This question is discussed in more detail below, under "Dictionary Trends."

    10. *Illustrative Quotations and Examples.* Larger dictionaries frequently provide quotations by writers, both contemporary and historical, which illustrate how particular words and phrases have been used in standard literature and popular sources like newspapers and mass-market magazines. Such quotations help to define words by showing their use in context. This technique is especially helpful in explaining the connotative senses of a word. Dictionaries may also include illustrative examples—made-up sentences and phrases—for the purpose of "forcing" definitional clarity.

11. *Synonyms and Antonyms.* Words of similar meaning (synonyms) and opposite meaning (antonyms) may be given for selected entries. Synonyms for the word *meager,* for example, might include *scanty, skimpy,* and *sparse,* with *ample* and *copious* as typical antonyms. Better dictionaries also provide synonymies or paragraph-length notes which discriminate shades of meaning among synonymous words.

12. *Graphics.* Drawings, diagrams, photographs, and other types of pictorial illustrations are often included to help define words visually. By way of example, the definition of the term *buttress* is made much clearer when accompanied by a line drawing or similar graphic.

13. *Supplementary Information.* Practically all general dictionaries include some nonlexical information—that is, material not directly related to words and their meanings. Such information is either located in the main body of the dictionary or in appendixes and may include brief biographies of famous people, important place-names, population statistics, historical tables, weights and measures, symbols and signs, lists of colleges and universities, chronologies of presidents and other heads of state, style manuals and proofreaders' marks, famous quotations, first names of men and women, punctuation and capitalization rules, forms of address, business correspondence style, maps, and important documents. Most dictionaries also provide an overview of the development of the English language, usually as part of the front matter.

DICTIONARY TRENDS

Dictionaries as we know them are a modern invention. They owe their basic composition to lexicographical innovations introduced in the seventeenth and eighteenth centuries and their present format to refinements which have occurred over the past 150 or so years. It is true that the Greeks and Romans compiled lists of words and that in medieval times a great many glossaries appeared, usually designed to explain difficult Latin words of a theological nature. The first dictionary printed in England—*Promptorum Parvulorum sive clericorum* (1499)—was an English-Latin vocabulary. Not until 1604, however, was the first entirely English dictionary issued.

Compiled by Robert Cawdrey and cumbersomely entitled *A Table Alphabeticall, conteyning and teaching the true writing and understanding of hard usuall English wordes, borrowed from the Hebrew, Greeke, Latine, or French &c.*, the work was, in the words of language authority Bergen Evans, "ludicrously meager in comparison to any modern dictionary," containing only about 3,000 words. Cawdrey freely plagiarized existing sources and was not above smart-aleck definitions. For example, he defined *degenerate* as "unlike his auncestours." Nonetheless, despite its limitations, Cawdrey's dictionary was a success with England's growing reading public and opened the way for more substantial compilations, such as Henry Cockeram's *The English Dictionarie: or, an Interpreter of Hard English Words*. Published in 1623, Cockeram's work was the first English-language wordbook to call itself a "dictionary." At the turn of the century (1702), *A New English Dictionary* appeared. Its compiler, John Kersey the Younger, is credited with being the first professional English lexicographer.

Two decades later, Nathaniel Bailey's *Universal Etymological English Dictionary* (1721) was published. It remained popular throughout the eighteenth century, undergoing some 30 editions. Bailey's dictionary can justifiably be called the first modern English dictionary. It was the first dictionary to try to include all the words in the language, not just hard or difficult terms; it was the first to use illustrative examples; it was the first to provide etymologies; it was the first to include pronunciations, word divisions, and graphics. No wonder it was popular. And no wonder it served as the foundation for Samuel Johnson's great and famous dictionary.

Dr. Johnson's *Dictionary of the English Language* (1755) has been called "one of the intellectual landmarks of the English-speaking people." True, Johnson imitated most of Bailey's lexicographical techniques and made liberal use of his word stock. But whereas Bailey was simply a schoolmaster turned dictionary-maker, Johnson was an accomplished scholar, as his remarkably clear and complete definitions and 118,000 well-chosen illustrative quotations from the classical literature indicate (though his etymologies are not so revered). Above all, Johnson's dictionary is a work of major historical significance because it authoritatively conveyed the "correct" meaning, spelling, and pronunciation of the words treated therein. In point of fact, Johnson was commissioned by a group of London booksellers to compile the dictionary with this purpose expressly in mind. At the time, national academies in Europe—most notably the Académie Française, founded in 1635 by Cardinal Richelieu and Louis XIII—were engaged in laying down the linguistic law for the major languages on the continent. The London literary establishment of its day looked to Dr. Johnson to provide the same sort of immutable standard for the English language, to "preserve the purity of its idiom," to save it from vulgar "corruption." Johnson himself spoke in a letter to the novelist Samuel Richardson of his "toils in settling a language," but toward the end the lexicographer came to realize that a living language cannot stop growing and changing, that its development might be arrested for a time but not stopped. Nevertheless, ever since Johnson's work the general dictionary has been viewed by most English-speaking people as a linguistic lawgiver.

In this country, small dictionaries of British origin were widely used in schools during the eighteenth century, even after the Revolution. The New England schoolmaster, Noah Webster, in some ways America's Dr. Johnson, set about changing this in the early 1800s when he published his first *Compendious Dictionary of the English Language* (1806). Although roughly based on a British work (Entick's *Spelling Dictionary*), the *Compendious* was the first substantial dictionary to deal with the American use of English. Of the 37,000 words included, more than 5,000 were native to the youthful United States (e.g., *chowder, skunk, lengthy, applicant, presidency, selectman*, and *congressional*). Webster also introduced American spellings (e.g., *honor* instead of *honour, music* instead of *musick*, and *center* instead

of *centre*). In addition, as an advocate of simplified spelling, Webster shortened some words (e.g., *plow* instead of *plough*). In 1807, Webster published
an abridged version of the *Compendious* under the title *Dictionary for
Schools.*

If Dr. Johnson's mission was to fix the English language, Noah Webster's
was to Americanize it. Fiercely nationalistic, both politically and linguistically, Webster championed what he called the "American language." He
argued that English as used in the United States need not be considered
an inferior strain or corruption of British English, but rather a separate
branch of the language with its own standards of usage. Not surprisingly,
he cared little for Dr. Johnson's role as English-language czar. "English is in
a state of progression," Webster wrote with some feeling in his introduction
to the 1806 *Compendious*, "even more rapid than before the great Dr. Johnson flattered himself that he might fix the language and put a stop to altera-
tions." Webster also attacked Johnson's work for its "blunders" and "multitude of errors."

In 1828, Noah Webster issued his tour de force. Entitled *An American
Dictionary of the English Language* (originally advertised as *A Dictionary
of the American Language*), the dictionary achieved great popularity, noted
particularly for its clear, concise definitions and its establishment of uniquely
American usages. Indeed, the dictionary was a linguistic Declaration of
Independence from England. Just as important, however, it served as the
foundation for the outstanding line of Merriam-Webster dictionaries which
have catered to the vocabulary needs of Americans and others since the
mid-1800s.

While Noah Webster and later the G. & C. Merriam Company (the firm
acquired the rights to Webster's dictionaries after his death in 1843) were
aggressively popularizing English American-style in this country, linguistic
scholars abroad were developing a new, rigorously scientific lexicography
based on the concept of "historical principles." Essentially, the new lexicography entailed the systematic tracking of every word in the language since
Anglo-Saxon times back to its Indo-European roots and providing illustrative quotations (authenticated and dated) for every meaning, spelling, and
pronunciation of every word. A number of substantial scholarly dictionaries
have been published on historical principles but none is more important
or more awe-inspiring than the *Oxford English Dictionary*, commonly
called the *OED*. It contains 15,500 pages, over 414,000 entries, and a staggering 1,827,306 illustrative quotations. First published as *A New English
Dictionary* and later reissued with corrections as the *OED*, the multivolume
work took almost 70 years to complete from the time it was first proposed
in the mid-nineteenth century. Publication stretched over three editors and
40 years, from 1884 to 1928. A supplement appeared in 1933 and at the present
time four new supplements are being published. Significantly, the *OED*'s
rationale is not to "fix" the English language but to describe it with as much
scientific accuracy as the historical sources permit.

With the important exception of the application of electronic technology
to dictionary-making, twentieth-century lexicography has been concerned
largely with the same issues and developments—both commercial and
scholarly—that dominated the previous century. Various refinements of

technique have been introduced to make dictionaries easier to use or more accurate as word guides. For instance, Clarence Barnhart, one of this country's premier lexicographers, introduced the schwa (ə) in trade dictionaries in 1947 in *The American College Dictionary*. The schwa is a phonetic pronunciation symbol which represents the most frequently heard vowel sound in American English (the *a* in *alone*, the *e* in *system*, the *i* in *easily*, the *o* in *gallop*, and the *u* in *circus*). Another twentieth-century refinement is the semantic or word frequency count. The number of times each word appears within a sample body of literature is recorded. By such means lexicographers can determine how frequently a particular word is used in various types of literature. This information is most useful when selecting which words to include in a school or adult dictionary.

The persistent question of the dictionary's cultural function flared anew in 1961 with the publication of *Webster's Third New International Dictionary*, Merriam-Webster's current unabridged edition, sometimes simply called *W3*. Language purists who regarded Merriam-Webster's 1934 Second Unabridged Edition as the "voice of authority" and a bulwark against popular misusage were outraged to discover that *W3* was "permissive." The new edition did not, for example, righteously condemn the use of *irregardless*, considered by some to be the height of grammatical illiteracy, but merely labeled it "nonstand." Nor were such words as *corny* and *tacky* labeled at all, though some critics insisted they should be "slang" or "colloquial." Indeed, the editors of *W3* proclaimed that "No word is invariably slang," and they abolished the usage label "colloquial." An acrimonious debate ensued over whether a dictionary should be "prescriptive" (tell how the language should be used) or "descriptive" (tell how the language is used). J. Donald Adams, the late *New York Times Book Review* columnist, called *W3*, "a gigantic flop," sniffing that "after the examination I have given it, I shall never turn again to the new Merriam-Webster." The late Wilson Follett, a noted language authority, vented his anger in an *Atlantic Monthly* article entitled "Sabotage in Springfield" (Springfield, Massachusetts, being the home of Merriam-Webster). The dictionary had its defenders, but most of the heat came from linguistic conservatives. Doubtless the controversy will continue, not perhaps so much about *W3* itself, which has survived its most vituperative critics, but generally about the role of the dictionary as prescriber or describer—as lawgiver or reporter.

Another emotional issue concerns the so-called dirty words and terms of ethnic or racial denigration. Until recently, such words were not included in general dictionaries. Now, however, due to our more relaxed attitudes about literary censorship, the use of such hitherto taboo words as *shit* and *fuck* is commonplace in both written and conversational speech. Should dictionaries, then, include this sort of vulgar vocabulary or, as in the past, ignore it? "All modern dictionary editors," writes Norman Hoss ("Words," *Penthouse*, January 1974, p. 36), "have taken it for granted that it is as much a part of their responsibility to record 'fuck' as to record 'eat.' However, it was not until the end of the sixties that an American lexicographer was permitted his professional conscience by a publisher." Hoss is referring to William Morris and *The American Heritage Dictionary* (1969). Increasingly, lexicographers are putting the offensive words in their dictionaries. Certain people inevitably will disapprove—usually parents and school boards—and occasionally we hear that some dictionary or other has been expelled from school or home for dirty talk. But the trend in the 1970s is toward candor not prudery.

"Who used that dreadful expression 'making out'?"

COPYRIGHT 1962. REPRINTED BY PERMISSION OF *Saturday Review* AND B. TOBEY.

Unquestionably, however, the most important twentieth-century development, as far as lexicography is concerned, has been the steadily increasing use of computer technology to assist dictionary compilation. This practical development is discussed in the next section, "Making and Selling Dictionaries."

MAKING AND SELLING DICTIONARIES

Compiling and marketing a quality dictionary is an expensive business. Merriam-Webster reportedly spent $3½ million to produce its Third Unabridged Edition in 1961. Five years later the smaller *Random House Dictionary* cost nearly the same, and in 1969 *The American Heritage Dictionary* topped $4 million, at the time "the largest investment in a single volume in history," according to the publisher. Because of the heavy expense of producing a decent dictionary, fly-by-night publishers have been known to pass off reprints of old dictionaries as new works. Not long ago, for instance, an abridged Webster published originally in 1858 was being sold under the title *The Student's Reference Dictionary*. In other cases publishers obtain new copyrights based on minimal revisions, usually accomplished by squeezing in a new word here and deleting an old one there. Respectable publishers of course scrupulously avoid such shoddy practices.

How is a good dictionary put together? Obviously, the first ingredient is sufficient capital to support a long-term project. Clarence Barnhart, who knows the dictionary business inside out, puts it this way: "A commercial dictionary is a very heavy expense, expensive to set and expensive to write and edit (even if the writing and editing are poorly done). If a dictionary is to sell, these costs cannot be passed on to consumers immediately as they can with many other products. Usually publishers plan to recover costs within a period of five years, but it often takes longer." (Quoted from Barnhart's article "General Dictionaries" in *American Speech*, Fall 1969, p. 173.) Equally important to a dictionary's eventual success are qualified people. Every dictionary of any magnitude requires an experienced editor who is trained as a lexicographer. A knowledgeable editorial staff, as well as authoritative linguistic and subject consultants, are also necessary.

Once the financial and human resources are assembled, the editors must set about formulating a word list from which their final vocabulary entries will be selected. A common practice throughout the history of English and American lexicography has been to consult—or cannibalize— existing dictionaries. Robert Cawdrey's 1604 *Table Alphabeticall* freely borrowed from earlier bilingual glossaries, and Dr. Johnson, the lexicographer par excellence, carefully perused Bailey's dictionary. Today, however, editors are more likely to compile their own word lists from scratch, thanks to the computer. A computer-assisted analysis of a large literature sample will enable the lexicographer not only to identify existing words but to accurately determine which words are most frequently used in different types of literature. *The American Heritage Dictionary* (1969) utilized this technique, drawing its 155,000 entries from a one-million-word computerized sample.

At the same time, the editors begin constructing a citation file. Citations are documented examples showing how words have been used by various writers and speakers, past and present. For older words, dictionaries compiled on historical principles like the *OED* provide a rich source for citations, but for newer words and new meanings of old words, an in-house citation file is indispensable. A dictionary's scholarly authority and intellectual integrity rest squarely on the quality (though not necessarily the size) of its citation file. In England, the practice of using citations goes back to the eighteenth century and the creative genius of Nathaniel Bailey and Dr. Johnson, although citations were used previously in dictionaries produced in classical times and later by the European academies like the Académie Française. Significantly, the use of citations in dictionary-making is an acknowledgment that the people and not lexicographers are the final authority concerning language usage. "Johnson illustrated the meanings of words by quotations from the writings of well-known authors," notes Bergen Evans in *Today's Education* (February 1970, p. 25). "And in so doing, he established the lexicographic principle that language is what usage makes it and that custom, in the long run, is the ultimate and only court of appeal in linguistic matters."

Among the major English-language dictionary publishers, Oxford University Press in England and Merriam-Webster in this country maintain the largest citation files. Obviously, citation files are not built overnight. Merriam, which dates back to the mid-nineteenth century, currently has over 12 million citation cards and adds about 200,000 new ones each year. Merriam editors spend an average of two hours a day reading all kinds of publications—books, newspapers, magazines—in search of new words and new meanings or connotations of old words. The broadcast media, also a rich source for new words and usages, is monitored in a similar manner. When a new word or meaning is found, the information is recorded on a card called a citation slip. As citation slips accumulate for a particular term, they form the body of evidence needed by lexicographers to determine if the word or phrase should be added to the dictionary and, if so, what it means in various contexts. Right now, for instance, dictionary-makers are watching the citational evidence mount for the phrase *do a number on*. Collins+World, publisher of *Webster's New World Dictionary* and Merriam competitor, reports having more than 100 slips for *do a number on* as of early 1977. The phrase, according to the citations, first appeared in the late 1960s and meant "to deceive," but now usually means "to affect in some devious manner." Once the decision has been made to add a new term to the dictionary, the citation slips go to editorial specialists who treat all dictionary aspects of the term, such as definitions, spelling, pronunciation, part of speech, syllabication, inflected forms, and etymology.

The best lexicographers go about their work in the most scientific, impartial manner humanly possible. Yet anything that entails as many subjective judgments as does dictionary-making is bound to contain some bias, however unintentional. For example, Sidney Landau, a contemporary American lexicographer, has observed that "all modern American dictionaries, reflecting the prevailing technological bias of our culture, give disproportionate emphasis, both in their choice of entries and in the fullness with which those entries are treated, to terms that are quantifiable or that are used in one of the disciplines studied in the universities, as compared with those that are qualitative or general. Terms deemed to be susceptible to definition in the precise language of science . . . are given disproportionate space." (Quoted from Landau's article "Little Boy and Little Girl" in *American Speech*, Fall/Winter 1970, p. 203.) Notwithstanding, dictionary-makers have come a long way since the eighteenth century when Dr. Johnson rather unscientifically defined *lexicographer* as "a writer of dictionaries, a harmless drudge."

Computer application to lexicography, an important modern development, has not eliminated potential bias nor the need for human judgment in dictionary-making. Computers cannot, for example, write definitions, although if so programmed they can match up related words. Basically, computers are capable of assisting the dictionary-making process in three distinct ways. First, as mentioned earlier, computers facilitate language use studies which determine how frequently each word in a literature sample occurs. Such studies, which realistically must be undertaken with the aid of a computer because of the very large sample required if the results are to be considered valid, permit lexicographers to know what words are used in what types and levels of literature, and how the frequency of each word compares with that of all other words in the same sample. Prior to this century such word studies were unknown. As Henry Kučera remarks in his essay "Computers in Language Analysis and in Lexicography" (in the front matter of *The American Heritage Dictionary*), "Linguists and lexicographers alike have found in the computer a new and useful tool that has not only made the analysis of language less laborious and less time-consuming but has also opened new insights into important problems of language usage." (See *The American Heritage Dictionary* profile for more information.)

Second, computers are now being used during the dictionary's preparation to perform such routine mechanical chores as sorting and alphabetizing words and other vocabulary data. *The Random House Dictionary*, for instance, instructed one of its computers to organize its word stock into 158 subject areas. Computers accomplish such tedious tasks far more quickly and efficiently than humans can. And third, computers are beginning to play an active role in the dictionary revision and printing process. By punching the dictionary's text on magnetic tape and storing it in the computer's vast memory, entries which require revision can be automatically retrieved. Individual entries are flashed on the screen of a computer-connected device called the cathode-ray-tube console (which looks like an ordinary television set). Editors working at the console are able to transmit their revisions directly to the magnetic tape. Composition machines set the type directly from the corrected tape. This process not only saves time but, in the long run, cuts production costs.

Lexicography, it has been said, combines the techniques of both science and art. Perhaps Albert Marckwardt, the distinguished language scholar, has expressed it best: "The painstaking accumulation of reliable data, consisting of thousands upon thousands of individual facts of the language; the proper classification of this data; and finally the formulation of sound conclusions from this mass of material—all illustrate the inductive process that is basic in every science. At the same time, the presentation of information about the language, the phrasing of definitions, and the ordering of word treatments demand of the lexicographer the ability to manipulate the language with economy and precision. The science without the art is likely to be ineffective; the art without the science is certain to be inaccurate." (Quoted from Marckwardt's preface to *Funk & Wagnalls Standard College Dictionary*, 1974.)

Bags of money, a committed publisher, knowledgeable and dedicated lexicographers, a strong citation file, electronic hardware, and a compatible blend of art and science are the necessary ingredients for sound contemporary lexicography. There is, however, one other important requirement, namely, continuity within the dictionary-making operation. The language does not stop changing with the publication of a new dictionary or new edition. A successful dictionary operation requires that lexicographical work be an ongoing process—that work not cease or slow down after the completion of a project. In this respect, one of the major complaints about American dictionary-making is what one distinguished critic has called "one-shot dictionaries." Allen Walker Read explains: "When the project is finished, the star editors are not retained . . . so that any later work would have to start from scratch again. An ongoing dictionary department, such as those of the Clarendon Press at Oxford, the G. & C. Merriam Co., or Clarence L.

Barnhart, Inc., is a *sine qua non* before American lexicography will be on a sound basis." (Quoted from Read's "Approaches to Lexicography and Semantics" in *Current Trends in Linguistics*, no. 10, 1970, p. 163). Of course this brings us full circle back to the question of money, for it takes enormous financial resources to maintain a continuing professional staff of lexicographers and researchers.

How profitable are dictionaries? Not very. Although approximately eight to ten million copies are sold annually in the United States alone, dictionaries are priced comparatively low, considering the amount of information the purchaser gets and the relatively high editorial and production costs. Publishers are fortunate if they receive as much as 8 percent profit on their dictionary investments, a meager return compared with profit margins in some other areas of publishing. Large sustained sales volume, not price, is the key to whatever profitability there is in publishing dictionaries.

As a result, the merchandising of dictionaries is a highly competitive—even cutthroat—business. Various gimmicks which make good advertising copy are used to stimulate sales, though they have little or nothing to do with the dictionary's real purpose or true quality. Some publishers, for example, tack on page after page of encyclopedic information which is ballyhooed as a great addition to the book but which most people never think to look for in a dictionary. Other publishers indulge in the number's game, boasting about and sometimes exaggerating or padding the number of entries or illustrations or etymologies in their dictionaries. A unique and highly successful bit of recent lexicographical gimmickry involves *The American Heritage Dictionary* and its usage panel. Capitalizing on the publicity stirred up over Merriam-Webster's so-called permissiveness, the publishers of *The American Heritage Dictionary* invited various well-known people (Margaret Mead, Edwin Newman, Isaac Asimov, and 100 others) to offer their opinions on questions concerning proper usage. As a publicity item the panel has been an outstanding success, but is *The American Heritage Dictionary* the better for it? (For further information on this question, see the profile of *The American Heritage Dictionary* in the "semi-unabridged" section of the *Buying Guide*.)

Hard-sell efforts concentrate on large, identifiable markets, such as college students and the federal government, which together account for roughly 40 percent of all dictionary sales. It has been charged, for instance, that Merriam-Webster, by far the largest dictionary publisher in this country, deliberately and artificially keeps dictionary prices low in order to win government contracts for dictionaries which are awarded on a low-bid basis. Other publishers pour enormous sums into very pointed advertising. Over $1 million was spent to promote *The American Heritage Dictionary* when it first appeared in 1969. Much of the promotional pitch was geared to the college market, like the ad featuring two scowling students under the caption: "You don't buy your old man's ideas. Why buy your old man's dictionary?" The reference to Merriam-Webster was unmistakable. In other instances publishers allow marketing considerations to influence editorial content. *Webster's New World Dictionary*, for example, does not include possibly offensive words because, according to its editor, "I know we couldn't sell a copy in Texas if we put them in." And when *The American Heritage Dictionary* initially appeared in 1969 there was a special Texas edition which deleted such words as *shit* and *fuck*.

In view of such competitive tactics, how do you determine which dictionary is the best investment for the college student, the federal government, the home, office, you? The name "Webster," which once upon a time distinguished Noah Webster's dictionaries and later those of the highly reputable G. & C. Merriam Company, can now be used by any publisher and is therefore no longer a guide to dictionary quality. The next section of the *Buying Guide*—"Choosing the Right Dictionary"—provides a checklist of criteria for evaluating a general dictionary.

CHOOSING THE RIGHT DICTIONARY

In her introduction to the 25th anniversary edition of *The Fountainhead*, Ayn Rand says she would not change a word of her famous novel except to correct one error. "The error is semantic: the use of the word 'egotist' in Roark's courtroom speech, while actually the word should have been 'egoist.' The error was caused by my reliance on a dictionary which gave such misleading definitions of these two words that 'egotist' seemed closer to the meaning I intended." In this case, the writer was simply using the wrong dictionary. Whereas she needed a large, reliable dictionary, capable of distinguishing words like *egotist* and *egoist* with authority and in some depth, she was using a small abridged item called *Webster's Daily Use Dictionary* (no longer in print). Never mind that "Webster" was in the title. Today, as has been pointed out, the name "Webster" means absolutely nothing as far as dictionary quality is concerned. Any publisher may use "Webster" in a dictionary's title and, because the general public still mistakenly venerates the term, you can be assured that many dictionaries of poor quality—as well as many of good quality—will bear the name "Webster."

How does a person determine if a dictionary is any good or not? The simplest and most effective way is to ask the dictionary some questions. The more questions you ask, and the more cogent the questions are, and the more dictionaries you ask questions of, the more likely you are to find *that* dictionary which best suits your needs. Ayn Rand, for example, would have been better off if she had carefully compared *Webster's Daily Use Dictionary* with others on the market before relying on it to write a book which required some precision of language. In his wacky autobiographical novel *A Fan's Notes*, Fred Exley relates how he goes about evaluating a dictionary. "To gauge the dictionary's breadth when buying it, I had looked up *thurible*, an Oriental-looking container in which one burns incense, and *gorp*, a freakishly obese person who eats constantly because he achieves a kind of erotic splendor when sitting on the throne. The former was listed, the latter not, and because the latter never is listed, because I don't to this day know where I ever heard the word, and because it didn't seem likely I'd be called upon to use it, I bought the dictionary anyway—it was cheap."

A similar though more seriously applied procedure is used when the U.S. government buys dictionaries. According to the most recent specifications developed by the Federal Supply Service of the General Services Administration (U.S. Federal Specification G-D-331D for Dictionaries, English; June 28, 1974), any dictionary purchased by the government must contain at least 16 of the following 20 terms: computer; escalator; fluorescent lamp; fluoridation; guided missile; H-bomb; jet plane, jet airplane or jet engine;

laser; launch pad or launching pad; lift-off; medicare; NATO; penicillin; spacecraft or spaceship; sputnik; stereophonic; subway; supersonic; UN or U.N.; and Zip Code or zip code. Additional terms are required for dictionaries containing 130,000 entries or more. These terms include antimissile missile; ball-point pen; bioastronautics; brainwash or brainwashing; CIA; genocide; gobbledygook or gobbledegook; karate; overkill; Peace Corps; seat belt; SEATO; snowmobile; and Xerox. In addition to checking to see if such terminology is included in the dictionary, government inspectors perform sample entry counts and test the quality of the dictionary's paper, binding, and printing. The government, however, makes no effort to evaluate the quality of a dictionary's definitions, etymologies, illustrative examples, etc. Clarence Barnhart has called the federal government's criteria for selecting dictionaries "laughable."

Unlike encyclopedias, which are usually sold door-to-door, most in-print dictionaries are available in bookstores. If a specific title is not in stock, it can be ordered through the store from the publisher. Note that some publishers offer two editions of the same dictionary—the retail or "trade" edition is sold in bookstores whereas the school or "text" edition is sold directly to educational institutions.

Dictionary Buying Guide recommends that prospective purchasers examine various dictionaries prior to deciding which one to buy. Consult the appropriate chart which follows in the "Dictionaries at a Glance" section and select a number of titles which meet your basic requirements in terms of price and size. Then study the individual profiles of these dictionaries in Part II. After consulting the profiles, narrow your selections to three or four dictionaries and then go to a bookstore and personally examine each title. Ask each dictionary reasonable questions based on your own vocabulary needs and experience with words. For instance, Ayn Rand might ask, "What is the meaning of *egotism* and *egoism*?" Cross-examine each dictionary. Judge and compare the responses. The following checklist, "Criteria for Evaluating a Dictionary," provides guidelines for framing the right questions to determine the quality and utility of general dictionaries.

CRITERIA FOR EVALUATING A DICTIONARY

Purpose and Scope

For whom is the dictionary compiled? Is it designed for a particular usership or for general home and office use? Is the dictionary unabridged (over 250,000 entries), semi-unabridged (130,000–250,000 entries), abridged (55,000–130,000 entries), or pocket-size (under 55,000 entries)? Does it contain all of the following dictionary components: main entries (in bold type); spelling and pronunciation (including variants); syllabication (i.e., word division); parts of speech; definitions (including denotative and connotative senses); etymologies (i.e., word histories); inflected forms (i.e., word variations prompted by change in tense, case, number, gender, etc.); run-on entries (i.e., derivative words formed by adding or dropping suffixes); usage labels (which denote geographical, field, currency, or cultural restrictions on a word); illustrative quotations or examples (which show how a word is used in context); and synonyms and antonyms? How extensive is the dictionary's coverage of these items?

Consumer Note: Studies estimate that the most studious people alive have vocabularies under 50,000 words. Other estimates indicate that the average adult recognizes up to 20,000 different words but ordinarily uses fewer than 12,000. Another study shows that 135 words comprise about 50 percent of most of our reading matter. Monitoring experiments conducted by Bell Telephone indicate that roughly 100 common words constitute over 75 percent of all conversations. These figures suggest that a good abridged dictionary in the neighborhood of 55,000–80,000 entries should meet the vocabulary needs of most people most of the time. College students, because of their exposure to larger and more sophisticated bodies of literature, will ordinarily need a semi-unabridged dictionary. Usually only scholars, writers, editors, teachers, and advanced university students will require an unabridged dictionary.

If you are buying a dictionary as a gift for a person entering college, be aware that occasionally professors of freshman English require the use of a specific dictionary.

Bear in mind that the number of entries in a dictionary is only a relative guide to its size and comprehensiveness. Number of entries tells you nothing about the dictionary's comparative quality. Note also that entry statistics can be calculated in a variety of ways. Some publishers may count only main entries, whereas others include main entries, inflected forms, run-on entries, and variants in the count. David Guralnik, the editor of *Webster's New World Dictionary*, puts it this way: "Most dictionaries of similar scope contain definitions for only a fraction of the total of vocabulary entries to which they lay claim, since many words are treated merely as run-ons. That is, they are entered after the definition of a related term, often syllabified and pronounced, but the reader is left to infer the meaning." (Quoted from Guralnik's article "The Making of a Dictionary" in *The Bulletin of the Cleveland Medical Library*, January 1977, p. 11.) Still other publishers may inflate their entry counts by including all words and phrases derived from self-explanatory prefixes like *un-* and *non-*. In an effort to make these quantitative data more meaningful for comparative purposes, the *Buying Guide* provides two separate statistics: the total entry count and the average number of words in the text of each main entry.

Authority

People, not machines, make dictionaries. Who are they? What are their qualifications? The professional editorial staff and consultants should be listed in the front matter of the dictionary. You might want to check the top names in such standard biographical sources as *Who's Who in America*, *American Men and Women of Science*, and the *Directory of American Scholars*. Is the publisher reputable? There are publishers who foist poorly compiled, out-of-date dictionaries on gullible consumers. A particularly odious practice is peddling reprints of old, unrevised dictionaries disguised as new works. Unless you have some knowledge of the book trade, assistance will be required to determine a publisher's standing. *Literary Market Place*, an annual Bowker directory, provides pertinent information about American publishers, such as the types of books each publishes, whether a dictionary or reference book department is maintained, and the number of books published each year. In addition, librarians can be informative about publishers' reputations. And of course, the *Buying Guide* includes this type of information. It is also important to determine if the dictionary's vocabulary selection and treatment are based on an adequate citation file. Finally, what is the history of the dictionary? Is it an established work which has undergone various editions or is it a new publication? The editor's preface should provide this information.

Consumer Note: To repeat, the name "Webster" can be used by any publisher, good or bad, and therefore has nothing whatsoever to do with a dictionary's worth. In alphabetical order, the prominent "names" associated with general commercial dictionaries today are: *American Heritage* (publisher: Houghton Mifflin); *Funk & Wagnalls Standard* (publishers: Funk & Wagnalls, T. Y. Crowell, and J. G. Ferguson); *Merriam-Webster* (publisher: G. & C. Merriam Co.); *Oxford* (publisher: Oxford University Press); *Random House* (publisher: Random House); and *Webster's New World* (publisher: Collins+World). The names *Macmillan* (Macmillan), *Thorndike-Barnhart* (Doubleday), and *World Book* (Field Enterprises) are prominent in the school dictionary field. A dictionary bearing any of these nine names presupposes authoritativeness.

Vocabulary Treatment

What is the quality of the lexicographical work? Are the definitions clear, accurate, current, complete? It has been said that dictionary-makers should "phrase their definitions with greater care than a lawyer uses in framing a millionaire's will." But there is a tendency among some lexicographers to define a word with other words even more unfamiliar or difficult. David Guralnik, in his *Cleveland Medical Library Bulletin* article cited above, characterizes this phenomenon as "the semantic merry-go-round that leads the reader [on] a wild chase from one entry to another only to bring him back in a mad finish to his original starting point." To evaluate the clarity, accuracy, recency, and thoroughness of a dictionary's definitions, look up a number of words you are familiar with and carefully study the definitions given. You might also ask someone you know who has specialized knowledge, say in biology or literature, to comment on the definitions of somewhat technical words, e.g., *photosynthesis* or *allegory*. As noted in the "How to Use This Book" section, the *Buying Guide* employed this evaluative technique. Definitions of numerous preselected words were checked by the author and consultants. The sample word list included aesthetic, cell, certiorari, existentialism, fast, formalism, funky, holism, jawbone, kerogen, meridian, misandry, mix, pathetic, redneck, thump, and visualization. Treatment of these words was compared in dictionaries of similar purpose and scope.

Of course, there is more to a dictionary than definitions. Are other dictionary components treated satisfactorily? If illustrative quotations or examples are provided, do they help clarify the meaning of words in context? Are the pronunciations and etymologies easy to comprehend and use? Are usage labels included and, if so, are they helpful? Are synonyms and antonyms provided in sufficient quantity? Are shades of meaning discriminated?

Consumer Note: The most current copyright date on the back of the title page gives you a reasonably good indication of the dictionary's recency. New copyrights, however, can be acquired with minimal revision. Any dictionary can obtain a new copyright, for example, by making minor plate revisions or simply by resetting a page here and there, adding an occasional new word or definition and deleting an old one of comparable length. It is necessary, therefore, to test the dictionary's up-to-dateness, no matter how current the copyright date is. Are such widely used and well-established recent words as *funky* and *jawboning* included? But it would be unfair to expect any dictionary to include words that have just been coined or are faddish in nature. As in the case of *do a number on*, lexicographers need time to determine if a new word or phrase is sufficiently durable to warrant inclusion in the dictionary. Numerous words coined for the moment—called "nounce" words (like *Chappaquiddickized*)—will never and should never find their way into any commercial dictionary.

Encyclopedic Features

Does the dictionary include nonlexical or encyclopedic information? If so, is it useful? Or is it simply window dressing designed to sell more dictionaries? Can the dictionary be purchased without the encyclopedic supplements? At what savings? Some critics believe that dictionaries should stick to what they know best—words. A few editions ago, the venerable *Reader's Adviser* (R. R. Bowker Co., 1964) complained that "Dictionaries, by trying to outdo one another, have undone themselves. They have trespassed upon encyclopedias, and are no longer the mere word catalogs, the collective biographies of words, which they were once . . . . The modern dictionary is a classical dictionary, a gazetteer, a who's who, a thesaurus of words and phrases, and a handbook of proverbs—all in one." Usually encyclopedic information is appended to the dictionary, but increasingly biographical and geographical entries are included in the main A–Z sequence.

Graphics

Are diagrams, drawings, photographs, maps, etc. included? Do they clarify or complement the entry they illustrate? The most important illustrations in a dictionary are verbal—that is, the quotations or made-up examples which aid definitional clarity by showing how words are used in context. Practically all dictionaries also include pictorial illustrations. They are usually not as plentiful nor as useful as verbal illustrations, except in the case of dictionaries for young children. A picture alone cannot adequately define a word, but graphics can provide a visual dimension to a definition if the word is something concrete, such as an animal, plant, invention, or architectural feature. It should also be noted that the new *Scott, Foresman Beginning Dictionary* (1976), a Thorndike-Barnhart production, has pioneered pictorial illustrations as definitional aids for abstract words like *affection, comparative, exotic,* and *neglect.* Possibly, because of the success *The American Heritage Dictionary* has enjoyed, due in part to its extensive and innovative use of graphics, adult dictionaries will pay more attention to pictorial illustrations in the future.

Physical Format

Is the dictionary well constructed physically? Does the binding appear to be sturdy and able to withstand heavy use? Is the paper durable and of good quality? Is the print large and sharp enough for easy reading? Are guide words printed at the top of each page? Does the dictionary lie flat when open, so that the volume can be left open on a desk or stand for ready consultation? Are the inner margins wide enough? Is the overall physical appearance attractive? That the dictionary is a "masterpiece of condensation" is doubtless true, but if the one you choose has print too small for your eyes or its physical size is too large for your study or desk, you have not chosen the right dictionary. An observation by Bill Katz (*Basic Information Sources*, 1974, p. 260) is also worth keeping in mind. Katz suggests "that many questionable works frequently give themselves away for the very lack of a pleasing format. This is more often the result of using old, worn plates from another dictionary than a design of the publisher. When the paper is of a poor quality, the typography running toward gray, and the illustrations obviously dated or inconsequential, this is a good warning signal that the dictionary is possibly inferior."

Summary

At this point you have read the appropriate critical profiles in Part II of the *Buying Guide* and examined several or more dictionaries at your bookstore. You are now in a reasonably good position to make an informed purchase decision. Moreover, during the course of reading Part I of the *Buying Guide*, you have gained a better idea about what a dictionary can and cannot do for you.

Compare the purpose and scope, authority, vocabulary treatment, encyclopedic features, graphics, and physical format of the several dictionaries under consideration. Add one more criterion: price. As already noted, dictionaries are real bargains when you consider how much information you get for your money. Dictionary prices do not vary that much from publisher to publisher, although there are considerable price differences between dictionaries of various sizes. Also, some dictionaries which pile on the encyclopedic supplements cost considerably more than the same dictionary sans supplements. With a dictionary, as with most things in life, the more you expect from it, the more you expect to pay for it. Obviously, an unabridged dictionary in the neighborhood of 500,000 entries will cost much more than a pocket dictionary purchased at a drugstore. But, in either case, the dictionary will be a bargain—if it is authoritative, clear and up-to-date, physically well made, and if it meets your vocabulary needs.

Other Critical Opinions

The more critical input you have, the more informed your choice will be. Time and energy permitting, you might want to consult the lengthy reviews produced by the Reference and Subscription Books Review Committee of the American Library Association and published in *Booklist* or the more compact notices in the *American Reference Books Annual*, *Library Journal*, and *Wilson Library Bulletin.* Citations to recent reviews are included at the end of each profile in Part II of the *Buying Guide.* Additional sources of critical information are described in Appendix B. All additional critical sources cited are readily available in most public libraries, unless otherwise noted.

DICTIONARIES AT A GLANCE: COMPARATIVE CHARTS

"Dictionaries at a Glance" consists of two comparative charts. The first chart provides quantitative information about the 58 general adult dictionaries evaluated in Part II of the *Buying Guide*. The second chart includes similar information about the 60 or so school and children's dictionaries covered in Part II.

The charts offer a convenient statistical overview of comparable dictionaries. Prospective dictionary purchasers who are serious about getting the best possible dictionary should consult the appropriate chart to determine which dictionaries meet their particular needs in terms of user suitability, vocabulary size, and price. Once the list of possibilities has been narrowed to a reasonable number of titles, the prospective buyer should carefully read the critical profiles in Part II for a detailed description and evaluation of the dictionaries selected. For instance, if you are choosing a dictionary as a gift for a high school student about to enter college, a quick perusal of the charts will guide you to the "semi-unabridged" category of "Adult Dictionaries." At this point you might want to read the profiles of all 14 dictionaries in this category or, if money is a prime consideration, you could look first at the profiles of those dictionaries which are most reasonably priced (and indeed, the prices range from $6.95 to $59.00).

CONSUMER NOTES ABOUT THE CHARTS

Do *not* make a final purchase decision about which dictionary to buy from the charts alone. The charts merely provide quantitative information about comparably sized dictionaries in convenient tabular form.

Be aware that quality and quantity are *not* necessarily related. Just because one dictionary has more entries or illustrative examples or etymologies than another does not automatically make it a better work or better investment. On the other hand, quantitative data—especially entry counts—are useful measures of the amount of information a dictionary contains. For each dictionary analyzed, the *Buying Guide* provides an estimate of the total number of entries. This figure includes both main entries and subentries, such as inflected forms, derivatives, variants, and idioms. The chart for adult dictionaries also includes an estimate of the number of words per entry. This quantitative measure, first suggested by Clarence Barnhart in his article "General Dictionaries" (*American Speech*, Fall 1969), permits further comparison based on dictionary size. A glance at the "unabridged" category, for example, indicates that *Funk & Wagnalls New Standard Dictionary* has approximately the same number of entries as *Webster's Third New International Dictionary*. But the next column—"Number of Words per Entry"— shows that *Webster's Third* provides significantly more information per entry than does *Funk & Wagnalls*. To repeat: This does not necessarily mean that *Webster's Third* is better than *Funk & Wagnalls*. It merely means that *Webster's Third* provides more information. To ascertain the quality of that information, users of the *Buying Guide* must consult the profiles in Part II.

In most instances, quantitative data has been supplied or verified by the publishers. Data provided by the publishers have been verified by the *Buying Guide* via sample counts. Publisher estimates were found to be generally reliable.

User and grade suitability classifications in the school and children's chart should be viewed as flexible guidelines, not ironclad rules. Be aware that grade levels sometimes bear scant relationship to a student's psychological age, verbal skills, intellectual maturity, or educational motivation. Bright, curious students at the middle school level, for example, who possess outstanding verbal ability may very well be ready for a high school or adult dictionary, whereas indifferent or slow middle school students may have difficulty with a beginning dictionary.

Be aware that price information quoted in the charts, current at the time the guide went to press in August 1977, is subject to change by the publishers at any time.

ADULT DICTIONARIES

SIZE AND USER CLASSIFICATION	TITLE, EDITION, AND CURRENT COPYRIGHT DATE	TOTAL ENTRIES	NUMBER OF WORDS PER ENTRY[1]	LOWEST RETAIL PRICE	PUBLISHER/DISTRIBUTOR
Unabridged 250,000+ Total Entries For Scholars, Teachers, Writers & Graduate Students	Funk & Wagnalls New Standard Dictionary (1963)	458,000	18	$62.50	Funk & Wagnalls; dist. by Crowell
	Random House Dictionary (Unabridged Ed., 1973)	260,000	17	35.00	Random House
	Webster's New Twentieth Century Dictionary (Unabridged 2nd Ed., 1975)	320,000	11	59.95	Collins+World
	Webster's Third New International Dictionary (3rd Unabridged Ed., 1976)	460,000	23	75.00	Merriam
Semi-Unabridged 130,000– 250,000 Total Entries For College Students & Advanced Senior High School Students Preparing for College	American College Dictionary (1970)	132,000	16	6.95	Random House
	American Heritage Dictionary (Larger Format Ed., 1975; New College Ed., 1976)	155,000	14	14.95 9.95	Houghton Mifflin
	Chambers Twentieth Century Dictionary (New Ed., 1972)	180,000	10	7.95 10.95	Littlefield, Adams; Two Continents
	Funk & Wagnalls Comprehensive Standard International Dictionary (Bicentennial Ed., 1973)	175,000	14	49.95	Ferguson; dist. by Crowell
	Funk & Wagnalls Standard College Dictionary (1974)	150,000	16	9.95	Funk & Wagnalls; dist. by Crowell
	Funk & Wagnalls Standard Dictionary (International Ed., 1976) 2 vols.	175,000	14	34.50	Ferguson

[1]Indicates the average number of words devoted to each entry recorded in the "Total Entries" column.

ADULT DICTIONARIES (*Continued*)

SIZE AND USER CLASSIFICATION	TITLE, EDITION, AND CURRENT COPYRIGHT DATE	TOTAL ENTRIES	NUMBER OF WORDS PER ENTRY[1]	LOWEST RETAIL PRICE	PUBLISHER/ DISTRIBUTOR
Semi-Unabridged (cont.)	Illustrated Heritage Dictionary and Information Book (1977)	155,000	14	34.95	Houghton Mifflin
	Living Webster Encyclopedic Dictionary (1975)	158,000	10	39.95	English Language Institute of America; dist. by Consolidated
	New Webster's Dictionary (College Ed., 1975)	158,000	10	9.95	Consolidated
	Random House College Dictionary (Revised Ed., 1975)	170,000	15	9.95	Random House
	Webster's New Collegiate Dictionary (8th Ed., 1976)	150,000	17	9.95	Merriam
	Webster's New World Dictionary (2nd College Ed., 1976; Soft-Cover Ed., 1976)	158,000	17	9.95 7.50	Collins+World
	Webster's Seventh New Collegiate Dictionary (Large Format Ed., 1974)	130,000	15	10.95	Merriam
	World Book Dictionary (1977), 2 vols.	225,000	23	59.00	Field
Abridged 50,000– 130,000 Total Entries For the Average Adult in	American Heritage Dictionary (Paperback Ed., 1976; Delta Special Ed., 1977)	55,000	12	1.95 3.95	Dell
	Concise Heritage Dictionary (1976)	55,000	12	5.95	Houghton Mifflin
	Concise Oxford Dictionary (6th Ed., 1976)	74,000	18	11.95	Oxford

	Title	Total Entries	Average¹	Price	Publisher
the Home or Office	Doubleday Dictionary (1975)	85,000	11	6.95	Doubleday
	English Larousse (1968)	60,000	20	17.50	Larousse
Also for Out-of-School Use by Middle and High School Students	Funk & Wagnalls Standard Desk Dictionary (New Updated Ed., 1977)	100,000	10	6.95	Funk & Wagnalls; dist. by Crowell
	Funk & Wagnalls Standard Encyclopedic Dictionary (1975)	100,000	10	18.95	Ferguson
	Larousse Illustrated International Encyclopedia and Dictionary (1972)	65,000	20	19.95	Larousse
	Merriam-Webster Dictionary (1974)	57,000	10	1.95	Pocket Books
	Merriam-Webster Dictionary for Large Print Users (1977)	57,000	10	27.50	G. K. Hall
	Oxford Illustrated Dictionary (2nd Ed., 1975)	65,000	15	20.00	Oxford
	Random House American Everyday Dictionary (1961)	60,000	10	2.50	Random House
	Scribner-Bantam English Dictionary (1977)	80,000	10	8.95	Scribners
	Webster's Concise Family Dictionary (1975)	57,000	10	5.95	Merriam
	Webster's Dictionary (New Ed., 1972)	75,000	8	2.50	Banner Press; dist. by Hippocrene Books
	Webster's New Ideal Dictionary (1973)	60,000	10	4.95	Merriam
	Webster's New World Dictionary (Compact School & Office Ed., 1974)	56,000	10	3.49	Collins+World

¹Indicates the average number of words devoted to each entry recorded in the "Total Entries" column.

ADULT DICTIONARIES (*Continued*)

SIZE AND USER CLASSIFICATION	TITLE, EDITION, AND CURRENT COPYRIGHT DATE	TOTAL ENTRIES	NUMBER OF WORDS PER ENTRY[1]	LOWEST RETAIL PRICE	PUBLISHER/ DISTRIBUTOR
Abridged (cont.)	Webster's New World Dictionary (2nd Concise Ed., 1975)	105,000	12	7.25	Collins+World
	Webster's New World Dictionary (Modern Desk Ed., 1976)	72,000	9	4.95	Collins+World
	Webster's New World Dictionary (100,000 Entry Ed., 1971)	100,000	10	3.95	New American Library
	Webster's New World Dictionary (Pocket-size Ed., 1975)	59,000	9	1.95	Popular Library
Pocket	Chambers' English Dictionary (1965)	30,000	7	1.95	Littlefield, Adams
Under 55,000 Total Entries	English Gem Dictionary (U.S. Ed., 1968)	33,000	9	2.45	Collins+World
For Simple, Quick Reference in the Home, Automobile, etc.	Follett Vest-Pocket Webster Dictionary (1975)	17,000	7	1.95	Follett
	Hugo Pocket Dictionary: English (1973)	30,000	6	1.95	Littlefield, Adams
	Langenscheidt Lilliput Webster (1957)	7,000	3	1.00	Hippocrene Books
	Langenscheidt's Universal Webster Dictionary (1958)	17,000	8	1.95	Hippocrene Books
	Little Oxford Dictionary (4th Ed., 1969)	35,000	10	4.75	Oxford
	New American Webster Handy College Dictionary (1972)	30,000	10	1.25	New American Library
	New Webster's Vest Pocket Dictionary (1976)	20,000	4	1.25	Dennison

	Total Entries	¹	Price	Publisher
Pocket Oxford Dictionary (5th Ed., 1969)	50,000	16	8.25	Oxford
Random House American Dictionary (1967)	30,000	5	1.65	Random House
Thorndike-Barnhart Handy Pocket Dictionary (New Revised Ed., 1955)	36,000	8	1.25	Bantam Books
Webster's Dictionary (no date)	20,000	3	1.95	Barnes & Noble
Webster's Dictionary (1975)	50,000	9	1.95	Dennison; also Path-mark Books
Webster's Dictionary for Everyday Use (1977)	50,000	9	2.50	Barnes & Noble
Webster's Encyclopedia of Dictionaries (New American Ed., 1975)	50,000	9	24.50	Ottenheimer
Webster's New World Handy Pocket Dictionary (1972)	30,000	5	1.95	Collins+World
Webster's New World Quick Reference Dictionary (1972)	30,000	5	1.00	Collins+World
Webster's New World Vest Pocket Dictionary (1972)	18,000	5	0.79	Collins+World

¹Indicates the average number of words devoted to each entry recorded in the "Total Entries" column.

SCHOOL AND CHILDREN'S DICTIONARIES

SIZE AND USER CLASSIFICATION	TITLE, EDITION, AND CURRENT COPYRIGHT DATE	GRADE SUITABILITY	TOTAL ENTRIES	LOWEST RETAIL OR SCHOOL PRICE	PUBLISHER/ DISTRIBUTOR
Secondary School					
75,000+ Total Entries	Macmillan Dictionary (1973)	9–12	90,000	$ 9.64*	Macmillan*
	Thorndike-Barnhart Advanced Dictionary (2nd Ed., 1974)	9–12	95,000	11.50 / 7.89*	Doubleday; Scott, Foresman*
For High School Students with Average or	Webster's New Students Dictionary (1974)	9–12	81,000	7.95 / 7.47*	Merriam; American Book Co.*
Above Average Verbal Skills	Webster's New World Dictionary (2nd College Ed., 1976; Special School Printing)	11–12	158,000	4.53*	Prentice-Hall*
	Webster's New World Dictionary (Students Ed., 1977)	9–12	108,000	8.95	Collins+World
	World Book Dictionary (1977), 2 vols.	7–12	225,000	59.00	Field
Middle School					
30,000–75,000 Total Entries	American Heritage School Dictionary (1972)	6–10	55,000	8.95	Houghton Mifflin
For Junior High School Students with Average or	Harcourt Brace Intermediate Dictionary (1968)	6–10	46,000	5.97	Harcourt Brace Jovanovich
	HBJ School Dictionary (1977)	6–10	46,000	5.97*	Harcourt Brace Jovanovich*
Above Average Verbal Skills	Holt Intermediate Dictionary (1967)	6–10	65,000	9.84*	Holt, Rinehart & Winston*
Also for Less Advanced High School Students	Macmillan School Dictionary (Revised Ed., 1977)	6–10	65,000	9.32*	Macmillan*

Title	Grades	Total Entries	Price	Publisher
Oxford School Dictionary (3rd Ed., 1974)	5–8	30,000	3.00	Oxford
Random House Dictionary (School Ed., 1973)	6–10	45,000	6.50*	Random House*
Thorndike-Barnhart Advanced Junior Dictionary (4th Ed., 1968)	7–10	65,000	9.50 / 7.14*	Doubleday; Scott, Foresman*
Thorndike-Barnhart Intermediate Dictionary (2nd Ed., 1974)	5–8	57,000	9.50 / 7.14*	Doubleday; Scott, Foresman*
Webster's Intermediate Dictionary (1972)	6–10	57,000	9.50 / 7.14*	Merriam American Book Co.*
Webster's Scholastic Dictionary (New Ed., 1976)	6–10	30,000	1.50	Airmont
Winston Dictionary for Schools (1967)	6–10	46,000	5.36*	Holt, Rinehart & Winston*

Elementary School
Under 50,000 Total Entries
For Children from Kindergarten to the Sixth Grade
Also for Less Advanced Middle School Students

Title	Grades	Total Entries	Price	Publisher
Charlie Brown Dictionary (1973)	K–3	2,400	7.95	Random House
Children's Dictionary (New & Revised Ed., 1970)	3–6	10,000	3.25	British Book Centre
Courtis-Watters Illustrated Golden Dictionary (Revised & Expanded Ed., 1965)	3–6	10,000	7.95	Western
Dictionary of Basic Words (1969)	2–8	21,000	14.95	Childrens Press
General Basic English Dictionary (1940)	3–8	20,000	5.00	Rowman & Littlefield
Ginn Beginning Dictionary (1973)	2–4	5,000	4.65*	Ginn*
Ginn Intermediate Dictionary (1974)	3–8	34,000	6.95*	Ginn*
Macmillan Beginning Dictionary (1976)	3–8	30,000	9.84*	Macmillan*

*Indicates a *text* edition, ordinarily available only to educational institutions.

SCHOOL AND CHILDREN'S DICTIONARIES (*Continued*)

SIZE AND USER CLASSIFICATION	TITLE, EDITION, AND CURRENT COPYRIGHT DATE	GRADE SUITABILITY	TOTAL ENTRIES	LOWEST RETAIL OR SCHOOL PRICE	PUBLISHER/ DISTRIBUTOR
Elementary School (cont.)	Macmillan Dictionary for Children (1976)	3–8	30,000	10.95	Macmillan
	New Horizon Ladder Dictionary (Revised Ed., 1970)	2–6	9,500	0.95	New American Library
	Oxford Children's Dictionary in Colour (1976)	1–3	15,000	6.00	Oxford
	Picture Dictionary for Children (Revised Ed., 1977)	K–3	5,000	3.95	Grosset & Dunlap
	Scott, Foresman Beginning Dictionary (1976)	3–8	25,000	10.95 7.50*	Doubleday; Scott, Foresman*
	Thorndike-Barnhart Beginning Dictionary (8th Ed., 1974)	3–8	26,000	8.50 5.97*	Doubleday; Scott, Foresman*
	Troll Talking Picture Dictionary (1974)	K–3	1,400	145.00*	Troll Associates*
	Webster's New Elementary Dictionary (1975)	3–8	32,000	5.95 6.27*	Merriam; American Book Co.*
	Webster's New World Dictionary for Young Readers (1976)	3–8	44,000	7.95	Collins+World
	Weekly Reader Beginning Dictionary (1973)	2–4	5,000	6.95	Grosset & Dunlap
	Word Wonder Dictionary (1966)	2–4	1,500	5.64*	Holt, Rinehart & Winston*
	Words to Know (1969)	K–3	1,200	5.95	Standard Educational
	Xerox Intermediate Dictionary (1974)	3–8	34,000	8.95	Grosset & Dunlap

	Title		Entries	Price	Publisher
Preschool	Cat in the Hat Beginner Book Dictionary (1964)	K–1	1,350	4.95	Random House
Under 5,000 Total Entries	Follett Beginning-to-Read Picture Dictionary (1959)	K–1	180	2.50	Follett
Heavily Illustrated	Golden Picture Dictionary (1976)	K–1	2,500	7.95	Western
For Very Young Children Beginning to Read	Grosset Starter Picture Dictionary (1976)	K–1	200	1.95	Grosset & Dunlap
	International Visual Dictionary (1973)	K–1	3,000	19.95	Carroll Book Service
	Little Golden Picture Dictionary (1959)	K–1	150	2.75	Western
For Use in the Home, Nursery, Day-Care Center, Kindergarten, etc.	My First Dictionary (1948)	K–1	650	3.50	Grosset & Dunlap
	My First Golden Dictionary (1957)	K–1	270	4.95	Western
	My First Picture Dictionary (Revised Ed., 1977)	K–1	800	6.94 / 3.99*	Lothrop, Lee & Shepard; Scott, Foresman*
Also for Less Advanced Elementary Students	My Pictionary (1970)	K–1	535	4.59 / 2.76*	Lothrop, Lee & Shepard; Scott, Foresman*
	My Second Picture Dictionary (1971)	K–3	4,000	7.17 / 5.40*	Lothrop, Lee & Shepard; Scott, Foresman*
	New Golden Dictionary (1972)	K–1	2,000	5.95	Western
	Picture Book Dictionary (New Ed., 1962)	K–1	166	4.50	Childrens Press
	Storybook Dictionary (1966)	K–3	2,500	6.95	Western
	Strawberry Picture Dictionary (1974)	K–1	375	3.50	Larousse
	Two Thousand Plus Index & Glossary (1977)	K–3	2,000	4.95	Macdonald-Raintree

*Indicates a *text* edition, ordinarily available only to educational institutions.

II

DICTIONARY PROFILES

ADULT DICTIONARIES

General adult dictionaries range in size from the very large *Webster's Third New International Dictionary* which comprises over ten million words and some 460,000 entries to the very small *Langenscheidt Lilliput Webster English Dictionary* with only 25,000 words and 7,000 very brief entries. For the purpose of comparative evaluation, the *Buying Guide* has divided all general adult dictionaries currently in print into four broad categories based on size: *unabridged* (250,000 or more entries); *semi-unabridged* (130,000–250,000 entries); *abridged* (55,000–130,000 entries); and *pocket* (under 55,000 entries).

Within these categories the dictionary profiles are arranged alphabetically by title. Profiles in the unabridged and semi-unabridged categories cover these standard evaluative criteria: Descriptive Information; Purpose and Scope; Authority; Vocabulary Treatment (Clarity, Accuracy, Thoroughness, Recency); Encyclopedic Features; Graphics; Physical Format; Summary; and Other Critical Opinions. Profiles for the smaller, less complex abridged and pocket dictionaries cover Descriptive Information; Contents; Summary; and Other Critical Opinions.

Always consult the index for specific dictionary titles.

UNABRIDGED DICTIONARIES

Funk & Wagnalls New Standard Dictionary

Descriptive Information

Full Title: **Funk & Wagnalls New Standard Dictionary of the English Language: Complete in One Volume.** *Editors:* Isaac K. Funk, Editor in Chief; Calvin Thomas, Consulting Editor; Frank H. Vizetelly, Managing Editor. *Publisher:* Funk & Wagnalls. *Distributor:* T. Y. Crowell Co. *Edition Reviewed:* 1963.

Classification: Adult—Unabridged. *Pages:* lxx, 2817. *Total Entries:* 458,000. *Average Entry Length:* 18 words. *Graphics:* 7,000. *Consultants:* 380. *Physical Size:* 9½ by 12½ in.; 31 cm. *LC:* 64-99. *ISBN:* 0-308-20005-5. *Lowest Retail Price:* $62.50.

Purpose and Scope

Funk & Wagnalls New Standard Dictionary is one of the largest general English-language dictionaries currently in print. The dictionary's basic aim, as expressed in the publisher's introductory statement, is "that the vocabulary should, first of all, embrace *all the live words* of the English language as used in the standard speech and literature of the day." Note that *F & W New Standard* emphasizes standard American English, but nonstandard words and phrases (e.g., slang and colloquial expressions) are included if widely used. Among the dictionary's 458,000 entries are 65,000 proper names, including 16,000 brief biographies and over 30,000 place-names. The dictionary also includes numerous regional meanings and pronunciations. A supplement containing new words and meanings is located in the front of the book. Comprising 34 pages and an estimated 4,000 entries, the supplement contains vocabulary (much of it scientific and technical) which entered the language in the 1950s and early 1960s. Obviously, a dictionary bearing 1963 as its most recent copyright date will lack coverage of new terms and meanings. Example: None of the following commonly encountered words and phrases is in the dictionary: *busing* (or *bussing*), *irregardless*, *medicaid*, *New Left*, *oxygen cycle*, *Pap smear*, and *reprography*.

Main entries are printed in boldface type. Information given includes spelling, syllabication, pronunciation (two different keys are provided for each pronunciation), part of speech designation, definitions, etymology, and derivatives (also in boldface type). Approximately 32,000 illustrative quotations and many more illustrative examples appear throughout. Some 7,500 synonym lists comprising more than 23,000 synonymous terms are provided. Usage labels indicate special or restrictive uses of certain words. *Certiorari*, for example, is labeled "law" and *maieutics* "rare." In the matter of the dictionary's role as describer or prescriber of language usage, *F & W New Standard* adheres to a middle course originally announced by Isaac Funk in 1893: "The chief function of a dictionary is to record usage; not, *except in a limited degree*, to seek to create it." Further along in the publisher's introduction, however, it is noted that "Words that are not used in the best literature" are labeled "colloquial," "slang," "cant," etc.

Authority

In 1893, Dr. Isaac Funk's *A Standard Dictionary of the English Language* appeared and was immediately recognized as a worthy competitor to Merriam-Webster's unabridged edition, at that time entitled *Webster's International Dictionary*. The *Standard* was reprinted in 1901 with a 13,000-word supplement. In 1913 it was completely revised and retitled *Funk & Wagnalls New Standard Dictionary of the English Language*. The dictionary has not been thoroughly revised since that time. Successive copyrights, including the 1963 edition under review, have been updated by deleting old material from the original plates to make room for new words and meanings. Essentially, *F & W New Standard* represents word knowledge as it existed prior to World War I. This fact alone seriously undercuts the dictionary's authority as a reliable guide to our language.

Isaac Kauffman Funk, listed as *F & W New Standard*'s editor, was a distinguished American lexicographer and publisher, but Dr. Funk died in 1912. The dictionary's Advisory Committee on Disputed Pronunciations comprised 25 outstanding scholars, but they are likewise now deceased. The same is true of the 375 subject consultants and editors listed in the front matter. The dictionary's original citation file was culled from "standard" writings. According to the publisher's introduction, "Practically all English literature from Chaucer's time to the present [1913] was ransacked for this purpose." Today, however, no citation file of the sort required to keep an unabridged dictionary up-to-date is maintained for *F & W New Standard*.

Vocabulary Treatment (Clarity, Accuracy, Thoroughness, Recency)

The dictionary is best known perhaps for giving the most recent or common meaning first, whereas Merriam-Webster gives definitions in historical order. The makers of *F & W New Standard* concede that scholarly lexicographical practice has been to give the current meaning last. "But this last meaning is precisely the one most commonly sought after," say the editors, and therefore the present meaning should be first. "Precedent should give way to convenience." To this day, all dictionaries bearing the names "Funk & Wagnalls" and "Standard" (both registered trademarks) give the most common meaning first, with successive definitions listed in order of declining frequency of use. Definitions are usually ample, as the words-per-entry figure (18) indicates. Definitions are also usually written in a clear, understandable manner. Sometimes, however, the style is stilted. Example: The first definition of the verb *mix* is "to cause to unite promiscuously into one mass, assemblage, or body; incorporate closely and indiscriminately together; mingle so as to render separately indistinguishable."

The dictionary's greatest weakness in the area of vocabulary treatment is its lack of currency. The treatment of words like *aesthetic* and *conceit* which have remained relatively static over the past 75 or so years is generally clear, accurate, comprehensive, and up-to-date. But in those instances—and there are thousands—where established words have undergone changes in meaning, *F & W New Standard* more often than not fails to include the new information. Example: The word *recision* is defined as "resection; a cutting off or pruning." The modern meaning of the word, however, is not given. Today *recision* is ordinarily used in connection with efforts to cancel or rescind (same Latin root) some political action, as in "The Equal Rights Amendment has passed in Montana but opponents are calling for *recision*." Example: The noun *mix* is variously defined as "a formula used in manufacture," "confusion caused by blundering" (labeled "colloq."), "dung; filth" (labeled "Prov. Eng."), and "a vile person; wretch." Not given, however, is the contemporary meaning of *mix* as a commercially prepared mixture of ingredients used for making mixed drinks, muffins, etc. Example: The adjective *gay* is accorded four different meanings but among all this information there is not so much as a hint that the most recent meaning of *gay* refers to homosexuality. Even more glaring is the great number of contemporary words and phrases not found anywhere in the dictionary. Users of *F & W New Standard* will look in vain for such terms as *decoupage*, *détente*, *holism*, *honcho*, *jawboning*, and *redneck*. Also missing are many modern compound words, such as *data bank*, *hard-core*, *minibike*, *mixed drink*, *plea bargaining*, and *spaced-out*. These terms, and numerous others like them, are not in the dictionary itself or in the new-word supplement in the front.

In other instances, definitions are inaccurate or misleading. Example: The biological meaning of the noun *cell* contains several errors, e.g., although the dictionary states "The envelop is absent in the white blood-corpuscles, in some of the lowest organisms," the fact of the matter is that all white blood cells have a membrane (or envelope), even the so-called low ones. Example: The one-line definition of *misandry* is "hatred of man," which can be confusing depending on how *man* is interpreted (actually the word means "hatred of men"). Example: The noun *existentialism* is not found in the main dictionary file but in the new-word supplement in the front. The definition summarizes Jean Paul Sartre's philosophy but makes no reference to Nietzsche, Kierkegaard, or other Germanic influences.

Other aspects of vocabulary treatment are reasonably satisfactory. The two pronunciation keys are effective and relatively easy to comprehend. The first key employs the Revised Scientific Alphabet which has a phonetic symbol for each distinct sound in the language. The second key is older but simpler, using only the letters of the alphabet with various diacritical marks to distinguish different sounds. In the area of spelling, both standard and variant forms are provided. In addition, simplified spelling is included for certain words, e.g., *although/altho*. Isaac Funk, like Noah Webster, was an advocate of simplified spelling, a popular lexical cause in the nineteenth century which ultimately generated more confusion than reform.

F & W New Standard's etymologies tend to be concise—perhaps too concise. Example: The etymology for *mix* is simply given as the Anglo-Saxon *miscian*. *Webster's Third New International Dictionary*, on the other hand, traces *mix* to the Middle English *mixen* which in turn originated from the Latin *mixtus*, the past participle of *miscere*, the Latin verb meaning "to mix." *Webster's Third* also refers to several Indo-European cognates, like the Greek *misgein* and the Old Irish *mescaim*.

The illustrative quotations are usually taken from classical (as opposed to modern) literature. In most cases, the quotations aid in understanding or differentiating word meanings, but not always. Sometimes the quotations are too airy or esoteric. Example: The second meaning of the verb *mix* is "to join in company; associate; as, to *mix* oneself with the crowd." Following this definition is a quotation from Addison's *Cato:* "To Heaven I swear,/To Heaven and all the powers that judge mankind,/Never to *mix* my plighted hands with thine." Unlike *Webster's Third*, author and source (dated) are cited for most quotations used in the dictionary.

Encyclopedic Features

As previously mentioned, *F & W New Standard* includes numerous biographical and geographical names in the main A–Z sequence. Much additional information of an encyclopedic nature can be found under such entries as *coffee*, *coin*, *dog*, *law*, *steam*, and *wheat*. Example: *Coin* includes a lengthy—and woefully out-of-date—table of foreign monetary equivalents. The appendix contains population data for all U.S. places with 5,000 or more people, based on the 1960 census. The appendix also includes a list of words whose pronunciation is frequently disputed and a glossary of foreign words and phrases commonly used in English. In all but a few instances, the encyclopedic material in *F & W New Standard* is readily available in other more likely and more current sources.

Graphics

F & W New Standard contains over 7,000 black-and-white line drawings and 36 full-page illustrations. The graphics are nearly always informative and complementary to the word being defined. As explained in the publisher's introduction, "As a rule, every illustration given in this work has been inserted to serve a definite purpose—to supplement verbal definition by pictorial demonstration. Often it is much easier to show by a picture what a thing really is than to define it by mere words." Example: The word *coin* is complemented by a full-page plate, "Examples of Remarkable Ancient Coins." Each coin is dated and described in considerable detail.

Physical Format

Like all unabridged dictionaries, *F & W New Standard* is so large that it requires a special dictionary or library stand. The volume weighs about 17 pounds and is 4½ inches thick. It is sturdily bound in a durable maroon buckramite binding. An excellent grade of paper has been used and the type, though small (5½ point) and old-fashioned, is usually legible. Guide words appear at the top of each three-column page, along with a concise version of both pronunciation keys. The inner and outer margins are sufficiently wide. Overall, the dictionary's physical construction is satisfactory, although the design is not modern.

Summary

Funk & Wagnalls New Standard Dictionary of the English Language aims to include "all live words" in the language. The emphasis is on "standard" language—that is, vocabulary used in the "best" literature. The dictionary also covers nonstandard words and phrases if widely used, but they are prescriptively labeled "slang," "colloquial," etc. Although 458,000 entries are claimed, at least 65,000 are proper names, mainly people and places. In addition, the dictionary includes much encyclopedic information in the main A–Z file.

F & W New Standard's history dates back to the nineteenth century. The present edition first appeared in 1913. Over the years, it has become best known perhaps for its relatively uncomplicated pronunciations, its emphasis on simplified spelling (now a lost cause), and its placement of the most common or frequently used meaning first (as opposed to the more scholarly historical order). The dictionary has also gained a reputation for clear, full, and authoritative definitions.

At the present time, however, the single most important fact about the dictionary is its lack of currency. Only minimal updating has occurred since 1913, and the relatively small new-word supplement in the front of the 1963 edition hardly suffices to keep a dictionary the size of *F & W New Standard* abreast of our living and changing language. Time and neglect have eroded *F & W New Standard*'s authority. Today the dictionary has no staff, no citation file, and an uncertain future.

In the unabridged class, *Webster's Third New International Dictionary* stands alone as the most reliable, comprehensive, and up-to-date general dictionary on the market today. The much smaller but less expensive *Random*

House Dictionary is also reliable and reasonably current. Although it lacks the depth and breadth of coverage provided by *Webster's Third*, *Random House* is easier to use, contains many useful encyclopedic features, and costs less than half as much. *Webster's New Twentieth Century Dictionary* has approximately the same scope as *Random House*, but it is not as current or as reliable. Although *F & W New Standard*'s coverage of the language historically is far superior to either *Random House* or *Webster's New Twentieth Century*, the dictionary's lack of currency makes it a questionable purchase.

Other Critical Opinions

Katz, William A. *Basic Information Sources*. Vol. 1 of *Introduction to Reference Work*, 2nd ed. (New York: McGraw-Hill, 1974), pp. 266–267.

Random House Dictionary

Descriptive Information

Full Title: **The Random House Dictionary of the English Language.**
Editors: Jess Stein, Editor in Chief; Laurence Urdang, Managing Editor.
Publisher: Random House. *Edition Reviewed:* Unabridged Edition, 1973.

Classification: Adult—Unabridged. *Pages:* xxxii, 2059. *Total Entries:* 260,000. *Average Entry Length:* 17 words. *Graphics:* 2,000. *Consultants:* 350. *Physical Size:* 9½ by 12 in.; 31 cm. *LC:* 74-129225. *ISBN:* 0-394-47176-8. *Lowest Retail Price:* $35.00.

Purpose and Scope

The Random House Dictionary of the English Language is the smallest of the four unabridged dictionaries. Some critics have questioned whether a dictionary under 300,000 total entries can be considered truly unabridged. The *Buying Guide* believes that the term *unabridged* is sufficiently elastic to include *Random House*. It must be emphatically stated, however, that *Random House* is no match for *Webster's Third New International Dictionary* in terms of scope and depth of coverage.

Jess Stein's preface clearly notes the dictionary's principal purpose: "If modern man is to function well in his society, one of his necessities, surely, is to keep pace with the dynamic growth of his language. To meet such a need *The Random House Dictionary of the English Language* has been prepared. It is an entirely new dictionary [in 1966], written in midcentury for twentieth-century users." The dictionary emphasizes words in current use. It includes the vocabulary of the contemporary businessman, professional, student, literate adult, and television viewer. In addition to standard present-day words and phrases, considerable attention is paid to new scientific and technical terms, idiomatic expressions, and slang and colloquialisms (though not vulgarisms). When *Random House* first appeared in 1966, it included many vogue words of the day, like *camp, frug, happening, kooky,* and *ratfink.* Recent revisions appear to have cooled it on fad words. Example: Such words as *deep-six, jawbone, New Left,* and *redneck* are included whereas *flat-out, honcho, mensch,* and *upfront* are not.

Among the dictionary's 260,000 entries there are numerous proper names.

These entries mainly consist of biographical and geographical names but also include historical and political events (e.g., *Jay's Treaty*) and titles of famous books (*Gone With the Wind*), plays (*The Man Who Came to Dinner*), poems (*Ode to a Nightingale*), operas (*La Bohème*), and works of art (*Mona Lisa*). Moreover, there is an extraordinary amount of encyclopedic information in the back of the dictionary.

Main entries are printed in boldface type. Information provided includes spelling, syllabication, pronunciation, part of speech designation, definitions, etymology, and derivatives (also in boldface type). More than 50,000 illustrative sentences and phrases and some 10,000 synonym studies are included. Usage labels indicate special or restrictive uses of certain words. For instance, *certiorari*, a legal term, is labeled "law" and *fubsy* "Brit. Dial." Concerning the dictionary's function as prescriber or describer of the language, *Random House* attempts to steer a "linguistically sound middle course." In his preface, the editor states that "the function of a dictionary [is] to provide the user with an exact record of the language he sees and hears." But, Stein continues, "That record must be *fully* descriptive. Since language is a social institution, the lexicographer must give the user an adequate indication of the attitudes of society toward particular words or expressions." Hence, *Random House* rather generously applies such restrictive cultural tags as "slang," "informal," and "nonstandard." In addition, certain controversial words (e.g., *irregardless*) have concise usage notes appended to the definition which offer some informed "do's and don'ts." The usage notes are prepared by Theodore M. Bernstein of the *New York Times*.

Authority

Random House, the newest of the big dictionaries, first appeared in 1966. According to the publisher, it took seven years and an estimated $3 million to make. The editor, Jess Stein, has been in the lexicography business for many years, beginning his career with Random House in 1945 as managing editor (under Clarence Barnhart) of the pathbreaking *American College Dictionary*. A well-qualified staff of 150 editors and lexicographers compiled *Random House*, assisted by 208 subject specialists. These specialists include such distinguished authorities as Charles M. Goren (cards), Kelsie B. Harder (given names), Gilbert Highet (mythology), William Kunstler (law), Robert Lekachman (economics), and Maurice F. Tauber (library science).

The editor's preface notes that, "In the preparation of the *RHD*, our permanent lexicographic staff made full use of its departmental resources— our large file of citations from newspapers, magazines, and books; glossaries and indexes; special dictionaries and lists; textbooks and concordances; reference books and learned studies, and so on." It would appear that *Random House* built its citation file from scratch, beginning in the late 1950s. The dictionary, however, contains no illustrative quotations, only made-up examples. Although it is described as "large," the *Random House* citation file can hardly be as impressive, at least in size, as the file Merriam-Webster has maintained over many years and which now contains more than 12 million citation slips.

Random House, on the other hand, does have the distinction of being the first general dictionary to utilize electronic data processing equipment in its compilation. (The more recent *American Heritage Dictionary* has also made good use of such hardware.) Specifically, four IBM computers were used to perform a variety of routine operations, including sorting the dictionary's vocabulary into 150 or so subject categories. A high-speed General Dynamics cathode-ray-tube printer was employed to produce a film copy of the dictionary which now serves to facilitate the production of revised editions.

Vocabulary Treatment (Clarity, Accuracy, Thoroughness, Recency)

Like *Funk & Wagnalls New Standard Dictionary, Random House* gives the most frequently used meaning first. Definitions tend to be reasonably up-to-date, accurate, and very clearly expressed. The dictionary falls down, however, in the area of thoroughness. Many definitions are too brief or incomplete. Example: The biological meaning of *cell* is superficial, lacks specificity, and lacks a diagram. Example: The term *existentialism* is defined as "the doctrine that man forms his essence in the course of the life he chooses to lead." This definition is skimpy, incomplete, and vague. The subentry *philosophical existentialism* is equally inadequate. Example: The word *holism* is defined as "the theory that whole entities, as fundamental components of reality, have an existence other than as the mere sum of their parts." But *holism* also refers to the concept that a part cannot be understood in isolation from the whole, a meaning which might be inferred from the *Random House* definition but is not explicitly stated.

Other words found to be skimpily or incompletely defined include *aesthetic, decoupage, gene, launder, macrame, photovoltaic,* and *radiation.* In addition, some newer terms, especially in the scientific and technical area, are omitted altogether: *busing* (or *bussing*), *cholestasis, ekistics, laetrile, mace* (the verb), *nitrofurantoin, Orwellian* (George Orwell, the novelist from whom the term derives, is listed but there is no mention of the novel *1984* that produced *Orwellian*), *oxygen cycle, renovascular,* and *Wankel engine.* Many active but less commonly used words are also omitted, e.g., *misandry.*

Words and phrases in *Random House* are adequately pronounced. The pronunciation system used in the dictionary involves primary and secondary stress marks, diacritical marks, and a few commonly recognized phonetic symbols. The system is fairly easy to understand. The full pronunciation key is given on the endpaper in the front of the book. A condensed key is conveniently provided at the bottom of each two-page spread. Variant pronunciations are included though not as abundantly as in *Funk & Wagnalls New Standard Dictionary* and *Webster's Third New International Dictionary.* Generally speaking, regional variants have been de-emphasized, although common regionalisms (e.g., krēk/krik) are included. Common British pronunciations are usually given, labeled "esp. Brit." Variant spellings are treated in a similar manner.

The dictionary's etymologies, prepared under the direction of Kemp Malone, a noted English-language scholar, are sufficient to meet the average user's needs. They are clear and accurate but usually not as full as those found in *Webster's Third.* John Ciardi, in a *Saturday Review* column (May 24, 1969, p. 39), described *Random House*'s etymologies as having "a tone of tidy but shallow efficiency."

The 50,000 illustrative examples, all written by the editors, have been called "unscholarly" and worse. For instance, Bill Katz writes in *Basic Information*

Sources (2nd ed., 1974, p. 267) that "The results are sometimes ludicrous. For example, quotations used to support 'begin,' 'contain,' and 'naked' are 'Where shall I begin?' 'This glass contains water.' 'The children swam naked in the lake.' More difficult words often slip by without quotations." It is true that silly illustrative examples can be found in *Random House* and that some words (e.g., *derisible; derision; derisive*) which need examples lack them. But what has not been generally recognized is that *Random House* has used a perfectly valid lexicographical technique developed by Dr. Edward L. Thorndike which employs made-up illustrations to "force" definitional clarity. Thorndike first used this device in school dictionaries but it has subsequently been adopted by lexicographers in the trade dictionary field. In the large majority of cases, the illustrative examples in *Random House* are quite helpful in clarifying definitions, particularly connotative senses. The dictionary also provides over 10,000 synonyms, many of which are treated in synonymies where similar words are discriminated.

Encyclopedic Features

As explained above (see Purpose and Scope), the main body of the dictionary includes considerable encyclopedic information in the form of biographical and geographical entries, as well as numerous entries covering specific works of music, art, and literature. More impressive, however, is the enormous amount of material appended to the dictionary. In addition to four concise bilingual dictionaries (French; Spanish; Italian; German), *Random House* offers a basic style manual, a list of major reference works, major dates in history, presidents and vice presidents of the United States, copies of the Declaration of Independence and the Constitution, and such geographical items as major ocean depths, principal lakes of the world, noted waterfalls of the world, major rivers of the world, deserts and volcanoes of the world, a 64-page color world atlas (maps prepared by C. S. Hammond & Co.), and a gazetteer of some 27,000 place-names keyed to the atlas. In all, the appended material accounts for approximately 400 of the dictionary's 2,000 pages.

Over the years, the publisher has made promotional hay with the dictionary's encyclopedic features. How valuable is such information in a dictionary? The *Buying Guide* believes that a dictionary should be judged essentially by how well it treats the language, not by how much nonlexical material is tacked on after the Z entries. Nevertheless, the wealth of factual material included in *Random House* does enhance its usefulness, particularly in the home or office which lacks a reliable general encyclopedia. It should be noted, however, that in some cases *Random House*'s encyclopedic information is out-of-date. Example: The list of countries of the world does not include such new African states as Zaire. Example: The Constitution of the United States fails to include the Twenty-sixth Amendment (voting age lowered to 18).

Graphics

Unlike *Funk & Wagnalls New Standard Dictionary*, which contains copious pictorial material, *Random House* is limited to 2,000 typically small black-and-white line illustrations, including a number of spot maps. The illustrations tend to emphasize animals, flowers, tools, and musical instruments. As a rule, they are clear and help define the word in question.

Physical Format

The light tan buckram binding is attractive and sturdy. Like all of the unabridged dictionaries, *Random House* comes with a jacket cover. The Imperial Bible paper is of the highest quality. The type is modern, exceedingly clear, and pleasing to the eye. Guide words appear at the top of each three-column page. The pronunciation key is printed at the bottom of every other page. Like most large dictionaries, *Random House* is thumb-indexed. Of the four unabridged dictionaries, *Random House* possesses the most inviting format, with *Webster's Third* a close second.

Summary

The Random House Dictionary of the English Language, the newest of the large dictionaries, is authoritative and reasonably up-to-date. First published in 1966, it is kept current by periodic revisions, the most recent occurring in 1973. The dictionary contains 260,000 total entries, including numerous proper names. This figure falls below the generally accepted standard for "unabridged" dictionaries, but the *Buying Guide* believes *Random House* is sufficiently large to serve the basic vocabulary needs of scholars, writers, editors, teachers, and advanced students.

The dictionary emphasizes the language as spoken and written at "mid-century." Considerable attention has been devoted to new terms brought forth by modern business, scientific, and technical developments. Coverage of such terminology, however, is not as broad as that found in *Webster's Third New International Dictionary*, the largest of the general unabridged dictionaries. Informal and nonstandard words and phrases, as well as idiomatic expressions, are well represented. Unlike *Webster's Third*, usage labels are generously applied. Vocabulary treatment tends to be satisfactory in every respect except thoroughness. Too often definitions are overly brief, vague, or incomplete. The made-up illustrative examples which have bothered some critics are usually helpful in "forcing" definitional clarity.

Random House provides an extraordinary amount of encyclopedic information, most of which is useful though hardly necessary if a good, up-to-date encyclopedia is readily available. The 2,000 small but clear black-and-white line drawings contribute to the dictionary's overall success. More impressive, however, are the dictionary's excellent physical qualities. The type is very legible and the format inviting. In practically every respect, *Random House* is a modern dictionary for modern people. Allen Walker Read has called *Random House* "without doubt the best dictionary of its decade."

In the unabridged class, *Webster's Third New International Dictionary* stands alone as the most reliable, comprehensive, and up-to-date general dictionary on the market today. *Random House*, although it lacks the depth and breadth of coverage provided by *Webster's Third*, is easier to use, contains many useful encyclopedic features, and costs less than half as much. *Webster's New Twentieth Century Dictionary* has much the same scope as *Random House*, but it is not as current or as reliable. Although *Funk & Wagnalls New Standard Dictionary*'s coverage of the language historically is far superior to either *Random House* or *Webster's New Twentieth Century*, the dictionary's lack of currency makes it a questionable purchase.

Other Critical Opinions

Booklist, April 1, 1967, pp. 803–807.

Katz, William A. *Basic Information Sources.* Vol. 1 of *Introduction to Reference Work*, 2nd ed. (New York: McGraw-Hill, 1974), pp. 267–268.

Webster's New Twentieth Century Dictionary

Descriptive Information

Full Title: **Webster's New Twentieth Century Dictionary of the English Language.** *Editor:* Jean L. McKechnie. *Publisher:* Collins+World. Former titles: *Webster's Universities Dictionary* (1940); *Webster's Standard Dictionary* (1907); *Webster's Imperial Dictionary* (1904); *Webster's Universal Dictionary* (1904). *Edition Reviewed:* Unabridged Second Edition—Deluxe Color Edition, 1975.

Classification: Adult—Unabridged. *Pages:* xiv, 2345. *Total Entries:* 320,000. *Average Entry Length:* 11 words. *Graphics:* 3,000. *Consultants:* None listed. *Physical Size:* 8½ by 11¼ in.; 29 cm. *ISBN:* 0-529-04852-3. *Lowest Retail Price:* $59.95.

Purpose and Scope

Webster's New Twentieth Century Dictionary of the English Language aims to "include virtually all those words that a prolific reader in English will ever be likely to investigate." The dictionary's emphasis is on "the active vocabulary of American English." Also included, however, are "a considerable number of obsolete, archaic, and rare words that are likely to be encountered in the earlier standard literature," such as *burthen*, an old form of the word *burden*. Numerous proper names—mostly classical, historical, and Biblical terms—are among the 320,000 total entries. Most general vocabulary terms are covered by *Webster's New Twentieth Century* although treatment tends to be more superficial than that provided by other unabridged dictionaries. But coverage in the area of modern scientific and technical terms is quite deficient. Examples: None of the following words is included in the dictionary: *cholestasis, ekistics, holism, laetrile, nitrofurantoin, patrifocal, renovascular, reprography, revanchism, ultrafiche*, and *Wankel engine*.

Main entries are printed in boldface type. Information given includes spelling, syllabication, pronunciation, part of speech designation, definitions, and etymology. Derivatives are always treated as main entries—that is, *cancer* and *cancerous* are separate entries. Illustrative quotations and examples are included "where it was felt that these would help give the connotative force of the word." In some instances, synonyms (though not antonyms) are provided, but they tend to be less plentiful than in other unabridged dictionaries. Usage labels are used to indicate locality, field, and frequency restrictions. Examples: One meaning of *mob* is labeled "in Australia." The term *mitosis* is labeled "in biology." *Moat* as a pond or lake is labeled "obs." In the matter of the dictionary as prescriber or describer of the language, *Webster's New*

Twentieth Century frequently uses the old-fashioned label "colloq." for non-standard words and meanings. Examples: *ain't*, *disinterested* (meaning uninterested), and *mad* (meaning angry) are all designated "colloq." A few words are tagged "slang." For instance, the word *jaw* (meaning to talk) is so labeled.

Authority

The title page carries the notation "Based upon the Broad Foundations Laid Down by Noah Webster." The introduction then proceeds to trace the dictionary's lineage back to Noah Webster's *Compendious Dictionary of the English Language*, initially published in 1806. (Merriam-Webster, on the other hand, traces its Websterian authority back to *An American Dictionary of the English Language*, published in 1828 and considered Webster's major lexicographical work.) The dictionary was first issued in 1941 as *Webster's New Twentieth Century Dictionary*, which is its current title, although it had previously appeared under the titles *Webster's Imperial Dictionary* (1904), *Webster's Universal Dictionary* (1904), *Webster's Standard Dictionary* (1907), and *Webster's Universities Dictionary* (1940).

The current edition appeared in 1955, published by the World Publishing Company, now Collins+World. Prepared by the publisher's editorial staff under the general direction of Jean L. McKechnie, this second edition represents a dramatic improvement over the previous one, which was mediocre at best. The second edition has been continuously revised since 1955, new copyrights being obtained every two or three years. The current copyright, 1975, still lists Miss McKechnie as the person with chief editorial responsibility. She does not appear in the standard biographical sources, nor are any other individuals named as consultants or staff members. The introduction to the dictionary does note, however, that the editorial staff utilizes the resources and files of *Webster's New World Dictionary of the American Language*, an authoritative semi-unabridged dictionary also published by Collins+World. Overall, *Webster's New Twentieth Century*'s authority is not clearly defined. Future editions should identify those editors, lexicographers, and specialists who are responsible for its contents.

Vocabulary Treatment (Clarity, Accuracy, Thoroughness, Recency)

Unlike practically all major dictionaries, and certainly all those in the unabridged category, *Webster's New Twentieth Century* lists its definitions in no particular order. *The Random House Dictionary*, for instance, gives the most frequently used definition first and *Webster's Third New International Dictionary* gives definitions in historical order. The editor's introduction explains: "Any effort to arrange each entry so that the prevailing current meaning is given first is doomed to failure, since for most words there are a number of senses, on different levels and in different fields, that have equal currency. The editors have, therefore, allowed practicality to determine their practice." What does "practicality" mean? "Where the historical order of senses seemed advisable, this order has been followed; where one meaning flows logically into another or others, this too has been indicated." This nebulous approach to definitional order is not one of the dictionary's most attractive qualities.

As has been already pointed out, the dictionary's announced scope includes "the active vocabulary of American English" but its coverage of the language of modern social science and the physical and biological sciences is spotty. Likewise, its definitions are often overly terse or simplistic. Example: Several connotations of the verb *mix* are either not included or incompletely defined. Example: The biological meaning of *cell* is vague and incomplete. Example: The genetic term *gene* has a fairly clear definition but it fails to include the chemical nature of the gene or its genetic function. Example: The technique of *decoupage* is defined as "the art of cutting out designs or illustrations from paper, foil, etc. and mounting them on a surface in a decorative arrangement." Missing from the definition is the information that decoupage is a permanent process which entails varnishing the designs or illustrations to a glossy finish.

The average number of words per entry is only 11, comparatively a very low figure for an unabridged dictionary which presumably treats its vocabulary in some depth. This low figure is partly due to the fact that *Webster's New Twentieth Century* treats every derivative as a main entry, and the derivatives are often defined simply by restating the root word. Example: The adjective *facetious* is defined as "lightly joking; jocular; jocose, especially at an in-appropriate time." Two synonyms—*witty* and *jocose*—are listed. The adverb *facetiously*, the next main entry, is merely defined as "in a facetious manner." And the noun *facetiousness*, the next main entry, is defined as "the quality of being facetious."

Generally speaking, the definitions are clear and reasonably accurate, as far as they go. But too often they are not thorough and hence are unreliable. Example: The term *existentialism* is clearly defined but the skimpy definition is misleading. *Existentialism* need not imply a "cult of nihilism and pessimism." Sometimes, too, the contemporary meaning of a word is not given. Example: The most recent meaning of *gay* (homosexual) is not given. Example: Two main entries are provided for *mace*. Both are designated nouns, the first meaning being a club-like weapon and the second a ground spice. Not given is *Mace* the chemical (a trade name) and the verb *mace*, meaning to spray with Mace. In addition as noted earlier, many new words in general use are not found in the dictionary, e.g., *honcho, medicaid*, and *Orwellian*. Some active but less frequently used words like *misandry* are also not included.

Other components of vocabulary treatment are likewise not always satis-factory. The pronunciation system, which uses only diacritical and stress marks, is simple but not precise. Etymologies are clear and accurate but they are sometimes too brief. Illustrative quotations and examples are provided though not as extensively as they should be in an unabridged dictionary. The quotations, which are not dated or fully identified, are also sometimes inap-propriate or of questionable value. Example: The second definition of the noun *mob* ("a disorderly assembly") is followed by this quotation from Madison: "Had every Athenian citizen been a Socrates, every Athenian assembly would still have been a *mob*." Finally, synonyms are infrequently provided and, when they are, they are usually not discriminated.

Encyclopedic Features

Webster's New Twentieth Century contains a number of encyclopedic supplements found in the back of the dictionary. They include a 40-page biographical dictionary, a smaller geographical dictionary, a dictionary of foreign words and phrases commonly used in English, a short list of standard abbreviations, forms of address, tables of weights and measures, signs and symbols, lists of U.S. presidents and vice presidents, copies of the U.S. Constitution, Declaration of Independence, and United Nations Charter, and lists of the major geographical features of the world. In addition, a limited amount of encyclopedic information is included in the main body of the dictionary.

The encyclopedic supplements total about 190 pages, far less than the similar supplements found in *The Random House Dictionary*. The material appended to *Webster's New Twentieth Century*, however, is relatively up-to-date. The inclusion of such material does enhance the value of the dictionary, especially when used in a home or office where a good, up-to-date general encyclopedia is not available. But in the final analysis, the dictionary must be judged by the quality of its coverage and treatment of the language, not by the number of its nonlexical supplements.

Graphics

Some 3,000 black-and-white line drawings are included throughout the dictionary. Small in size, they clearly illustrate such terms as *base molding, cockroach, forceps, semiquaver,* and *thermos bottle.* In 1972, 32 full-color plates were added to the dictionary, hence its designation as "Deluxe Color Edition." The plates, which all follow pages 786 and 1554, cover such diverse topics as aircraft, human anatomy, automobiles, styles of painting through the ages, the solar system (which fails to identify the moon), various types of plants and animals, and state flags. The plates are always pretty and sometimes informative, but they are not related to the vocabulary entries in any discernible way. Practically speaking, the color plates are little more than promotional fodder, and "Deluxe Color Edition" seems to be an overstatement of fact.

Physical Format

The large 12-pound volume is not quite as tall as the other unabridged dictionaries but it is very thick (4½ inches). The brown buckram binding appears to be strong; it should withstand heavy use without ill effects. The medium weight paper is of reasonably good quality. The type, while legible, is unevenly printed and sometimes excessively light. The review copy provided by the publisher was missing pages 947 through 978. A condensed pronunciation key appears at the bottom of each three-column page with guide words printed at the top. The volume is thumb-indexed and comes with a brightly colored jacket cover.

Summary

Webster's New Twentieth Century Dictionary of the English Language traces its ancestry back to Noah Webster's little *Compendious Dictionary of the English Language* (1806). The dictionary first appeared under its present title in 1941. A work of poor quality, that edition was transformed into a respectable dictionary when *Webster's New Twentieth Century* underwent a complete and rigorous revision in 1955. Since that time the Unabridged Second Edition has been kept relatively current via continuous revision.

The dictionary emphasizes the "active vocabulary of American English." Its coverage, while not scandalously bad, is especially deficient in the area of modern scientific and technical terms. The dictionary also fails to include many new words, phrases, and meanings which have recently entered the language. Vocabulary treatment, though usually clear, is not always current. But the greatest weakness of *Webster's New Twentieth Century* is its cursory treatment of vocabulary. Too often definitions are simply a string of synonyms. At best, users get only a bare-bones sense of the meaning; at worst they may be misled. Other aspects of the dictionary's vocabulary treatment— pronunciation, illustrative quotations, etymologies, and synonyms—are simple and often superficial.

The dictionary offers considerable encyclopedic information, though not as much as *The Random House Dictionary*. The black-and-white pictorial illustrations are a plus, but the 32 full-color plates have little purpose beyond being good promotional copy. The physical format, though generally satisfactory, is a poor third when compared with *Random House* and *Webster's Third New International Dictionary*.

In the unabridged class, *Webster's Third New International Dictionary* stands alone as the most reliable, comprehensive, and up-to-date general dictionary on the market today. *The Random House Dictionary*, although it lacks the depth and breadth of coverage provided by *Webster's Third*, is easier to use, contains many useful encyclopedic features, and costs less than half as much. *Webster's New Twentieth Century* has much the same scope as *Random House*, but it is not as current or as reliable. The key word which describes *Webster's New Twentieth Century* is "superficial." Although *Funk & Wagnalls New Standard Dictionary*'s coverage of the language historically is far superior to either *Random House* or *Webster's New Twentieth Century*, the dictionary's lack of currency makes it a questionable purchase.

Other Critical Opinions

Booklist, December 1, 1957, pp. 181–187.

Webster's Third New International Dictionary

Descriptive Information

Full Title: **Webster's Third New International Dictionary of the English Language.** *Editors:* Philip Babcock Gove, Editor in Chief, and the Merriam-Webster Editorial Staff. *Publisher:* G. & C. Merriam Co. *Edition Reviewed:* Third Unabridged Edition, 1976.

Classification: Adult—Unabridged. *Pages:* 81a, 2662. *Total Entries:* 460,000. *Average Entry Length:* 23 words. *Graphics:* 3,000. *Consultants:* 202. *Physical Size:* 9¼ by 13 in.; 32 cm. *ISBN:* 0-87779-101-5 (Blue Sturdite); 0-87779-106-6 (Imperial Buckram). *Lowest Retail Price:* $75.00 (Blue Sturdite).

Purpose and Scope

Webster's Third New International Dictionary of the English Language, the largest and most prestigious dictionary published in the United States, covers the general English-language vocabulary in use since 1755, the date of Dr. Johnson's famous *Dictionary of the English Language*. Words obsolete prior to that date are not included in the dictionary unless, according to the editor's preface, they are "found in well-known major works of a few major writers," for instance, Shakespeare. The late Philip B. Gove, editor of *Webster's Third*, states the dictionary's fundamental purpose this way: "Comprehensiveness requires maximum coverage with a minimum of compromise. The basic aim is nothing less than coverage of the current vocabulary of standard written and spoken English."

The dictionary now includes approximately 460,000 entries counting the vocabulary covered in the separately published supplement *6,000 Words* (G. & C. Merriam Co., 1976). When *Webster's Third*, hereafter referred to simply as *W3*, first appeared in 1961 it added some 100,000 new words and meanings not found in the previous unabridged edition, *Webster's New International Dictionary* (Second Edition, 1934), hereafter *W2*. Much of the new vocabulary derived from scientific and technical developments which have occurred since the 1930s, especially, reports Dr. Gove in his preface, "in physical science (as in electronics, nuclear physics, statistics, and soil science), in technology (as in rocketry, communications, automation, and synthetics), in medicine, and in the experimental phases of natural science." Notably, some 250,000 obsolete words and phrases were dropped from *W2*, which included among its 600,000 entries all words in use since 1500, as well as all words found in the works of Chaucer (1340–1400).

Another important difference in the scope of the two dictionaries concerns encyclopedic information. Whereas *W2* included many proper names and much factual material in the main vocabulary, along with extensive biographical and geographical supplements, *W3* excludes most of this kind of information. Indeed, among the four in-print unabridged dictionaries, *W3* contains the least nonlexical material. Dr. Gove cites the "demands for space" as the chief reason for this policy, as well as the dictionary's increased emphasis on its "linguistic" function. As Gove explains, *W3* "confines itself strictly to generic words and their functions, forms, sounds, and meanings as distinguished from proper names that are not generic." In this sense, *W3* is more purely a dictionary than any of its unabridged rivals.

Another major difference between the two editions is that *W3* dropped most foreign words and phrases, except those which are now part of the English language (e.g., *tour de force*). Another is that *W3* dropped the simplified spellings found in *W2*, perhaps the death knell for the spelling reform so eagerly sought by Noah Webster, Isaac Funk, and other nineteenth-century lexicographers. And yet another difference is that *W3* added many compound words formed by combining two or more elements, either by running them together (e.g., *redneck*), or hyphenating them (e.g., *hand-me-down*), or using the alphabet's so-called zero form, the blank space (e.g., *mixed drink*).

Still another significant difference between *W2* and *W3* concerns the application of restrictive usage labels. Whereas *W2* rather freely identified certain words and usages as culturally or socially inferior via such labels as "slang" and "colloquial," *W3* strikes a much less prescriptive stance. "Accuracy in addition to requiring freedom from error and conformity to truth," says Dr. Gove in his preface, "requires a dictionary to state meanings in which words are in fact used, not to give editorial opinion on what their meanings should be." The pejorative label "colloquial" was entirely discarded and "slang" used much more sparingly, being replaced by the neutral "nonstandard." As described in Part I of the *Buying Guide* (see "Dictionary Trends"), *W3*'s "permissiveness" caused a firestorm of criticism from conservative self-appointed guardians of the language. And, although *W3* appears to have outlasted its most vocal critics, the issue is far from dead, as the popular success of the *American Heritage Dictionary*'s usage panel suggests.

Main entries are printed in boldface type. Information provided includes spelling, syllabication, pronunciation, part of speech designation, definitions, etymology, and inflected forms (also in boldface type). More than 200,000 illustrative quotations and examples are provided. The quotations represent some 14,000 different authors, many of them contemporary writers. Numerous synonyms are discriminated in over 1,000 synonym paragraphs. Antonyms, which were included in *W2*, have been dropped. Usage labels (other than those indicating social status) are provided, although subject field labels are applied much less frequently than in the previous edition or the other unabridged dictionaries. Examples: The first meaning of the adjective *capable* ("able to take in, contain, receive, or accommodate") is labeled "archaic." The third sense of the thirteenth meaning of the noun *lift* (elevator) is labeled "chiefly Brit." But the legal term *stare decisis* is not labeled "law," although the definition makes it clear that *stare decisis* is used only in a legal sense.

Authority

W3's genealogy is impeccable. The dictionary traces its origins back to Noah Webster's famous *American Dictionary of the English Language*, initially published in 1828. The present publisher, G. & C. Merriam Company, acquired the rights to Webster's dictionary after his death in 1843, and soon thereafter issued a revised edition under the editorship of Webster's son-in-law, Chauncey A. Goodrich, a Yale University professor. Successor editions in the unabridged series include the *American Dictionary of the English Language* (1864), edited by Noah Porter, president of Yale; *Webster's International Dictionary* (1890), also edited by Porter; *Webster's New International Dictionary* (1909), edited by William Torrey Harris and F. Sturges Allen; and *Webster's New International Dictionary* (Second Edition, 1934), edited by William Allan Neilson and Thomas A. Knott. *W3* first appeared in 1961. New copyrights, indicating periodic revisions, have been registered every five years since 1961.

W3 was in preparation for ten years. Estimates indicate that it required over $3.5 million and 757 "editor-years" to produce. Philip Gove, the principal editor, was an academician prior to joining Merriam-Webster in 1946. He served as editor in chief until his death in 1972. The supporting editorial staff is impressive. All of the 13 associate editors bring excellent credentials to their work. The same is true of the 125 assistant editors and editorial assistants listed in the front of the book. Gove rightly notes in his preface that "This staff is in effect a faculty which specializes in different branches of knowledge much as a small college faculty does." In addition, 202 outside consultants are identified. Their qualifications are outstanding.

W3's ultimate authority rests on its imposing citation file, now grown to over 12 million slips (or examples of recorded usage). Some 4½ million such examples were collected by the editorial staff between 1936 and 1960. These citations, drawn from a variety of contemporary sources, are the ones most frequently quoted as verbal illustrations in *W3*. Like all commercial unabridged dictionaries, *W3* also draws upon the great research dictionaries like the *Oxford English Dictionary* for citational evidence of an historical nature.

Vocabulary Treatment (Clarity, Accuracy, Thoroughness, Recency)

Unlike the other in-print unabridged dictionaries, *W3* continues the Websterian tradition of listing definitions in historical order, giving the earliest known meaning first and the most recent meaning last. Definitional treatment stresses what editor Gove calls "the three cardinal virtues of dictionary making: accuracy, clearness, and comprehensiveness." In an effort to achieve these virtues more perfectly, *W3* introduced a new method of defining words. The technique involves constructing a self-contained analytical phrase which represents one complete sense of the word being defined. The analytical phrases, which are set apart by heavy black colons, contain as little punctuation as possible. Example: The first definition of the verb *mix*, which has seven different senses, is as follows (illustrative examples omitted): "to stir, shake, or otherwise bring together (different substances) with a loss of separateness or identity: cause to be scattered or diffused throughout: combine (as the ingredients of smokeless powder) in one mass: intermingle thoroughly: put as an ingredient: combine with or introduce into a mass already formed: put in disorder: JUMBLE." Each of the phrases set off by colons is a complete sense of the first meaning of *mix*. The synonymic JUMBLE, which appears in small capitals, "should not be considered a definition but a cross-reference to a definition of equivalent meaning." Each of the remaining seven numbered definitions of *mix* is treated in a similar manner.

Almost without exception, *W3*'s definitions are clear and accurate. Example: The definition of the term *existentialism* is the longest, fullest, and most knowledgeable among the four in-print unabridged dictionaries. There is also a cross-reference to *Christian Existentialism* which is equally clear and accurate. Example: The noun *misandry* is accurately defined as "a hatred of men." *W3* is the only one of the four dictionaries which treats this word competently. Thoroughness of definition is attested to by the average number of words (23) accorded each entry. The definitions are likewise up-to-date. The 1961 third edition is revised periodically, a new copyright appearing every five years. In addition, the supplement *6,000 Words* (1976) is now available. (See the section "New Words" under "Special-Purpose Dictionaries and Wordbooks" for additional information about *6,000 Words*.)

Most other aspects of vocabulary treatment are satisfactory, although the pronunciation system has been roundly criticized as being too technical for the average dictionary user. A total of 79 different symbols are involved, including letters of the alphabet (with and without diacritical marks), a variety of stress marks, and numerous phonetic symbols, some of which might be too difficult for the layperson to master. Unlike the other in-print unabridged dictionaries, *W3* does not include a condensed pronunciation key on every page or two-page spread. Instead, the key only appears on the endpapers and in the front matter. It should also be noted that *W3*'s pronunciations reflect "general cultivated conversational usage, both informal and formal," whereas *W2* gave pronunciations that represented formal platform speech.

W3 methodically provides variant spellings whenever there is a legitimate question about a word's accepted orthography. Examples: discernible/discernable; labeled/labelled; sizable/sizeable. Preferred British spellings are also profusely given, labeled "Brit." One oddity about *W3*'s vocabulary treatment is its lack of capitalization. For instance, there are two entries for the word *Brooklyn*, one as an adjective (as in Brooklyn streets) and the other as a noun meaning in bowling "a hit in which the ball strikes the headpin to the left of center." In both instances, the main entry is entered as *brooklyn* followed by the note "usu cap"—that is, usually capitalized. Indeed, the only proper name capitalized as a main entry is the word *God*. Critics have generally denounced *W3*'s punctuation and specifically its lack of capitalization, one reviewer declaring that the policy has been carried to "an absurd extreme."

The etymologies are quite full. They are the work of Charles R. Sleeth, one of *W3*'s associate editors, and they are usually superior to those found in the other unabridged dictionaries. An etymological innovation is the introduction of the label ISV, meaning International Scientific Vocabulary. This descriptive device is applied to the etymologies of scientific and technical terms "when their language of origin is not positively ascertainable but they are known to be current in at least one language other than English." The term *cholesterol* is an example.

The 200,000 illustrative quotations and examples are mostly contemporary in source and tone. For instance, the following authors or publications are quoted within the entry for the verb *mix: Saturday Review;* J. D. Magee; Walter Goodman; H. S. Canby; *Springfield* (Mass.) *Daily News; American Guide Series;* D. W. Brogan; Erle Stanley Gardner; *Times Literary Supplement;* Ellen Glasgow; Louis Auchincloss; Bertrand Russell; H. O. Taylor; Carl Alpert; and Zechariah Chafee. The dictionary has been faulted by some critics for quoting the likes of Erle Stanley Gardner and even—yes—Mickey Spillane. Wilson Follett, in his savage attack on *W3* ("a scandal and a disaster") in the January 1962 *Atlantic Monthly*, wrote that "the great preponderance of latter-prose, little of it worth repeating and a good deal of it hardly worth printing in the first place, is likely to curtail by years the useful life of the *Third New International.*" *W3*'s editors, on the other hand, point out that the illustrative quotations chosen represent language as it is typically used today, "rather than in atypical uses often found in imaginative literature." Regrettably, the quotations are not dated nor are sources cited in the case of individual authors.

Encyclopedic Features

The dictionary contains much encyclopedic information in the form of tables on such topics as archaeology, book sizes, colors, dyes, ocean currents, shotgun gauges, major stars, chemical elements, important planets, and weights and measures. Biographical and geographical entries, however, are excluded. But note that Merriam-Webster publishes *Webster's New Geographical Dictionary, Webster's Biographical Dictionary,* and *Webster's American Biographies.* These reference works provide more thorough coverage of people and places than can be found in the encyclopedic supplements of the other unabridged dictionaries.

Graphics

The 3,000 black-and-white line drawings located throughout the dictionary are small but clear. They accompany such terms as *bandage, doublet, emmy, goatee, martha washington table, pew, rigging screw,* and *sloop.* The emphasis is on articles of clothing, furniture, instruments, and implements. In every instance, the drawings visually clarify or enhance the meaning of the terms they accompany.

Physical Format

The volume is naturally large, weighing 13 pounds. The publisher conveniently sells a table-top stand ($19.95) and a dictionary table ($49.95), both designed to hold *W3.* The two bindings currently available—Blue Sturdite and Imperial Buckram—are sturdy and should wear well, even with very heavy use. Different grades of paper—regular and india—are used in the two editions. Both grades are of excellent quality. Merriam-Webster's Times Roman type, introduced in 1961 with the initial publication of *W3,* is compact and legible. The quality of the printing is outstanding.

The three-column page layout effectively utilizes the available space. *W2* had what was known as the "divided page," a layout which entailed two alphabetical sequences, one at the top, listing the standard vocabulary, and, the other at the bottom, giving variant spellings, inflected forms, certain derivatives, words formed by self-explanatory prefixes like *non-,* and archaic and obsolete words. This feature, referred to by some critics as "basement storage," has fortunately not been retained in *W3.* But despite the clean, compressed look of the page layout, there is at least at first glance, in the words of one critic, "too many tricky little symbols." These symbols are, of course, all explained and, in most cases, are not difficult to grasp. Nevertheless, *W3* is a large, complex dictionary which can be intimidating to casual users. In this respect, the smaller and somewhat less complicated *Random House Dictionary* is more inviting to use.

Summary

Webster's Third New International Dictionary of the English Language is the latest in Merriam-Webster's line of unabridged dictionaries which dates back to Noah Webster's famous *American Dictionary of the English Language* (1828). First published in 1961, *W3* (as *Webster's Third* is called) covers words and phrases in general use since 1755. Its coverage of the vocabulary of modern science and technology is particularly noteworthy, although all areas of the language are covered satisfactorily. Treatment of vocabulary is outstanding in almost all respects. The definitions are lucid, accurate, extremely thorough, and up-to-date. In addition, a supplement to the dictionary entitled *6,000 Words* was issued in 1976. (See the section "New Words" under "Special-Purpose Dictionaries and Wordbooks" for additional information about *6,000 Words.*)

Another impressive feature of the dictionary is its extensive provision of illustrative quotations, many of them from contemporary sources. The detailed etymologies are excellent. On the negative side, the pronunciation system is probably too technical and complicated for most users, the lack of capitalization of proper nouns and adjectives (e.g., *brooklyn*) is disconcerting, and, though the type is quite legible and the page layout neat and clean, the dictionary gives the impression of being crowded with many symbols, some unfamiliar.

W3 is unquestionably *the* American dictionary of this generation. When it appeared in 1961, however, many well-known writers on language usage like Jacques Barzun, Dwight Macdonald, and Wilson Follett bitterly attacked it. These critics were not so much concerned that the dictionary was smaller in terms of total entries (450,000 versus 600,000) than the preceding edition published in 1934. Nor were they particularly disturbed by *W3*'s complex pronunciation system or the fact that the encyclopedic information included in the second edition had been dropped from the new edition. Rather, what touched off an unprecedented paroxysm of abuse was *W3*'s failure, according to its critics, to provide prescriptive standards denoting good usage. In a word, *W3* was "permissive."

Today the debate has cooled and *W3* is generally recognized as *the* authoritative big dictionary, despite its sparing use of restrictive labels. Bergen Evans, a respected dictionary authority, puts it this way: "It is a very great book. No scholar, no teacher of literature, no library, no lawyer, no editor, no business office can afford to be without it." Nevertheless, it is true that *W3* does not abundantly provide the sort of usage information which some people expect to find in a dictionary. As a result, there are still some who prefer the 1934 Second Edition. And, although it has been out of print for many years, used copies are occasionally available on the secondhand market, usually at $100 or more a copy. Libraries especially may want to have both editions available.

A question often asked is when will *W4* be published? The average interval between Merriam-Webster's unabridged editions has been about 23 years. This means that *Webster's Fourth* is probably not due until the mid-1980s. A Merriam-Webster executive, however, has told the *Buying Guide* that "tremendous progress" is currently being made toward the compilation of a new edition. It was further indicated that *W4* would not appear before 1980 at the earliest and that, due to rising production costs, the new edition *might* be published in parts on a volume-by-volume basis.

Comparatively speaking, *Webster's Third New International Dictionary* stands alone as the most reliable, comprehensive, and up-to-date general unabridged dictionary on the market today. The *Random House Dictionary*, although it lacks the depth and breadth of coverage provided by *W3*, is easier to use, contains many useful encyclopedic features, and costs less than half as much. *Webster's New Twentieth Century Dictionary* has much the same scope as *Random House*, but it is not as current or as reliable. Although *Funk & Wagnalls New Standard Dictionary*'s coverage of the language historically is far superior to either *Random House* or *Webster's New Twentieth Century*, the dictionary's lack of currency makes it a questionable purchase.

Other Critical Opinions

Booklist, July 1, 1963, pp. 871–874.

Katz, William A. *Basic Information Sources*. Vol. 1 of *Introduction to Reference Work*, 2nd ed. (New York: McGraw-Hill, 1974), pp. 265–266.

Sledd, James, and Wilma R. Ebbitt, eds. *Dictionaries and That Dictionary* (Chicago: Scott, Foresman, 1962). This book is a collection of articles and reviews, pro and con, about *W3*. Larger public and most academic libraries should have a copy of the book.

SEMI-UNABRIDGED DICTIONARIES

American College Dictionary

Descriptive Information

Full Title: **The American College Dictionary.** *Editors:* Clarence L. Barnhart, Editor in Chief; Jess Stein, Managing Editor. *Publisher:* Random House. *Edition Reviewed:* 1970.

Classification: Adult—Semi-unabridged. *Pages:* xxviii, 1444. *Total Entries:* 132,000. *Average Entry Length:* 16 words. *Graphics:* 1,500. *Consultants:* 355. *Physical Size:* 7 by 10 in.; 25 cm. *LC:* 70-115027. *ISBN:* 0-394-40002-X (plain); 0-394-40001-1 (thumb-indexed). *Lowest Retail Price:* $6.95.

Purpose and Scope

The American College Dictionary (*ACD*) was, when first published in 1947, "the latest record of current usage made by any dictionary staff since World War II." The dictionary, which has been periodically updated through the 1960s, includes some 60,000 scientific and technical terms, many of which were generated in the early postwar era. Also included among the dictionary's 132,000 entries are 5,000 names of people, a similar number of places, some commonly used foreign words and phrases, standard abbreviations, and the like.

In addition, like *Webster's New World Dictionary* (Second College Edition), *ACD* is strong in the area of Americanisms (e.g., *bunco, lynch law, peachy, pea jacket, robber baron*), due in large measure to its extensive use of the scholarly multivolumed *Dictionary of American English on Historical Principles* (University of Chicago, 1938). Likewise, considerable emphasis has been placed on usage levels and regional differences. In this respect, Clarence Barnhart notes in his introduction that "A dictionary should tell you what is commonly accepted usage and wherein different classes of speakers or regions differ in their use of the language. We have taken special pains to give an accurate record of the distribution of usage (*Colloq., Slang, Brit., U.S.,* etc.)."

Authority

When *ACD* appeared in 1947, it received rave reviews. The editor, Clarence L. Barnhart, brought impeccable qualifications and many new ideas to the work. He began his career as a lexicographer in the 1930s with the textbook publisher Scott, Foresman & Company. During that period, he and Dr. Edward L. Thorndike, an educational psychologist, introduced a number of important innovations into American dictionary-making. The so-called Thorndike Revolution included the use of word frequency studies to determine what vocabulary should be covered in the dictionary and how it should be treated; the use of made-up illustrative sentences and phrases designed to "force" definitional clarity; and the use of the schwa (ə), a pronunciation symbol borrowed from the International Phonetic Alphabet which represents the most frequently heard vowel sound in American English. When Barnhart accepted Random House's offer to build a new dictionary completely from scratch, he brought these innovative ideas and techniques with him.

Barnhart was assisted by a distinguished group of lexicographers, linguists (foremost of whom was Leonard Bloomfield who wrote the book on modern linguistics), editors, and subject specialists. Jess Stein, currently editor of *The Random House Dictionary*, served as managing editor. The Editorial Advisory Committee comprised Bernard Block, Leonard Bloomfield, Charles C. Fries, W. Cabell Greet, Irving Lorge, and Kemp Malone. The language scholars in charge of usage levels and dialect distribution included Albert C. Baugh, Sir William A. Craigie, Mitford M. Mathews, and Allen Walker Read. The subject consultants included Ralph Linton (anthropology), Robert M. MacIver (political theory), Owen Lattimore (China and Japan), Bruce Rogers (typography), and Gardner Murphy (psychology). In all, some 350 very well-qualified people were involved in the production of *ACD*. Barnhart was not exaggerating when he notes in the introduction that *ACD* was the "first abridged dictionary to be prepared by a staff larger than is usually assembled for an unabridged dictionary."

The old but highly regarded *Century Dictionary and Cyclopedia* and *The New Century Dictionary* (see Appendix A for descriptions of both of these out-of-print titles) were used to compile *ACD*'s basic word list. But the modern vocabulary derived from the Lorge-Thorndike Semantic Count, a word frequency study based on a 4½-million-word sample. Among other things, the study revealed that, at the time, the contemporary vocabulary of science and technology was not being adequately covered by comparable dictionaries. Barnhart and his associates, therefore, made a particular effort to produce a college dictionary which was up-to-date in the area of scientific and technical terminology. It must be kept in mind, however, that *ACD* has never been fully revised. Spot revisions using the original plates did occur through the 1950s and 1960s with the most recent copyright date 1970. But at the present time *ACD*'s authority is weakened due to onsetting old age.

Vocabulary Treatment (Clarity, Accuracy, Thoroughness, Recency)

The most common or frequently used meaning is given first. The definitions are exceptionally clear, simplicity of treatment being a high editorial priority. The definitions also tend to be sufficiently detailed. In some instances, however, newer words (e.g., *existentialism* and *holism*) are not defined as thoroughly as might be expected in a college-level dictionary. In other cases, the definitions are not up-to-date or use outdated terminology (e.g., *cell* and *photovoltaic*). In a few instances, definitions are at least partially inaccurate based on today's knowledge. Example: The biological term *gene* is biochemical in nature, not "probably" so. Moreover, genes do not develop "into a hereditary character" but rather into *codes* for the character. And to say that the gene "reacts with the environment" is a confusing and/or meaningless statement. But the greatest single problem with *ACD* is the vocabulary, which is not treated at all. None of the following relatively new but commonly used words is included in the dictionary: *data bank, decoupage, funky, honcho, kerogen, Pap smear, reprography, shtick, time-sharing,* and *visualization*. Nor are new meanings of such words as *launder, leverage, modulus,* and *residual* found in *ACD*.

Other aspects of vocabulary treatment are satisfactory. The pronunciation system is comparatively easy to use and quite precise. The schwa, which caused much debate when it was introduced in 1947 (it had been used earlier in the Thorndike-Barnhart school dictionaries), has now been widely accepted by trade dictionary editors. Common variant pronunciations and spellings are usually given, though not always. Example: the word *inalienable* is listed but the less common *unalienable* is not, despite the fact that the Declaration of Independence speaks of *un*alienable rights. The etymologies, prepared under the supervision of Kemp Malone (who did the same for the more recent *Random House Dictionary*), are concise and, when the dictionary was first published, it included some word origins not found in comparable dictionaries, especially in the area of Americanisms, American-Indian words, and some Romance language words.

Illustrative phrases (though no quotations) are abundantly provided throughout the dictionary. Example: the verb *mix* has 12 senses, five of which are accompanied by phrases like "to mix business and pleasure" and "to mix a little soda into the flour." The provision and treatment of synonyms are excellent. Care has been taken to include an illustrative example for every synonym. Moreover, synonyms and antonyms are keyed by number to the corresponding definition. Example: The synonym paragraph accompanying the verb *mix* keys the synonyms *consort* and *mingle* to the ninth meaning, "to associate, as in company."

Encyclopedic Features

As previously noted, *ACD* includes many nonlexical entries (especially famous people and places) in the main body of the dictionary. Indeed, it was one of the first general dictionaries to put all entries (including people, places, events, abbreviations, etc.) in one main alphabet, a feature which has been widely imitated by other dictionaries. The small amount of appended material consists of a list of signs and symbols, a usage and style manual, and a directory of colleges and universities.

Graphics

The 1,500 small black-and-white line drawings are legible, captioned, and complementary to the words they accompany. They include spot maps (about 300) and representations of plants and animals (actual sizes of the animals are given in the caption) as well as objects like clothing, instruments, and types of buildings.

Physical Format

The dictionary is well bound, uses a fine quality opaque Bible paper, and has small but very readable type. Guide words are printed at the top of each two-column page; condensed etymological and pronunciation keys appear at the bottom. Overall, this desk-size dictionary has an attractive, modern format.

Summary

When *The American College Dictionary* appeared in 1947, it represented the vanguard of American lexicography. Its innovative methods and superlative scholarship far outstripped other dictionaries' in its class at the time. Today, *ACD* remains a useful but much less impressive dictionary. Its definitions, pronunciation system, etymologies, illustrative examples, etc. are clear and usually informative, but the passage of time has had an effect. Although *ACD* has undergone periodic plate revisions since 1947, the updatings have not kept pace with changes in the language. The estimated life of a college dictionary today is about ten or at most fifteen years, after which time it should be thoroughly revised or dropped. *ACD* is now 30 years old—still remarkable in some respects but definitely showing its age. In point of fact, Random House is putting its lexicographical energies into *The Random House Dictionary* and *The Random House College Dictionary*, not *ACD*.

Comparatively speaking, *ACD* cannot be recommended over the five leading college dictionaries. It is simply not as up-to-date and hence as reliable as the five leading semi-unabridged college dictionaries: *The American Heritage Dictionary* (New College Edition), *Funk & Wagnalls Standard College Dictionary*, *The Random House College Dictionary*, *Webster's New Collegiate Dictionary*, and *Webster's New World Dictionary* (Second College Edition).

Other Critical Opinions

Booklist, June 15, 1964, pp. 927–930.
Katz, William A. *Basic Information Sources*. Vol. 1 of *Introduction to Reference Work*, 2nd ed. (New York: McGraw-Hill, 1974), p. 270.

American Heritage Dictionary (*New College Edition*)

Descriptive Information

Full Title: **The American Heritage Dictionary of the English Language.** *Editors:* William Morris, Editor; Fernando de Mello Vianna, Editorial Director; Norman Hoss, Managing Editor. *Publishers:* American Heritage Publishing Co., Inc., and Houghton Mifflin Co. *Edition Reviewed:* New College Edition, 1976.

Classification: Adult—Semi-unabridged. *Pages:* l, 1550. *Total Entries:* 155,000. *Average Entry Length:* 14 words. *Graphics:* 4,000. *Consultants:* 200. *Physical Size:* 7½ by 10¼ in.; 26 cm. (Standard or Larger Format Edition is 8½ by 11¼ in.; 28 cm.) *LC:* 76-86995. ISBN: 0-395-20359-7 (New College Edition, plain); 0-395-20360-0 (New College Edition, thumb-indexed); 0-395-09066 (Standard or Larger Format Edition, thumb-indexed). *Lowest Retail Price:* $9.95.

Purpose and Scope

The American Heritage Dictionary of the English Language is published in several editions. The New College Edition reviewed here has the same text and number of entries as the Standard or so-called Larger Format Edition. The only differences between these editions are that the latter is physically larger and only available with thumb-index at $14.95. The dictionary is also published in abridged editions under the titles *The Concise Heritage Dictionary* (55,000 entries) and *The American Heritage School Dictionary* (55,000 entries). There is also an abridged 55,000-entry paperback edition under the title *The American Heritage Dictionary of the English Language* which has exactly the same text as *The Concise Heritage.* And McGraw-Hill (which owns the American Heritage Publishing Co.) apparently publishes the 155,000-entry version under the title *The Heritage Illustrated Dictionary of the English Language* (International Edition). Finally, Houghton Mifflin now publishes the 155,000-entry work with encyclopedic supplements under the title *Illustrated Heritage Dictionary and Information Book.* In this review, *American Heritage* refers to the New College Edition, dated 1976.

The basic 155,000-entry dictionary first appeared in 1969, an entirely new work compiled from scratch. It is the newest major American dictionary (not counting such smaller abridged items as *The Doubleday Dictionary* and *The Scribner-Bantam English Dictionary,* published in 1975 and 1977 respectively). From the beginning the American Heritage line of dictionaries has been promoted vigorously. Over $1 million was budgeted for promotion even before the dictionary reached the bookstores. As *Time* put it (May 11, 1970, p. 96), *American Heritage* "was brought out last September with the kind of hoopla usually reserved for new detergents." The dictionary has sold phenomenally well in its various editions and is now among the country's most popular reference works.

In addition to being popular, *American Heritage* is a well-produced dictionary. Its vocabulary represents a balanced selection of words and phrases from contemporary American English. The editor, William Morris, indicates the dictionary's scope in his introduction: "The vocabulary recorded here, ranging from the language of Shakespeare to the idiom of the present day, is that of the educated adult." Among the idioms of the day included in *American Heritage* are all the notorious four-letter words and their derivatives. Example: the verb *fuck* has a 12-line entry, complete with informative and easy to understand etymology. Derivatives include *fuck up* and *fuck with* but not *fuck over.* All the definitions are labeled "vulgar" and, for good measure, some are tagged "vulgar slang." Among the other leading college dictionaries, *Webster's New Collegiate Dictionary* and *The Random House College Dictionary* also include four-letter words, whereas *Funk & Wagnalls Standard College Dictionary* and *Webster's New World Dictionary* do not.

American Heritage attempts to be a "with-it" dictionary. It was born during the Vietnam era of protest and confrontation and, perhaps as a result, the editors were encouraged to break at least some lexicographical traditions. In addition to being the first general dictionary to include obscenities, the dictionary is more profusely illustrated than other college dictionaries. It has wide white margins with plenty of open space, a sharp contrast to the usually crowded dictionary page. It uses such terms as *way-out* (labeled "informal" by the dictionary) in its definitions. See, for example, the definition of *funky*. Its etymologies avoid the traditional abbreviations ("OE," "OF," "OHG," "OL," "ON," etc.) which turn off or stymie many users. The entire thrust of *American Heritage* is ease of use. Real efforts have been made to make the dictionary "readable." William Morris explains: "To many people a dictionary is a forbidding volume, a useful but bleak compendium, to be referred to hastily for information, such as spelling and pronunciation. Yet what a dictionary ought to be is a treasury of information about every aspect of words, our most essential tools of communication. It should be an agreeable companion."

Another innovative aspect of *American Heritage* is its usage panel. Now headed by Edwin Newman (NBC news commentator and author of *Strictly Speaking* and *A Civil Tongue*), the panel comprises about 100 celebrities who comment on examples of questionable usage (e.g., *My watch runs good*). The editors then tally the responses and report on how the panel members responded (86 percent condemn *My watch runs good*). This information is then incorporated into the dictionary in some 800 usage notes. For example, several other uses and abuses of *good* as an adverb are presented in a lengthy note accompanying the entry for *good*, the adjective. The usage-panel concept is obviously a reaction—or perhaps overreaction—to the charge of permissiveness which was hurled at *Webster's Third New International Dictionary* in the early 1960s. William Morris notes that *American Heritage* was prepared "at a time when the language, already a historical melting pot, is under constant challenge—from the scientist, the bureaucrat, the broadcaster, the innovator of every stripe, even the voyager in space." Therefore, the dictionary "would faithfully record our language, the duty of any lexicographer, but it would not, like so many others in these permissive times, rest there. On the contrary, it would add the essential dimension of guidance." Morris is, of course, referring to Merriam-Webster's alleged "permissiveness."

Other dictionaries provide informative usage notes. *The Random House Dictionary*, for instance, includes notes prepared by Theodore Bernstein of the *New York Times*, who is also a member of the *American Heritage* panel. Bernstein is an authority on the use of the language and therefore his views are worth having. But in the case of the *American Heritage* panel, is Peter Hurd, the artist, a language expert? Is Senator Mark Hatfield from Oregon an authority? Is Margaret Mead? Is Red Smith the sportscaster? Is Gloria Steinem? Not really, but they make good advertising copy. Rochelle Girson, who reviewed the dictionary in *Saturday Review* (September 27, 1969, pp. 25–26), raises another question about the usage panel as a "guidance" device: "Since the arbiters have proved far from unanimous on what is or is not acceptable as the King's American English (we almost elected a president who always says 'myself' when he means 'me'), ample license is provided for non-U [a Britishism meaning non-Upper Class] expressions by simply going along with the opinion of the minority who upheld them." And, in a number of cases (e.g., the word *laundered* in connection with campaign funds), the panel is split about 50-50 as to what constitutes correct usage.

Authority

The American Heritage Dictionary is co-published by the American Heritage Publishing Company and Houghton Mifflin, the well-known Boston firm. The American Heritage Publishing Company also publishes the handsome magazines *American Heritage, Americana,* and *Horizon.* The dictionary, initially published in 1969, has undergone what the publishers call "major revisions" in 1971, 1973, and 1976. The original edition was costly—the *Saturday Review* labeled it "a $4-million lexicographical spectacle."

The people who originally compiled *American Heritage* were well qualified for the job. William Morris, the editor, has had much experience at making both dictionaries and encyclopedias. Among his books are the *Harper Dictionary of Contemporary Usage* and the three-volume *Dictionary of Word and Phrase Origins.* Morris, it should be pointed out, is no longer the editor, although his name continues to appear on the title page. Fernando de Mello Vianna is now designated as editorial director, Dictionary Division, of Houghton Mifflin. There is a large supporting editorial staff of 106, including a board of linguists which is composed of six distinguished specialists. In addition, there are 82 subject consultants listed in the front matter. And, of course, the usage panel adds another 100 or so prominent names to the dictionary's authority list.

Vocabulary selection as well as illustrative citations derive from a computer-generated word frequency study conducted at Brown University in the mid-1960s. The study encompassed a total sample of 1,014,232 words drawn from a collection of texts called the *Standard Corpus of Present-Day Edited American English.* Computer analysis revealed exactly 50,406 different words in the one-million-word sample. The most frequently used words are *the* (occurring 69,971 times), *of* (36,411 times), *and* (28,852 times), *to* (26,149 times), and *a* (23,237 times). The word *he* (9,543 times) was tenth on the list whereas *she* occurred only 2,859 times, which tells something about sexism as well as word frequencies. This language research, which continues the work pioneered by Edward L. Thorndike and Clarence L. Barnhart in the 1930s, provides *American Heritage* with a balanced vocabulary list as well as requisite citational evidence.

Vocabulary Treatment (Clarity, Accuracy, Thoroughness, Recency)

Unlike other dictionaries, *American Heritage* lists the "central" or essential meaning first, rejecting both the methods of Merriam-Webster (historical order) and Funk & Wagnalls (most commonly used meaning first). The definitions tend to be up-to-date, accurate, and clear. "Our aim," says the editor, "has been to phrase definitions in concise, lucid prose." This is achieved in almost every instance. The definitions are not always thorough, however. For instance, the three-line definition of *gene* is accurate as far as it goes but, compared with other leading college dictionaries, the definition is superficial, e.g., it neglects the chemical nature of genes. Such terms as *decoupage, existentialism, holism, macrame,* and *visualization* are likewise not fully treated. Strangely enough, this "with-it" dictionary provides no entry for the verb *mace* (to be sprayed with the chemical Mace), although *Maced.,* the abbreviation for Macedonia and Macedonian, is included. Generally speaking, the definitions are not as extensive or as comprehensive as those found in such competitors as *Webster's New World Dictionary* and *Webster's New Collegiate Dictionary.*

The pronunciation system is relatively clear and simple. Variant pronunciations have been de-emphasized, though the most common variants (e.g., rōōf/rŏŏf) are given. Oddly, first names of people entered in the dictionary are not pronounced, e.g., *Kenyatta* is pronounced but not *Jomo; Kierkegaard* is pronounced but not *Sören.* Spelling variants are usually given. Examples: *inalienable/unalienable; labeled/labelled; sizable/sizeable* are found in the dictionary but *discernable* (variant of *discernible*) is not. As noted earlier, the 40,000 etymologies avoid the standard abbreviations and symbols in an effort to make word origins (which are really part of a word's central definition) as accessible as possible to the average user. The etymologies tend to be brief but clear. An effort has been made to trace each word, when possible, back to its Indo-European roots. These roots are listed and explained in detail in the appendix.

Only about 6,000 illustrative quotations are used in the dictionary. The quotations, which are usually attributed to such standard American and English authors as Daniel Defoe, Arthur Conan Doyle, Sinclair Lewis, and Jack London, derive from the collection of texts called the *Standard Corpus of Present-Day Edited American English* which comprised the dictionary's original word sample. Occasionally, a contemporary writer like J. P. Donleavy or Pauline Kael is cited. Unfortunately, the quotations are not identified as to date or source. In addition, some 20,000 staff-written illustrative sentences and phrases appear throughout. The many synonym studies are a useful feature. All synonyms are discriminated—that is, shades of meaning among similar words are explained.

Encyclopedic Features

The main body of the dictionary includes some 10,000 biographical and geographical entries, briefly identifying such famous persons as Samuel Adams, Thomas Malthus, and Florenz Ziegfeld, and such varied places as the Gulf of Aden and Zion National Park in Utah. The only appended material concerns the Indo-European origins of the English language. There are also seven long, informative articles on specialized language topics in the front of the book. Henry Kučera's article "Computers in Language Analysis and in Lexicography" is an especially significant addition to the dictionary literature.

Graphics

The editor's introduction refers to the several thousand black-and-white pictorial illustrations in the dictionary as a "notable advance in dictionary design." This statement is not an exaggeration. The graphics, which include many photographs and some 200 specially drawn locator maps representing every country in the United Nations, are all small but exceptionally clear. Unlike other American dictionaries, the illustrations are placed in the wide outer margins, a design pattern characteristic of the French Larousse line of dictionaries and encyclopedias. The illustrations are usually instructive and fully complement the words they accompany. But one critic (John B. White in his article "Pictures at a Definition; a Marginal Critique," *Wilson Library Bulletin*, March 1971) has complained that margin space is "underutilized" and that some of the pictures are placed too far from the words they illustrate. For instance, writes Professor White, if the reader "looks for the word 'vermiculàte' . . . on page 1423, will his eye wander to the window of the Louvre on page 1422 which is intended to illustrate it?" The point is well taken. In the final analysis, however, *American Heritage* is among the best illustrated general adult dictionaries currently on the market. *The World Book Dictionary* also stands high in this regard.

Physical Format

American Heritage is also among the most attractively produced adult dictionaries currently available. The red binding with gold lettering is both handsome and durable. The paper quality is satisfactory and the offset printing very legible. Particularly inviting is the Times New Roman type, chosen for its readability. The page layout, the most appealing of any adult English-language dictionary available today, is clean-cut and uncluttered by what editor Morris has called "dictionary shorthand." The ample margins, which contain illustrations or simply "run white," help the dictionary avoid what Morris views as the "cramped runarounds characteristic of most American dictionaries." Consumers should note that the Standard (or Larger Format) Edition is somewhat oversized for a desk dictionary, but not so large that it requires a stand.

Summary

The American Heritage Dictionary of the English Language, first published in 1969, is the newest general dictionary of substance on the American scene. In many ways it is an innovative dictionary which has caused the same sort of lexicographical waves that the now tired *American College Dictionary* did 30 years ago. Among *American Heritage*'s outstanding qualities are "readability" (not usually associated with dictionaries) and the absence of excessive dictionary symbols and abbreviations (or "dictionary shorthand"), excellent typography and inviting format, clear and up-to-date treatment of the 155,000 total vocabulary which derived from a computer sample of one million words, and provision of some 4,000 interesting and informative graphics, including many photographs and locator maps of countries.

Less impressive is the dictionary's much touted usage panel, a group of 100 or so celebrities who pontificate on troublesome questions of usage and grammar. The resulting 800 usage notes, which report the panel's verdicts in percentages similar to baseball averages, are dogmatic, sometimes confusing, and often quixotic. The panel's chief merit appears to be the free publicity it generates for the dictionary. A more important criticism of the dictionary is its sometimes superficial or overly concise treatment of vocabulary. Definitions especially are often less extensive than those found in such competing dictionaries as *Webster's New Collegiate Dictionary* and *Webster's New World Dictionary* (Second College Edition). And in some instances, pronunciations, etymologies, and illustrative examples are not as amply provided as in other leading college dictionaries.

Most authorities agree that there is not a great deal of difference among the better dictionaries in the college category. With that caveat, the *Buying Guide* believes that for all-around performance—clear, current, thorough, and authoritative coverage and treatment of vocabulary as well as appealing design and serviceable format—*Webster's New Collegiate Dictionary* and *Webster's New World Dictionary* (Second College Edition) are the best buys. Second choices are the innovative and attractively produced *American Heritage Dictionary* (New College Edition) and the authoritative *Random House College Dictionary. Funk & Wagnalls Standard College Dictionary*, though competitive with the others, is the last among equals.

Other Critical Opinions

American Reference Books Annual 1970, pp. 49–50 (in Vol. 2); also 1974 edition (review by Frances Neel Cheney), p. 451.
Booklist, February 1, 1972, pp. 437–438.
Consumer Bulletin (review by W. T. Johnston), January 1970, p. 14+.
Katz, William A. *Basic Information Sources.* Vol. 1 of *Introduction to Reference Work*, 2nd ed. (New York: McGraw-Hill, 1974), pp. 260–262; 268.
Lynes, Russell, "After Hours: Usage, Precise and Otherwise," *Harper's Magazine*, April 1970, pp. 32–36.
National Review (review by Guy Davenport), January 27, 1970, pp. 92–94.
Saturday Review (review by Rochelle Girson), September 27, 1969, pp. 25–26.
White, John B. *"The American Heritage Dictionary:* Pictures at a Definition; A Marginal Critique," *Wilson Library Bulletin*, March 1971, pp. 674–678. See also William Morris's reply ("White's Time, Not White Space, Was Wasteful") in the same issue, pp. 679–680.

Chambers Twentieth Century Dictionary

Descriptive Information

Full Title: **Chambers Twentieth Century Dictionary.** *Editor:* A. M. Macdonald. *Publishers:* Littlefield, Adams; also Two Continents. Former title: *Chamber's Twentieth Century Dictionary of the English Language. Edition Reviewed:* New Edition, 1972.

Classification: Adult—Semi-unabridged. *Pages:* xii, 1649. *Total Entries:* 180,000. *Average Entry Length:* 10 words. *Graphics:* None. *Consultants:* None listed. *Physical Size:* 5½ by 8½ in.; 22 cm. *LC:* 73-14842. *ISBN:* 0-8226-0500-7. *Lowest Retail Price:* $7.95.

Purpose and Scope

Chambers Twentieth Century Dictionary, according to the publisher's preface, intends "to provide, in convenient and easily legible form, a comprehensive vocabulary aid for the present-day reader, speaker and writer of English." Among its estimated 180,000 total entries are all the words (29,066) found in Shakespeare's works as well as the poetry of Milton and Spenser, the novels of Scott, and the Bible (Authorized Version). In addition, this British dictionary includes an enormous number of foreign words and phrases commonly used in English, a reflection of Great Britain's increasing ties to Europe via the Common Market community. There has also been an effort to bridge "the hitherto largely artificial gulf between 'English' and 'American English'" by including some Americanisms, e.g., *baseball, catalog, clobber, cookie, diaper, drugstore, hanky-panky,* and *sneaker.*

What in previous editions of *Chambers Twentieth Century* had been excluded as nonstandard or colloquial English is now likely to be included. As explained in the preface, "The hitherto somewhat rigid barrier between formal and colloquial English is collapsing to such an extent that some contemporary fiction is virtually unintelligible to those without a wide colloquial vocabulary." Thus, the dictionary has added such informal terms as *ass, bloke, bloody, blood-and-thunder, bullshit, hell for leather, pimp, shoot the works, turn off,* and *turn on.* In addition, the American user will find numerous Britishisms, like *blighter, bonkers, bugger off, crikey* (also *cricky* and *crickey*), *gaffer, nappy, tumble up, zebra crossing,* and *zed.* The dictionary liberally applies such restrictive labels as "colloquial," "slang," and "vulgar."

Authority

The dictionary was first published in 1901 under the title *Chamber's Twentieth Century Dictionary of the English Language* and has undergone several extensive revisions since that time. The 1972 New Edition is a thorough revision and enlargement of the 1952 edition. The dictionary is published by the Edinburgh firm of W. & R. Chambers, a reputable Scottish publishing house, and reissued in this country by Littlefield, Adams, and Two Continents. The editor, A. M. Macdonald, is known in British lexicographical circles as an experienced dictionary-maker. Aside from Ms. Macdonald, the only names listed as having editorial responsibility for the work are two assistant editors, E. Kirkpatrick and P. Kerr. There is no indication of linguistic and subject consultants, nor is the dictionary's citation file (if any) mentioned. The contents of the dictionary, however, are generally reliable and, given the publisher and editor's good standing, *Chambers Twentieth Century* can be considered authoritative.

Vocabulary Treatment (Clarity, Accuracy, Thoroughness, Recency)

The most common meaning is usually, though not always, entered first, followed by older meanings of the word. The definitions, which emulate the Merriam-Webster definitional style, tend to be clear and current but much too brief, as the words-per-entry figure (10) suggests. Only skeletal definitions are provided for such complex terms as *cell, holism, radiation,* and *visualisation* (the American spelling *visualization* is also indicated). The dictionary is especially weak in thoroughly defining words in the area of science and technology. Example: The biological term *gene* is inadequately defined. Aside from a reference to DNA (the gene's chemical makeup), the three-line definition lacks specifics. General and literary vocabulary terms fare much better, but they too are quite concisely defined. In some instances contemporary connotations are lacking. Example: None of the contemporary meanings of *funky* is included. Example: The only general current meaning of *pathetic* given is "affecting the emotions of pity, grief, sorrow: touching." The more recent connotation of *pathetic* as inferior or inadequate (as in a *pathetic* swing) is not given. And many words found in the contemporary American lexicon are not included in the dictionary, e.g., *busing* (or *bussing*), *data bank, decoupage, deep space, groupie, hoagie* (or *hoagy*), *honcho, jawbone* (or *jawboning*), *mensch, Pap smear, redneck,* and *Wankel engine.* Overall, *Chambers Twentieth Century* is relatively current for British English but deficient in American English. But its main weakness is superficial or overly brief definitions.

Another problem with the dictionary is its policy of entering words which share a common root as run-on derivatives under the common word. For instance, *pathetic* is entered as a derivative of *pathos; aesthetic* is found under *aesthesia.* The editors say that this has been done to save space and note that "cross-references have been included where these seemed necessary." Cross-references are not always included, however. Moreover, it is disconcerting not to find such terms as *aesthetic, anxiety, morale, pathetic,* and *reduction* in alphabetical sequence. In addition, derivatives are not entered alphabetically under the main entry, "but in a more logical form." The editors explain: "The direct derivatives, i.e., the headword [main entry] with an inseparable suffix, come first. These are followed by compound words beginning with the headword and then by phrases containing the headword." At best, the procedure is awkward.

Other aspects of vocabulary treatment are not always satisfactory. The pronunciation system is uncomplicated but imprecise. It involves no phonetic symbols, only simple respelling with diacritical and stress marks. Standard British pronunciations are given but regional variants are ignored. Preferred American pronunciations, however, are often provided, e.g., the American *LABratory* is indicated along with the English *laBORatory.* Many American spellings are also given. The etymologies are usually informative but brief. (A. M. Macdonald, the editor, has also prepared the new edition of the *Chambers Etymological English Dictionary* published in 1960.) No illustrative quotations or examples are included, although words and meanings associated with a particular author like Shakespeare, Milton, or Spenser are so designated. Example: The word *minute-jack* is labeled "Shak." Sometimes the title of the work in which the word appears is cited, but usually not. No explanation is offered for this inconsistency. Synonyms and antonyms are not provided.

Encyclopedic Features

Unlike most of the dictionaries in the semi-unabridged category, *Chambers Twentieth Century* does not include well-known people and places in the main vocabulary. Proper adjectives (e.g., *Dantean*), eponyms (*Stradivarius*), and certain historical groups and movements (*Kitkat Club*) are briefly covered, however. A small amount of nondictionary information is found in the appendixes: a list of quotations from foreign languages, abbreviations and symbols, musical signs, English first names for both men and women, and some common mathematical symbols. In addition, the Greek and Russian alphabets are given, along with some terse notes on how American spelling and pronunciation differ from the British.

Graphics

None.

Physical Format

This dictionary is physically compact, being a squat 8½ inches tall and 2½ inches thick. The red binding is striking but of unexceptional quality. A good grade of paper has been used and the print is clear. The 1972 edition under review has a somewhat larger typeface than the previous 1952 edition. Nevertheless, the type remains noticeably smaller than that found in the other dictionaries in this category. The two-column page layout, unrelieved by any drawings or other graphics, is crowded and uninviting. A condensed pronunciation key is printed at the bottom of each page but not on the endpapers. Overall, the format is unsatisfactory.

Summary

Chambers Twentieth Century Dictionary, published by the Edinburgh publisher W. & R. Chambers Ltd., and reissued in this country by both Littlefield, Adams and Two Continents Publishing Group, first appeared in 1901 and was last revised in 1972. That edition, which is reviewed here, contains approximately 180,000 total entries comprising standard British English, including all the vocabulary used by such great writers as Shakespeare and Milton. Current terms are also included in abundance, especially British idioms. Moreover, considerable effort has been made to cover American English and, although many familiar contemporary Americanisms (like *funky* and *jawboning*) are not included, the dictionary's scope is impressive.

The definitions are usually clear and current but too frequently the treatment is overly concise or superficial. This criticism is especially true in the case of scientific and technical terminology. The space-saving system of entering derivatives like *morale* under the root word *moral* is sometimes confusing and always bothersome. Other deficiencies include the lack of illustrative quotations or examples, synonyms and antonyms, and graphic illustrations. In addition, the typography is unsatisfactory when compared with the leading dictionaries in the semi-unabridged class.

American students of English literature from Shakespeare through the eighteenth century might find this inexpensive British dictionary a handy supplementary desk reference. It will not, however, fill the need for a substantial, well-rounded college dictionary like *Webster's New Collegiate Dictionary*, *Webster's New World Dictionary* (Second College Edition), *The American Heritage Dictionary* (New College Edition), or *The Random House College Dictionary*.

Other Critical Opinions

American Reference Books Annual 1974 (review by Bohdan S. Wynar), pp. 451–452.

Wilson Library Journal (review by Charles A. Bunge), March 1974, p. 599.

Funk & Wagnalls Comprehensive Standard International Dictionary

Descriptive Information

Full Title: **Funk & Wagnalls Comprehensive Standard International Dictionary.** *Editor:* Sidney I. Landau, Editor in Chief. *Publisher:* J. G. Ferguson Publishing Co. *Distributor:* T. Y. Crowell Co. Alternate titles: *Funk & Wagnalls Standard Comprehensive International Dictionary; Funk & Wagnalls New Comprehensive International Dictionary of the English Language* (Encyclopedic Edition). *Edition Reviewed:* Bicentennial Edition, 1973.

Classification: Adult—Semi-unabridged. *Pages:* xx, 1929. *Total Entries:* 175,000. *Average Entry Length:* 14 words. *Graphics:* 1,200. *Consultants:* 60. *Physical Size:* 9 by 11½ in.; 29 cm. *LC:* 74-150152. *ISBN:* 0-308-10109-X. *Lowest Retail Price:* $49.95.

Consumer Note

This dictionary is practically a verbatim reprint of *Funk & Wagnalls Standard Dictionary of the English Language* (International Edition), a new work in 1958 and only minimally revised since that time. In 1970, J. G. Ferguson Publishing Company of Chicago acquired exclusive rights to the International Edition and subsequently reissued it in two different formats under the titles: (1) *Funk & Wagnalls Comprehensive Standard International Dictionary* (called the Bicentennial Edition; also called the Encyclopedic Edition under an alternate title—see "Descriptive Information"); and (2) *Funk & Wagnalls Standard Dictionary of the English Language* (still called the International Edition, but issued in two volumes).

Both dictionaries have virtually the same lexical contents. The main difference between the two is that the so-called Bicentennial Edition has much more appended encyclopedic information, most of it filler reprinted from other sources. Also, the Bicentennial Edition is published in a single volume with a red, blue, and gold binding, whereas the International Edition appears in two volumes with a two-tone blue binding. Note also that the Bicentennial Edition sells for $49.95 whereas the International costs only $34.50.

Incredibly, the Reference and Subscription Books Review Committee of the American Library Association reviewed *Funk & Wagnalls Comprehensive Standard International Dictionary* (Bicentennial Edition) as a new work, not once mentioning in the laudatory two-page review that the Bicentennial Edition is virtually the same as the International Edition. (See *Booklist*, January 15, 1975, pp. 511–512.) Fortunately for librarians and other consumers, Charles Bunge warned in his column "Current Reference Books" (*Wilson Library Bulletin*, September 1974, pp. 93–94) that the dictionary was nothing more than a reprint of *Funk & Wagnalls Standard Dictionary of the English Language* (International Edition), plus some unimpressive "encyclopedic supplements."

See the profile of *Funk & Wagnalls Standard Dictionary of the English Language* (International Edition) which follows in this section for a detailed evaluation of the lexical contents of *Funk & Wagnalls Comprehensive Standard International Dictionary* (Bicentennial Edition).

Other Critical Opinions

Booklist, January 15, 1975, pp. 511–512.
Wilson Library Bulletin (review by Charles A. Bunge), September 1974, pp. 93–94.

Funk & Wagnalls Standard College Dictionary

Descriptive Information

Full Title: **Funk & Wagnalls Standard College Dictionary.** *Editor:* Sidney I. Landau, Editor in Chief. *Publisher:* Funk & Wagnalls. *Distributor:* T. Y. Crowell Co. Former title: *Funk & Wagnalls New College Standard Dictionary. Edition Reviewed:* 1974.

Classification: Adult—Semi-unabridged. *Pages:* xxvi, 1606. *Total Entries:* 150,000. *Average Entry Length:* 16 words. *Graphics:* 3,000. *Consultants:* 100. *Physical Size:* 7½ by 10 in.; 25 cm. *LC:* 72-13007. *ISBN:* 0-308-10053-0 (plain); 0-308-10054-9 (thumb-indexed). *Lowest Retail Price:* $9.95.

Purpose and Scope

Funk & Wagnalls Standard College Dictionary, like all the dictionaries in Funk & Wagnalls' "Standard" series, emphasizes what the editors call "Standard English"—that is, "The language of cultivation, being that normally used by the leading part of the community, and that most widely understood within the English-speaking world [and that which] has high prestige and is considered to be the 'upper' level." In addition, the dictionary includes "Nonstandard English" words and expressions (such as dialect, slang, and technical terms) but only if they are widely used or related in some way to standard vocabulary. Nonstandard words and meanings are strictly labeled, e.g., "dial.," "slang," and "illit." Special subject fields are also labeled, e.g., "bot.," "chem.," and "photog." Some 260 usage notes are included and the general tone is prescriptive.

F & W Standard College provides fairly balanced coverage of the words, phrases, and expressions college students may encounter. The dictionary's jacket cover especially notes the "broad" coverage of scientific and technical terms. The *Buying Guide* finds, however, that the other leading college dictionaries like *Webster's New Collegiate Dictionary* and *Webster's New World Dictionary* provide better coverage in the area of science and technology. Sometimes *F & W Standard College* fails to include basic scientific terms. Example: The bituminous material *kerogen*, a petroleum-like substance found in oil shale which will play a role in easing the energy crisis, is not found in the dictionary. Nor are such relatively new but widely used technical terms as *data bank, deep space, laetrile, oxygen cycle, patrifocal, renovascular, reprography,* and *time-sharing. F & W Standard College* is also less likely to include recently coined words and phrases, e.g., *hoagie* (or *hoagy), honcho,* and *Orwellian* are not in the dictionary.

Among the 150,000 entries are some 4,000 biographies of important people, both living and dead. There are also many geographical entries as well as standard abbreviations, some trade names, and commonly used foreign words and expressions. *F & W Standard College* has the distinction of providing more Canadianisms than any other comparably sized dictionary. Over 500 words and phrases native to Canada are included, such as proper nouns like *Bluenose,* loanwords like *shaganappi* (borrowed from the Indian but not so designated in the dictionary), and regionalisms like *longliner* and *longlinerman.* Walter S. Avis, the dictionary's consultant on Canadianisms, contributes an informative essay called "Canadian English" which is found in the front matter.

Authority

F & W Standard College was first published in 1963, replacing the dated *Funk & Wagnalls New College Standard Dictionary* which initially appeared in 1922. *F & W Standard College* is actually a condensed version of *Funk & Wagnalls Standard Dictionary* (International Edition), a 175,000-entry work published in 1958 under the editorial supervision of S. Stephenson Smith, but now edited by Sidney I. Landau. *F & W Standard College* is, in turn, the source of *Funk & Wagnalls Standard Desk Dictionary* (which, in turn, is the same dictionary as *Funk & Wagnalls Standard Encyclopedic Dictionary*). In addition, *F & W Standard College* formed the A–Z dictionary portion of *The Reader's Digest Great Encyclopedic Dictionary,* now fortunately defunct (see Appendix A).

In a very large number of cases, *F & W Standard College* gives exactly the same definitions, pronunciations, etymologies, etc. as found in the *Funk & Wagnalls Standard Dictionary* (International Edition) published in 1958 and only minimally revised since that time. Thus, *F & W Standard College's* basic authority derives from the International Edition, which is still in print and is reviewed in this section. Both dictionaries now list the same editor, Sidney I. Landau, a reputable American lexicographer. The 29-member advisory board, headed by Allen Walker Read, includes such distinguished names as Albert C. Baugh, Margaret M. Bryant, Frederic G. Cassidy, Albert H. Marckwardt, and Marjorie Nicolson. Also listed is a 35-member editorial staff plus a number of consultants, most of them academicians.

The *Buying Guide* understands that a citation file is maintained for *F & W Standard College,* but that it is by no means a master file comparable to that required to keep a sizable dictionary truly current.

Vocabulary Treatment (Clarity, Accuracy, Thoroughness, Recency)

As with all Funk & Wagnalls dictionaries, the most frequently used meaning is given first. The definitions, like those in *The American Heritage Dictionary* and *The Random House College Dictionary,* tend to be concisely stated but not always up-to-date, accurate, and thorough. Example: Parts of the definition of *gene* are inaccurate and unclear. For instance, the gene is not a "protein" molecule as stated. And the long phrase "as a unit or in various biochemically determined combinations" is vague and confusing. Example: The adjective *aesthetic* ignores the philosophical and psychological aspects of the word, as well as connotations involving taste and criticism. Example: The noun *decoupage* is incompletely defined as "the art of decorating a surface with cutouts of foil, paper, etc." A second meaning is even less helpful: "Something done in decoupage." Many other words such as *cell, existentialism, holism, macrame, radiation*, and *visualizaton* are inadequately defined. In other instances (e.g., *funky, impressionist, launder, leverage*, and *pathetic*), the most current meaning is not included.

The pronunciation system is clear and reasonably accurate. Variant spellings are given when appropriate, as are variant pronunciations. The etymologies, prepared by Albert H. Marckwardt, an outstanding authority, appear after the definitions. Numbering some 30,000, the etymologies are brief but clear. No illustrative quotations are provided. There are, however, many illustrative phrases used throughout the dictionary which augment or clarify meanings. Over 1,000 synonym lists (which are not discriminated) and synonym paragraphs (which are discriminated) accompany such words as *futile, gay, mix*, and *row*. Another useful synonymic device is the provision of "collateral adjectives"—that is, related terms having a foreign origin, e.g., the collateral adjective for *day* is *diurnal*.

Encyclopedic Features

Most of the nondictionary material contained in *F & W Standard College* is in the main A–Z text in the form of biographical and geographical entries. The dictionary also appends a number of useful items, including lists of colleges and universities, given names for men and women, signs and symbols, and reference guides covering punctuation, capitalization, style in correspondence, and manuscript preparation. All of this material will be useful to the college student.

Graphics

F & W Standard College provides over 3,000 small black-and-white line drawings, including 85 spot maps, throughout the text. In every instance the illustrations are carefully chosen to complement the words they accompany. Preference is given to the unfamiliar over the familiar, e.g., there is a drawing for *Canada goose* but none for the more familiar *canary*.

Physical Format

The dictionary's plain black pyroxylin binding with gold lettering is strong and durable. The typeface is clear, easy to read, and gives the impression of modernity. A good quality opaque paper has been used. The two-column page layout is satisfactory, though not as appealing as *The American Heritage Dictionary*. Guide words appear at the top of each page and the pronunciation key at the bottom of every other page. Overall, the dictionary's appearance is pleasing and its physical construction sound.

Summary

Funk & Wagnalls Standard College Dictionary, a 150,000-entry work first published in 1963 as the successor to *Funk & Wagnalls New College Dictionary* (1922), is a modified version of *Funk & Wagnalls Standard Dictionary* (International Edition), a 175,000-entry work originally published in 1958. Much of the same material appears verbatim in both dictionaries.

The dictionary purports to cover "Standard English" as well as some nonstandard vocabulary which is widely used. Restrictive labels are heavily applied to dialect, slang, and specialist terms. The coverage is fairly well balanced, although newer words and scientific and technical terms are frequently not included. A particular effort has been made to cover Canadianisms. Definitions tend to be reasonably clear but not always up-to-date, accurate, or thorough. Other aspects of the vocabulary treatment are satisfactory, as are the graphics and physical format. The dictionary is continuously revised within the framework of the 1963 text. A comparison of the 1963 and 1974 copyrights shows that many pages are exactly the same.

James Sledd, writing in *Consumer Reports* (November 1963) when *F & W Standard College* initially appeared, observed that "Flipping the pages, I saw little to disturb an old impression that reputable desk dictionaries are much of a muchness, with the Funk & Wagnalls 'Standard' being perhaps a little simpler, a little less professional, a little less strenuously scientific than such a competitor as 'Webster's Seventh New Collegiate.' That highly impressionistic judgment was not greatly changed by more detailed examination." Professor Sledd's opinion is still on target today.

The *Buying Guide* believes that for all-around performance—clear, current, thorough, and authoritative coverage and treatment of vocabulary, as well as appealing design and serviceable format—*Webster's New Collegiate Dictionary* and *Webster's New World Dictionary* (Second College Edition) are the best buys. Second choices are the innovative and attractively produced *American Heritage Dictionary* (New College Edition) and the authoritative *Random House College Dictionary*. *Funk & Wagnalls Standard College Dictionary*, though competitive with the others, is the last among equals.

Other Critical Opinions

American Reference Books Annual 1974, p. 452.
Booklist, June 15, 1964, pp. 935–938.
Wilson Library Bulletin (review by Charles A. Bunge), March 1974, p. 598.

Funk & Wagnalls Standard Dictionary (International Edition)

Descriptive Information

Full Title: **Funk & Wagnalls Standard Dictionary of the English Language.** *Editors:* Sidney I. Landau, Editor in Chief (since 1965); S. Stephenson Smith, Supervising Editor (1958–1965). *Publisher:* J. G. Ferguson Publishing Co. *Edition Reviewed:* International Edition (also called Comprehensive International Edition on cover and spine), 1976.

Classification: Adult—Semi-unabridged. *Volumes:* 2. *Pages:* xx, 1697. *Total Entries:* 175,000. *Average Entry Length:* 14 words. *Graphics:* 1,200. *Consultants:* 60. *Physical Size:* 8½ by 11¼ in.; 29 cm. *LC:* 69-11209. *ISBN:* 0-308-10111-1. *Lowest Retail Price:* $34.50 the set.

Purpose and Scope

Funk & Wagnalls Standard Dictionary of the English Language (International Edition) aims to provide "the widest possible coverage of both the established word stock of English and of the rapidly expanding vocabularies of the arts, sciences, trades, and professions." Like all Funk & Wagnalls dictionaries bearing the name "Standard" (a registered trademark), this dictionary emphasizes standard English currently in use. Those nonstandard terms which are included are forthrightly labeled "dial.," "slang," and so on. As explained in the introduction, "the most important label is the one that is not here. As the best style is the absence of it, so the 'best' words in our language are those needing no label that make up general-purpose English. A writer who is a general practitioner will usually stick to this level of standard English."

F & W Standard, which first appeared in 1958 as a completely new work, includes among its 175,000 entries some 14,000 proper names, mostly people and places. Also included are a number of words and expressions indigenous to Canada, e.g., *longliner* and *longlinerman*. Overall, the vocabulary coverage is fairly well balanced, although many newer but hardly esoteric scientific terms are not included. Example: Energy-conscious Americans will increasingly encounter the word *kerogen*, a petroleum-like substance found in oil shale but not found in *F & W Standard*. Nor are *data bank, deep space, laetrile, oxygen cycle, patrifocal, renovascular, reprography*, and *time-sharing* in the dictionary. Nor are such recently coined but standard words and phrases as *busing* (or *bussing*—the noun), *hoagie* (or *hoagy*), *impressionist* (meaning one who does comic impressions), *Orwellian*, and *self-destruct* included in the dictionary. This is not to imply that there are no current words or meanings in *F & W Standard*, e.g., *gay* (as in homosexual), *groupie, happening*, and *jawbone* are defined.

Authority

F & W Standard, a semi-unabridged dictionary which stands between the unabridged 458,000-entry *Funk & Wagnalls New Standard Dictionary* (1913) and the smaller 150,000-entry *Funk & Wagnalls Standard College Dictionary* (1963), first appeared in 1958 as an entirely new work, although it naturally drew upon the lexicographical experience and resources of the Funk & Wagnalls operation which dates back to the nineteenth century. S. Stephenson Smith served as supervising editor until 1965 when Sidney I. Landau became editor in chief. Allen Walker Read headed a distinguished editorial advisory board comprising 28 English-language scholars, including Albert C. Baugh, Frederic G. Cassidy, Albert H. Marckwardt, Mitford M. Mathews, and Frederick A. Pottle. In addition, the editors utilized some 60 consultants, most of whom are or were associated with large corporations. Smith's editorial staff of 29 included William Morris (who went on to edit *The American Heritage Dictionary*) and Laurence Urdang (who subsequently went to Random House and did the first edition of *The Random House College Dictionary*).

F & W Standard is unquestionably an authoritative dictionary. Significantly, it has sired all of the dictionaries currently in the Funk & Wagnalls line except for the old *Funk & Wagnalls New Standard*, the unabridged dictionary which was first issued in 1913. Specifically, *Funk & Wagnalls Comprehensive Standard International Dictionary* (Bicentennial Edition) is merely a reprint of *F & W Standard* with many pages of encyclopedic matter added; *Funk & Wagnalls Standard College Dictionary* is an abridged version of *F & W Standard; Funk & Wagnalls Standard Desk Dictionary* is in turn an abridgment of the college dictionary; *Funk & Wagnalls Standard Encyclopedic Dictionary* is merely a reprint of the desk dictionary with some encyclopedic matter added; and the now out-of-print *Reader's Digest Great Encyclopedic Dictionary* was merely a reprint of the college dictionary with much encyclopedic matter added.

Vocabulary Treatment (Clarity, Accuracy, Thoroughness, Recency)

As with all Funk & Wagnalls dictionaries, the most commonly used meaning is given first. The definitions tend to be clear but not always up-to-date, accurate, and thorough. Example: the adjective *aesthetic* is very skimpily defined. The definition ignores the philosophical and psychological aspects of the word, as well as connotations concerning taste and criticism. Example: The definition of *gene* is not completely accurate, e.g., genes are found in every cell, not just in gametes; also, genes are not the carriers of "specific physical factors" but rather of the coded information necessary to synthesize specific proteins. Nor is the gene's chemical nature given—it is simply called a "chemically complex unit." Example: The meaning of *cell* as used in biology is superficial and garbled. The cell's wall is not "semipermeable" as stated, nor is there any mention of the two basic types of cells. Example: *Radiation* is defined only in terms of particle radiation. The definition is inaccurate, incomplete, and out-of-date. Many other words such as *decoupage, existentialism, holism, macrame*, and *visualization* are likewise poorly defined. In other instances the most current meaning of a word is not included. Example: *busing* (or *bussing*), *launder, leverage*, and *pathetic*.

The pronunciation system is relatively simple to understand and use. It entails the use of letters of the alphabet combined with familiar diacritical and stress marks. Variant spellings and pronunciations are de-emphasized. The etymologies, estimated at 50,000, appear at the end of the entries. They trace native English words back to their Old English form when possible. The etymologies are brief but clear. No illustrative quotations are provided, although many illustrative phrases which focus or clarify meanings are included. Approximately 12,000 synonyms (some discriminated, some not) accompany such words as *complex, futile, gay, hazard, mix, poverty*, and *shelter*. Another useful synonymic device is the provision of "collateral adjectives"—that is, related words having a foreign origin, e.g., the collateral adjective for *day* is *diurnal*.

Encyclopedic Features

The dictionary per se covers 1,466 pages in the two volumes. The remaining 230 pages are devoted to "Special Supplementary Features" found at the back of volume two. The material is a mishmash including a handbook on grammar and usage, a discussion by Albert Marckwardt on how to improve your vocabulary and spelling, tips on how to write "The Library Research Paper," a dictionary of quotations, a glossary of mythological names, concise descriptions of the world's religions, how to start a club and conduct meetings, and such documents as the U.S. Constitution and the United Nations Charter. In addition, the main body of the dictionary includes numerous entries covering famous people and places.

Graphics

There are about 1,200 small black-and-white line drawings throughout the dictionary proper which amplify word meanings. Also scattered throughout are 32 full-color plates (both photographs and reproductions) of such items as peasant costumes, game fish, famous bridges and canals, mushrooms, modern paintings, the Seven Wonders of the World, reptiles, shells, dated photographs of life in the U.S.S.R., and rare and precious stones. Unfortunately, these plates are not related to the words they presumably help define. Example: A plate showing various models of early sailing ships follows page 962. The entry for *ship* is on page 1161. The entry contains no cross-reference to the plate. The plates are usually pretty but have little value except perhaps to the browser.

Physical Format

F & W Standard is published in two volumes. The two-tone blue Sturdite binding appears to be sturdy and is attractive. The paper is of good quality and the 8-point type easy on the eyes. The three-column page has guide words at the top and the pronunciation key at the bottom of every odd-numbered page. Overall, the dictionary is well constructed but is considerably larger than the average desk dictionary. Together the two bulky volumes weigh close to 8 pounds.

Summary

Funk & Wagnalls Standard Dictionary of the English Language (International Edition) was first published in 1958 as a new work. The dictionary originally included some of this country's foremost language scholars among its editors and advisers. Significantly, it has sired every Funk & Wagnalls dictionary currently in print, with the exception of the old (1913) unabridged *Funk & Wagnalls New Standard Dictionary*. Since 1958 the dictionary has been kept up-to-date via continuous revision but the revisions have been modest, usually only involving the addition of a small number of new words and the deletion of a similar number of older terms. The dictionary has never been thoroughly revised.

Like all Funk & Wagnalls dictionaries, *F & W Standard* concentrates on "Standard English." Nonstandard vocabulary (dialect, slang, etc.) is included if widely used and is assiduously labeled "slang" and so forth. The coverage is fairly good although newer words and scientific and technical terms are often not found in the dictionary. Vocabulary treatment is mediocre. Words and phrases are usually defined in a clear manner but the definitions tend to be insufficient, sometimes inaccurate, and not always current. The pronunciation scheme, etymologies, illustrative phrases (but no quotations), and synonymies are adequate. The dictionary has been dressed up with pretty color plates and much encyclopedic matter, but these features generally produce more informational smoke than fire. It should also be noted that, while *F & W Standard* has a satisfactory format, the two-volume work is considerably larger than desk-size.

Although the lexical content of *F & W Standard* and *Funk & Wagnalls Standard College Dictionary* (which derives directly from *F & W Standard*) is often quite similar or exactly the same, the college dictionary is much less expensive ($9.95 as opposed to $34.50) and therefore preferable. When compared with the other leading college dictionaries, *Funk & Wagnalls Standard College* is the last choice. For all-around performance—clear, current, thorough, and authoritative coverage and treatment of vocabulary as well as appealing design and serviceable format—*Webster's New Collegiate Dictionary* and *Webster's New World Dictionary* (Second College Edition) are the best buys. Second choice are the innovative and attractively produced *American Heritage Dictionary* (New College Edition) and the authoritative *Random House College Dictionary*.

Other Critical Opinions

None. There are, however, two recent reviews available of *Funk & Wagnalls Comprehensive Standard International Dictionary* (Bicentennial Edition, 1973). This dictionary has exactly the same lexical content as *Funk & Wagnalls Standard Dictionary* (International Edition) but adds about 300 more pages of "encyclopedic supplements."

Incredibly, the Reference and Subscription Books Review Committee of the American Library Association reviewed the so-called Bicentennial Edition as a new work, not once mentioning in the laudatory two-page review that the Bicentennial Edition is virtually the same as the International Edition. (See *Booklist*, January 15, 1975, pp. 511–512.) Fortunately for librarians and other consumers, Charles Bunge warned in his column "Current Reference Books" (*Wilson Library Bulletin*, September 1974, pp. 93–94) that the dictionary was merely a reprint with some 300 pages of filler appended.

See the Consumer Note on *Funk & Wagnalls Comprehensive Standard International Dictionary* (Bicentennial Edition) for further information.

Illustrated Heritage Dictionary and Information Book

Descriptive Information

Full Title: **The Illustrated Heritage Dictionary and Information Book.** *Editors:* Fernando de Mello Vianna, Editorial Director, and the American Heritage Dictionary Staff. *Publisher:* Houghton Mifflin Co. *Edition Reviewed:* 1977.

Classification: Adult—Semi-unabridged. *Pages:* l, 1966. *Total Entries:* 155,000. *Average Entry Length:* 14 words. *Graphics:* 4,000. *Consultants:* 200. *Physical Size:* 8½ by 11¼ in.; 28 cm. *LC:* 77-2138. *ISBN:* 0-395-25441-8. *Lowest Retail Price:* $34.95.

Consumer Note

The *Illustrated Heritage Dictionary and Information Book* has exactly the same dictionary contents as the 155,000-entry *American Heritage Dictionary* (1976). Indeed, *The Illustrated Heritage Dictionary and Information Book* consists of the Standard (also called Larger Format) Edition of the dictionary, plus about 400 pages of supplementary material, including a style manual, much illustrated information about American history, a section featuring American quotations, a concise five-language dictionary (French, Italian, Spanish, and German with English equivalents), a four-color world atlas, a guide to the metric system, and a directory of U.S. and Canadian colleges and universities.

Note that *The Illustrated Heritage Dictionary and Information Book* costs $34.95. Note also that *The American Heritage Dictionary* (Standard or Larger Format Edition) can be purchased for $14.95. This means that the 400 pages of encyclopedic supplements in *The Illustrated Heritage Dictionary and Information Book* cost the consumer $20.00. That is much too expensive for a potpourri of information tacked on to a reasonably priced dictionary. Moreover, the same dictionary can be acquired for $9.95 in the New College Edition.

See the profile of *The American Heritage Dictionary* in this section of the *Buying Guide* for additional information about the dictionary contents of *The Illustrated Heritage Dictionary and Information Book.*

Living Webster Encyclopedic Dictionary

Descriptive Information

Full Title: **The Living Webster Encyclopedic Dictionary of the English Language.** *Editor:* Dana F. Kellerman. *Publisher:* English Language Institute of America. *Distributors:* Consolidated Book Publishers (New York and Chicago); Dabco Industries (Glenview, Ill.); Webster Dictionary Co. (New York). *Edition Reviewed:* 1975.

Classification: Adult—semi-unabridged. *Pages:* xxx, 1360. *Total Entries:* 158,000. *Average Entry Length:* 10 words. *Graphics:* 24 plates. *Consultants:* 29. *Physical Size:* 8½ by 11¼ in.; 29 cm. *LC:* 76-146839. *ISBN:* 0-8326-0001-6. *Lowest Retail Price:* $39.95.

Purpose and Scope

The Living Webster Encyclopedic Dictionary of the English Language, according to the publisher's preface, aims to cover "all but the most technical and the most esoteric words from our ever-expanding storehouse of knowledge." In actuality, the 158,000 entries cover only words and phrases in active use. Practically all obsolete or archaic words and meanings have been excluded. The vocabulary offerings include many newer words and some nonstandard terms (e.g., *jaw* meaning to talk or gossip) which are labeled "slang" or "colloq." Many recently coined words in general usage, however, are not found in *Living Webster*. Example: *busing* (or *bussing*), *data bank*, *decoupage, groupie, hoagie* (or *hoagy*), *jawbone* (and *jawboning*), *motor home, Orwellian,* and *self-destruct.* Also, some relatively simple and widely encountered scientific and technical terms are omitted, e.g., *kerogen, laetrile, oxygen cycle,* and *Wankel engine.* Unlike most semi-unabridged dictionaries, *Living Webster* does not include biographical and geographical entries either in the main body of the dictionary or as encyclopedic supplements.

Authority

The *Living Webster's* frontispiece is a portrait of Noah Webster. The preface states that "Our dictionary carries on it the name *Webster* in recognition of and respect for the American lexicographer, Noah Webster, whose work in the standardization of American usage and pronunciation set the guides for those of us who follow." A full-page advertisement for the dictionary in the *New York Times* (January 10, 1976, p. 42) credits Webster as the "inspiration" behind *Living Webster.* Perhaps. But this dictionary, like many others bearing the name "Webster," has no real connection with the nineteenth-century works of Noah Webster, nor indeed does it emulate many of Webster's lexicographical principles.

Living Webster, first published in 1971, was prepared by an editorial and production staff of 95, working under the general supervision of Dana F. Kellerman. Kellerman is not known in American lexicographical circles nor included in the standard biographical sources. There are also 29 contributors and consultants listed, including some university professors, a few authors and librarians, and several well-known names, notably Roy H. Copperud, Julius Lester, Mario Pei, and the late Mark Van Doren. Dr. Pei has contributed "A Historical Sketch of the English Language" which is printed in the front of the dictionary. The publisher, the English Language Institute of America, a Chicago firm, has no reputation to speak of in the dictionary publishing field. No mention is made of the dictionary's citation file (if any) or other scholarly sources used in the preparation of *Living Webster.* Quite possibly the dictionary derives at least partially from the *New Webster Dictionary* (1964), a mediocre work issued by Consolidated Book Publishers and now out of print (see Appendix A). Note also that Consolidated currently publishes an illustrated version of *Living Webster* under the title *New Webster's Dictionary* (College Edition). Under these circumstances, *Living Webster* cannot be considered an authoritative dictionary.

Vocabulary Treatment (Clarity, Accuracy, Thoroughness, Recency)

When more than one meaning is given for a word, the "preferred sense" is given first with the "following senses according to common usage." If a word lacks "a clear preferred use, the order of definitions is arbitrary." All of this is quite vague and antithetical to the Websterian tradition of giving meanings in historical order. The definitions themselves are usually clear and fairly current but not always precise. The biggest fault with the definitions, however, is their general lack of depth. Example: The definition of *gene* lacks specifics, omitting, for example, both the chemical nature of the gene and its actual function. Example: The adjective *aesthetic* (also *esthetic*) is simply defined as "pertaining to the study of taste or beauty; pertaining to the sense of the beautiful." The definition is skimpy, uncomprehensive, inadequate, and relatively uninformative. Such entries as *cell, conceit, mix, pathetic, radiation,* and *visualization* are representative of the many words not sufficiently defined by *Living Webster.*

Other aspects of vocabulary treatment are equally poor. The simple and imprecise pronunciation system uses only the letters of the alphabet with a few diacritical and accent marks. Variant pronunciations and spellings are sometimes given, sometimes not. Example: The variant of *inalienable* is *unalienable.* The variant was used by Jefferson in the Declaration of Independence but it is not found in *Living Webster.* The etymologies are concise and sometimes uninformative. No illustrative quotations are included and only occasionally do illustrative phrases appear. This lack of illustrative examples is a serious deficiency in a dictionary the size of *Living Webster.* Also, there are no synonymies, although sometimes the definitions are little more than a series of similar words strung together.

Encyclopedic Features

Living Webster appends 16 encyclopedic supplements, including color plates of various national and state flags; dictionaries of synonyms and antonyms, foreign words and phrases, and abbreviations; popular quotations; a student's and writer's guide to grammar and manuscript preparation; brief biographical sketches of the American presidents through Gerald Ford; a secretaries' guide to business correspondence; and tables giving compound interest, multiplication, and measurements. The material is quite similar to that included with the several Funk & Wagnalls encyclopedic dictionaries. Such information is usually readily available in a reliable, up-to-date encyclopedia in the home or school or public library. In that light, the dictionary must be judged on the basis of its vocabulary coverage and treatment, not its pages of encyclopedic extras.

Graphics

The 1,158 pages of purely dictionary contents contain no pictorial illustrations of any kind. The encyclopedic supplements do include a few illustrated sections, e.g., flags of the world. The lack of drawings and diagrams for such entries as *buttress, cell, jet engine, phaeton,* and *tetrahedron* further diminishes the dictionary's definitions.

Physical Format

The large (6 pounds; 11¼ inches high; 3 inches thick) volume is bound in sturdy brown boards with gold lettering. The pages are gilt-edged all around. A modestly good quality paper has been used and the type is clear and readable. The three-column page, unrelieved by any graphics, has guide words at the top of each page and a condensed pronunciation key at the bottom of each two-page spread. Overall, the physical format of *Living Webster* is satisfactory.

Summary

The Living Webster Encyclopedic Dictionary of the English Language, first published in 1971, claims a tenuous connection with Noah Webster and his lexicographical principles. The claim is unfounded. The dictionary almost exclusively devotes itself to words in current usage. Most standard vocabulary can be found in the dictionary, but inevitably some newer words are not included. *Living Webster's* treatment of vocabulary is seriously deficient in several important respects. Specifically, the definitions lack depth; there are no illustrative quotations; there are too few illustrative phrases; there are no synonyms in the main dictionary (a 34-page list of undiscriminated synonyms is found, however, among the encyclopedic supplements); and there are no pictorial illustrations in the main dictionary. The encyclopedic material in the back of the dictionary comprises some 200 pages and is a mishmash of this and that.

Living Webster, which is also published in an illustrated version by Consolidated Book Publishers under the title *New Webster's Dictionary* (College Edition), is actively promoted through newspaper advertisements, frequently offering "bargain" prices. A recent ad in the *New York Times Book Review* (March 6, 1977), for instance, quoted a price of $19.95 plus $2.25 for freight and crating. The dictionary is also distributed through the American Automobile Association by Dabco Industries for $14.95 plus $1.00 postage and handling. The advertisements tend to greatly overstate the virtues of *Living Webster:* "In short, if you had but one book to choose in life, [*Living Webster*] should be it. It is perhaps the most comprehensive, utilitarian, *entertaining* single volume ever published."

In reality, *Living Webster* is the worst dictionary in the semi-unabridged category. It is totally inferior to such substantial and well-rounded desk dictionaries as *Webster's New Collegiate Dictionary*, *Webster's New World Dictionary* (Second College Edition), *The American Heritage Dictionary* (New College Edition), and *The Random House College Dictionary*. Note also that *Living Webster* is grossly overpriced, even when offered at "bargain" rates.

New Webster's Dictionary

Descriptive Information

Full Title: **New Webster's Dictionary of the English Language.** *Editor:* Dana K. Kellerman. *Publisher:* Consolidated Book Publishers. *Edition Reviewed:* College Edition, 1975.

Classification: Adult—Semi-unabridged. *Pages:* xxxii, 1824. *Total Entries:* 158,000. *Average Entry Length:* 10 words. *Graphics:* 800. *Consultants:* 29. *Physical Size:* 7 by 10 in.; 26 cm. *LC:* 75-18559. *ISBN:* 0-8326-0035-0. *Lowest Retail Price:* $9.95.

Consumer Note

New Webster's Dictionary of the English Language (College Edition) is a verbatim reprint of *The Living Webster Encyclopedic Dictionary of the English Language.* Aside from their titles, the major differences between the two dictionaries are that *New Webster's* includes some 800 small black-and-white line drawings (mostly of plants and animals) whereas *Living Webster* completely lacks illustrations in the main dictionary section, and that *Living Webster* appends much encyclopedic filler not found in *New Webster's*. *New Webster's* is also a poorly printed volume but it costs significantly less than *Living Webster* ($9.95 as opposed to $39.95). Neither dictionary treats its vocabulary covered in any depth. Neither is recommended under any circumstances.

For a full assessment of the lexical contents of *New Webster's*, see the profile of *Living Webster* in this section of the *Buying Guide*.

Random House College Dictionary

Descriptive Information

Full Title: **The Random House College Dictionary.** *Editor:* Jess Stein, Editor in Chief. *Publisher:* Random House. *Edition Reviewed:* Revised Edition, 1975.

Classification: Adult—Semi-unabridged. *Pages:* xxxii, 1568. *Total Entries:* 170,000. *Average Entry Length:* 15 words. *Graphics:* 1,500. *Consultants:* 400. *Physical Size:* 7 by 10 in.; 25 cm. *LC:* 75-4858. *ISBN:* 0-394-43500-1 (plain); 0-394-43600-8 (thumb-indexed). *Lowest Retail Price:* $9.95.

Purpose and Scope

The Random House College Dictionary is based on the larger 260,000-entry *Random House Dictionary of the English Language* (Unabridged Edition), which first appeared in 1966. In terms of total entries, *Random House College* (170,000 entries) currently leads the other major college dictionaries: *The American Heritage Dictionary* (155,000 entries); *Funk & Wagnalls Standard College Dictionary* (150,000 entries); *Webster's New Collegiate Dictionary* (150,000 entries); and *Webster's New World Dictionary* (158,000 entries). As the *Buying Guide* has noted elsewhere, the number of entries has nothing to do with the comparative quality of dictionaries. Yet it would appear that publishers and their promotion departments place great stock in achieving a statistical advantage. William Morris, the original editor of *The American Heritage Dictionary*, has deplored this sort of entry race, noting that many dictionaries inflate their entry counts by adding flocks of words formed with self-explanatory prefixes like *un-*, *non-*, and *sub-*. Says Morris (*Wilson Library Bulletin*, March 1971, p. 680), "Random House's so-called 'unabridged' dictionary is a particularly flagrant offender in this regard. These lists of undefined entries constitute 'padding' of a very low order and are designed solely to run up inflated 'entry counts'." *Random House College*, it should be noted, employs the same technique.

In any event, *Random House College* is some 90,000 entries smaller than its parent *The Random House Dictionary*. The emphasis in both dictionaries is on the standard vocabulary of the present day, with considerable attention paid to new scientific and technical terms, idiomatic expressions, and new coinages. In most instances the coverage is very similar in both dictionaries, except that the larger work includes more technical terms. Example: A simple comparative check of one small portion of each dictionary reveals that the unabridged *Random House Dictionary* includes the following terms that the college version does not: *club topsail* (nautical term), *club wheat* (a type of wheat), *clump block* (nautical term), *Clurman, Harold* (a drama critic), *Clusium* (the ancient name of *Chiusi*), *clustered* (an architectural term), *clusterhead pink* (an herb), *cluster leg* (furniture term), and *cluster point* (a math term).

As is the case with other Random House dictionaries (like *The American College Dictionary*), *Random House College* includes practically all its material in a single alphabet (colleges and universities and English given names being the exceptions). Among the 170,000 entries are over 7,000 biographies, a similar number of place-names, some 3,500 abbreviations, and numerous idioms. Usage labels are abundantly used to denote particular geographical, subject, and cultural restrictions on nonstandard words and meanings.

Authority

The dictionary draws its authority from the larger *Random House Dictionary*, an authoritative work which is described with the unabridged dictionaries in this part of the *Buying Guide*. It should be noted that *Random House College* was initially published in 1968. Laurence Urdang was the editor in chief of that edition and Stuart Berg Flexner the managing editor. Jess Stein is now the editor. The 1975 revised edition added some 15,000 entries to the first edition, increasing the total count from 155,000 to 170,000. Also, 50 new consultants were recruited for the revised edition, including such prominent people as Erik Erikson, John Knowles, and Jack Valenti.

Vocabulary Treatment (Clarity, Accuracy, Thoroughness, Recency)

When words have more than one definition, the most commonly used meaning is given first. The definitions are usually current, accurate, and clearly expressed. But, like *The Random House Dictionary*, *Random House College* sometimes lacks thorough treatment in the area of definitions. Example: The definition of *gene* is quite vague as to what a gene actually is and what it does. Note that the definition is exactly the same as the one given in *The Random House Dictionary* (Unabridged Edition). Example: The definition of *cell* as used in biology is very brief and nonspecific. The same is true of such terms as *aesthetic, decoupage, holism, photovoltaic,* and *radiation*.

Other aspects of vocabulary treatment are satisfactory. The pronunciation system is relatively uncomplicated and easy to grasp. The most common pronunciation and spelling variants are usually provided. The etymologies, which number some 40,000, are brief but clear. Although there are no illustrative quotations, 30,000 or more illustrative sentences and phrases help clarify or amplify meanings. The 5,000 synonym lists which discriminate shades of meaning among similar words are helpful.

Encyclopedic Features

The dictionary includes numerous biographical and geographical entries in the main alphabetical sequence. In addition, there are several non-lexical items appended to the dictionary, including standard signs and symbols, a directory of colleges and universities, a list of male and female given names, and a concise style manual.

Graphics

Random House College includes approximately 1,500 small black-and-white line drawings throughout the dictionary. Almost all of these illustrations are reprinted from the unabridged version. A few, however, are unique to the college dictionary, e.g., the diagram accompanying *cell*. In most cases the drawings are helpful as definitional aids.

Physical Format

The bright red cloth binding with gold lettering is both attractive and strong. An excellent quality of thin but durable Bible paper has been used. The type, though small, is clear and reasonably kind to the eyes. The two-column page has guide words at the top and a condensed pronunciation key at the bottom of odd-numbered pages. Generally speaking, *Random House College* has both a pleasing and sturdy format.

Summary

The Random House College Dictionary is an abridgment of *The Random House Dictionary of the English Language* (Unabridged Edition). The first edition of *Random House College* (1968) contained about 155,000 entries, and the revised edition (1975) added some 15,000 new words and meanings, bringing the current entry total to 170,000. As such, *Random House College* is the quantitative leader among the major college dictionaries, as the publisher's advertisements are quick to point out. But dictionary consumers should be aware that the "entry race" has nothing to do with relative dictionary quality. Dictionaries ultimately must be judged on their lexical contents, not their entry counts.

Like the parent dictionary, *Random House College* covers the active vocabulary of the 1970s very well. Scientific, technical, and commercial terms are emphasized, as are generally accepted new words. The dictionary usually provides clear, up-to-date definitions. Sometimes, however, the definitions are not as full as they might be. Other aspects of vocabulary treatment are satisfactory.

Most authorities agree that there is not a great deal of difference among the better dictionaries in this group. With that caveat, the *Buying Guide* believes that for all-around performance—clear, current, thorough, and authoritative coverage and treatment of vocabulary as well as appealing design and serviceable format—*Webster's New Collegiate Dictionary* and *Webster's New World Dictionary* (Second College Edition) are the best buys. Second choices are the innovative and very attractively produced *American Heritage Dictionary* (New College Edition) and the authoritative *Random House College Dictionary*. *Funk & Wagnalls Standard College Dictionary*, though competitive with the others, is the last among equals.

Other Critical Opinions

Wilson Library Bulletin (review by Charles A. Bunge), September 1969, p. 104.

Webster's New Collegiate Dictionary

Descriptive Information

Full Title: **Webster's New Collegiate Dictionary.** *Editor:* Henry Bosley Woolf, Editor in Chief. *Publisher:* G. & C. Merriam Co. Former titles: *Webster's Seventh New Collegiate Dictionary* (1963–1972); *Webster's New Collegiate Dictionary* (1949–1961); *Webster's Collegiate Dictionary* (1898–1948). *Edition Reviewed:* Eighth Edition, 1976.

Classification: Adult—Semi-unabridged. *Pages:* 32a, 1536. *Total Entries:* 150,000. *Average Entry Length:* 17 words. *Graphics:* 900. *Consultants:* 205. *Physical Size:* 7 by 10 in.; 25 cm. *LC:* 75-33335. *ISBN:* 0-87779-338-7 (plain); 0-87779-339-5 (thumb-indexed); 0-87779-340-9 (Buksyn binding). *Lowest Retail Price:* $9.95.

Purpose and Scope

Webster's New Collegiate Dictionary (Eighth Edition) is modeled after the unabridged *Webster's Third New International Dictionary* (1961). According to the editor's preface, *Webster's New Collegiate* "is a general dictionary edited for use in school or college, in the office, and in the home—in short, wherever information about English words is likely to be sought." The dictionary's scope is largely limited to vocabulary in active use, although some rare and obsolete words are included, particularly if they appear in the English classics (Shakespeare, Milton, Austen, Dickens, et al.). "The average user," states the editor, "should rarely have occasion to look for information about the vocabulary of present-day English that is not available within these pages."

The collegiate edition contains far fewer entries than the unabridged (150,000 as opposed to 460,000). Many technical, archaic, variant, and esoteric terms found in *Webster's Third* are omitted from the collegiate. Example: A comparative sample of one small portion of both dictionaries shows that the unabridged includes the following entries that the collegiate does not: *clubster* (a variant of *clubstart*, English dialect for stoat), *club stripe* (a clothing term), *club tie* (clothing term), *club tooth* (used in connection with watches), *clubweed* (a plant), *club wheat* (a type of wheat), *clubwoman* (a woman active in clubs), *cluif* (Scottish variant of *cloof*), *cluj* (defined as "of or from the city of Cluj, Romania"), and *clum* (a British variant of the past tense of *climb*).

In addition, many of the definitions in *Webster's Third* are abridged in the collegiate edition. Example: The verb *cluck* is defined in its several denotative and connotative senses in both dictionaries, but the unabridged edition gives somewhat fuller definitions, e.g., "to make a clicking sound with the tongue often expressive of alarm, distress, or concern; *also:* to express interest or concern" as opposed to the collegiate's "to make a clicking sound with the tongue: to express interest or concern." As might be expected, the unabridged edition provides many more illustrative quotations and examples than does the smaller collegiate.

Like *Webster's Third* (but unlike the other leading college dictionaries), *Webster's New Collegiate* does not give biographical and geographical information in the main body of the dictionary. This sort of encyclopedic material is appended in the back of the book. Abbreviations and commonly used foreign words and phrases are, however, in the main dictionary file. The previously taboo four-letter words like *fuck* have been added to *Webster's New Collegiate* (they were excluded from earlier editions). Many new words in general usage are also included, usually with a clarifying illustrative quote or phrase, e.g., *busing, data bank, deep-six, deep space, groupie, hoagie, minibike, Pap smear, red-neck,* and *time-sharing* all appear in the dictionary. Only a few of the *Buying Guide*'s sample words were not found in *Webster's New Collegiate*, e.g., *laetrile, mensch,* and *upfront.* Following the policy set by *Webster's Third,* such restrictive labels as "substandard," "slang," and "nonstandard" are used quite sparingly. In some instances, *Webster's New Collegiate* even drops labels used in the larger dictionary. Example: Whereas *Webster's Third* labels the noun *cluck* meaning "a stupid or naive person" as "slang" the collegiate edition does not. Unquestionably, *Webster's New Collegiate* is descriptive in the cultural sense whereas the other major college dictionaries tend to be prescriptive, with *The American Heritage Dictionary* the most didactic of all.

Authority

Merriam-Webster's line of collegiate dictionaries dates back to 1898. *Webster's Seventh New Collegiate Dictionary* (1963) was the first edition based on *Webster's Third.* In 1973 the Eighth Edition appeared, representing a completely revised version. It includes some 22,000 new words and meanings not found in the previous edition. *Webster's Seventh New Collegiate* (130,000 entries) remains in print, however, in a large format edition called "Big 7" (8½ by 11 in.; 28 cm.) which features easy-to-read type. According to a Merriam-Webster official, the Seventh Edition "is sold essentially as a promotion item for special uses." It sells for $10.95.

All Merriam-Webster's general dictionaries base their vocabulary selection and treatment on citations, following the practice introduced by Dr. Johnson in his famous dictionary and continued by Noah Webster and other reputable American dictionary-makers of the nineteenth century. *Webster's New Collegiate* ultimately derives its authority from the larger *Webster's Third* which in turn is based on the massive citational evidence which Merriam-Webster has systematically collected over many years. In addition, *Webster's New Collegiate* draws upon the excellent full-time staff of linguists and subject specialists maintained by the firm.

Vocabulary Treatment (Clarity, Accuracy, Thoroughness, Recency)

Meanings are listed in historical order, a Websterian tradition. The more than 150,000 entries include an estimated 191,000 separate definitions. The definitions, while not always as fully treated as in the unabridged *Webster's Third,* are clear, relatively precise, admirably up-to-date, and sufficiently detailed to meet the average adult user's needs. The latter conclusion is reinforced by the relatively high number of words (17) accorded each entry. The same definitional technique used in *Webster's Third* is employed in the collegiate edition. The system entails providing a self-contained analytical phrase for each meaning. Definitional phrases and numbered meanings are separated by means of a heavy dark colon. Example: The noun *oscilla-*

tion is defined as "1: the action or fact of oscillating: VIBRATION 2: VARIA-TION, FLUCTUATION 3: a flow of electricity changing periodically from a maximum to a minimum; *esp:* a flow periodically changing direction 4: a single swing (as of an oscillating body) from one extreme limit to the other." Note that synonymic words in small capitals (e.g., VIBRATION) are cross-references, not definitions.

Other components of vocabulary treatment are generally satisfactory, although the modified diacritical pronunciation system (the same as used in *Webster's Third*) might cause some users difficulty. The etymologies, which precede the definitions, are usually adequate. There are some 27,000 illustrative examples, including 3,000 quotations from (says one advertisement) "poets, comics, critics and presidents" as well as classical and contemporary writers. This figure represents far fewer illustrative examples than the 200,000 found in *Webster's Third*. *Webster's New Collegiate* provides about 2,000 synonyms in 760 synonym paragraphs. Those synonyms "believed to present special problems" are clearly discriminated whereas those with a readily understood "shared meaning element" are merely listed. The dictionary also provides 1,200 antonyms. *Webster's Third* and *Webster's Seventh New Collegiate* do not include antonyms.

It should also be noted here that the publisher has recently established a Language Research Service which is available without charge to owners of *Webster's New Collegiate* and other Merriam-Webster dictionaries. According to the information on the dictionary's jacket cover, "The Language Research Service will answer *your* questions about words and their usage. Word origins and pronunciations, shades of meaning, variants and slang, new coinages, changes in usage over the centuries—*specific* questions about any of these will be answered promptly, accurately, and concisely." The questioner must, however, enclose a stamped, self-addressed envelope. Questions should be addressed to: Language Research Service, Merriam-Webster Dictionaries, Box 1424, Springfield, Mass. 01101. As far as the *Buying Guide* is aware, this service is unique among American dictionary publishers.

Encyclopedic Features

The Merriam-Webster collegiate line has traditionally placed certain types of encyclopedic information in the back of the dictionary. *Webster's New Collegiate* (Eighth Edition) includes approximately 6,000 biographies and some 12,500 place-names, as well as a directory of colleges and universities and a basic style manual, in the appendix. There are also 550 or so foreign expressions in the back that "occur frequently in English texts but that have not become part of the English vocabulary." Note that many commonly used foreign words and phrases like *tour de force* are included in the main dictionary file. Note also that the vocabulary rhymes and lists of English given names which were appended in the Seventh Edition have been dropped from the Eighth.

Graphics

The 900 small black-and-white line drawings found throughout the dictionary are helpful aids to clarifying or augmenting definitions, but they are not a noteworthy feature. The illustrations tend to emphasize the unusual (e.g., a *DNA* molecular model; Queen Elizabeth I in a *farthingale;* a *purse seine*) rather than the usual variety of plants and animals so frequently depicted in college and desk dictionaries.

Physical Format

Webster's New Collegiate's physical construction is very good. The less expensive (plain) edition has a grey Lexotone binding and the thumb-indexed edition a pyroxylin red linen binding. Both are good-looking and sturdy. A special smooth-finish offset paper is used which appears to be strong and is glare-free. The same sharp, clear type (Times Roman) used in *Webster's Third* is found in the collegiate edition. The overall page design is pleasing but not as appealing or as innovative as *The American Heritage Dictionary*.

Summary

Webster's New Collegiate Dictionary (Eighth Edition) is America's best-selling dictionary. Since it first appeared in 1973, replacing *Webster's Seventh New Collegiate Dictionary* (1963), the Eighth Edition has sold over a million copies a year. The reason is simple: *Webster's New Collegiate* is an outstanding dictionary. Based on the authoritative unabridged *Webster's Third New International Dictionary*, the collegiate edition provides thorough, accurate, precise, and up-to-date treatment of the English language as it has evolved in the 1970s. Prospective purchasers should be aware, however, that *Webster's New Collegiate*, following the lead of *Webster's Third*, does not abundantly provide the sort of usage labels ("slang," etc.) which some users expect to find in a dictionary. The coverage is well balanced among the various areas of general knowledge. Especially well covered, however, are the words and phrases which make up our literary vocabulary. For instance, the obsolete sense of *crude* (as "immature") is included because it occurs in Milton's oft-studied poem *Lycidas*. The coverage and treatment of the contemporary vocabulary of science and technology are also noteworthy.

Dictionary consumers should realize that *Webster's Seventh New Collegiate Dictionary* (1963) is still in print in a special large format (8¾ by 11 in.; 28 cm.) with easy-to-read type. This special edition, which sells for $10.95, should not be confused with *Webster's New Collegiate Dictionary* (Eighth Edition) which is the latest in Merriam-Webster's collegiate line.

Most authorities agree that 90 percent or so of the lexical content of the leading college dictionaries is roughly the same. Detailed analyses by the *Buying Guide* tend to confirm that opinion. With that caveat, the *Buying Guide* believes that for all-around performance—clear, current, comprehensive, and authoritative coverage and treatment of vocabulary as well as appealing design and serviceable format—*Webster's New Collegiate Dictionary* and *Webster's New World Dictionary* (Second College Edition) are the best buys. Both are superior college dictionaries, with *Webster's New Collegiate* perhaps having the edge when it comes to treatment of scientific and literary terms and *Webster's New World* out front in coverage of Americanisms and etymological depth. Second choices are the innovative and attractively produced *American Heritage Dictionary* (New College Edition) and the authoritative *Random House College Dictionary*. *Funk & Wagnalls Standard College Dictionary*, though competitive with the others, is the last among equals.

Other Critical Opinions

American Reference Books Annual 1974 (review by Christine L. Wynar), pp. 452–453.
Booklist, November 1, 1973, pp. 251–253.
Katz, William A. *Basic Information Sources*. Vol. 1 of *Introduction to Reference Work*, 2nd ed. (New York: McGraw-Hill, 1974), p. 269.
Wilson Library Bulletin (review by Charles A. Bunge), June 1973, p. 866.

Webster's New World Dictionary (Second College Edition)

Descriptive Information

Full Title: **Webster's New World Dictionary of the American Language**. *Editor:* David B. Guralnik, Editor in Chief. *Publisher:* Collins+World. *Edition Reviewed:* Second College Edition, 1976.

Classification: Adult—Semi-unabridged. *Pages:* xxxvi, 1692. *Total Entries:* 158,000. *Average Entry Length:* 17 words. *Graphics:* 1,500. *Consultants:* 26. *Physical Size:* 7¼ by 10 in.; 25 cm. (Deluxe Color Edition is 8¼ by 11½ in.; 29 cm. and Soft-Cover Edition is 5¼ by 8 in.; 21 cm.) *LC:* 75-39572. *ISBN:* 0-529-05324-1 (plain); 0-529-05326-8 (thumb-indexed); 0-529-05328-4 (Deluxe Color Edition); 0-529-05327-6 (Soft-Cover Edition). *Lowest Retail Price:* $9.95; also $7.50 paper.

Purpose and Scope

Webster's New World Dictionary of the American Language (Second College Edition) provides a vocabulary, according to the editor's foreword, "chosen to meet the needs of students and others in this particular period of history." The dictionary's range is quite broad. Included among its 158,000 entries are common words and phrases in current usage, many scientific and technical terms of recent coinage, numerous modern compound words and phrases, some 5,500 idiomatic expressions, a considerable amount of slang and other nonstandard vocabulary, and thousands of brief biographical and geographical items. As the dictionary's full title suggests—*Webster's NEW WORLD Dictionary of the AMERICAN Language*—the major emphasis is on English as written and spoken in the United States. Over 14,000 Americanisms are identified (by means of a small star) and defined. For instance, each of the following words is preceded by a star: *jackknife, jackleg, jacklight, jack pine, jackpot, jack rabbit,* and *jacksmelt*. In addition, in some cases particular meanings of a word are designated as Americanisms, e.g., the slang senses of the verb *goose* ("to prod suddenly and playfully in the backside so as to startle," etc.).

In most instances, the sample words preselected by the *Buying Guide* are found in *Webster's New World*. Not covered are *cholestasis, laetrile, oxygen cycle*, *reprography*, *ultrafiche*, and *upfront*, among others. *Orwellian* is listed but not defined, and the current meanings of *launder* and *mace* are not given. Also, the dictionary's scope does not include the so-called four-letter words, or terms of racial and ethnic denigration. David Guralnik, the editor, suggests that the former "are so well known as to require no explanation" and the latter (the "true obscenities") are "encountered with diminishing frequency these days." He also indicates that the controversial words are omitted "on the practical grounds that there is still objection in many quarters to the appearance of these terms in print and that to risk keeping this dictionary out of the hands of some students by introducing several terms that require little if any elucidation would be unwise." The *Buying Guide* disagrees with these arguments. Most reputable dictionaries, including the new supplements to the *Oxford English Dictionary*, now include such words. In many instances, these terms (e.g., *fuck*) have a large variety of informal meanings and derivations. To exclude them from the dictionary on either practical or lexicographical grounds is not defensible in the 1970s.

Webster's New World, like *The American Heritage Dictionary*, *Funk & Wagnalls Standard College Dictionary*, and *The Random House College Dictionary* but unlike its major rival *Webster's New Collegiate Dictionary*, provides numerous restrictive labels to indicate nonstandard vocabulary (e.g., technical terms, dialect, slang, and colloquialisms). There are also many usage notes. Example: The note accompanying the word *irregardless* (identified as an Americanism) is "a substandard or humorous redundancy for REGARDLESS." (REGARDLESS is printed in small capitals to signify a cross-reference.) According to the editor, the usage notes and restrictive labels represent an "informed collective determination" by the dictionary's editorial staff.

Authority

Webster's New World (Second College Edition) first appeared in 1970, replacing the initial edition published in 1953. That dictionary derived from the 142,000-entry *Webster's New World Dictionary* (Encyclopedic Edition), a two-volume work published in 1951 and now out of print. The Encyclopedic Edition, which took ten years to prepare, was compiled from scratch by a 94-member staff headed by David Guralnik and Joseph Friend. The project was sponsored by World Publishing Company (now Collins+World), a trade publisher which at the time included several inexpensive general English-language dictionaries of very modest quality on its list. Users of the *Buying Guide* should note that *Webster's New World* is not an abridgment of the larger *Webster's New Twentieth Century Dictionary*, an undistinguished work also published by Collins+World. Note also that these dictionaries and the publisher are in no way connected with the G. & C. Merriam Company which publishes a line of dictionaries with similar titles.

Webster's New World is a highly authoritative dictionary. As indicated, David Guralnik, the editor, has been with the dictionary from the start and is one of this country's senior lexicographers. Mitford M. Mathews, editor of the prestigious *Dictionary of Americanisms*, is responsible for the 14,000

Americanisms in the dictionary. William E. Umbach, a professor at the University of Redlands, prepared the etymologies, one of the dictionary's strongest features. Like Guralnik, Dr. Umbach was associated with the work from its inception in the 1940s. In addition, there is a permanent editorial staff of some 30 people, as well as 26 special contributing editors, most of whom are university professors at midwestern institutions.

The dictionary also derives its authority from a constantly growing citation file. "These citations," says David Guralnik, "constitute what we like to think of as the life's blood of our lexicographical program." At the present time, the file contains nearly a million slips. *Webster's New World* has also drawn on the personal files of Mitford Mathews since he joined the staff in 1957 as a special consulting editor. The editors likewise use the *Oxford English Dictionary* and other research dictionaries prepared on historical principles, as well as the files of the scholarly language journal *American Speech*. Increasingly, *Webster's New World* is being recognized as one of our leading general dictionaries. For instance, several years ago the *New York Times* selected *Webster's New World* (Second College Edition) as its dictionary of first reference. More recently, the Associated Press and United Press International did the same.

Vocabulary Treatment (Clarity, Accuracy, Thoroughness, Recency)

Like *Webster's New Collegiate Dictionary*, *Webster's New World* arranges its definitions in historical order, with the etymology preceding the earliest meaning. "The result," states the editor, "is a single coherent paragraph that clearly shows the history and development of the word and the relationship among the meanings, rather than an assemblage of fragmented bits of disconnected information." The definitions are almost always clear, reliable, up-to-date, and reasonably detailed (although, as noted below, illustrative examples are not always provided in sufficient quantity). Example: The eight-line definition of *gene* is only slightly less clear and thorough than the one in *Webster's New Collegiate Dictionary*, which has the best overall definition of the term among the college dictionaries. The definition is accurate except for one minor error (the gene itself is not composed of protein). Example: The verb *mix* has five precisely defined meanings as a transitive verb, the first being "to put or blend together in a single mass, collection, or compound." Three senses of the word as an intransitive verb follow. The more recent meaning of *mix* as a noun (as in cake *mix* or cement *mix*) is also given. This meaning is designated as an Americanism. The pronunciations given "are those used by cultivated speakers in normal, relaxed conversation." The pronunciation system, which is easy to follow, entails a phonetic key consisting of 24 consonant and 19 vowel sounds, including the schwa. Numerous common variant pronunciations and spellings are provided.

The etymologies are one of the dictionary's glories. In the first edition (1951), Harold Whitehall, chairman of the Linguistics Department at Indiana University, and William Umbach, then at Case Institute of Technology, prepared fresh etymologies based on contemporary language research, some of it original. An effort was made, for example, to trace native English words back to their Indo-European base. The result was fuller and more informative word histories than had heretofore appeared in a desk-size dictionary. The Second College Edition (1970) has continued this emphasis on full etymological information. Example: Following the definition of the second main entry for the word *funky* ("having an earthy quality or style derived from early blues") there is a lengthy, informative etymology which traces the cant term to both "Negro argot" and its earlier Latin roots. The etymology also serves to bring out additional senses of *funky* ("smelly, hence musty, earthy"). Example: The origins of American place-names are given. The user learns, for instance, that *Florida* is a Spanish word derived from the Latin which literally means "abounding in flowers."

Less impressive are the illustrative examples. No quotations are provided, only staff-written phrases, e.g., to *mix* work and play. Like *The Random House College Dictionary*, *Webster's New World* uses these phrasal illustrations to "force" definitional clarity. Usually the illustrations are helpful but in some instances words which need illustrative examples do not have them. Example: All of the following words, taken from one small sample, lack illustrative examples: *depurate*, *depute*, *deracinate*, *dereism*, *derelict*, *deride*, *de rigueur*, *derision*, *derisive*, *dervish*, *descry*, and *desensitize*. The last word, *desensitize*, for instance, is defined as "to take away the sensitivity of; make less sensitive," but the contemporary usage of the word (to become inured to violence and war; to lose one's moral sensitivity) is not brought out, in part for want of an apt illustrative quotation or example.

About 800 synonym studies appear throughout the dictionary, accompanying such words as *intrude*, *mix*, and *sentimental*. Shades of meaning are discriminated, e.g., "that is *mawkish* which is sentimental in a disgustingly weak, insincere, or exaggerated way [a *mawkish* soap opera]." Another useful synonymic feature is the inclusion of cross-references (printed in small capitals) at the end of some entries. Example: The third meaning of the noun *glutton* is "a furry, northern animal (*Gulo gulo*) related to the marten and weasel but larger: the American variety is the WOLVERINE." Note also that all definitions of plants and animals include their scientific names.

Encyclopedic Features

Unlike *Webster's New Collegiate Dictionary*, *Webster's New World* includes the names of people, Biblical and legendary figures, places, foreign expressions, abbreviations, and so forth in the main dictionary file, not in various appendixes in the back. The dictionary does, however, include lists of American and Canadian colleges and universities in the back, as well as a helpful "Guide to Punctuation, Mechanics, and Manuscript Form" and the usual tables of weights and measures, signs, and symbols, and proofreaders' marks with sample copy.

Graphics

Webster's New World includes approximately 1,500 small black-and-white line drawings throughout the text. They are quite clear and usually informative complements to the written definition. Some spot maps are also provided. The Deluxe Color Edition, which has exactly the same text as the Second College Edition, adds 36 pages of color illustrations. They depict such standard items as flags, animals, and jewels. Although the color plates are attractive and placed relatively close to the subject being illustrated, they are not specifically related to any entry. Their value is more aesthetic than informational. The Deluxe Color Edition also prints the small line drawings and guide words at the top of each page in blue. This edition costs $15.00, as opposed to $9.95 for the plain hardcover edition and $7.50 for the paper edition. Whether the two-color page and 36 four-color plates are worth an extra $5.00 is questionable. The dictionary is also available in a deluxe leather edition at $35.00.

Physical Format

The plain and thumb-indexed editions are standard desk-size whereas the Deluxe Color Edition is somewhat larger. All of the hardcover editions are bound in an attractive, sturdy noncloth material called Lexide, but the imitation leather covers of the paperback edition will quickly become dog-eared. A good quality nonglare paper has been used. The modern type is large, distinctive, and quite clear, although the print in the review copy provided by the publisher was excessively light on some pages. Guide words appear at the top of each page and a condensed pronunciation key at the bottom of odd-numbered pages. Overall, the dictionary's format is satisfactory but not as appealing as *The American Heritage Dictionary*'s.

Summary

Webster's New World Dictionary of the American Language (Second College Edition) contains 158,000 entries which represent the most commonly encountered words and phrases in the English language as written and spoken in the United States today. In the tradition of Noah Webster, the dictionary provides especially good coverage and treatment of Americanisms—that is, words and idioms which have originated in this country. In general, the vocabulary treatment is first-rate. The definitions tend to be up-to-date, clearly and precisely written, and sufficiently detailed. The pronunciation system is relatively easy to grasp, discriminated synonyms are abundantly provided, and nonstandard vocabulary is usually so labeled. The fullness of the etymologies is without parallel among college dictionaries. A unique feature of *Webster's New World* is the provision of etymological information for American place-names (states, cities, rivers, etc.). On the negative side, illustrative quotations are not provided and illustrative examples are sometimes lacking in instances where they might enhance definitional clarity, particularly connotative senses.

Webster's New World is a highly authoritative dictionary, but unlike its principal competitor, *Webster's New Collegiate Dictionary*, it does not have a long or especially illustrious history. Instead, *Webster's New World* was prepared in the 1940s under the sponsorship of a publisher (the now defunct World Publishing Company) not noted for lexicographical achievements. Nevertheless, when the dictionary was issued in the early 1950s, critics immediately recognized it as a sound work. In 1970 a completely revised and considerably improved edition appeared. Since that time, *Webster's New World* has steadily achieved recognition as one of the best college dictionaries on the market.

Most authorities agree that 90 percent or so of the lexical content of the leading college dictionaries is roughly the same. Detailed analyses by the *Buying Guide* tend to confirm that opinion. With that caveat, the *Buying Guide* believes that for all-around performance—clear, current, comprehensive, and authoritative coverage and treatment of vocabulary as well as appealing design and serviceable format—*Webster's New Collegiate Dictionary* and *Webster's New World Dictionary* (Second College Edition) are the best buys. Both are superior college dictionaries, with *Webster's New Collegiate* perhaps having the edge when it comes to treatment of scientific and literary terms and *Webster's New World* out front in coverage of Americanisms and etymological depth. Second choices are the innovative and attractively produced *American Heritage Dictionary* (New College Edition) and the authoritative *Random House College Dictionary*. *Funk & Wagnalls Standard College Dictionary*, though competitive with the others, is the last among equals.

Other Critical Opinions

American Reference Books Annual 1974 (review by Francis J. Witty), p. 453.
Booklist, March 15, 1974, pp. 750–752.
Katz, William A. *Basic Information Sources.* Vol. 1 of *Introduction to Reference Work*, 2nd ed. (New York: McGraw-Hill, 1974), p. 270.

Webster's Seventh New Collegiate Dictionary (Large Format Edition)

Descriptive Information

Full Title: **Webster's Seventh New Collegiate Dictionary.** *Editors:* Philip Babcock Gove, Editor in Chief; Henry Bosley Woolf, Managing Editor. *Publisher:* G. & C. Merriam Co. *Edition Reviewed:* Large Format Edition, 1974.

Classification: Adult—Semi-unabridged. *Pages:* 1244. *Total Entries:* 130,000. *Average Entry Length:* 15 words. *Graphics:* 600. *Physical Size:* 8¾ by 11¼ in.; 29 cm. *ISBN:* 0-87779-314-X. *Lowest Retail Price:* $10.95.

Consumer Note

Webster's Seventh New Collegiate Dictionary, initially published in 1963, has been superseded by *Webster's New Collegiate Dictionary* (Eighth Edition), which first appeared in 1974. The publisher, however, has issued a Large Format Edition of *Webster's Seventh*, mainly for promotional purposes. The dictionary is made available to booksellers at a reduced wholesale price. This results in a higher profit margin at the retail level and is thus used as an inducement for dealers to stock the Merriam-Webster line of dictionaries. As a "traffic-builder book," as the publisher calls it, *Webster's Seventh* serves a useful commercial purpose. In addition, *Webster's*

Seventh remains a relatively current and authoritative dictionary (it is based on *Webster's Third New International Dictionary*, the latest unabridged edition). Moreover, its large format with easy-to-read type will appeal to consumers in the market for a college dictionary with big print. On the other hand, this edition (called "Big 7" by the publisher) is larger than desk-size and hence not as handy as *Webster's New Collegiate Dictionary* (Eighth Edition). But the most important point is that consumers should not confuse *Webster's Seventh New Collegiate Dictionary* (Large Format Edition) as the latest in the firm's "Collegiate" line. Consumers who want the most recent "Collegiate" should carefully check to see that they have the Eighth Edition, called *Webster's New College Dictionary*, which currently bears a 1976 copyright and is updated every year.

World Book Dictionary

Descriptive Information

Full Title: **The World Book Dictionary**. *Editors:* Clarence L. Barnhart and Robert K. Barnhart. *Publisher:* Field Enterprises Educational Corp. Former title: *The World Book Encyclopedia Dictionary*. *Edition Reviewed:* 1977.

Classification: Adult—Semi-unabridged. *Volumes:* 2. *Pages:* 124 (colored paper), 2430. *Total Entries:* 225,000. *Average Entry Length:* 23 words. *Graphics:* 3,000. *Consultants:* 156. *Physical Size:* 8¾ by 11¼ in.; 29 cm. *LC:* 76-23524. *ISBN:* 0-7166-0277-6. *Lowest Retail Price:* $59.00 the set.

Purpose and Scope

The World Book Dictionary, according to the editor's introduction, "contains 225,000 terms in the working vocabulary of English—the vocabulary used by educated people to communicate with each other and needed by them to understand the world they live in and the world of the past." Although it does contain some rare and esoteric terms, the dictionary is emphatically devoted to general words and phrases in current usage. The editors explain: "By concentrating on vocabulary in actual use, this dictionary is able to provide fuller definitions and more illustrative sentences than it could if it were to include all possible obsolete, archaic, or excessively technical terms. By limiting entries to the really useful ones, entries are easier to find and space is gained in which to explain them adequately."

World Book Dictionary's coverage of the live vocabulary of present-day English is quite comprehensive. With only a few exceptions (e.g., *nitrofurantoin*), the sample terms preselected by the *Buying Guide* are included in the dictionary. Indeed, the dictionary's general range is equal to or surpasses that of the leading college dictionaries. *World Book Dictionary*, however, does not include the so-called four-letter words. On the other hand, numerous slang and informal terms are defined, including many idiomatic expressions, e.g., *go to the dogs, dog eat dog, dog in the manger, dog it*, and *let sleeping dogs lie*. For instance, all of the following recently coined words are covered: *deep-six, flat-out, groupie, honcho, jawbone, shtick* (or *schtick*), and *up-front*. Note that such vocabulary is appropriately labeled "slang" or "informal." Many Americanisms (e.g., *busing* or *bussing; hoagie* or *hoagy*) are likewise included. They are labeled "U.S." Usage notes are provided for certain troublesome terms. Example: The adjective *irregardless*, labeled "informal," is said to be "not considered good usage."

World Book Dictionary is designed to complement the publisher's well-known *World Book Encyclopedia*, a 22-volume general reference work for student and family use. An effort has been made to insure that every word used in the encyclopedia is defined in the dictionary. But the dictionary does not include biographical, geographical, and other encyclopedic-type material which is readily available in the encyclopedia. However, many proper adjectives (e.g., *Wordsworthian*), proper nouns (e.g., *Chicano*), and commonly used trademarks (e.g., *Xerox*) are covered in the dictionary. Names of plants and animals are entered in both the dictionary and the encyclopedia, but the latter treats them more fully, including provision of scientific names and classifications. According to the editors, *The World Book Encyclopedia* and *The World Book Dictionary* "are the only encyclopedia and dictionary that are edited to supplement each other. Together, they form a reference library for the family as well as the classroom." It is further noted that the annual supplement to the encyclopedia, *The World Book Year Book*, contains a special dictionary section on the year's new words and meanings.

World Book Dictionary, then, is first and foremost for those who own *World Book Encyclopedia*. But the dictionary can be profitably used by both students and adults without reference to the encyclopedia. As indicated, the dictionary's scope is essentially that of the typical college dictionary which treats a sizable vocabulary (150,000–170,000 entries) in some depth for a fairly sophisticated audience. Conversely, *World Book Dictonary*'s purpose is more akin to the school dictionary (30,000–90,000 entries) which is principally concerned with vocabulary instruction via simplified treatment and explanation by example (both verbal and visual). In short, *World Book Dictionary* uniquely—and very successfully—combines the best qualities of two different types of dictionaries. The result is a dictionary with a broader potential appeal and usership than any other on the market today.

Authority

The dictionary initially appeared in 1963 under the title *The World Book Encyclopedia Dictionary*. In 1967 the title was shortened to the current *World Book Dictionary*. The dictionary is updated annually but in 1976 it received a thorough overhaul, being completely revised, reset, and substantially enlarged. From the beginning *World Book Dictionary* has been recognized as a work of impeccable authority. Prepared by Clarence L. Barnhart, the dean of American lexicographers, and his staff at Clarence L. Barnhart, Inc. (one of the few permanent commercial dictionary operations in this country), the dictionary is the largest and most impressive work in the distinguished line of Thorndike-Barnhart school dictionaries. Vocabulary selection and treatment are based on the Barnhart citation file which currently contains well over three million slips. The slips, which have been accumulating over the past 25 years, "are culled from a wide sampling of contemporary magazines, newspapers, scholarly and technical journals, and books." This work, conducted by the full-time Barnhart staff as well as commissioned readers, is an international endeavor: "Correspondents from Australia, Canada, Great Britain, South Africa, and other parts of the English-speaking world regularly furnish evidence of new regional usages."

In addition to the prestigious Thorndike-Barnhart logo, the dictionary has a 46-member international editorial advisory committee which includes such eminent English-language authorities as Margaret M. Bryant, Frederic G. Cassidy, Hans Kurath, Albert H. Marckwardt, and Robert P. Stockwell. The dictionary also lists over 100 subject consultants who provide comments and suggestions in some 70 fields of knowledge. Consultants include Clive Barnes (dance), H. J. Eysenck (psychology), Morris Fishbein (medicine), Chandler B. Grannis (publishing), Stanley Kunitz (literature), and Dore Schary (motion pictures). Finally, 37 editors and artists from Field Enterprises are identified as having a hand in the project.

Vocabulary Treatment (Clarity, Accuracy, Thoroughness, Recency)

When a word has more than one definition, the most frequently used meaning is given first. *World Book Dictionary* follows the Thorndike Barnhart principle that definitions ought to be written in simpler language than the word being defined. The dictionary's definitions tend to be exceptionally clear, up-to-date, and reliable. They are usually more conversational and hence less concise than the definitions in the leading college dictionaries. This tendency helps account for the dictionary's extraordinarily high average-words-per-entry figure (23). Example: The entry *Pap test* or *smear* is defined as "a test used to diagnose certain cancers, in which exfoliated cells of organs, such as the cervix, stomach, or uterus, are obtained, smeared on a glass slide, and stained for microscopic examination." The definition is followed by an illustrative quotation: "*The 'Pap smear' is effective in spotting potential cancers of the cervix.*" The quotation, identified simply as from *Harper's*, is followed by an etymological note about Dr. George N. Papanicolaou who developed the test. Compare this information, for instance, with the entry *Pap smear* in *Webster's New Collegiate Dictionary:* "a method for the early detection of cancer employing exfoliated cells and a special staining technique that differentiates diseased tissue—called also *Papanicolaou test, Pap test.*" Etymological information precedes the definition but there is no illustrative quotation or example. The entries in both dictionaries are accurate and informative, but *World Book Dictionary*'s is more relaxed, more readable, and more expansive but no less thorough. It should also be noted that *World Book Dictionary* definitions are, according to the publisher, stated "in language suited to the level of understanding of the likely user. They are written to the grade level of the student most likely to look them up." Hence the biological term *cell*, for example, will be defined on a more elementary level than a term like *Pap smear*.

The pronunciation system used by *World Book Dictionary*, adapted from the International Phonetic Alphabet, utilizes individual letters of the English alphabet, combinations of letters (e.g., *zh*), diacritical and stress marks, and the schwa (which Clarence Barnhart originally introduced into American dictionaries in the 1940s). Also, five non-English sounds are represented, e.g., *N* as in the French *bon.* The system is both precise and not difficult to comprehend. The complete pronunciation key is printed in the front matter on page 124 but not on the endpapers in either volume. Although an abbreviated key is reproduced at the bottom of odd-numbered pages, future editions of *World Book Dictionary* would do well to include the full key on the endpapers, particularly since they are now blank. The pronunciations given "are those which the editors consider to be in current use among educated speakers of English in the United States, and in representative areas of Canada." Common variant pronunciations and spellings are provided. Syllabication is indicated by thin vertical lines rather than the usual hyphens or centered dots.

As the *Pap smear* entry shows, the dictionary frequently provides illustrative quotations and/or examples to clarify or amplify meanings. Although the quotations are undated and identified only by the person or publication being quoted, they are an essential part of the dictionary's successful effort to define complicated terms in a fairly simple yet precise manner. Example: The definition of *existentialism* is augmented by the quotation "*Existentialism, as expounded by Sartre, is not pessimistic in the nihilist sense, but is a doctrine of fortitude and even hope.*" This quote, identified as coming from the *New York Times*, not only further explains the term but adds an extra connotative dimension to the definition. Aside from the unabridged *Webster's Third New International Dictionary*, *World Book Dictionary* offers more useful illustrative quotations and examples than any general dictionary available today. The quotations are mainly drawn from contemporary sources (often British authors and magazines), but classical writers are also represented, especially to explain figurative meanings. Example: The fourth and last sense of the noun *jaws* is labeled "figurative" and defined as "the seizing action or capacity of any devouring agency, as of death or time." The accompanying illustrative quotation is from Tennyson: "*Into the jaws of Death, / Into the mouth of Hell Rode the six hundred.*" Also, strenuous efforts have been made by the editors to eliminate sexism and sexist terminology from the definitions, quotations, and examples.

The etymologies, while not as full as those found in several of the leading college dictionaries, are quite sufficient for the average student or adult user. Like *The American Heritage Dictionary*, standard etymological terms (e.g., "Old French") are written out instead of being abbreviated as in most dictionaries. In point of fact, *World Book Dictionary* (again like *American Heritage*) avoids typical "dictionary shorthand" wherever and whenever possible, preferring to spell out such labels as "slang," "informal," "British slang," "botany," "archaic," and "Middle Dutch" in an effort to achieve greater readability. The standard etymological symbols < (derived or taken from) and + (and) are used, however. Synonyms are abundantly provided. A useful feature is the inclusion of cross-references to synonym studies which discriminate similar words. Example: At the end of the entry for the adjective *capable* there is a note: "See syn. under *able*." At the end of the entry *able* there is a synonym paragraph which discriminates *able*, *capable*, and *competent*. Precise distinctions are clarified by illustrative examples which accompany each word.

Encyclopedic Features

The dictionary contains practically no encyclopedic information, either in the main body of the work or appended in the back. As explained earlier (see Purpose and Scope), the dictionary does not attempt to duplicate material available in *The World Book Encyclopedia*. Although some users may find the dictionary's lack of biographical and geographical entries an inconvenience, the editors correctly point out that, "Excluding such encyclopedic information from the dictionary means that more space can be given to word meanings, illustrative sentences, usage notes, word origins and histories, synonyms, and illustrations." Note that the unabridged *Webster's Third New International Dictionary* excludes encyclopedic material for the same reason. It should be mentioned, however, that *World Book Dictionary* does provide a number of excellent special features in the front matter. This material includes step-by-step instructions for preparing term papers and book reports; graded vocabulary building exercises (from grade three through the college level); easy-to-understand discussions of English-language history and new developments in linguistic theory (e.g., the concept of "transformational grammar" is simply and clearly explained); and a potpourri of useful information about languages other than English, including codes and ciphers and internationally recognized signs and symbols.

Graphics

World Book Dictionary now has over 3,000 black-and-white line drawings designed to visually supplement or clarify the vocabulary terms they complement. All of the drawings are new (as of 1976), created especially for the dictionary by Field Enterprise staff artists, two researchers, and ten free-lance artists commissioned for the project. A unique feature is that multiple illustrations are sometimes provided for terms which have more than one meaning. For instance, there are six different drawings for the word *bridge* showing a highway bridge, the bridge of a ship, the bridge of a nose, a bridge used in billiards, etc. The illustrations, some of which are two columns wide, tend to emphasize scientific topics, e.g., *brain*, *cell*, *cloud*, *distributor*, *electromagnet*, *interior angle*, *microfiche*, *otoscope*, *radiolarian*, and *suspension system*. Illustrated entries are denoted by an asterisk. Cross-references are also used when necessary to relate the drawings to appropriate entries. Example: Under *conjugation* there is a diagram of a conjugation of spirogyra. At the end of the entry *spirogyra*, there is a note: "See diagram under *conjugation*." Overall, the drawings are superior to those found in other general dictionaries.

Physical Format

The dictionary's two-volume format (A–K; L–Z) is a drawback when many entries are being checked at random. In addition, the volumes are larger than desk-size and hence somewhat inconvenient for home or office use. The volumes are also quite heavy, weighing 5 pounds apiece. But beyond these complaints, which involve handling ease, *World Book Dictionary* is a superbly designed and constructed work. The thumb-indexed volumes are attractively bound in a strong pyroxylin fabric which will withstand very heavy and even rough use. A special coated 30-pound weight white English-finish litho paper has been used. It is glare-free and of excellent quality. The same kind of paper is used in the front matter except it is tan in color and somewhat heavier. The sans-serif Spectra type is handsome, modern, and exceptionally readable. The main entries are printed in dark bold type, the definitions in lightface type, and the illustrative quotations and examples in italic. This variation of type contributes to the dictionary's pleasing appearance and readability. The three-column page layout is enhanced by the "ragged" (or unjustified) edges on the right-hand side of each column of type. This innovative typographical feature also improves the dictionary's readability by reducing hyphenation and eliminating uneven spacing between words on a line. The ragged look also adds variety to the usually monotonous dictionary page. Among the large general dictionaries *World Book Dictionary* and *The American Heritage Dictionary* have the most inviting and creative formats.

Summary

The World Book Dictionary, first published in 1963 and substantially revised in 1976, is the largest dictionary in the prestigious Thorndike-Barnhart school line. Moreover, its approximately 225,000 entries give *World Book Dictionary* a range equivalent to the leading college dictionaries in the semi-unabridged category. It is also designed to complement the publisher's popular *World Book Encyclopedia*, a multivolume reference set for student and family use. The dictionary, however, is an independent work and can be used without reference to the encyclopedia. It is published in two bindings, the Renaissance at $59.00 for both volumes and the Aristocrat at $69.00.

The dictionary's vocabulary treatment is admirably lucid, remarkably current, entirely reliable, and sufficiently expansive to meet the English-language needs of users from young students at the middle school level to inquiring adults and college students. Particularly noteworthy is the large number of idiomatic expressions covered in the dictionary. Other outstanding features include the dictionary's unimpeachable authority, its simplified yet thorough definitions, its numerous and carefully chosen illustrative quotations and examples, its appealing typography and general readability, its lack of off-putting abbreviations and dictionary symbols, its effective use of graphics, its precise yet easily understood pronunciation key, its useful and in some instances unique supplementary material on language located in the front matter, and its vigorous program of annual revision and updating.

On the negative side, the two-volume format (A–K; L–Z) is simply not as handy to use as the more customary single volume. (Several years ago the publisher offered a one-volume edition to schools and libraries, but this edition is no longer available.) Moreover, the volumes are physically larger than desk-size and therefore not as convenient to handle or store. The complete pronunciation key, though printed in the front matter, is not

readily accessible to the casual user. Future editions should consider printing the full key on the endpapers (which are currently blank). Finally,
there is the question of price. Most frequently, the dictionary is sold at a
reduced price in combination with *The World Book Encyclopedia*. The dictionary is also offered to schools and libraries at a discount price. Note,
however, that both the dictionary and the encyclopedia are only sold
through local *World Book* representatives (who are listed in the yellow
pages). Neither the dictionary nor the encyclopedia is available through
the usual trade channels—that is, through retail bookstores. Individual
consumers who want only the dictionary must buy it through the publisher's local representative at a cost of $59.00. This price is rather steep
when you consider that the unabridged *Webster's Third New International
Dictionary* costs only $16.00 more and *The Random House Dictionary*
(Unabridged Edition) can be acquired for about half the price. Or when
you consider that the leading college dictionaries (*Webster's New Collegiate
Dictionary; Webster's New World Dictionary; The American Heritage
Dictionary; The Random House College Dictionary; Funk & Wagnalls
Standard College Dictionary*) can all be acquired for under $10.00.

Clearly, *World Book Dictionary* is one of the finest general dictionaries
currently on the American market. It has a wider potential usership (from
young students to inquisitive adults) than any other dictionary available.
Unfortunately, its high price and limited method of distribution render
it noncompetitive with other dictionaries in its class. The *Buying Guide*
believes, however, that if *The World Book Dictionary* were published in
a smaller one-volume, desk-size trade edition of, say, 150,000–175,000
entries it would, to put it idiomatically, knock the competition dead.

Other Critical Opinions

American Reference Books Annual 1970, pp. 51–52 (in vol. 2); also *Ameri-
can Reference Books Annual* 1972 (review by Sally Wynkoop), pp. 467–
468; also *American Reference Books Annual* 1977 (review by Bohdan S.
Wynar), pp. 521–522.
Booklist, November 1, 1976, pp. 422–423.
Katz, William A. *Basic Information Sources.* Vol. 1 of *Introduction to
Reference Work*, 2nd ed. (New York: McGraw-Hill, 1974), p. 271.
Wilson Library Bulletin (review by Charles A. Bunge), September 1976,
p. 91.

ABRIDGED DICTIONARIES

American Heritage Dictionary (Paperback Edition)

Descriptive Information

Full Title: **The American Heritage Dictionary of the English Language.
Paperback Edition.** *Editors:* Peter Davies and the American Heritage Dictionary Staff. *Publisher:* Dell Publishing Co. *Edition Reviewed:* Paper-

back Edition (based on the Hardcover Edition; William Morris, Editor), 1976.

Classification: Adult—Abridged. *Pages:* xii, 820. *Total Entries:* 55,000. *Average Entry Length:* 12 words. *Graphics:* 300. *Physical Size:* 4¼ by 7 in.; 18 cm. *Lowest Retail Price:* $1.95 paper.

Contents

The American Heritage Dictionary of the English Language (Paperback Edition), which has exactly the same text as *The Concise Heritage Dictionary*, contains 55,000 entries selected from the 155,000-entry semiunabridged edition of the dictionary. The vocabulary includes all of the completely different words (50,406) identified in the one-million-word computer sample used to produce the larger edition in 1969, plus new words which have entered the language over the past six or seven years. The entries are often abridged versions of those found in the larger dictionary. In many instances, words treated as main entries in the larger dictionary are simply entered as derivatives in the Paperback Edition. Example: The adjective *discernible* is defined as "perceptible; distinguishable" in the 155,000-entry edition but is merely listed as a subentry of the verb *discern* in the smaller edition. Etymologies and usage notes (derived from the American Heritage Usage Panel) are carried over into the Paperback Edition, but all synonym studies are omitted. About 300 of the larger dictionary's 4,000 graphics are reproduced in the paper edition. Most are spot maps. The type, though clear, is quite small and the page layout in no way resembles the innovative design which distinguishes the larger edition.

Summary

The dictionary is an abridgment of the 155,000-entry *American Heritage Dictionary of the English Language*, originally published in 1969 and continuously revised since that time. Moreover, the Paperback Edition is a photographically reduced reprint of *The Concise Heritage Dictionary*. The text of the paper and concise editions is exactly the same (including graphics). The only difference between the two editions involves physical format. *Concise Heritage* is hardbound and physically larger (including more readable type) whereas the Paperback Edition is softcover and smaller. Also, the *Concise Heritage* costs $5.95.

The $1.95 mass market paper edition has been enormously successful. Dell, the publisher, claims some six million copies currently in print. In July 1977, a more expensive trade paperback edition (a Delta Special) was issued. Sold only in bookstores, this edition costs $3.95 and comes in a special Permalin binding which is washable and tear-resistant. However, it has the same text as the $1.95 edition.

The three leading abridged paperback dictionaries currently available are *The American Heritage Dictionary* (55,000 entries), *The Merriam-Webster Dictionary* (57,000 entries), and *Webster's New World Dictionary* (Pocket-size Edition; 59,000 entries). Each can be acquired for $1.95. Each derives its authority from a well-known and highly reputable larger dictionary. And each is a good buy—if you want an inexpensive abridged dictionary.

For further information, see the profile of *The American Heritage Dictionary* in the "semi-unabridged" section and the note on *The Concise Heritage Dictionary* which follows.

Concise Heritage Dictionary

Descriptive Information

Full Title: **The Concise Heritage Dictionary.** *Editor:* The American Heritage Dictionary Staff. *Publisher:* Houghton Mifflin Co. *Edition Reviewed:* 1976.
Classification: Adult—Abridged. *Pages:* xii, 820. *Total Entries:* 55,000. *Average Entry Length:* 12 words. *Graphics:* 300. *Physical Size:* 6 by 9¼ in.; 24 cm. *LC:* 76-4047. *ISBN:* 0-395-24522-2. *Lowest Retail Price:* $5.95.

Consumer Note

The Concise Heritage Dictionary, an abridgment of the 155,000-entry *American Heritage Dictionary,* has exactly the same contents as *The American Heritage Dictionary* (Paperback Edition). The only difference between the two dictionaries is that *Concise Heritage* is hardbound and has a larger format, including a relatively large typeface. Also, *Concise Heritage* costs $5.95 as opposed to the Paperback Edition, which is available for $1.95 and in a more durable binding for $3.95.

Concise Heritage (55,000 entries) compares favorably with the out-of-date *Random House American Everyday Dictionary* (60,000 entries), with the attractive *Webster's Concise Family Dictionary* (57,000 entries), with the well-designed *Webster's New Ideal Dictionary* (60,000 entries), and with *Webster's New World Dictionary* (Compact School and Office Edition; 56,000 entries). Except for the *Random House American Everyday Dictionary,* each of these dictionaries will adequately serve the rudimentary vocabulary needs of adults and secondary school students.

For further information about *Concise Heritage,* see the profile of *The American Heritage Dictionary* (Paperback Edition) which immediately precedes this one. See also the profile of the 155,000-entry *American Heritage Dictionary* in the "semi-unabridged" section of the *Buying Guide.*

Other Critical Opinions

Booklist, January 15, 1977, p. 746.

Concise Oxford Dictionary

Descriptive Information

Full Title: **The Concise Oxford Dictionary of Current English.** *Editor:* J. B. Sykes. *Publisher:* Oxford University Press. *Edition Reviewed:* Sixth Edition, 1976.
Classification: Adult—Abridged. *Pages:* xxiii, 1368. *Total Entries:* 74,000. *Average Entry Length:* 18 words. *Graphics:* None. *Physical Size:* 5¾ by

8¾ in.; 22 cm. *ISBN:* 0-19-861121-8 (plain); 0-19-861122-6 (thumb-indexed). *Lowest Retail Price:* $11.95.

Contents

The Concise Oxford Dictionary of Current English first appeared in 1911 under the editorship of Henry Watson Fowler and F. G. Fowler. Often cited as *COD*, the dictionary is based on the monumental *Oxford English Dictionary*, a research dictionary of impeccable authority. As the present editor, J. B. Sykes, explains in his preface to the Sixth Edition, the compilers of *COD* also utilized the large citation file assembled for the current supplements to the *Oxford English Dictionary*, a four-volume set which is in progress. The Sixth Edition, which first appeared in 1976, is a substantial revision of the Fifth Edition (1964).

COD contains some 40,000 main entries, plus 34,000 derivatives, compounds, and abbreviations. As the full title suggests, the emphasis is strictly on vocabulary in current usage. Scientific and technical terms frequently encountered in the popular press tend to be included. Likewise, there is a fair representation of current slang and colloquial expressions, including the so-called four-letter words. The Sixth Edition greatly increased the dictionary's coverage and treatment of American English. Americanisms are identified by means of an asterisk, e.g., **bum, *bunco, *cookie, *mad* (meaning angry). In addition, words and meanings unfamiliar to American users are so indicated by light parallel lines, e.g., ‖ *biscuit* (meaning cookie), ‖ *lift* (meaning elevator), ‖ *public house* (meaning a bar). Biographical and geographical terms are not included in the dictionary, although some proper names are defined, e.g., *Jansenist, Jehovah, Jekyll and Hyde*.

The definitions tend to be very clear, precise, and up-to-date. Illustrative phrases are sometimes used to clarify meanings, but there are no quotations. The etymologies are quite brief but informative. Usage labels are liberally provided to identify subject fields (such as "law," "math.," and "naut.") and various informal usages (such as slang, colloquial, jocular, derogatory, and vulgar—all of which are abbreviated when used as labels, e.g., "sl."). Regrettably, there are no synonyms or antonyms indicated. Usually the pronunciation given involves only diacritical and stress marks, but in some instances the entry is phonetically respelled. Note that *COD* provides only one "standard" pronunciation, that "associated especially with Southern England." The introduction further notes that "No attempt is made here to show the many variations heard in educated speech in Northern England, the rest of the British Isles, the United States, and the rest of the English-speaking world."

The dictionary uses numerous space-saving devices, such as entering compounds and idioms as subentries of the main word, e.g., *time-sharing* is found in a very long and crammed paragraph under *time*. Another device used to conserve space is the tilde or "swung dash," a symbol (~) which represents the main entry when it is repeated, e.g., ~-*sharing*. In addition, *COD* employs a great many abbreviations in the definitions, etymologies, etc. Example: The adjective *futile* is defined as "useless, ineffectual, vain, frivolous; hence or cogn. *futility*." To find out what *cogn.* means, the user must turn to the list of about 500 abbreviations located in the front of the dictionary. Although *COD* is attractively printed, it has a cramped, intimidating look about it which will be off-putting to the average American user. And there are no graphics to break up the page.

Summary

The Concise Oxford Dictionary of Current English is a standard British desk dictionary which derives its authority from the prestigious *Oxford English Dictionary* and its supplements. The *Concise* (or *COD*, as it is frequently called) dates back to 1911, when the first edition was prepared by the Fowler brothers, famous English-language authorities. The Sixth Edition, issued in 1976, continues the honorable tradition established by *COD* over the years. Limited to vocabulary in active usage, the dictionary is up-to-date, precise, and clear. The new edition has greatly expanded coverage and treatment of American English, although American pronunciations are not given. The dictionary's greatest limitation is its excessive use of abbreviations and space-saving devices. Users may be frustrated or baffled by *COD*'s many symbols and cramped page layout, unrelieved by any pictorial illustrations.

Whatever its limitations, *COD* is an extremely popular small dictionary in Great Britain. In the United States it is generally recognized as the best British desk dictionary, although there is practically no competition except for the semi-unabridged *Chambers Twentieth Century Dictionary* (which is much larger at 180,000 entries), the encyclopedic *English Larousse* (which lacks the lexical depth of *COD*), and *The Oxford Illustrated Dictionary* (which bases its vocabulary on an earlier edition of *COD*). In the final analysis, libraries of any consequence should have a copy of the latest edition of *COD*, but the individual American consumer will be better off in most instances with an American-produced dictionary.

Other Critical Opinions

American Reference Books Annual 1977 (review by Koert C. Loomis, Jr.), p. 521.
Library Journal (review by B. Hunter Smeaton), October 15, 1976, p. 2161.
Wilson Library Bulletin (review by Charles A. Bunge), January 1977, pp. 439–440.

Doubleday Dictionary

Descriptive Information

Full Title: **The Doubleday Dictionary for Home, School, and Office.** *Editors:* Sidney I. Landau, Editor in Chief; Ronald J. Bogus, Managing Editor. *Publisher:* Doubleday & Co. *Edition Reviewed:* 1975.

Classification: Adult—Abridged. *Pages:* xxviii, 906. *Total Entries:* 85,000. *Average Entry Length:* 11 words. *Graphics:* 970. *Physical Size:* 5¾ by 8½ in.; 22 cm. *LC:* 74-3543. *ISBN:* 0-385-04099-7 (plain); 0-385-03368-0 (thumb-indexed). *Lowest Retail Price:* $6.95.

Contents

The Doubleday Dictionary for Home, School, and Office is one of the newest dictionaries on the American scene. Unlike most abridged dictionaries, it is not based on a larger work. The main emphasis has been to create a dictionary which, "though compact in size, would compare in coverage of the general vocabulary with much larger dictionaries." The editor, Sidney I. Landau, further notes in his preface that most obsolete and archaic terms are excluded from the dictionary and that the etymologies have been "condensed." He also says that "Technical definitions that could be conveyed adequately by general definitions were also omitted," whatever that means. "By such means," continues Landau, "we were able to give fuller coverage to the general and scientific vocabulary than any other dictionary of comparable size had ever attempted."

Actually, the dictionary's coverage is erratic. Example: The technical terms *ekistics* and *Pap smear* are included but not *holism* or *time-sharing*. The legal term *certiorari* is defined but not *stare decisis*. The most recent meanings of *gay* and *launder* are given but not *busing* (or *bussing*) or *impressionist*. Such new coinages as *hoagie* and *Wankel engine* are found in *Doubleday Dictionary* but *deep-six, deep space, flat-out, groupie, honcho, patrifocal*, and *reprography* are not. Likewise, the so-called dirty words are included but not terms of racial or ethnic denigration. Abbreviations, countries of the world, and some other proper nouns and adjectives are defined in the main dictionary file (e.g., *Dark Ages, Darwinism, Holy Roman Empire*) but biographies and place-names (including countries) are entered in separate lists in the back. A noteworthy feature of the geographical list is inclusion of zip codes for cities and towns with 15,000 or more population. Authorized post office abbreviations of U.S. states are also given. The dictionary also contains a number of Canadianisms (e.g., *mainstreeting*) and a short essay on Canadian English in the front of the book.

Doubleday Dictionary's treatment of vocabulary is in no way comparable with that found in the leading semi-unabridged dictionaries. The definitions are often skimpy and incomplete. This criticism is especially true of scientific and technical terms. Although the dust jacket proclaims "Thousands of illustrative quotations," only illustrative phrases (e.g., "to *mix* business with pleasure") are provided. The etymologies are quite limited, the synonyms are not discriminated, and the usage notes, though helpful when provided, are few and far between. Usage labels tend to be applied inconsistently in the area of subject fields, e.g., *cell* is labeled "biol." whereas *gene* is not labeled at all. Usage labels to indicate social status are limited to "slang" (e.g., *funky*), "informal" (e.g., *funk*), and "nonstand." (e.g., *irregardless*). Albert H. Marckwardt, chairman of the dictionary's five-member advisory committee, contributes a helpful essay in the front matter discussing usage. The pronunciation key is reasonably detailed and easy to comprehend. The pictorial illustrations, which include spot maps, are exceedingly small but not without informational value. The print is small and uninviting but legible.

Summary

The Doubleday Dictionary for Home, School, and Office, first published in 1975, is a reputable but not entirely satisfactory dictionary. Its 85,000 entries include many new words and meanings but omit others. Some commonly encountered technical terms are included, others are not. Some words associated with a particular subject field are so labeled, others are not. In short, the dictionary is erratic. Moreover, vocabulary treatment is frequently superficial. Definitions and etymologies, for instance, tend to be overly brief. Synonyms are not discriminated and the illustrative phrases (there are no quotations) are not always helpful or plentiful enough. The physical format is generally unappealing.

Doubleday Dictionary is quite comparable in both vocabulary coverage and treatment to the *Scribner-Bantam English Dictionary* (1977), which contains 80,000 entries. There are some differences between the two (for instance, *Scribner-Bantam* has much larger type and discriminates synonyms, but lacks illustrative examples, pictorial illustrations, and usage notes), but the key point for consumers is price. Whereas the cheapest edition of *Scribner-Bantam* is $8.95, *Doubleday Dictionary* can be purchased for $6.95 (which is only one dollar more than the much smaller *Concise Heritage Dictionary* and *Webster's Concise Family Dictionary*). Considering the price factor, as well as the limitations of both dictionaries, *Doubleday Dictionary* is a better buy than *Scribner-Bantam*. On the other hand, one of the better college dictionaries (150,000–170,000 entries) can be acquired for $9.95 or $10.95. In practically all instances, the consumer will be better off investing in a good semi-unabridged dictionary (e.g., *Webster's New Collegiate Dictionary*, *Webster's New World Dictionary*, *The American Heritage Dictionary*, *The Random House College Dictionary*) than opting for a superficial desk dictionary like *Doubleday Dictionary* or *Scribner-Bantam*.

Other Critical Opinions

American Reference Books Annual 1976, p. 541.
Booklist, July 15, 1975, p. 1204.
Library Journal (review by B. Hunter Smeaton), January 15, 1975, p. 110.
Wilson Library Bulletin (review by Charles A. Bunge), April 1975, p. 598.

English Larousse

Descriptive Information

Full Title: **English Larousse.** *Editor:* O. C. Watson. *Publisher:* Librairie Larousse. *Distributor:* Larousse & Co. Original title: *Longmans English Larousse. Edition Reviewed:* 1968.

Classification: Adult—Abridged. *Pages:* 1343. *Total Entries:* 60,000 (48,000 words; 12,000 encyclopedic terms). *Average Entry Length:* 20 words (includes encyclopedic entries). *Graphics:* 1,000. *Consultants:* 100. *Physical Size:* 5¾ by 8¼ in.; 21 cm. *Lowest Retail Price:* $17.50.

Contents

English Larousse, originally published in Great Britain under the title *Longmans English Larousse*, is an encyclopedic dictionary modeled on the popular French desk dictionary *Petit Larousse Illustré* (also titled *Nouveau*

Petit Larousse in 1968). The French Larousse line of encyclopedic dictionaries is based on the principle that "access to language and access to general knowledge are taken as one and indivisible." Hence *English Larousse* not only covers basic vocabulary terms in current usage but also provides encyclopedic information about well-known people, places, events, etc. One significant difference between *Petit Larousse Illustré* and *English Larousse* is that the French work divides the lexical and encyclopedic entries into two separate lists whereas *English Larousse* includes all entries in one alphabetical sequence. There are approximately 48,000 dictionary entries and 12,000 encyclopedic terms.

English Larousse, according to the editor, was prepared "by a team of English and American scholars, working under editorial control from the Larousse headquarters in Paris." The book, which took seven years to complete, appeared in 1968 and has never been revised, although the editor, O. C. Watson, indicates in his preface (dated January 1, 1968) that "the book will be constantly kept up-to-date in revised impressions if its usefulness is proved." Note, however, that a somewhat larger and slightly modified version of *English Larousse* appeared in 1972 under the title *Larousse Illustrated International Encyclopedia and Dictionary*. (This work is in print and is reviewed in this section of the *Buying Guide*.)

Watson notes that the book's chief lexicographical sources were *Webster's Third New International Dictionary* and *The Shorter Oxford English Dictionary*. Common active words and phrases like *aesthetic, capable, conceit, going to the dogs, lift, pathetic*, and *sizable* (and *sizeable*) are found in *English Larousse*. The definitions are reasonably clear and accurate. They are also sufficiently detailed for an abridged dictionary. Omitted from the dictionary, however, are many new standard and commonly used technical terms. Example: *busing* (or *bussing*), *certiorari, data bank, data processing, decoupage, ekistics, holism, kerogen, laetrile, Pap smear, revanchism*, and *time-sharing*. Also omitted are many new meanings of older words (e.g., the verb *mace*) and most current slang and all vulgarisms (e.g., *fuck, funky, gay, groupie*). Also omitted are practically all obsolete and archaic terms as well as derivatives of words whenever, according to the editor, "meaning or usage could be taken as requiring no special explanation: nouns ending in '-er' or '-ness,' adverbs in '-ly,' adjectives in '-less,' '-like,' '-able,' and many negatives beginning with 'in-' and 'non-.'"

Words and phrases which are defined often include several or more illustrative examples. This feature helps account for the dictionary's relatively high words-per-entry (20) figure. The etymologies are usually very brief and not always helpful. American and British meanings are labeled "Am." and "Br." and nonstandard, informal, or colloquial meanings are simply labeled "pop." (popular). For instance, *lift* meaning to steal is labeled "pop." and *lift* meaning elevator is labeled "Br." The pronunciation key unfortunately utilizes a number of unfamiliar phonetic symbols. American and British pronunciations and spellings are usually given.

The encyclopedic entries derive mainly from the *Grand Larousse Encyclopédique* and the *Statesman's Year-Book*. The emphasis is on biographies and place-names. Because *English Larousse* is now ten years old, some of the information is out-of-date. Example: According to the book,

Eisenhower, De Gaulle, and Khrushchev are still alive; the country of Zaire does not exist; men have yet to walk on the moon; and the U.S. Constitution contains only 25 amendments. Encyclopedic entries vary in length from one or two lines to articles of several pages (e.g., the entry *France*). The longer articles also help account for the book's high words-per-entry figure.

The three-column page is illustrated with a variety of graphics, including photographs, art reproductions, spot maps, and line drawings. These illustrations are usually small and in black-and-white. They include many portraits of famous people (e.g., Franco, Lenin, Nehru, Roosevelt) and instructional diagrams (e.g., the digestive system). In addition, the book contains several full-page color plates on such subjects as North America, South America, and Europe. Although the plates brighten up the book, they are unrelated to the articles they presumably complement. Example: The article *Africa* is on pages 14–16 whereas the color plates showing African scenes follow page 376. There is no cross-reference from the article to the plates. The print is small and excessively light in several places.

Summary

English Larousse, an encyclopedic dictionary modeled on the famous French *Petit Larousse Illustré*, is an authoritative work containing approximately 48,000 vocabulary entries and 12,000 encyclopedic articles. The dictionary portion is limited largely to standard words and meanings in current usage. Because the book has not been revised since it first appeared in 1968, new terms which have entered the language over the past decade are not included. Like all Larousse productions, *English Larousse* is fairly heavily illustrated with photographs, maps, and diagrams. Except for a few full-page color plates scattered throughout the book, the graphics are useful complements to the text, enhancing or clarifying the definitions or articles.

If *English Larousse* were not a decade old (and hence ten years out-of-date), it would compare favorably with *The Oxford Illustrated Dictionary* (Second Edition, 1975), which also contains much encyclopedic information among its 65,000 total entries. *Oxford Illustrated*, however, represents the British perspective, both informationally and lexicographically, whereas *English Larousse* is more European and American centered. Although both *English Larousse* and *Oxford Illustrated* are reputable works with some attractive features, neither can be recommended as a first purchase for most American consumers. *English Larousse* is too dated and *Oxford Illustrated* too British oriented. Note also that a somewhat enlarged and modified edition of *English Larousse* was published in 1972 under the title *Larousse Illustrated International Encyclopedia and Dictionary*. (For further information, see the profile of *Larousse Illustrated* which follows in this section.)

Funk & Wagnalls Standard Desk Dictionary

Descriptive Information

Full Title: **Funk & Wagnalls Standard Desk Dictionary.** *Editor:* Sidney I. Landau, Editor in Chief. *Publisher:* Funk & Wagnalls. *Distributor:* T. Y.

Crowell Co. Former title: *Funk & Wagnalls New Desk Standard Dictionary.* *Edition Reviewed:* New Updated Edition, 1977.

Classification: Adult—Abridged. *Pages:* 896. *Total Entries:* 100,000. *Average Entry Length:* 10 words. *Graphics:* 400. *Physical Size:* 6¼ by 8½ in.; 22 cm. *ISBN:* 0-308-10280-0 (plain); 0-308-10272-X (thumb-indexed). *Lowest Retail Price:* $6.95.

Contents

Funk & Wagnalls Standard Desk Dictionary was initially published in 1964. It is an abridgment of *Funk & Wagnalls Standard College Dictionary*, a 150,000-entry semi-unabridged dictionary which first appeared in 1963. As is the case with all dictionaries in the Funk & Wagnalls line, vocabulary coverage emphasizes "standard" words and phrases. Nonstandard vocabulary is included if it is widely used or related in some way to standard vocabulary. Nonstandard terms are labeled "slang" or "illit." Again, like all other dictionaries bearing the Funk & Wagnalls name, *Funk & Wagnalls Standard Desk* gives the most common or frequently encountered meaning first, a tradition which dates back to the nineteenth century and Isaac Funk, who initiated the line. Vocabulary treatment is satisfactory in most respects. (See the detailed analysis of *Funk & Wagnalls Standard College Dictionary* in the "semi-unabridged" section of the *Buying Guide* for further information about vocabulary coverage and treatment.)

In 1977 a "New Updated Edition" of *Funk & Wagnalls Standard Desk* appeared. In reality, the dictionary has not been thoroughly revised since its publication in 1964. The periodic revisions which have occurred over the years (1966, 1969, 1975, 1977) have been quite minor, sometimes involving the addition and deletion of only a thousand or so words and sometimes only changes in the supplementary material in the back of the dictionary. The editor, Sidney I. Landau, has written in the preface to his newer *Doubleday Dictionary* (1975) that "Dictionaries may be updated by the substitution of some new entries for old entries, and for the first few years after publication, such a procedure may work very well. But when a dictionary passes the ten- or fifteen-year-old mark, updating takes on a desperate character. Substituting a few new entries for old entries in such a book is like bailing out a swamped boat with a sieve. . . . Only a fresh examination of the entire range of possible entries, with careful attention to examples of current usage and the assistance of special consultants in the sciences and other fields, can provide an adequate basis for a thoroughly up-to-date dictionary." If Landau is right (and the *Buying Guide* believes he is), *Funk & Wagnalls Standard Desk* needs a thoroughgoing overhaul.

The dictionary includes a good deal of supplementary reference material, such as a pronouncing gazetteer, a biographical dictionary, and a useful style manual. The physical format is satisfactory. Noteworthy is the clear, large 7-point type which enhances readability.

Summary

Funk & Wagnalls Standard Desk Dictionary is an abridgment of the semi-unabridged *Funk & Wagnalls Standard College Dictionary*. In turn, *Funk & Wagnalls Standard College* is a somewhat smaller, slightly modified version of *Funk & Wagnalls Standard Dictionary* (International Edition), a 175,000-entry work originally published in 1958. All of these Funk & Wagnalls dictionaries are authoritative but they have now reached the point where thorough revisions are required. *Funk & Wagnalls Standard Desk,* for instance, carries a 1977 copyright but its essential vocabulary coverage and treatment are 20 years old.

Funk & Wagnalls Standard Desk (100,000 entries) competes directly with *Webster's New World Dictionary* (Second Concise Edition; 105,000 entries). In addition, it is comparable in size to the recently published *Doubleday Dictionary* (1975; 85,000 entries) and *The Scribner-Bantam English Dictionary* (1977; 80,000 entries). All of these abridged dictionaries are comparably priced. *Funk & Wagnalls Standard Desk,* however, is the last choice among the four, mainly because it is the least current in overall coverage and treatment.

For further information about *Funk & Wagnalls Standard Desk*'s vocabulary coverage and treatment, see the detailed analysis of *Funk & Wagnalls Standard College Dictionary* in the "semi-unabridged" section of the *Buying Guide.* Note also that *Funk & Wagnalls Standard Encyclopedic Dictionary* is simply a reprint of an earlier edition of *Funk & Wagnalls Standard Desk* with various reference supplements added. A consumer note about the encyclopedic edition follows.

Funk & Wagnalls Standard Encyclopedic Dictionary

Descriptive Information

Full Title: **Funk & Wagnalls Standard Encyclopedic Dictionary.** *Editor:* Sidney I. Landau, Editor in Chief. *Publisher:* J. G. Ferguson Publishing Co. *Edition Reviewed:* 1975.

Classification: Adult—Abridged. *Pages:* xii, 1140. *Total Entries:* 100,000. *Average Entry Length:* 10 words. *Graphics:* 550. *Physical Size:* 8½ by 11¼ in.; 29 cm. *LC:* 66-26533. *Lowest Retail Price:* $18.95.

Consumer Note

This dictionary has essentially the same lexical contents as *Funk & Wagnalls Standard Desk Dictionary,* first published in 1964 and only minimally revised since that time. The main differences between the two titles concern number of encyclopedic supplements, physical size, and cost. *Funk & Wagnalls Standard Encyclopedic Dictionary* appends some 200 pages of "Special Reference Supplements" (a mishmash of material from synopses of the world's major religions to various historical documents), most of which are not included in *Funk & Wagnalls Standard Desk Dictionary.* The encyclopedic edition is physically larger (having an 8 by 11 in. page size) than the desk version (6 by 9 in. page size). The larger page is accomplished by photographic enlargement. And the encyclopedic edition sells for $18.95 as opposed to the desk dictionary which can be purchased for as little as $6.95. The consumer is advised that $12.00 (the difference between $6.95 and $18.95) is simply too much to pay for various reference supplements which contain information (some of it dated) readily available in a reliable general encyclopedia.

Note also that *Funk & Wagnalls Standard Desk Dictionary* (and, therefore, *Funk & Wagnalls Standard Encyclopedic Dictionary*) is an abridgment of *Funk & Wagnalls Standard College Dictionary* which in turn derived from *Funk & Wagnalls Standard Dictionary* (International Edition, 1958). Among all of the in-print Funk & Wagnalls dictionaries, the college edition (150,000 entries at $9.95) is the best buy.

See the profile of *Funk & Wagnalls Standard Desk Dictionary* immediately preceding for additional information.

Other Critical Opinions

Booklist, April 1, 1969, pp. 845–852.

Larousse Illustrated International Encyclopedia and Dictionary

Descriptive Information

Full Title: **Larousse Illustrated International Encyclopedia and Dictionary.** *Editor:* O.C. Watson. *Publisher:* World Publishing Co. *Distributor:* Larousse & Co. *Edition Reviewed:* 1972.

Classification: Adult—Abridged. *Pages:* 1564. *Total Entries:* 65,000 (50,000 words; 15,000 encyclopedic terms). *Average Entry Length:* 20 words (includes encyclopedic entries). *Graphics:* 3,000. *Physical Size:* 8¾ by 11¼ in.; 29 cm. *LC:* 72-84242. *ISBN:* 0-529-04894-9 (Trade Edition); 0-529-04895-7 (Deluxe Edition). *Lowest Retail Price:* $19.95.

Contents

Larousse Illustrated International Encyclopedia and Dictionary is intended as an American equivalent of the famous French encyclopedic dictionary *Petit Larousse Illustré.* Indeed, several trademarks of the Larousse line of reference works are readily evident. First, *Larousse Illustrated* includes both general vocabulary and encyclopedic information. The two are presented in separate A–Z sections. Part I, the encyclopedia, includes approximately 15,000 entries (e.g., *Argentina; Mayflower Compact; Van Buren, Martin*) and Part II, the dictionary, covers some 50,000 entries which, according to the editor's preface, comprise "the vocabulary of the living language, without slang or cant terms and without archaisms." Second, the work is characteristic of the French Larousse line in that many illustrative examples are included in the dictionary. As O. C. Watson, the editor, notes, "Pierre Larousse insisted that a dictionary without examples was a mere skeleton." And third, *Larousse Illustrated* is heavily, colorfully, and creatively illustrated with photographs, reproductions of paintings and other works of art, and diagrams. According to Watson, the graphics are intended as "a natural extension of the text."

Actually, *Larousse Illustrated* is a somewhat modified, slightly enlarged version of *English Larousse* (originally published in 1968 in Great Britain as *Longmans English Larousse*). *English Larousse* remains in print and is available in the U.S. (see the profile in this section of the *Buying Guide*). Major differences between the two works include arrangement, number of illustrations, and physical size. *Larousse Illustrated*, as noted, divides the dictionary and encyclopedic contents into two alphabets whereas *English Larousse* puts all entries into one A–Z sequence. *Larousse Illustrated* contains over 3,000 full-color illustrations whereas *English Larousse* has only 1,000 small black-and-white graphics, except for a few color plates. *Larousse Illustrated* is a large oversized volume (8¾ by 11¼ in.) whereas *English Larousse* is desk-size. Other differences include the fact that *Larousse Illustrated* has a few thousand more entries than *English Larousse* (e.g., *cinderblock; Ochoa, Severa;* and *Ochs, Adolph* are found in the former but not the latter). Also, *Larousse Illustrated* has been Americanized as far as preferred spellings and pronunciations are concerned.

Summary

Larousse Illustrated International Encyclopedia and Dictionary is an authoritative work which derives from the 1968 *English Larousse* (originally published as *Longmans English Larousse*). Both works are modeled on the popular French encyclopedic dictionary *Petit Larousse Illustré. Larousse Illustrated*, published in the U.S. in 1972, is a somewhat modified, slightly enlarged, Americanized version of *English Larousse*. Neither work has ever been revised and both are somewhat out-of-date, the material now being a decade old.

Larousse Illustrated can appropriately be compared with *The Oxford Illustrated Dictionary* (Second Edition, 1975) which contains about the same number of total entries and includes some, though not as much, encyclopedic information. *Oxford Illustrated* is more current than *Larousse Illustrated* but, on the other hand, it has a pronounced British orientation whereas *Larousse Illustrated* is more international in perspective. Neither work is entirely satisfactory for American users, especially when price is taken into account. For the same amount ($20), the consumer can buy one of the leading semi-unabridged dictionaries (e.g., *Webster's New Collegiate Dictionary, Webster's New World Dictionary, The American Heritage Dictionary,* and *The Random House College Dictionary*) plus an up-to-date almanac like *Information Please Almanac* or *World Almanac and Book of Facts*—and still have a few dollars left over.

See the profile of *English Larousse* in this section of the *Buying Guide* for further information about the vocabulary coverage and treatment found in *Larousse Illustrated.*

Other Critical Opinions

American Reference Books Annual 1974 (review by Christine L. Wynar), p. 24.

Booklist, November 15, 1973, pp. 297–298.

Kister, Kenneth F., ed. *Encyclopedia Buying Guide* (New York: R. R. Bowker Co., 1976), pp. 158–162.

Wilson Library Bulletin (review by Charles A. Bunge), February 1973, p. 521.

Merriam-Webster Dictionary

Descriptive Information

Full Title: **The Merriam-Webster Dictionary.** *Editor:* Henry Bosley Woolf, Editor in Chief. *Publisher:* Pocket Books. Former titles: *Merriam-Webster Pocket Dictionary* (1947); *New Merriam-Webster Pocket Dictionary* (1964). *Edition Reviewed:* 1974.

Classification: Adult—Abridged. *Pages:* 848. *Total Entries:* 57,000. *Average Entry Length:* 10 words. *Graphics:* None. *Physical Size:* 4¼ by 7 in.; 18 cm. *ISBN:* 0-671-80558-4. *Lowest Retail Price:* $1.95 paper.

Contents

The Merriam-Webster Dictionary, a paperback dictionary sold in drugstores and at newsstands as well as in bookstores, contains some 57,000 entries which, according to the editor's preface, "constitute the core of the English language." The vocabulary covered derives from Merriam-Webster's unabridged *Webster's Third New International Dictionary.* Definitional authority ultimately rests on Merriam's huge, carefully maintained citation file. Obviously, vocabulary treatment (like the coverage) is considerably abridged in *The Merriam-Webster Dictionary.* Definitions tend to be very brief though up-to-date and accurate. A few concise etymologies are provided but most words are merely defined. No illustrative quotations or examples are given. Some synonyms are listed but not discriminated. The appendix includes American cities and towns with a population of 12,000 or more, as well as a lengthy list of foreign words and phrases. All in all, this is a typical abridgment, useful only to those seeking superficial information about the basic or most common words and phrases in the language.

Note that *The Merriam-Webster Dictionary* has exactly the same text and pagination as *Webster's Concise Family Dictionary*, a hardcover edition available for $5.95. In addition, *The Merriam-Webster Dictionary for Large Print Users*, published in 1977 by G. K. Hall at $27.50, also has the same text as *The Merriam-Webster Dictionary* and *Webster's Concise.*

Summary

The Merriam-Webster Dictionary is an authoritative abridgment of the outstanding unabridged *Webster's Third New International Dictionary.* The dictionary first appeared in 1947 under the title *Merriam-Webster Pocket Dictionary.* In 1964 (after the appearance of *Webster's Third* in 1961), a new edition was issued, appropriately called the *New Merriam-Webster Pocket Dictionary.* The present edition (which has dropped the word *Pocket* from the title) appeared in 1974. It is a verbatim reprint (photographically reduced) of *Webster's Concise Family Dictionary.* Aside from the distinctive titles, the only differences between the two editions involve size, binding, and price. *Webster's Concise* is hardbound and physically larger (including very large, readable type) whereas *Merriam-Webster Dictionary* is paperbound and pocket-size. As noted, *Webster's Concise* costs $5.95 whereas the paper edition can be purchased for $1.95. Note also that *The Merriam-Webster Dictionary for Large Print Users*, published in 1977 by G. K. Hall at $27.50, has the same text as *The Merriam-Webster Dictionary* and *Webster's Concise.*

The three leading abridged paperback dictionaries currently available are *The American Heritage Dictionary* (55,000 entries), *Merriam-Webster Dictionary* (57,000 entries), and *Webster's New World Dictionary* (59,000 entries). Each is priced at $1.95. Each derives its authority from a well-known and highly reputable larger dictionary. And each is a good buy.

For further information, see the profile of *Webster's Third New International Dictionary* in the "unabridged" section and the Consumer Note on *Webster's Concise Family Dictionary* which follows in this section.

Other Critical Opinions
American Reference Books Annual 1977, pp. 522–523.

Merriam-Webster Dictionary for Large Print Users

Descriptive Information

Full Title: **The Merriam-Webster Dictionary for Large Print Users.** *Editor:* Henry Bosley Woolf, Editor in Chief. *Publisher:* G. K. Hall & Co. (by arrangement with G. & C. Merriam Co.). *Edition Reviewed:* 1977.

Classification: Adult—Abridged. *Pages:* 1119. *Total Entries:* 57,000. *Average Entry Length:* 10 words. *Graphics:* None. *Physical Size:* 8½ by 11 in.; 29 cm. *LC:* 77-1497. *ISBN:* 0-8161-6459-2. *Lowest Retail Price:* $27.50 plus shipping and handling.

Consumer Note

The Merriam-Webster Dictionary for Large Print Users is a verbatim reprint of *Webster's Concise Family Dictionary. The Merriam-Webster Dictionary,* a paperback edition published by Pocket Books, also has exactly the same text and pagination. The large print edition reproduces definitions in 12-point type, main entries in 14-point type, and guide words at the top of the page in 18-point type. Nonglare paper has been used. See the profile of *Merriam-Webster Dictionary* immediately preceding for further information about vocabulary coverage and treatment. The *Buying Guide* questions the high price of the large print edition. Why is it that the same dictionary sells for $5.95 when entitled *Webster's Concise Family Dictionary* and $27.50 when issued as *The Merriam-Webster Dictionary for Large Print Users?*

Oxford Illustrated Dictionary

Descriptive Information

Full Title: **The Oxford Illustrated Dictionary.** *Editors:* Text edited by J. Coulson, C. T. Carr, Lucy Hutchinson, and Dorothy Eagle; Second Edition revised by Dorothy Eagle with the assistance of Joyce Hawkins. *Publisher:* Oxford University Press. *Edition Reviewed:* Second Edition, 1975.

Classification: Adult—Abridged. *Pages:* xx, 998. *Total Entries:* 65,000. *Average Entry Length:* 15 words. *Graphics:* 800. *Physical Size:* 6½ by 9½ in.; 24 cm. *ISBN:* 0-19-861118-8. *Lowest Retail Price:* $20.00.

Contents

The Oxford Illustrated Dictionary, first published in 1962 and thoroughly revised in 1975, attempts to "combine the essential features of an encyclopedia and of a dictionary in the ordinary sense; that is to say, a work which [deals] not only with words and phrases, but also with the things for which these words and phrases stand." This statement of purpose, quoted from an introductory note to the first edition, concisely summarizes the dictionary's present intention. The user will find in one alphabet such basic vocabulary terms as *aesthetic, crude, futile, lift, pathetic,* and *sizeable* (but not *sizable*) along with such people, places, and things as *Buller, Sir Redvers Henry* (a nineteenth-century Irish soldier); *Clackmannanshire* (formerly a county in Scotland); *Mermaid Tavern; Rhea* (of Greek mythology); and the *Trans-Siberian Railway.* In all, there are about 2,000 people and 1,300 places covered. Coverage rarely exceeds more than a few lines.

Not found in *Oxford Illustrated,* however, are such fairly recent but quite common terms as *busing* (or *bussing*), *data bank, discernible* (although *discern* is included), *groupie, irregardless, mixed drink, oxygen cycle, Pap smear,* and *time-sharing.* Nor are such people, places, and things as *Bryant, William Cullen* (the poet); *Federal Trade Commission; Hoover, J. Edgar; Miami; Mojave Desert; New Orleans;* and *Stevenson, Adlai E.* covered. The preface suggests that the vocabulary coverage should "be adequate for the reader who consults the book for ordinary dictionary purposes." This generalization might be true for British readers but not for Americans.

Oxford Illustrated's general coverage is based on the vocabulary included in *The Concise Oxford Dictionary* (often cited as *COD*), a popular British desk dictionary. Note, however, that the most recent edition of *COD* (the sixth) appeared in 1976, a year after the present (second) edition of *Oxford Illustrated.* This simply means that the vocabulary base for the revised *Oxford Illustrated* reflects the coverage provided by the fifth edition of *COD* (first issued in 1964). This point takes on added significance when it is realized that the new (1976) edition of *COD* has greatly expanded the dictionary's coverage of American terms and usage.

Vocabulary treatment in *Oxford Illustrated* is less thorough than in *COD.* The editors explain, for instance, that illustrative examples "have been more sparingly used so as to obtain a wider scope for treatment of things." Indeed, illustrative examples (there are no quotations) have been all but eliminated. The definitions are brief but usually clear and precise. Few etymologies are provided and there are practically no synonyms, except in some cases where a short string of similar words are used as definitions, e.g., one meaning of *capable* is given as "able, gifted, competent." British spellings and pronunciations are preferred with U.S. variants so labeled. And like *COD,* several space-saving devices have been used. For instance, practically all derivatives are treated as subentries of the root word. Hence, the phrase *New Deal* is found under *deal* and *hard-core* under *hard.* The so-called "swung dash" is also used to conserve space. It is a symbol (~) which stands for the root word when it is repeated, e.g., ~*-core.* In addition, a multitude of abbreviations are used in the dictionary. Overall, *Oxford Illustrated* is attractively printed but the page layout gives the impression of being crowded and cluttered with strange symbols and abbreviations.

Unlike *COD*, however, *Oxford Illustrated* contains many instructive graphics. They are all black-and-white line drawings but some are two or three columns in width. The drawings are usually presented in sufficient detail and clearly drawn. The editors note that "subjects chosen for illustration are those which can be defined more clearly by this means than verbally." Entries illustrated include *bat, drum, grasshopper, lamp, muscle* (the illustration covers half a page and shows the muscles of the human body), *samovar, saw,* and *windmill.*

Summary

The Oxford Illustrated Dictionary, first published in 1962 and issued in a thoroughly revised second edition in 1975, bases its general vocabulary coverage on that provided by *The Concise Oxford Dictionary,* an authoritative British desk dictionary also published by Oxford University Press. Unlike, *COD,* however, *Oxford Illustrated* contains numerous encyclopedic entries (mainly people and places) and some 800 excellent line drawings. American dictionary consumers should be aware that *Oxford Illustrated*'s coverage and treatment are British in perspective. Also, British spelling and pronunciation are preferred, although common American variants are given. Although the dictionary is handsomely printed (as are all Oxford University Press reference books), the use of various space-saving techniques like the "swung dash" (~) gives the typical page a cramped, crowded, and somewhat forbidding appearance.

One dictionary authority referred to the first edition of *Oxford Illustrated* as "a *Petit Larousse* manqué"—meaning a failed or abortive English version of the famous French desk dictionary, *Petit Larousse Illustré.* In some respects, this criticism is still valid. *Oxford Illustrated,* for instance, lacks the colorful graphics, the international perspective, and the encyclopedic depth of *Petit Larousse Illustré* and its English-language counterpart, *Larousse Illustrated International Encyclopedia and Dictionary* (1972), which in turn derives from *English Larousse,* a British version of *Petit Larousse Illustré* published in 1968.

Both *Oxford Illustrated* and *Larousse Illustrated International Encyclopedia and Dictionary* contain roughly the same number of entries and both are authoritative reference works. Neither work, however, is entirely satisfactory for American users, especially when price is taken into account. For the same amount as *Oxford Illustrated* or *Larousse Illustrated* costs ($20), the consumer can purchase one of the leading semi-unabridged dictionaries (e.g., *Webster's New College Dictionary, Webster's New World Dictionary, The American Heritage Dictionary,* and *The Random House College Dictionary*) plus an up-to-date almanac like *Information Please Almanac* or *World Almanac and Book of Facts*—and still have a few dollars left over.

Other Critical Opinions

American Reference Books Annual 1976 (review by Francis J. Witty), pp. 539–540.
Booklist, April 15, 1976, p. 1214.

Choice, November 1975, p. 1141.
Library Journal (review by B. Hunter Smeaton), July 1975, 'p. 1309.
Wilson Library Bulletin (review by Charles A. Bunge), October 1975, p. 121.

Random House American Everyday Dictionary

Descriptive Information

Full Title: **The Random House American Everyday Dictionary.** *Editor:* Jess Stein. *Publisher:* Random House. Alternate titles: *The American Dollar Dictionary; The American Everyday Dictionary;* and *Modern American Dictionary. Edition Reviewed:* 1961.

Classification: Adult—Abridged. *Pages:* 570. *Total Entries:* 60,000. *Average Entry Length:* 10 words. *Graphics:* 135. *Physical Size:* 6½ by 9½ in.; 25 cm. *Lowest Retail Price:* 2.50.

Contents

The Random House American Everyday Dictionary, which has been issued under various titles over the years (see above), is an abridgment of *The American College Dictionary*. Both dictionaries initially appeared in 1949 and were very well received by critics. At the present time, however, both are past their prime and it appears that Random House, the publisher, has no plans for major revisions of either title.

American Everyday contains 60,000 entries which represent the basic vocabulary in common usage. Obviously newer terms are not covered. Moreover, new meanings of older words are not included, e.g., *gay, happening, launder, leverage, mace,* and *mix.* Vocabulary treatment is quite simplified. There are no etymologies, no illustrative quotations or examples, and no synonyms or antonyms. The definitions are usually clear but sometimes overly brief. The pronunciation key is uncomplicated and easy to understand. There are some very small black-and-white line drawings which add little to the dictionary's overall value. The hardcover binding is cheap and will not withstand even modestly heavy use. The paper is of poor quality and has begun to yellow.

Summary

The Random House American Everyday Dictionary, an inexpensive hardcover dictionary, was first published in 1949 and last revised in 1961. It is dreadfully out-of-date. In its day, however, it was a good dictionary buy, being an abridgment of the authoritative *American College Dictionary*. But today, despite its low price, *American Everyday* cannot compete with the newer, more current hardbound desk dictionaries in the 55,000–60,000-entry category, such as *The Concise Heritage Dictionary, Webster's Concise Family Dictionary,* and *Webster's New World Dictionary* (Compact School & Office Edition).

Scribner-Bantam English Dictionary

Descriptive Information

Full Title: **The Scribner-Bantam English Dictionary.** *Editors:* Edwin B. Williams, General Editor; Walter D. Glanze, Managing Editor. *Publisher:* Charles Scribner's Sons. *Edition Reviewed:* 1977.
Classification: Adult—Abridged. *Pages:* 40a, 1093. *Total Entries:* 80,000. *Average Entry Length:* 10 words. *Graphics:* None. *Physical Size:* 6½ by 9½ in.; 24 cm. *LC:* 76-53585. *ISBN:* 0-684-14871-4 (plain); 0-684-14879-X (thumb-indexed). *Lowest Retail Price:* $8.95.

Contents

The Scribner-Bantam English Dictionary is the newest dictionary of any consequence on the American scene. First published in 1977, *Scribner-Bantam* is unrelated to any larger dictionary. Its 80,000 total entries represent the standard vocabulary of English as well as some informal words and meanings which are labeled "slang," "colloq.," "vulgar," "offensive," etc. As noted in the introductory section, "this dictionary leans toward being prescriptive. . . . When the average intelligent reader opens a dictionary, he or she wants to know the 'correct' spelling or pronunciation or meaning of a word and is not interested in reading what the majority of speakers of the language tend to say."

Scribner-Bantam is said to rest its authority on "all the English dictionaries in print, on other printed and spoken sources, and on consultation with authorities in many fields." The general editor, the late Edwin B. Williams, was a well-known language scholar until his death in 1975 at the age of 83. Seven other experienced editors are listed in the front matter, along with 22 editorial consultants. Interestingly, neither Scribners nor Bantam (a paperback publisher) has previously published a general English-language dictionary. No mention is made of a citation file or word frequency counts.

According to the flyleaf of the jacket cover, the dictionary's coverage is limited to "the most frequently used words in American English." In the introductory notes, the editors also state that "A strong feature of this Dictionary is the amount of space given to the contemporary world of electronics, nuclear physics, ecology, surgery, space flight, etc." In reality, *Scribner-Bantam*'s coverage is quite shallow. None of the following scientific and technical terms is included in the dictionary, although they are encountered everyday in newspapers, magazines, and on television: *data bank, ekistics, kerogen, laetrile, modulus, oxygen cycle, photovoltaic, recision, renovascular, revanchism, reprography,* and *time-sharing*. In addition, such new but commonly used words as *busing* (or *bussing*), *funky, hoagie* (or *hoagy*), *mensch, Orwellian,* and *upfront* are not covered. Nor are the latest meanings of such terms as *impressionist, launder,* and *mix* given in *Scribner-Bantam*. As might be expected, the so-called four-letter words and terms of racial or ethnic slur are also omitted. The dictionary does include, however, many biographical and geographical entries. Example: *Key, Francis Scott; Key West; Khrushchev, Nikita; King, Martin Luther, Jr.; Kinshasa; Kipling, Rudyard*. There are also some common abbreviations like *K.K.K.* and *K.O.*

Vocabulary treatment also tends to be superficial in most respects. The definitions, which are advertised as being "succinct," "no-nonsense," "straight to the point," and as having "transparent clarity," are all too frequently incomplete, fragmentary, and inadequate. Such terms as *cell, conceit, facetious, gene, hard-core, radiation,* and *visualization* are so skimpily defined as to be practically worthless to any serious user. In some instances the definitions are simply erroneous. Example: The relatively new word *groupie* is inaccurately defined as a "female admirer and follower of male members of the beat generation." The *Buying Guide* doubts if Bob Dylan, the Beatles, Rolling Stones, et al. qualify as part of the 1950s "beat generation."

Scribner-Bantam completely lacks illustrative examples of any kind. It also lacks pictorial illustrations of any kind. It also lacks usage notes, except for such labels as "slang" and "substandard." Etymologies, which are sparingly provided, are quite brief. On the positive side, the dictionary's pronunciation key is fairly simple to use and comprehend. More impressive is the provision of many excellent synonym studies. In addition, cross-references are provided throughout to these studies, e.g., there is a reference at the end of *gay* to *cheerful,* under which there is a lengthy paragraph which discriminates such similar words as *cheery, sprightly, gay, merry, mirthful, gleeful,* and *hilarious.* Antonyms are also indicated but not discriminated. *Scribner-Bantam* also provides the Latin names for all plants and animals entered in the dictionary. Likewise, atomic weights, numbers, and symbols are given for chemical elements.

The dictionary's physical format is satisfactory. Although the two-column page is unrelieved by any graphics, the print is exceptionally large and bold. Also, the margins are rather wide, giving the page layout an uncluttered appearance. The binding is sturdy.

Summary

The Scribner-Bantam English Dictionary initially appeared in 1977. For the time being, it is the newest general dictionary available. Eventually there will be a paperback edition, but at present *Scribner-Bantam* is only published in hardcover. The dictionary claims to cover "the most frequently used words in American English," as well as many new scientific and technical terms. The *Buying Guide,* however, found numerous gaps in the vocabulary coverage. Moreover, vocabulary treatment is shallow in most areas. Definitions are often overly concise, there are no illustrative examples of any kind, etymologies are few and far between, and there is not a single pictorial illustration in the book. On the other hand, the pronunciation system is simple to use and the synonym studies are excellent. The physical format is satisfactory, especially the large, bold typeface.

Scribner-Bantam is quite comparable in both vocabulary coverage and treatment to the *Doubleday Dictionary* (1975), which claims 85,000 entries. There are some differences between the two (for instance, *Scribner-Bantam* has much larger print and discriminates synonyms but lacks *Doubleday Dictionary*'s illustrative examples, graphics, and usage notes), but the key difference for consumers is price. Whereas the cheapest edition of *Scribner-Bantam* is $8.95, *Doubleday Dictionary* can be purchased for $6.95. Considering the price differential as well as the limitations of both dictionaries, *Doubleday Dictionary* is a better buy than *Scribner-Bantam.* On the other hand, one of the better college dictionaries (150,000–170,000 entries) can be acquired for $9.95 or $10.95. In practically all instances, the consumer will be better off investing in a good semi-unabridged dictionary (e.g., *Webster's New Collegiate Dictionary*, *Webster's New World Dictionary*, *The American Heritage Dictionary*, *The Random House College Dictionary*) than opting for a superficial desk dictionary like *Doubleday Dictionary* or *Scribner-Bantam*.

Other Critical Opinions

Library Journal (review by B. Hunter Smeaton), April 1, 1977, p. 788.

Webster's Concise Family Dictionary

Descriptive Information

Full Title: **Webster's Concise Family Dictionary.** *Editor:* Henry Bosley Woolf, Editor in Chief. *Publisher:* G. & C. Merriam Co. *Edition Reviewed:* 1975.

Classification: Adult—Abridged. *Pages:* 848. *Total Entries:* 57,000. *Average Entry Length:* 10 words. *Graphics:* None. *Physical Size:* 6¼ by 9½ in.; 24 cm. *ISBN:* 0-87779-039-6. *Lowest Retail Price:* $5.95.

Consumer Note

Webster's Concise Family Dictionary, first published in 1975, has exactly the same contents as *The Merriam-Webster Dictionary* (1974), an abridged paperback dictionary published by Pocket Books. The only differences between the two, aside from their titles, are that *Webster's Concise* is hardbound, has a much larger typeface, and costs $5.95, whereas *Merriam-Webster Dictionary* is paperbound, has small print, and costs only $1.95. *The Merriam-Webster Dictionary for Large Print Users*, published in 1977 by G. K. Hall at $27.50, also has the same text as *Webster's Concise* and *Merriam-Webster Dictionary*.

Webster's Concise (57,000 entries) compares favorably with other hardbound abridged dictionaries in the 55,000–60,000-entry class. It is preferable to the outdated *Random House American Everyday Dictionary* (60,000 entries), more attractively printed than *Webster's New World Dictionary* (Compact School and Office Edition; 56,000 entries), and comparable in quality to *The Concise Heritage Dictionary* (55,000 entries) and another Merriam-Webster abridgment entitled *Webster's New Ideal Dictionary* (60,000 entries). With the exception of the *Random House American Everyday*, any of these dictionaries will adequately serve the rudimentary vocabulary needs of adults and secondary school students.

For further information about the contents of *Webster's Concise*, see the profile of *The Merriam-Webster Dictionary* in this section of the *Buying Guide*.

Other Critical Opinions

American Reference Books Annual 1977 (review by Francis J. Witty), p. 523.

Webster's Dictionary

Descriptive Information

Full Title: **Webster's Dictionary.** *Editor:* A. M. Macdonald. *Publisher:* Banner Press; Copyright by Pyramid Communications, Inc. *Distributor:* Hippocrene Books. Original title: *Chambers Etymological English Dictionary.* *Edition Reviewed:* New Edition, 1972.

    Classification: Adult—Abridged. *Pages:* 604. *Total Entries:* 75,000. *Average Entry Length:* 8 words. *Graphics:* None. *Physical Size:* 5¼ by 7½ in.; 20 cm. *Lowest Retail Price:* $2.50 paper.

Consumer Note

    This so-called Webster's dictionary is a very thinly revised version of *Chambers Etymological English Dictionary* (New Edition), edited by A. M. Macdonald and published in 1966 in Great Britain by W. & R. Chambers, Ltd. The Banner Press edition, which carries a 1972 copyright by Pyramid Communications, Inc., is somewhat smaller than *Chambers Etymological* (75,000 entries versus 85,000) and has added a few recent American terms, e.g., *zip code.* Essentially, *Chambers Etymological* is a scholarly British work which emphasizes word origins. Despite the Banner Press edition's note on the cover and title page which reads "Special School and Reference Edition," this work is not suitable for use in American schools.

    The dictionary does have some value, however, as an etymological work. For further information, see the brief profile of *Chambers Etymological English Dictionary* in the section on special-purpose dictionaries and word-books under "Etymology and History of Words."

Webster's New Ideal Dictionary

Descriptive Information

Full Title: **Webster's New Ideal Dictionary.** *Editor:* Merriam-Webster Staff. *Publisher:* G. & C. Merriam Co. Former titles: *Webster's Ideal Dictionary* (1961–1967); *Webster's New Practical Dictionary* (1951–1960). *Edition Reviewed:* 1973.

    Classification: Adult—Abridged. *Pages:* 8a, 663. *Total Entries:* 60,000. *Average Entry Length:* 10 words. *Graphics:* None. *Physical Size:* 6¾ by 8½ in.; 22 cm. *ISBN:* 0-87779-149-X. *Lowest Retail Price:* $4.95.

Contents

    Webster's New Ideal Dictionary contains approximately 40,000 main entries, about 60,000 total entries, and some 74,000 individual definitions. The present edition of the dictionary was initially published in 1968, being based on the unabridged *Webster's Third New International Dictionary.* Earlier editions—*Webster's Ideal Dictionary* and *Webster's New Practical Dictionary*—were based on the previous unabridged edition. The brief preface notes that obsolete, rare, and highly technical words and meanings are omitted from the dictionary. "The vocabulary thus becomes a list of the words most likely to be looked up by any person searching for a meaning, a pronunciation, or a syllabication." There are also a number of supplements, including a list of standard abbreviations, a pronouncing vocabulary of common English given names, a concise list of foreign words and phrases frequently encountered in English, a table of chemical elements, a copy of the Declaration of Independence and the U.S. Constitution, and an alphabetical directory of U.S. places with a population of 12,000 or more (1970 population figures are given).

Vocabulary treatment is quite simplified. Only spelling, syllabication, part of speech, and definitions are provided. The definitions are abridgments of those found in the larger Merriam-Webster dictionaries. No etymologies, illustrative quotations or examples, or graphics are given. The definitions sometimes include synonymic terms (printed in lightface small capital letters) which are intended as cross-references from one entry to another. The two-column page, though unrelieved by any pictorial illustrations, is pleasing to the eye. The print is legible but not large.

Summary

Webster's New Ideal Dictionary, a rather simple and inexpensive abridgment of larger Merriam-Webster dictionaries, is designed for the user with basic, unsophisticated vocabulary needs. Aside from simplified definitions and standard spellings and pronunciations, the dictionary has little to offer. There are no etymologies, no illustrative quotations or examples, no graphics, and no synonyms (although the cross-references are synonymic in nature). *Webster's New Ideal* (60,000 total entries) compares reasonably well with other hardbound abridged dictionaries in the 55,000–60,000-entry class. It is preferable to the outdated *Random House American Everyday Dictionary* (60,000 entries), more attractively designed than *Webster's New World Dictionary* (Compact School and Office Edition; 56,000 entries), and comparable in quality to *The Concise Heritage Dictionary* (55,000 entries) and another Merriam-Webster abridgment entitled *Webster's Concise Family Dictionary* (57,000 entries), which was published in 1975. *Webster's Concise* has approximately the same vocabulary as *Webster's New Ideal,* although the former is somewhat more up-to-date.

Webster's New World Dictionary (Compact School & Office Edition)

Descriptive Information

Full Title: **Webster's New World Dictionary: Compact School & Office Edition.** *Editor:* David B. Guralnik, Editor in Chief. *Publisher:* Collins+ World. *Edition Reviewed:* Compact School & Office Edition, 1974.

Classification: Adult—Abridged. *Pages:* 507. *Total Entries:* 56,000. *Average Entry Length:* 10 words. *Graphics:* None. *Physical Size:* 5½ by 8 in.; 21 cm. *LC:* 74-5545. *ISBN:* 0-529-03069-1. *Lowest Retail Price:* $3.49.

Contents

The Compact School & Office Edition of *Webster's New World Dictionary,* according to the back of the title page, "is based upon and includes material from *Webster's New World Dictionary, Second College Edition*," which was published in 1972. The Second College Edition, a semi-unabridged dictionary, is one of the best works in that category.

The Compact School & Office Edition, like all abridged dictionaries in the 55,000–60,000-entry class, includes only those words in active usage. Obsolete, rare, and highly technical terms are omitted, as is most slang. The dictionary also contains eight pages of encyclopedic material in the back, including tables of weights and measures, lists of the U.S. states and largest cities with population figures, and punctuation rules.

Vocabulary treatment is very brief and sometimes superficial. The definitions of course are condensed from the Second College Edition of *Webster's New World*. They tend to be as full or fuller than other dictionaries of comparable size. The etymologies, however, are quite limited and very few illustrative phrases (there are no quotations) are included. The pronunciation key is relatively uncomplicated. There are no graphics. The print is rather small and unattractive. The binding, however, is reasonably strong—a plus considering the dictionary's inexpensive price.

Summary

Webster's New World Dictionary (Compact School & Office Edition) derives from the same dictionary's excellent Second College Edition. It is a simple abridgment designed for those who have simple vocabulary needs. It compares reasonably well with other hardbound abridged dictionaries in the 55,000–60,000-entry category. It is preferable to the outdated *Random House American Everyday Dictionary* (60,000 entries) and is as useful though not as attractively designed as *The Concise Heritage Dictionary* (55,000 entries), *Webster's Concise Family Dictionary* (57,000 entries), and *Webster's New Ideal Dictionary* (60,000 entries). Note that the Compact School & Office Edition of *Webster's New World Dictionary* is a couple of dollars cheaper than the others. As such it is a good buy—if a simple abridgment will meet your vocabulary needs.

Webster's New World Dictionary (Second Concise Edition)

Descriptive Information

Full Title: **Webster's New World Dictionary of the American Language: Second Concise Edition.** *Editor:* David B. Guralnik, General Editor. *Publisher:* Collins+World. *Edition Reviewed:* Second Concise Edition, 1975.

Classification: Adult—Abridged. *Pages:* xiv, 882. *Total Entries:* 105,000. *Average Entry Length:* 12 words. *Graphics:* 632. *Physical Size:* 6¾ by 10 in.; 25 cm. *LC:* 75-7616. *ISBN:* 0-529-05267-9 (plain); 0-529-05268-7 (thumb-indexed). *Lowest Retail Price:* $7.25.

Contents

The Second Concise Edition—not to be confused with the Second College Edition—of *Webster's New World Dictionary* is an abridgment of the 158,000-entry Second College Edition, which is one of the best dictionaries in the semi-unabridged category. According to David B. Guralnik, the editor of both editions, the Concise Edition is for those "who want a comprehensive and up-to-date dictionary, but who have less need for the extensive etymologies, highly technical or arcane terms, rare meanings, and certain other features found in the Second College Edition. For such persons, the Second Concise Edition should prove highly serviceable." It is further noted that the 105,000 entries in the Second Concise Edition were chosen because of their "frequency of occurrence in general publications and books of general interest."

As suggested, vocabulary treatment is somewhat abridged in the Second Concise Edition. For instance, a comparison of the entry *lift* in both editions shows that two technical meanings given in the Second College Edition have been dropped from the Concise. More important, the lengthy synonym study which discriminates such similar terms as *lift, raise, elevate, hoist,* and *boost* in the College Edition has been dropped from the Concise. A check reveals that all synonym paragraphs have been omitted from the Concise Edition. Also, as the editor mentioned, etymologies are condensed or omitted in the Concise. Example: The etymology for *funky* in the College Edition traces the word's origin back to the French *funkier* meaning to smoke which derived possibly from the Vulgar Latin *fumicare.* All of this information is omitted from the Concise Edition, although an abbreviated etymology is provided. The Concise Edition includes the same field and usage labels and illustrative examples as found in the College Edition, but for some reason left unexplained, Americanisms (e.g., *bunco, funky, minibus*) which are prominently identified (by a small star) in the College Edition are not so indicated in the Concise.

Both dictionaries include all entries in a single alphabet, including numerous abbreviations, biographies, and place-names. Several useful supplements appended to the College Edition, however, are omitted from the Concise, e.g., directories of U.S. colleges, universities, and junior colleges. The College Edition contains about 1,500 small black-and-white graphics, the Concise Edition exactly 632. Like the College Edition, the Concise is sturdily bound, attractively printed, and well designed.

Summary

Webster's New World Dictionary (Second Concise Edition) is an abridgment of the larger *Webster's New World Dictionary* (Second College Edition), one of the outstanding college dictionaries on the American market today. The Second Concise Edition, which contains 105,000 entries, retains many of the fine features of the College Edition, although as a rule the etymologies have been condensed, technical meanings dropped, and in all instances the excellent synonym studies omitted. Both dictionaries are generally up-to-date and provide clear, accurate, and reasonably thorough definitions.

The Concise Edition of *Webster's New World Dictionary* competes directly with *Funk & Wagnalls Standard Desk Dictionary* (100,000 entries). In addition, it is comparable in size to the recently published *Doubleday Dictionary* (1975; 85,000 entries) and *The Scribner-Bantam English Dictionary* (1977; 80,000 entries). The Second Concise Edition of *Webster's New World* is clearly superior to *Funk & Wagnalls Standard Desk,* which sorely needs a complete overhaul. But in the case of the two newer abridged works, there is no clear-cut choice. For instance, *Scribner-Bantam* has excellent synonym studies which *Doubleday Dictionary* and *Webster's New World* (Second Concise Edition) lack, but *Scribner-Bantam* lacks illustrative examples, graphics, and usage notes. In the final analysis, however, *Webster's New World* is generally preferable because of the fullness of its definitions and its overall authority derived from the Second College Edition. For further information about the vocabulary coverage and treatment in the Second Concise Edition, see the detailed analysis of *Webster's New World Dictionary* (Second College Edition) in the "semi-unabridged" section of the *Buying Guide*.

Webster's New World Dictionary (*Modern Desk Edition*)

Descriptive Information

Full Title: **Webster's New World Dictionary of the American Language: Modern Desk Edition.** *Editor:* David B. Guralnik, Editor in Chief. *Publisher:* Collins+World. *Edition Reviewed:* Modern Desk Edition, 1976.

Classification: Adult—Abridged. *Pages:* x, 566. *Total Entries:* 72,000. *Average Entry Length:* 9 words. *Graphics:* 400. *Physical Size:* 6¾ by 9½ in.; 25 cm. *LC:* 76-24952. *ISBN:* 0-529-05333-0. *Lowest Retail Price:* $4.95.

Contents

The editor's foreword notes that "This *Modern Desk Edition* of *Webster's New World Dictionary* is an abridgment of the popular *Second College Edition* of *WNWD*. . . . Through a judicious selection of vocabulary and a careful compression of the definitions and other lexical material, the editors have managed to bring together the answers to most of the questions that people generally ask about words they read and use." In the hierarchy of *Webster's New World* dictionaries, the Modern Desk Edition (72,000 entries) stands between the larger Second Concise Edition (105,000 entries) and the smaller Compact School & Office Edition (56,000 entries). The source of all of these editions, as well as the 100,000 Entry Edition (published by New American Library in paperback) and the 59,000-entry Pocket-size Edition (published by Popular Library), is the authoritative Second College Edition (158,000 entries), one of the best dictionaries in the semi-unabridged category.

As the editor indicates, vocabulary treatment in the Modern Desk Edition has been compressed. Unlike the Second College Edition, the Modern Desk includes no synonyms, has very brief etymologies, provides relatively few illustrative examples, and has quite short definitions. Vocabulary coverage includes names of people and places. The 400 or so small black-and-white graphics are usually helpful and the pronunciation key is fairly easy to comprehend. The binding and printing are satisfactory.

Summary

The Modern Desk Edition of *Webster's New World Dictionary* is one of several abridgments of the semi-unabridged Second College Edition of the dictionary, an excellent work which has few peers in its class. The Modern Desk Edition will be useful to those who have relatively simple vocabulary needs. It favorably compares in terms of vocabulary coverage and treatment with the newer and somewhat larger *Doubleday Dictionary* (1975; 85,000 entries) and *Scribner-Bantam English Dictionary* (1977; 80,000 entries). In the long run, however, the *Buying Guide* believes that the average dictionary consumer will be better off investing in one of the good semi-unabridged dictionaries on the market (e.g., *Webster's New Collegiate Dictionary; Webster's New World Dictionary*—Second College Edition; *The American Heritage Dictionary*—New College Edition; or *The Random House College Dictionary*), any of which can be purchased for under $10.

Webster's New World Dictionary (100,000 Entry Edition)

Descriptive Information

Full Title: **Webster's New World Dictionary of the American Language: The 100,000 Entry Edition.** *Editor:* David B. Guralnik, General Editor. *Publisher:* New American Library. *Edition Reviewed:* The 100,000 Concise Entry Edition, 1971.

Classification: Adult—Abridged. *Pages:* xiv, 882. *Total Entries:* 100,000. *Average Entry Length:* 10 words. *Graphics:* 600. *Physical Size:* 5¼ by 8 in.; 21 cm. *LC:* 70-144113. *Lowest Retail Price:* $3.95 paper.

Consumer Note

The 100,000 Entry Edition of *Webster's New World Dictionary*, originally issued as the Concise Edition, is a paperback abridgment of the 158,000-entry Second College Edition of *Webster's New World Dictionary*. Consumers should be aware, however, that the 100,000 Entry Edition has been superseded by the Second Concise Edition (1975) which contains 105,000 entries and is more up-to-date. The Second Concise Edition is only available in hardcover at $7.25 from Collins+World. Presumably New American Library (a paperback publisher) will in due course issue a paperbound edition of the Second Concise Edition. In the meanwhile, consumers are advised to avoid the 100,000 Entry Edition last copyrighted in 1971.

Webster's New World Dictionary (Pocket-size Edition)

Descriptive Information

Full Title: **Webster's New World Dictionary of the Language: Pocket-size Edition.** *Editor:* David B. Guralnik, Editor in Chief. *Publisher:* Popular Library. *Edition Reviewed:* Pocket-size Edition, 1975.

Classification: Adult—Abridged. *Pages:* viii, 696. *Total Entries:* 59,000. *Average Entry Length:* 9 words. *Graphics:* 200. *Physical Size:* 4¼ by 7 in.; 18 cm. *Lowest Retail Price:* $1.95 paper.

Contents

Webster's New World Dictionary (Pocket-size Edition) is an inexpensive mass-market paperback—meaning that it is sold at newsstands, drugstores, and variety stores as well as bookstores. The Pocket-size Edition is, according to the editor's foreword, "based upon and extracted from the materials prepared for *Webster's New World Dictionary*, Second College Edition," an authoritative and up-to-date semi-unabridged dictionary. Vocabulary coverage is limited to words and phrases frequently encountered in popular reading matter, the broadcast media, etc. The editor notes that "The selection of vocabulary items has been made largely on the basis of frequency of occurrence within our vast citation file and from various word-count lists." Also included among the vocabulary are numerous biographical and geographical entries. Vocabulary treatment (like the coverage) is considerably abridged. Definitions tends to be concise as are the 25,000 etymologies. Some illustrative phrases are provided but synonyms are omitted altogether. The 200 or so line drawings are very small and not always useful. All in all, this is a typical paperback abridgment of a much larger and more detailed dictionary.

Summary

The Pocket-size Edition of *Webster's New World Dictionary* is an authoritative abridgment of the 158,000-entry Second College Edition, which is one of the best semi-unabridged dictionaries currently on the market. The Pocket-size Edition is limited in its coverage to the basic or most common vocabulary terms. Treatment is equally limited. The dictionary compares favorably, however, with the other two leading abridged paperback dictionaries available. Whereas *Webster's New World Dictionary* (Pocket-size Edition) has 59,000 entries, *The American Heritage Dictionary* (Paperback Edition) has 55,000 entries and *The Merriam-Webster Dictionary* 57,000 entries. Each is priced at $1.95. Each derives its authority from a well-known and highly reputable larger dictionary. And each is a good buy—if you want an inexpensive abridged dictionary. Note also that the Pocket-size Edition of *Webster's New World Dictionary* is sold as part of Popular Library's "Desk Top Reference Set," a six-volume paperback library in its own handy slipcase. The set, which sells for only $9.45, includes Charlton Laird's *Webster's New World Thesaurus*, Nurnberg and Rosenblum's *How to Build a Better Vocabulary*, Flesch and Lass's *A New Guide to Better Writing*, Nila Smith's *Speed Reading Made Easy*, and *The New York Times Guide to Reference Materials*, as well as the dictionary.

For further information, see the profile of *Webster's New World Dictionary* (Second College Edition) in the "semi-unabridged section" of the *Buying Guide*.

Other Critical Opinions

American Reference Books Annual 1976 (review by Francis J. Witty), p. 544.

POCKET DICTIONARIES

Chambers' English Dictionary

Descriptive Information

Full Title: **Chambers' English Dictionary.** *Editor:* T. C. Collocott. *Compilers:* A. B. Anderson and J. E. Arkieson. *Publisher:* Littlefield, Adams. *Edition Reviewed:* 1965.

Classification: Adult—Pocket. *Pages:* iv, 380. *Total Entries:* 30,000. *Average Entry Length:* 7 words. *Graphics:* None. *Physical Size:* 5 by 8 in.; 20 cm. *Lowest Retail Price:* $1.95 paper.

Contents

The foreword states that the compilers' aim "has been to include all words which are likely to be met within the course of ordinary reading. Accordingly, the work comprises some 20,000 words which are fully defined, and nearly 10,000 more, the meanings of which follow readily from the definitions given in the main heading." The definitions "have been made as simple as accuracy allows" and in many instances illustrative sentences or phrases accompany definitions. The pronunciation system used is quite simple. Etymologies and synonyms are not provided.

Apparently, *Chambers' English Dictionary* derives directly from the larger *Chambers Etymological English Dictionary* (New Edition, 1964), a reputable British work edited by A. M. Macdonald. (The etymological dictionary is briefly described in the section covering special-purpose dictionaries and wordbooks under "Etymology and Word Histories.") For instance, both dictionaries define *canard* as "a false rumour," but *Chambers Etymological* provides an etymology whereas *Chambers' English* does not. The next word in both dictionaries is *canary.* *Chambers' English* defines the term as "a light sweet wine from the *Canary* Islands: a song-bird (finch) found in the Canary Islands.—*adj.* canary-coloured, bright yellow." *Chambers Etymological* has exactly the same definition except the wording at the end is slightly altered. The next word in the etymological dictionary is *can-can* ("an immodest dance of French origin") but the term is omitted from *Chambers' English.*

The vocabulary selection in *Chambers' English* may indeed serve the needs of the average British user but such terms as *Candlemas, caoutchouc, capapie,* and *cassowary* are not the sort of words American readers will encounter with any great frequency. In addition, spelling and pronunciation of all words and phrases in *Chambers' English* are British. No American variants are given. The dictionary is paperbound and printed on good paper, but the typeface gives the impression of being old.

Summary

Chambers' English Dictionary, apparently an abridgment of *Chambers Etymological English Dictionary* (New Edition, 1964), is a British work which has little to offer American dictionary users. The vocabulary selection and treatment are based on English not American usage. Moreover, the dictionary is now almost 15 years old. If the American consumer wants a small British dictionary, the *Buying Guide* recommends *The Pocket Oxford Dictionary* or the smaller *Little Oxford Dictionary.*

English Gem Dictionary

Descriptive Information

Full Title: **English Gem Dictionary: U.S. Edition.** *Editor:* J. B. Foreman, General Editor. *Publisher:* William Collins Sons & Co. *Distributor:* Collins+ World. Alternate title: *Collins American Gem Dictionary. Edition Reviewed:* U.S. Edition, 1968.

Classification: Adult—Pocket. *Pages:* ix, 629. *Total Entries:* 33,000. *Average Entry Length:* 9 words. *Graphics:* None. *Physical Size:* 3¼ by 4¼ in.; 12 cm. *ISBN:* 0-00-548332-9. *Lowest Retail Price:* $2.45 paper (Leatheroid).

Contents

The *English Gem Dictionary* (U.S. Edition), also called *Collins American Gem Dictionary*, provides brief definitions of some 33,000 words and phrases. The vocabulary coverage includes basic terms encountered in everyday reading and conversation, as well as some rather esoteric entries, e.g., *blancmangé, blesbok*, and *Buchmanite*. Such terms could readily be omitted from future American editions of this little dictionary. It is part of the publisher's well-known "Gem" series which includes a number of bilingual pocket dictionaries ranging from an English-Spanish work to one covering English-Malay. All of the dictionaries in the "Gem" series range from 32,000 to 55,000 entries, are 3¼ by 4½ inches in size, are bound in flexible Leatheroid covers, and cost $2.45.

Vocabulary treatment in *English Gem*, as might be expected, is quite simple. In addition to concise definitions, entries provide part-of-speech labels, spelling and syllabication, and occasionally usage labels. Pronunciation information is usually limited to accent marks. As is common in British dictionaries, derivatives are entered as subentries of the main or root word, e.g., *composer* and *composition* are entered under the root word *compose*. There is considerable supplementary material found in the back of the dictionary. Example: Common abbreviations, foreign words and phrases frequently used in English, metric equivalents, chemical symbols, American presidents, and first names of men and women. The format is satisfactory.

Summary

English Gem Dictionary (U.S. Edition), part of the publisher's "Gem" dictionary series, is also titled *Collins American Gem Dictionary* (on the cover and spine). The dictionary has not been revised for ten years and some of the vocabulary entries seem a trifle arcane, e.g., *Mae West* ("inflated lifejacket worn by airmen"), *magilp* (or *megilp*), and *mahout* (an "elephant driver"). Vocabulary treatment is limited to short definitions, spelling, syllabication, and part-of-speech labels. Overall, the dictionary is authoritative and will prove useful to those who need only bare bones information about common words. Its coverage and treatment compare favorably with other dictionaries of similar size, e.g., the *Hugo Pocket Dictionary*, *The Little Oxford Dictionary*, *The Random House American Dictionary*, *The Thorndike-Barnhart Handy Pocket Dictionary*, and *Webster's New World Handy Pocket Dictionary*. Note that, as the *Buying Guide* was going to press, *English Gem Dictionary* (U.S. Edition) was reported out of print, at least for the present.

Follett Vest-Pocket Webster Dictionary

Descriptive Information

Full Title: **Follett Vest-Pocket Webster Dictionary.** *Editors:* Arthur Norman and Robert E. Allen. *Publisher:* Follett Publishing Co. *Edition Reviewed:* Revised & Enlarged Edition, 1975.

Classification: Adult—Pocket. *Pages:* 304. *Total Entries:* 17,000. *Average Entry Length:* 7 words. *Graphics:* 200. *Physical Size:* 3 by 5¼ in.; 14 cm. *LC:* 65-13066. *ISBN:* 0-695-80611-9. *Lowest Retail Price:* $1.95 paper.

Contents

The *Follett Vest-Pocket Webster Dictionary* succinctly defines most of the essential or familiar words in the language. But the preface notes that "Research has shown that dictionary users rarely or never look for the meaning or spelling of common, everyday words like *be, and, is, not, of, or, to,* etc. By omitting such words, this dictionary has made room for thousands of modern terms and definitions not usually included in a work of this size— terms such as *biodegradable, bioastronautics, parapsychology, REM, hallucinogen, transsexual, counterinsurgency* . . . and many others too numerous to mention." Word treatment is quite superficial, as might be expected. Example: The adjective *capable* is simply spelled, syllabified, identified as an adjective, and defined as "having skill." Example: The noun *yesterday* is merely defined as "the day before this." There is no indication of the word's connotative meaning, i.e., a short time ago. The dictionary also contains about 200 very small black-and-white line drawings which illustrate such terms as *derrick, forge, iron lung,* and *pineapple.* The drawings are too simple in most instances to enhance or complement the definitions they accompany. In addition, there are some 25 pages of encyclopedic information at the back, including geographical material about the world's continents, oceans, rivers, waterfalls, largest cities, and U.S. states.

Summary

The *Follett Vest-Pocket Webster Dictionary*, a small paperbound work, is reasonably up-to-date and provides a fairly good selection of basic vocabulary terms, except for very common words like *if, and, not, to,* and *but* which have been deliberately omitted to make room for some frequently used technical words. The definitions are exceedingly brief and not always precise.

The small drawings add little to the dictionary's contents, but the appended encyclopedic information might be useful to those who lack access to a general encyclopedia or almanac. The dictionary compares well with *Langenscheidt's Universal Webster Dictionary*, which is the same size but much older, and *Webster's New World Vest Pocket Dictionary*, a work with the same number of entries but less expensive.

Hugo Pocket Dictionary: English

Descriptive Information

Full Title: **Hugo Pocket Dictionary: English.** *Editors:* D. M. Caswell and R. Batchelor-Smith. *Publisher:* Hugo's Language Books Ltd. *Distributor:* Littlefield, Adams. Alternate title: *Hugo English Dictionary* (on spine and cover). *Edition Reviewed:* 1973.

Classification: Adult—Pocket. *Pages:* v, 632. *Total Entries:* 30,000. *Average Entry Length:* 6 words. *Graphics:* None. *Physical Size:* 2¾ by 4½ in.; 11 cm. *ISBN:* 0-085285-049-2. *Lowest Retail Price:* $1.95.

Contents

The *Hugo Pocket Dictionary: English*, a small hardbound pocket dictionary compiled in Great Britain, covers common words and phrases. The definitions are quite brief. Occasionally usage labels are provided, e.g., *cop* meaning policeman is labeled "sl"—that is, "slang." Pronunciations, etymologies, illustrative samples, and spelling variants, however, are all omitted. As is the case with most British-produced dictionaries, derivatives are entered as subentries of the root word, e.g., *composer, composition, compositor*, and *composure* are all found under *compose*. There is no supplementary or appended material. The dictionary is prepared by the same firm which publishes the well-known "Hugo" bilingual dictionaries.

Summary

The *Hugo Pocket Dictionary: English* is a relatively up-to-date but very limited pocket dictionary, designed mainly for travelers. It is quite comparable in most respects to the *English Gem Dictionary* (U.S. Edition). The vocabulary coverage, treatment, and arrangement are similar in both dictionaries. *Hugo Pocket* also compares favorably with the other British pocket work, *The Little Oxford Dictionary*, as well as three American dictionaries of the same size: *The Random House American Dictionary*, *The Thorndike-Barnhart Handy Pocket Dictionary*, and *Webster's New World Handy Pocket Dictionary*.

Langenscheidt Lilliput Webster English Dictionary

Descriptive Information

Full Title: **Langenscheidt Lilliput Webster English Dictionary.** *Compiler:* Sidney Fuller. *Publisher:* Langenscheidt. *Distributor:* Hippocrene

Books. Alternate title: *The Little Webster* (on cover and spine). *Edition Reviewed:* 1957.

Classification: Adult—Pocket. *Pages:* 640. *Total Entries:* 7,000. *Average Entry Length:* 3 words. *Graphics:* None. *Physical Size:* 1½ by 2 in.; 5 cm. *Lowest Retail Price:* $1.00 paper (vinyl).

Contents

The *Langenscheidt Lilliput Webster English Dictionary* has the distinction, for what it's worth, of being physically the smallest general adult dictionary in print. It is so small that it fits comfortably in the palm of a person's hand. Obviously, its contents are quite limited. The compiler notes in his preface that "In order to gain as much space as possible for words which we felt the reader might really need to look up, we decided to leave out as many words of [the] simple kind as we could." Thus users of the *Lilliput Webster* will find such words as *paradigm, paradox, paragon, paralysis,* and *paramour* in the dictionary but not common words like *as, girl, head, if, little, prepare,* and *the.* The only information provided for each entry is a very brief definition, usually of two or three words. Example: The word *aesthetics* is defined as "science of the beautiful." Accent marks are also indicated. The print is, of course, very small though legible. The one-column page, though tiny, is not overcrowded. The binding is blue vinyl with gold lettering.

Summary

The tiny *Langenscheidt Lilliput Webster English Dictionary* is more a conversation piece than a serious work of lexicography. It offers very brief and not really satisfactory definitions of some 7,000 familiar but relatively complex words. For reasons of space, "everyday words" like *and, crude,* and *simple* are omitted. Comparatively speaking, the *Lilliput Webster* most resembles the *Follett Vest-Pocket Webster Dictionary,* another very small pocket work which also excludes common words.

Langenscheidt's Universal Webster Dictionary

Descriptive Information

Full Title: **Langenscheidt's Universal Webster: An English Dictionary.** *Compilers:* Sidney Fuller and R. Fuller. *Publisher:* Langenscheidt. *Distributor:* Hippocrene Books. *Edition Reviewed:* 1958.

Classification: Adult—Pocket. *Pages:* 416. *Total Entries:* 17,000. *Average Entry Length:* 8 words. *Graphics:* None. *Physical Size:* 3 by 4¼ in.; 11 cm. *Lowest Retail Price:* $1.95 paper (vinyl).

Contents

Langenscheidt's Universal Webster: An English Dictionary is a small pocket work produced under the auspices of the German publishing house Langenscheidt. The dictionary provides only definitions, syllabication, and part-of-speech labels. The definitions, however, are relatively full and often include illustrative examples. For instance, the word *mix* has three distinct meanings, one of which ("keep company with") is clarified by the illustrative sentence "he mixes with strange people." According to the compilers' preface, the dictionary intends to include "all the words in everyday use, as well as modern technical terms, and the names of plants, animals and minerals. . . . In addition, we have incorporated the more difficult words which a reader of English is likely to come across in newspapers and books, and which for the most part are of Latin or French derivation." Aside from being somewhat dated now (e.g., *détente* is not found in the dictionary), *Langenscheidt's Universal Webster* achieves its purpose quite well. The binding (yellow vinyl) and print are satisfactory.

Summary

Langenscheidt's Universal Webster: An English Dictionary defines its 17,000 entries as fully as can be expected in a very small dictionary. Though somewhat smaller than the *English Gem Dictionary* (U.S. Edition) and *Hugo Pocket Dictionary: English*, it is comparable in terms of vocabulary treatment, physical size, and price. All three dictionaries are prepared abroad and will be most useful to the traveler. *Langenscheidt's Universal Webster* also compares favorably with the similar-sized *Follett Vest-Pocket Dictionary* (17,000 entries) and *Webster's New World Vest Pocket Dictionary* (18,000 entries). *Langenscheidt's Universal Webster*, however, is now 20 years old and needs a new edition to bring its vocabulary up-to-date.

Little Oxford Dictionary

Descriptive Information

Full Title: **The Little Oxford Dictionary of Current English.** *Editor:* Jessie Coulson. *Compiler:* George Ostler. *Publisher:* Oxford University Press. *Edition Reviewed:* Fourth Edition, 1969.

Classification: Adult—Pocket. *Pages:* vi, 687. *Total Entries:* 35,000. *Average Entry Length:* 10 words. *Graphics:* None. *Physical Size:* 3¾ by 5 in.; 13 cm. *ISBN:* 0-19-861114-5. *Lowest Retail Price:* $4.75.

Contents

The Little Oxford Dictionary of Current English is the peewee in the prestigious Oxford family of dictionaries, which includes the 13-volume *Oxford English Dictionary*, the 2-volume *Shorter Oxford English Dictionary*, the desk-size *Concise Oxford Dictionary*, the slightly larger *Oxford Illustrated Dictionary*, and *The Pocket Oxford Dictionary*. *Little Oxford* is based on the somewhat more extensive vocabulary found in *Pocket Oxford* (50,000 entries). *Little Oxford* was first published in 1930, revised in 1937 and 1941, and last issued in 1969 (Fourth Edition).

Like the other dictionaries bearing the name "Oxford," *Little Oxford* is very much a British production. Only British spellings and pronunciations are given. Such words as *lift* and *bonnet* ("hinged cover over engine of motor-vehicle") are given their peculiar English meanings, but American terms like *busing* (or *bussing*) and *softball* are not included at all. In addition, the various space-saving devices typical of British dictionaries are used. For instance, the tilde or "swung dash" (~) is used to represent the the root word when it is repeated. And derivatives, compounds, and idioms are entered as subentries of the root word, e.g., *companionable* and *companionship* are found under the main entry *companion*. These space-saving techniques give the dictionary a cluttered, cramped appearance.

Summary

The Little Oxford Dictionary of Current English, a somewhat abridged version of the 50,000-entry *Pocket Oxford Dictionary*, is an authoritative small work which has all of the good and bad qualities associated with the Oxford line of dictionaries. American users, unless they have a special need for British meanings and spellings, will find *Little Oxford* a bit rarefied. It is preferable, however, to *Chambers' English Dictionary*, a British work of comparable size (30,000 entries).

Other Critical Opinions

American Reference Books Annual 1970, p. 49 (in Vol. 2).

New American Webster Handy College Dictionary

Descriptive Information

Full Title: **The New American Webster Handy College Dictionary**. *Editors:* Albert Morehead and Loy Morehead. *Publisher:* New American Library. *Edition Reviewed:* Revised & Updated, 1972.

Classification: Adult—Pocket. *Pages:* 574. *Total Entries:* 30,000. *Average Entry Length:* 10 words. *Graphics:* 350. *Physical Size:* 4¼ by 7 in.; 18 cm. *LC:* 55-10446. *Lowest Retail Price:* $1.25 paper.

Contents

The New American Webster Handy College Dictionary, an inexpensive paperback, purports to provide "more than 100,000 definitions of useful words." In addition to meanings of common words and phrases, the dictionary includes spelling, syllabication, and pronunciation information. The pronunciation key is relatively simple and easy to comprehend. According to the front matter, *New American Webster* has been "Prepared and Edited" by the National Lexicographic Board, a now defunct organization of which Albert H. Morehead, (who died in 1966) was chairman and general editor. In addition to Loy Morehead, listed as co-editor of the dictionary, six editorial staff members are identified, along with some 60 subject consultants, most of whom are now retired or deceased.

Vocabulary selection and treatment leave something to be desired. For instance, *aesthetic* is not included in the dictionary, unless the user thinks to look under *esthetic* (a variant spelling). Other quite common terms (e.g., *macrame*) are not covered nor are many newer words and phrases. Scientific and technical terms are very superficially defined. Example: The biological meaning of *cell* is given as "the structural unit of organic life" and *gene* is defined as "an element in the germ cell, concerned with the transmission of hereditary characteristics." Some usage labels are provided, e.g., *mad* meaning angry is labeled "colloq." The small black-and-white illustrations tend to depict ordinary things. For instance, there is an illustration for *buzzard* but none for *buttress*. There are several appendixes, including a list of abbreviations, place-names, foreign words and phrases, and new words (such as *Afro-American* and *medicaid*). The papercover binding appears to be satisfactory but the print is sometimes blurry and too dark.

Summary

The New American Webster Handy College Dictionary is a reasonably up-to-date albeit superficial paperbound dictionary. At the low price of $1.25 it is not a bad deal, but dictionary users with serious vocabulary needs will, of course, want a larger, more authoritative work. *New American Webster* compares reasonably well with other similar-sized paperback dictionaries. For example, the more reputable *Thorndike-Barnhart Handy Pocket Dictionary* and *The Random House American Dictionary* are both now out-of-date and *Webster's New World Handy Pocket Dictionary*, though relatively up-to-date, is even more superficial than *New American Webster*.

New Webster's Vest Pocket Dictionary

Descriptive Information

Full Title: **New Webster's Vest Pocket Dictionary.** *Editor:* None listed. *Publisher:* Commonwealth Books, Inc. *Distributor:* Dennison Manufacturing Co. Alternate title: *Dennison Webster's English Dictionary* (on cover). *Edition Reviewed:* 1976.

Classification: Adult—Pocket. *Pages:* 192. *Total Entries:* 20,000. *Average Entry Length:* 4 words. *Graphics:* None. *Physical Size:* 2¾ by 5½ in.; 14 cm. *LC:* 75-39798. *Lowest Retail Price:* $1.25 paper.

Contents

New Webster's Vest Pocket Dictionary—also called the *Dennison Webster's English Dictionary*—provides only simple pronunciations, spelling, syllabication, part-of-speech labels, and very brief definitions. Example: The noun *cell*, which has a number of meanings, is defined in *New Webster's Vest Pocket* as "tiny room, smallest bit of living matter, unit of organization." Connotations are usually not given. Example: The word *buttonhole* is defined as "slit in garment for button." The meaning of the verb *buttonhole* as to detain in conversation is not given. Also, derivatives are often not included. Example: The verb *discern* is entered along with the noun form *discernment* (entered as a subentry simply as *-ment*) but *discernible*, the adjectival form, is not given. The vocabulary selection is generally good, although there are occasional anomalies. Example: Why is *narghile* ("oriental form of pipe smoking") included but not *gene?* Some brief information about punctuation and the metric system is found in the back of the dictionary. The print is very small.

Summary

New Webster's Vest Pocket Dictionary—or the *Dennison Webster's English Dictionary*, as it is called on the cover—is a quite small, superficial paperback dictionary which provides only basic vocabulary information. Its word list is fairly up-to-date. The dictionary compares favorably with other vest-pocket dictionaries currently in print, namely, the *Follett Vest-Pocket Webster Dictionary*, which was revised in 1975 and contains about 17,000 entries, and *Webster's New World Vest Pocket Dictionary*, which has some 18,000 entries and costs only $0.79. Note that *New Webster's Vest Pocket* has practically the same text as an item called *Webster's Dictionary*, published by Barnes & Noble.

Pocket Oxford Dictionary

Descriptive Information

Full Title: **The Pocket Oxford Dictionary of Current English.** *Compilers:* F. G. Fowler and H. W. Fowler; Revised by E. McIntosh. *Publisher:* Oxford University Press. *Edition Reviewed:* Fifth Edition, 1969.

Classification: Adult—Pocket. *Pages:* xxiv, 1052. *Total Entries:* 50,000. *Average Entry Length:* 16 words. *Graphics:* None. *Physical Size:* 4¼ by 6¾ in.; 17 cm. *ISBN:* 0-19-861113-7. *Lowest Retail Price:* $8.25.

Contents

The Pocket Oxford Dictionary of Current English, now in its Fifth Edition (1969), is one of the most popular small general dictionaries in those areas of the world where English—especially British English—is used. Although relatively small both in terms of vocabulary entries and physical size, *Pocket Oxford* includes an enormous amount of lexical information about 50,000 common words, phrases, and idiomatic expressions. Actually, *Pocket Oxford* is an abridgment of *The Concise Oxford Dictionary* (or *COD*), a general dictionary of nearly 75,000 entries now in its Sixth Edition (1976). It should be noted that the present edition of *Pocket Oxford* is based on the Fifth Edition (1964) of *COD*. This point is significant because the 1964 edition of *COD* was much more British centered than the more recent 1976 edition, which pays greater attention to American English.

Pocket Oxford first appeared in 1924, the work of the Fowler brothers, famous British-language authorities. Revised editions were issued in 1934, 1939, 1942, and most recently 1969. In the preface to the First Edition, the Fowlers note that "The bad dictionary, on a word that has half a dozen distinct meanings, parades by way of definition half a dozen synonyms, each of them probably possessed of several senses besides the one desired, and fails to add the qualifications and illustrations that would show the presumably ignorant reader how far each synonym is coextensive with his word. . . . To avoid this vice has been the chief aim of the C.O.D. and of this abridgement alike." Certainly *Pocket Oxford* provides fuller vocabulary treatment than any other dictionary in the pocket category. Its very high words-per-entry figure (16) supports this point. Indeed, the dictionary is comparable in terms of vocabulary treatment to the abridged dictionaries, which fall in the 55,000–130,000-entry range.

The definitions are quite full, considering the size of the work. Numerous illustrative examples are provided, e.g., one of the meanings given for *aesthetic* is "in good taste," which is followed by the example "~ *wallpaper.*" Concise etymologies are also included. The etymologies were revised in the Fifth Edition by G. W. S. Friedrichsen, currently Oxford's principal etymologist. The Oxford system of phonetic respelling (when required) provides reliable pronunciations, but American users should be aware that the pronunciations are those preferred in Great Britain. As in *COD* and other Oxford dictionaries, various space-saving schemes are used, such as entering derivatives under the root word, e.g., *composite* is found as a subentry of *compose*. In addition, as the example a few lines above shows, the dictionary uses the "swung dash" (~) to represent the main word when it is repeated. Also, many abbreviations are used throughout the book. Although *Pocket Oxford* is handsomely printed, the page layout has a cramped, intimidating appearance which may frustrate or turn off American users.

Pocket Oxford has two appendixes, one covering standard abbreviations and the other offering guidance on the pronunciation of non-English words. In addition, there is a very useful 32-page "Supplement of Australian and New Zealand Words," a specialized lexicon of some 1,100 words and phrases prepared by R. W. Burchfield, now Oxford University Press's chief lexicographer.

Summary

The *Pocket Oxford Dictionary of Current English* is an abridgment of *The Concise Oxford Dictionary* (*COD*) which in turn derives from the monumental *Oxford English Dictionary*, the multivolume research dictionary which stands as the greatest general historical resource available on the English language. *Pocket Oxford* in turn has spawned the smaller 35,000-entry *Little Oxford Dictionary*. These excellent credentials are further enhanced by the impeccable authority of the dictionary's founding editors, F. G. and H. W. Fowler, two of the towering names in English-language usage.

Pocket Oxford, perhaps because of its convenient size and manageable vocabulary (50,000 entries), has achieved worldwide popularity, particularly where British English is spoken or studied. The work, first issued in 1924, is now in its Fifth Edition (1969) and doubtless a Sixth Edition is currently in preparation, an assumption based on the appearance of the Sixth Edition of *COD* in 1976.

Pocket Oxford, like *COD* and *Little Oxford*, is not a first-choice small dictionary for American users. Despite its relatively full vocabulary treatment and illustrious authority, *Pocket Oxford* is very much a British dictionary. Its pronunciations, spellings, definitions, and illustrative examples are British in tone and fact. In addition, users may be frustrated or turned off by the dictionary's many abbreviations, space-saving devices, and crowded page layout, which is unrelieved by any graphics. Libraries, which will want a reliable British-made dictionary, would be better off acquiring the larger (but still desk-size) *COD*, along with the Oxford research dictionaries (*The Shorter Oxford English Dictionary* in two volumes and the multivolume *Oxford English Dictionary*).

See the profile of *The Concise Oxford Dictionary* in the "abridged dictionaries" section of the *Buying Guide* for additional information.

Other Critical Opinions

American Reference Books Annual 1970, p. 49 (in Vol. 2).

Random House American Dictionary

Descriptive Information

Full Title: **The Random House American Dictionary.** *Editor:* Jess Stein. *Publisher:* Random House. Former title: *The American Vest Pocket Dictionary. Edition Reviewed:* 1967.

Classification: Adult—Pocket. *Pages:* 318. *Total Entries:* 30,000. *Average Entry Length:* 5 words. *Graphics:* None. *Physical Size:* 3 by 5½ in.; 14 cm. *LC:* 67-20650. *ISBN:* 0-394-40050-X. *Lowest Retail Price:* $1.65 flexible covers.

Contents

The Random House American Dictionary is a vest-pocket abridgment of the 60,000-entry *Random House American Everyday Dictionary* which in turn derives from *The American College Dictionary.* As has been pointed out, both *American Everyday* and the semi-unabridged *American College* are now clearly dated. The same is true of *Random House American.* It first appeared in 1951 and was last revised in 1967. Obviously many new but commonly used terms are omitted from the dictionary, e.g., *busing* (or *bussing*), *data bank, détente, hard-core, macrame, New Left, redneck,* and *time-sharing.* On the other hand, because the dictionary's vocabulary essentially represents words active in the immediate post-World War II era, *Random House American* contains a number of somewhat esoteric entries, e.g., *Mae West* (defined as "inflatable life preserver"), *M-day* ("mobilization day"), and *mule skinner* ("driver of mules").

Vocabulary treatment is limited to very brief definitions, elementary pronunciation information, part-of-speech labels, and occasional usage labels. For instance, *mule skinner* is labeled "U.S." and *mad* meaning angry is "colloq." There are about 20 pages of supplementary information in the back, including spelling rules, brief emergency first aid, a table of calories, a page on detecting counterfeit money, some basic gazetteer data, forms of address, how to compute interest, lists of commonly misspelled and mispronounced words, and "General Orders of the Armed Forces of the

United States." The dictionary is sturdily bound for a paperback book. The print, though small, is legible.

Summary

The *Random House American Dictionary*, once one of our best vest-pocket works, is now out-of-date, as are *The Random House American Everyday Dictionary* and the larger *American College Dictionary* from whence it comes. Vocabulary treatment is quite superficial, limited mostly to very brief definitions. The dictionary is not as good a buy as *Webster's New World Handy Pocket Dictionary*, a pocket dictionary of comparable size (30,000 entries) and price ($1.95). Nor is it preferable to *The New American Webster Handy College Dictionary*, which lacks the authority of *Random House American* but is more up-to-date and less expensive. And even though it is older, *The Thorndike-Barnhart Handy Pocket Dictionary* (New Revised Edition, 1955) has the edge on *Random House American* in terms of size (36,000 entries), fullness of coverage, and price. The consumer should bear in mind that none of these dictionaries provides more than very basic vocabulary information.

Thorndike-Barnhart Handy Pocket Dictionary

Descriptive Information

Full Title: **The Thorndike-Barnhart Handy Pocket Dictionary.** *Editor:* Clarence L. Barnhart. *Publisher:* Doubleday & Co. *Distributor:* Bantam Books. *Edition Reviewed:* New Revised Edition, 1955.

Classification: Adult—Pocket. *Pages:* xxvi, 451. *Total Entries:* 36,000. *Average Entry Length:* 8 words. *Graphics:* None. *Physical Size:* 4¼ by 7 in.; 18 cm. *ISBN:* 0-553-10058-0. *Lowest Retail Price:* $1.25 paper.

Contents

The *Thorndike-Barnhart Handy Pocket Dictionary* is an abridgment of the now out-of-print but justly famous *Thorndike-Barnhart Comprehensive Desk Dictionary*, a work of some 80,000 carefully selected vocabulary entries intended principally for secretarial use. Published in 1951 in a trade edition by Scott, Foresman & Co., *The Thorndike-Barnhart Comprehensive Desk* has apparently been replaced by the more recent (1975) *Doubleday Dictionary for Home, School, and Office* which is also in the 80,000-entry category (but not a Thorndike-Barnhart work). The paperback abridgment, however, remains in print, available from Bantam Books. The dictionary is now over 20 years old but because of its judicious vocabulary selection it is still useful, though in need of a thorough updating. For instance, such recently introduced but frequently encountered words and phrases as *busing* (or *bussing*), *data bank*, and *détente* are not found in the dictionary, nor are the latest meanings of such terms as *gay* and *mix*. Vocabulary treatment is limited to definitions, pronunciations, parts of speech, and syllabication. The definitions are reasonably full, considering the size of the dictionary. The physical format is satisfactory.

Summary

An abridgment of the authoritative *Thorndike-Barnhart Comprehensive Desk Dictionary* (1951; now out-of-print), *The Thorndike-Barnhart Handy Pocket Dictionary* was *the* outstanding small paperback dictionary in the 1950s and early 1960s. The dictionary has not been revised, however, since 1955 and, though still useful in many respects, its age is definitely showing. It is not as up-to-date as *Webster's New World Handy Pocket Dictionary* and *The New American Webster Handy College Dictionary*, both comparably sized at 30,000 entries.

Webster's Dictionary (Barnes & Noble)

Descriptive Information

Full Title: **Webster's Dictionary**. *Editor:* None listed. *Publisher:* Barnes & Noble. *Edition Reviewed:* No date or edition given.

Classification: Adult—Pocket. *Pages:* 285. *Total Entries:* 20,000. *Average Entry Length:* 3 words. *Graphics:* None. *Physical Size:* 3¾ by 5¼ in.; 13 cm. *Lowest Retail Price:* $1.95 paper (with vinyl jacket).

Contents

This edition of *Webster's Dictionary* is published by Barnes & Noble Books, a division of Harper & Row. The back of the title page notes, however, that the book is "published under arrangement with Ottenheimer Publishers, Inc." Ottenheimer, a Baltimore (Md.) firm, is responsible for several works of inferior quality (e.g., *Webster's Encyclopedia of Dictionaries;* see Consumer Note under that entry in this section) and any dictionary bearing its name should not be purchased unless it has been carefully and personally examined by the consumer. The back of the title page also indicates the dictionary was printed in Italy. There is no indication, however, of editorship or date of publication. But the definitions, in most instances, are either the same as or condensed versions of those found in the 20,000-entry *New Webster's Vest Pocket Dictionary* (1976), distributed by Dennison Manufacturing Co. Example: Each dictionary defines *cell* as "tiny room, smallest bit of living matter, unit of organization." Vocabulary coverage is also practically the same. Example: Both dictionaries fail to cover the term *gene* but rather oddly do include the word *narghile* (defined in both dictionaries as "oriental form of pipe smoking").

New Webster's Vest Pocket Dictionary is a reasonably up-to-date but superficial little dictionary. The same can be said of *Webster's Dictionary*. But whereas *New Webster's* is a fairly well-printed item selling for $1.25, *Webster's Dictionary* is very poorly printed but sells for $0.70 more. One disconcerting feature of *Webster's Dictionary* is the space-saving technique of continuing a definition on the line above the main entry. Example: The word *lunge* is defined as "thrust forward." The last syllable of "forward," however, is printed on the line above the entry *lunge*, crammed into a free space left from the definition of the preceding entry and set off by a bracket. The dictionary is paperbound with a bright green vinyl slip-on jacket.

Summary

Webster's Dictionary, published by Barnes & Noble by arrangement with Ottenheimer Publishers, has much the same text as *New Webster's Vest Pocket Dictionary* (1976), a generally current but very limited little dictionary distributed by Dennison Manufacturing Company. *Webster's Dictionary*, however, costs more ($1.95 as opposed to $1.25 for *New Webster's*) and is quite poorly printed. Consumers are advised to avoid *Webster's Dictionary* bearing the Barnes & Noble imprint.

Webster's Dictionary (Dennison)

Descriptive Information

Full Title: **Webster's Dictionary.** *Editor:* John Gage Allee. *Publishers:* Dennison Manufacturing Co.; also Pathmark Books. Alternate title: *Webster's Dictionary for Everyday Use.* Former title: *Webster's Dictionary of the American Language.* *Edition Reviewed:* 1975.

Classification: Adult—Pocket. *Pages:* 446. *Total Entries:* 50,000. *Average Entry Length:* 9 words. *Graphics:* None. *Physical Size:* 5¼ by 7¾ in.; 20 cm. *Lowest Retail Price:* $1.95 paper.

Contents

Several editions of *Webster's Dictionary* edited by John Gage Allee are in print. Both Dennison Manufacturing Company and Pathmark Books publish identical versions under the simple title *Webster's Dictionary.* They appear in a large paperback format and are printed on cheap paper. Barnes & Noble Books, a division of Harper & Row, publishes exactly the same dictionary under the title *Webster's Dictionary for Everyday Use.* All three of these editions of the Allee dictionary bear a 1958 copyright by the Literary Press and more recent copyrights by Ottenheimer Publishers, Inc., a Baltimore (Md.) publisher. Specifically, the Pathmark book has a 1973 copyright, the Dennison a 1975 copyright, and the Barnes & Noble a 1977 copyright. All three editions, however, have virtually the same contents and format. The same dictionary has also been published by Ottenheimer under the title *Webster's Dictionary of the American Language.* This edition is apparently no longer on the market. In addition, the Allee dictionary forms the general dictionary portion of *Webster's Encyclopedia of Dictionaries*, an omnium-gatherum of various wordbooks published in a single volume by Ottenheimer. (See the Consumer Note on *Webster's Encyclopedia of Dictionaries* which follows in this section of the *Buying Guide.*)

Webster's Dictionary, edited by John Gage Allee, was once a respectable work. The 50,000 entries cover a fairly broad vocabulary range and the treatment, while not as detailed as that found in larger dictionaries, includes concise etymologies, pronunciations, parts of speech, and relatively full definitions. The dictionary, however, is woefully out-of-date at the present time, despite the recent copyrights. For instance, such new but commonly used terms as *busing* (or *bussing*), *data bank*, *data processing*, *decoupage*, *détente*, *hard-core*, *motor home*, and *time-sharing* are not covered. Nor are the most recent meanings of such words as *gay, leverage, mace, mix,* and *residual* found in the dictionary. On the other hand, the dictionary does include such esoteric entries as *caracole* (defined as "to wheel," from the Spanish), *Mae West* ("an inflatable life-jacket"), and *ranee* or *rani* ("in India, a queen or wife of a prince"). Moreover, many definitions are simply not appropriate for present-day users. Example: The noun *cock* has one definition ("a pile of hay"). The noun *faggot* or *fagot* has one definition ("a bundle of sticks for fuel; a bundle of steel rods cut for welding"). The noun *macrame* has one definition ("a coarse fringe"). Overall, the dictionary is not suitable for any sort of use today, no matter what title it appears under.

Summary

Webster's Dictionary, edited by John Gage Allee, is an inferior, out-of-date work which should be avoided by dictionary consumers. The dictionary, which bears various recent copyrights and appears under several different titles, can be identified by the name Oppenheimer Publishers, Inc. on the reverse side of the title page. The dictionary is frequently sold for $0.50 and up in discount stores, supermarkets, etc. It is a bad buy at any price.

Webster's Dictionary for Everyday Use

Descriptive Information

Full Title: **Webster's Dictionary for Everyday Use.** *Editor:* John Gage Allee. *Publisher:* Barnes & Noble. Alternate title: *Webster's Dictionary.* *Edition Reviewed:* 1977.

Classification: Adult—Pocket. *Pages:* 446. *Total Entries:* 50,000. *Average Entry Length:* 9 words. *Graphics:* None. *Physical Size:* 5¼ by 7¾ in.; 20 cm. *Lowest Retail Price:* $2.50 paper.

Consumer Note

Webster's Dictionary for Everyday Use, a paperback dictionary published by Barnes & Noble Books (a division of Harper & Row), has exactly the same text as *Webster's Dictionary*, published in papercover editions by both Dennison Manufacturing Company and Pathmark Books. Although the dictionary bears a recent copyright (1977), it is very much out-of-date and not recommended. The copyright is held by Ottenheimer Publishers, Inc., a firm located in Baltimore, Md. See the profile of *Webster's Dictionary* (edited by John G. Allee) above for further information about vocabulary contents of this dictionary. Consumers should also note that this dictionary, which Barnes & Noble sells for $2.50, is frequently found in discount stores and supermarkets for as little as $0.50. It is a bad buy at any price.

Webster's Encyclopedia of Dictionaries

Descriptive Information

Full Title: **Webster's Encyclopedia of Dictionaries: 12 Complete Dictionaries in One.** *Editor* (general dictionary): John Gage Allee. *Publisher:* Ottenheimer. *Edition Reviewed:* New American Edition, 1975.

Classification (general dictionary): Adult—Pocket. *Pages:* 446 (general dictionary; 1246 (all 12 dictionaries). *Total Entries:* 50,000 (general dictionary); 150,000 (all 12 dictionaries). *Average Entry Length* (general dictionary): 9 words. *Graphics:* Color plates in front; maps in back. *Physical Size:* 8½ by 11 in.; 28 cm. *Lowest Retail Price:* $24.50.

Consumer Note

Webster's Encyclopedia of Dictionaries, printed in large type, is a collection of 12 different dictionaries. The general dictionary has the same contents as *Webster's Dictionary* (published by Dennison Manufacturing Company and Pathmark Books) and *Webster's Dictionary for Everyday Use* (published by Barnes & Noble). These titles all bear relatively recent copyrights but in actuality the work is very much out-of-date. In each instance, the copyright is held by Ottenheimer. For further information about the contents of *Webster's Dictionary*, see the profile preceding in this section.

The remaining 11 dictionaries which make up *Webster's Encyclopedia of Dictionaries* include a crossword puzzle dictionary (copyright 1957); a Bible dictionary (1958); a book of quotations (1963); a dictionary of synonyms, antonyms, and homonyms (1965); a music dictionary (1961); a rhyming dictionary (1963); a legal dictionary (1965); a medical dictionary (1963); an outline of American history (1975); and an atlas and gazetteer (1966).

Webster's Encyclopedia of Dictionaries is a jumble of miscellaneous material which is either out-of-date or inferior in quality or both. By no stretch of the imagination is the volume worth $24.50.

Webster's New World Handy Pocket Dictionary

Descriptive Information

Full Title: **Webster's New World Handy Pocket Dictionary.** *Editor:* David B. Guralnik, Editor in Chief. *Publisher:* Collins+World. Alternate title: *Webster's New World Quick Reference Dictionary. Edition Reviewed:* 1972.

Classification: Adult—Pocket. *Pages:* iv, 316. *Total Entries:* 30,000. *Average Entry Length:* 5 words. *Graphics:* None. *Physical Size:* 3 by 5½ in.; 14 cm. *LC:* 70-147261. *ISBN:* 0-529-03088-8. *Lowest Retail Price:* $1.95 paper (with vinyl jacket).

Contents

Webster's New World Handy Pocket Dictionary, a small paperbound dictionary with a vinyl slip-on jacket, provides simplified definitions, pronunciations, and usage labels for some 30,000 active words and phrases. The vocabulary, based on that found in the College and Concise Editions of *Webster's New World Dictionary*, is relatively up-to-date, although current meanings of some words (e.g., *gay* and *mace*) are not given. Treatment is quite superficial, as the words-per-entry figure (5) suggests. A number of supplements are included in the back covering punctuation, abbreviations, weights and measures, cities and countries, American presidents, and wedding anniversaries. There is also a perpetual calendar.

Summary

Webster's New World Handy Pocket Dictionary, derived from the larger dictionaries in the New World line, is a reasonably current and authoritative dictionary for very simple information. It is more up-to-date but less thorough than *The Thorndike-Barnhart Handy Pocket Dictionary* (New Revised Edition, 1955). *The Random House American Dictionary*, which is practically the same size (30,000 entries) as *Webster's New World Handy Pocket*, is not as up-to-date. *The New American Webster Handy College Dictionary*, also 30,000 entries and published in a revised edition in 1972, lacks *Webster's New World Handy Pocket's* authority but it is just as current, more thorough, and costs less. Of course, all of these dictionaries are quite superficial and will not satisfy users with serious vocabulary needs. Note that *Webster's New World Handy Pocket Dictionary* also appears in a slightly different format as *Webster's New World Quick Reference Dictionary*.

Other Critical Opinions

American Reference Books Annual 1974 (review by Francis J. Witty), p. 453.

Webster's New World Quick Reference Dictionary

Descriptive Information

Full Title: **Webster's New World Quick Reference Dictionary.** *Editor:* David B. Guralnik, Editor in Chief. *Publisher:* Collins+World. Alternate title: *Webster's New World Handy Pocket Dictionary. Edition Reviewed:* 1972.

Classification: Adult—Pocket. *Pages:* iv, 316. *Total Entries:* 30,000. *Average Entry Length:* 5 words. *Graphics:* None. *Physical Size:* 3 by 5½ in.; 14 cm. *LC:* 70-147261. *ISBN:* 0-529-03091-8. *Lowest Retail Price:* $1.00 paper.

Consumer Note

Webster's New World Quick Reference Dictionary is, according to the title page, a "new format printing" of *Webster's New World Handy Pocket Dictionary* (see profile immediately preceding for further information). The only differences between the two titles are price and format. The *Quick Reference* costs only $1.00 (as opposed to $1.95 for the *Handy Pocket*) and the *Quick Reference* has a "flip-top" format similar to a note pad—that is, the binding is at the top of the page instead of along the left-hand margin. Note also that *Quick Reference* has flexible imitation leather covers for its binding whereas *Handy Pocket* comes with a vinyl slip-on jacket.

Other Critical Opinions

American Reference Books Annual 1974 (review by Francis J. Witty), p. 453.

Webster's New World Vest Pocket Dictionary

Descriptive Information

Full Title: **Webster's New World Vest Pocket Dictionary**. *Editor:* Clark C. Livensparger, Supervising Editor. *Publisher:* Collins+World. Alternate title: *New Vest Pocket Webster Dictionary.* Former title: *Vest Pocket Webster Dictionary. Edition Reviewed:* 1972.

Classification: Adult—Pocket. *Pages:* iv, 188. *Total Entries:* 18,000. *Average Entry Length:* 5 words. *Graphics:* None. *Physical Size:* 3 by 5½ in.; 14 cm. *ISBN:* 0-529-0486-5. *Lowest Retail Price:* $0.79 paper.

Contents

Webster's New World Vest Pocket Dictionary—also called the *New Vest Pocket Webster Dictionary*—is a reasonably current little dictionary which merely provides very brief definitions, parts of speech, and pronunciations for the more difficult words. Only the most common standard words are included. Definitions are based on the larger dictionaries bearing the "Webster's New World" name. Supplementary material includes abbreviations, weights and measures, punctuation information, brief geographical entries, and a list of state flowers. The dictionary is bound in maroon paper covers which resemble imitation leather.

Summary

Webster's New World Vest Pocket Dictionary—also entitled the *New Vest Pocket Webster Dictionary*—has been published since 1943 when it was known as the *Vest Pocket Webster Dictionary.* With only 18,000 entries, the dictionary has very limited value except to spell and briefly define the most common words. It compares favorably with the *Follett Vest-Pocket Webster Dictionary, Langenscheidt's Universal Webster Dictionary*, and the *New Webster's Vest Pocket Dictionary*, all of which have about the same number of entries as *Webster's New World Vest Pocket* but cost somewhat more. None of these dictionaries, however, will adequately serve the person with serious vocabulary needs.

SCHOOL AND CHILDREN'S DICTIONARIES

School and children's dictionaries, like general adult dictionaries, cover words and phrases commonly used in both the written and spoken language. In some instances, the larger school dictionaries are not greatly different from those prepared for general adult use. Indeed, such works as *The World Book Dictionary* and the *Macmillan Dictionary* can be used interchangeably—and profitably—as either an adult or student dictionary. But generally speaking, school and children's dictionaries do possess several features which distinguish them from adult dictionaries. These characteristics include vocabulary selection by grade level based on word frequency studies, provision of relatively simple definitions augmented and clarified by numerous illustrative examples, use of large and inviting type, and inclusion of many graphics throughout the text as both complements to the written definition and as attention-getting devices.

In addition, school dictionaries are usually marketed differently than adult dictionaries, which are sold as *trade* editions through established retail outlets like bookstores, drugstores, variety stores, supermarkets, and the like. School dictionaries on the other hand are usually merchandised as *text* editions—that is, they are normally sold only to educational institutions at a discount through publisher or distributor representatives. Often text editions include a property stamp on the front endpaper. Text editions may also be published with additional instructional material in the front matter and with separately published supplementary material, such as student workbooks or teachers' guides. In many cases a dictionary will appear in both a trade and text edition. Ordinarily the contents of both editions are the same, except for any additional preparatory and supplementary material. It should also be noted that individual consumers can usually acquire a text edition if they contact the publisher directly or order through a local bookstore. The individual consumer, however, will not ordinarily receive the discount accorded schools and libraries.

Once upon a time school dictionaries were simply watered down versions of adult dictionaries. All of this changed, however, in the 1930s and 1940s with the pioneering work of Dr. Edward L. Thorndike, an eminent psychologist who taught at Columbia University's famed Teachers College. What Thorndike did essentially was apply the techniques of educational psychology to the business of lexicography. During those two decades, Thorndike, with the assistance of Clarence L. Barnhart, produced three graduated dictionaries for students from the third through the twelfth grades. Perhaps the foremost ingredient in what has become known as the "Thorndike revolution" is the compilation and use of word or semantic frequency studies which indicate what words occur and how often in certain types of literature and, in the case of reading matter for children and young adults, at what grade level words occur and at what frequency. Thorndike published his first frequency count in 1921. A revision of that work by Thorndike and Irving Lorge appeared in 1944. Entitled *Teachers' Word Book of Thirty Thousand Words*, it is still in print (Teachers College Press, $10.95).

Over the years other word frequency counts have been produced, usually accomplished with the assistance of the computer, which is uniquely suited to perform the sort of laborious work such counts entail. Among the most useful and most recent frequency counts are these two works: *The American Heritage Word Frequency Book* (compiled by John B. Carroll, Peter Davies, and Barry Richman; published by Houghton Mifflin, 1971, at $25.00), a computer analysis of over five million words of running text from over a thousand carefully selected publications for children in grades three through nine; and *The Living Word Vocabulary; the Words We Know . . . A National Vocabulary Inventory* (compiled by Edgar Dale and Joseph O'Rourke; published by Field Enterprises Educational Corporation and distributed by Dome, Inc., 1976, at $39.95), a computer analysis of over 43,000 words based on word familiarity tests given to school and college students throughout the United States at various grade levels. Such studies not only assist lexicographers in the selection and treatment of vocabulary in school dictionaries but they are also useful to English teachers concerned with vocabulary building, teachers of remedial reading, writers and editors of instructional materials, and reviewers of such materials.

Thorndike was also responsible for introducing the extensive use of clarifying illustrative sentences and phrases in school dictionaries. Illustrative quotations, usually from classical or well-known contemporary writers, had long been used in large adult dictionaries but before Thorndike the technique had not been applied to works as small as school dictionaries, which normally range between 25,000 and 95,000 entries. Significantly, Thorndike applied his knowledge and experience as an educator and psychologist when preparing definitions. In particular, he used illustrative examples to "force" definitional clarity. As Allen Walker Read has written (in *Consumer Reports*, March 1964, p. 145), "Thorndike did not merely 'cut down' the book or 'shorten' the definitions: he constructed them with the psychology of the child in mind. . . . Thus under the word *camouflage* he reduced the definition to only two words, 'disguise; deception'; but the sentence he added brought it to life for children: 'The white fur of a polar bear is a natural *camouflage*, for it prevents its being easily seen against the snow.'"

Dr. Thorndike died in 1949 and his original Thorndike-Century dictionary series is now out-of-date. But Clarence L. Barnhart and his company (Clarence L. Barnhart, Inc.) have continuously revised the dictionaries. In the 1950s the series was expanded to four dictionaries, covering the beginning elementary grades (*Thorndike-Barnhart Beginning Dictionary*), the upper elementary grades (*Thorndike-Barnhart Junior Dictionary*), the middle school grades (*Thorndike-Barnhart Advanced Junior Dictionary*), and the high school grades (*Thorndike-Barnhart High School Dictionary*). In recent years, the titles of the series have changed and at the present time there are again three basic Thorndike-Barnhart school dictionaries (the *Beginning, Intermediate,* and *Advanced*). Note that the latest elementary Thorndike-Barnhart dictionary is entitled the *Scott, Foresman Beginning Dictionary* (1976). There is also the large *World Book Dictionary* (225,000 entries) which is more than a school dictionary although it utilizes the Thorndike-Barnhart lexicographical techniques discussed above. With the exception of *The World Book Dictionary* (which is published by Field Enterprises and usually sold in combination with *The World Book Encyclopedia*), Thorndike-Barnhart dictionaries are published by Doubleday (trade editions) and Scott, Foresman (text editions). The important point for dictionary consumers to remember, however, is that the name Thorndike-Barnhart means school dictionaries of the highest quality.

There are other good school dictionaries on the market, including those published by Merriam-Webster, Collins+World, Macmillan, and Harcourt Brace Jovanovich. In addition, a number of picture dictionaries for preschool children are available. The following section of the *Buying Guide* briefly comments on school and children's dictionaries currently available from American publishers and distributors. In addition, several titles specially designed for teaching English as a second or foreign language are identified. For purposes of comparative analysis, the *Buying Guide* has divided all school and children's dictionaries into four broad categories based on grade level: Secondary School (for high school students); Middle School (for junior high school students); Elementary School (for students from kindergarten to the sixth grade); and Preschool (for very young children not yet in school). Within these categories the dictionary profiles are arranged alphabetically by title. As indicated in the table of contents, those titles which are specifically useful for teaching English as a foreign language follow the "Preschool Dictionaries." Consult the index for specific dictionary titles.

SECONDARY SCHOOL DICTIONARIES

Macmillan Dictionary

Descriptive Information

Full Title: **Macmillan Dictionary.** *Editors:* William D. Halsey, Editorial Director; Judith S. Levey, Executive Editor; Christopher G. Morris, Managing Editor. *Publisher:* Macmillan Publishing Co. *Edition Reviewed:* Text Edition, 1973.

Classification: School & Children—Secondary School. *Grade Suitability:* Grade 9 through 12. *Pages:* G26, 1158. *Total Entries:* 90,000. *Graphics:* 1,800. *Physical Size:* 8¼ by 10¼ in.; 26 cm. *LC:* 79-183135. *School & Library Price:* $9.64.

Comments

The *Macmillan Dictionary* claims some 90,000 main entries and about 120,000 different definitions. The definitions are quite full and include many illustrative examples. Also included are clear etymologies, numerous synonym studies, helpful usage notes, and approximately 1,800 instructional drawings, many of them in two colors (either green or orange and white). The vocabulary represents "the language of contemporary America." Attention has been paid to current idioms, although many contemporary slang terms are conspicuously omitted, e.g., *funky, groupie, spaced-out*, and the homosexual meaning of *gay*. People (e.g., *Hemingway, Ernest*), places (*Hermon, Mount*), mythological names (*Hesperides*), biblical names (*Hezekiah*), abbreviations (*H.I.H.*), and things (*Hippocratic oath*) are all included in the main alphabet. There are no encyclopedic supplements. How the 90,000 entries were selected is not indicated, although the editors express thanks to the staff of the *Merit Students Encyclopedia* for "extensive assistance" in preparing the dictionary. Perhaps the text of the encyclopedia served as a vocabulary source? The book is very well bound and attractively produced. *Macmillan Dictionary* is the largest of three dictionaries bearing the Macmillan name. The others are the *Macmillan School Dictionary* (for middle school use) and the *Macmillan Dictionary for Children* (for elementary school use). Overall, this is an excellent series of dictionaries. Certainly, the *Macmillan Dictionary* competes well with the other titles in the secondary school category.

Other Critical Opinions

American Reference Books Annual 1974, p. 452.
Wilson Library Bulletin (review by Charles A. Bunge), May 1973, p. 798.

Thorndike-Barnhart Advanced Dictionary

Descriptive Information

Full Title: **Thorndike-Barnhart Advanced Dictionary.** *Editor:* Clarence L. Barnhart. *Publishers:* Doubleday & Co. (Trade Edition); Scott, Foresman & Co. (Text Edition). Former Titles: *Thorndike-Barnhart High School Dictionary* (1952–1972); *Thorndike-Century Senior Dictionary* (1941–1951). *Edition Reviewed:* Second (Trade) Edition, 1974.

Classification: School & Children—Secondary School. *Grade Suitability:* Grade 9 through 12. *Pages:* 29, 1186. *Total Entries:* 95,000. *Graphics:* 1,300. *Physical Size:* 8 by 9½ in.; 24 cm. *ISBN:* 0-385-07543-X (trade). *Lowest Retail Price:* $11.50; to schools & libraries, $7.98.

Comments

The *Thorndike-Barnhart Advanced Dictionary* is an up-to-date, authoritative dictionary for high school students. It provides excellent vocabulary coverage of words and phrases which might be encountered by students. Biographical and geographical entries are included in a single alphabet along with common words and phrases, abbreviations, idiomatic expressions, and frequently used scientific and technical terms. New words and meanings are usually found in the dictionary, e.g., *funky* and the most recent meaning of *gay* (homosexual) are included. The definitions are reasonably thorough, almost always augmented by helpful illustrative examples. Etymologies are provided and in this edition such abbreviations as *L* ("Latin") and *OE* ("Old English") are spelled out for the convenience of the student. The pronunciation key, long an outstanding feature of the Thorndike-Barnhart series, is clear and precise. The black-and-white graphics, which include small historical maps, help clarify the entries they accompany. The book is sturdily bound and handsomely printed. The Second Edition (1974) of *Thorndike-Barnhart Advanced Dictionary* continues the tradition of excellence which has characterized the Thorndike-Barnhart line of school dictionaries for more than a generation. The *Thorndike-Barnhart Advanced Dictionary* is a first choice dictionary for classroom use in American high schools.

Other Critical Opinions

American Reference Books Annual 1974 (review by Francis J. Witty), p. 455.
Katz, William A. *Basic Information Sources*. Vol. 1 of *Introduction to Reference Work*, 2nd ed. (New York: McGraw-Hill, 1974), pp. 271–272.

Webster's New Students Dictionary

Descriptive Information

Full Title: **Webster's New Students Dictionary.** *Editor:* Merriam-Webster Staff. *Publishers:* G. & C. Merriam Co. (Trade Edition); American Book Co. (Text Edition). Alternate title: *Webster's New Students Dictionary: High School Dictionary* (on spine). Former title: *Webster's Students Dictionary for Upper School Levels* (1938–1963). *Edition Reviewed:* Trade Edition, 1974.

Classification: School & Children—Secondary School. *Grade Suitability:* Grade 9 through 12. *Pages:* 10a, 1050. *Total Entries:* 81,000. *Graphics:* 535. *Physical Size:* 6¾ by 9½ in.; 24 cm. *ISBN:* 0-87779-180-5 (trade). *Lowest Retail Price:* $7.95; to schools, $7.47.

Comments

Webster's New Students Dictionary first appeared in 1964, replacing *Webster's Students Dictionary for Upper School Levels*. The dictionary is thoroughly revised every five years, with the next revision scheduled for 1979. According to the brief preface, *Webster's New Students* has been compiled especially for high school students, its entries being selected "chiefly on the basis of their occurrence in textbooks and supplementary reading in all subjects of the high school curriculum." The dictionary's authority ultimately rests with the unabridged *Webster's Third New International Dictionary* and the very large citation file maintained by the publisher. The definitions are reasonably full. They are augmented by carefully framed illustrative examples, some 15,000 etymologies, and more than 600 synonym studies. The graphics are quite small black-and-white line drawings which add little to the dictionary's reference value. The book is adequately bound and printed. *Webster's New Students* is the largest and most advanced of the three Merriam-Webster school dictionaries. The other titles in the series are *Webster's Intermediate Dictionary* (for middle school students) and *Webster's New Elementary Dictionary* (for elementary school students). This line of dictionaries is a fine one, but it is not the equal of the Thorndike-Barnhart series, the leader in school dictionaries for nearly 40 years.

Other Critical Opinions

American Reference Books Annual 1976 (review by Lillian L. Shapiro), p. 543.
Booklist, September 15, 1976, pp. 200, 202.

Webster's New World Dictionary (*Special School Printing*)

Descriptive Information

Full Title: **Webster's New World Dictionary of the American Language: Second College Edition.** *Editor:* David B. Guralnik, Editor in Chief. *Publisher:* Prentice-Hall (by arrangement with Collins+World). *Edition Reviewed:* Second College Edition—Special School Printing, 1976.

Classification: School & Children—Secondary School. *Grade Suitability:* Grade 11 through 12. *Pages:* xxxvi, 1692. *Total Entries:* 158,000. *Graphics:* 1,500. *Physical Size:* 7¼ by 10 in.; 25 cm. *LC:* 75-39572. *ISBN:* 0-13-944504-8. *School Price:* $4.53.

Consumer Note

Webster's New World Dictionary of the American Language (Second College Edition) is too advanced for most secondary school students. Juniors and seniors in high school, however, who are planning to attend college will find this excellent semi-unabridged dictionary a helpful resource. As the title implies, the emphasis is on the language as used in the United States. Many terms in the dictionary are designated as Americanisms, e.g., *funky, funnies, make the fur fly,* and the verb *furlough. Webster's New World* is also noted for its full etymological information, including the origin of American place-names. But unlike the high school dictionaries in the Thorndike-Barnhart, Macmillan, and Merriam-Webster series, *Webster's New World* is not designed with the secondary school student in mind.

The Special School Printing sold by Prentice-Hall to educational institutions for $4.53 is identical in contents to the trade edition published by Collins+World for $9.95. The only very minor differences between the two publications are that the Special School Printing has a property stamp on the front endpaper where the trade edition has a map showing regional American dialects. Also, the trade edition comes with a dust jacket and the School Printing does not. For more information about *Webster's New World Dictionary* (Second College Edition), see the profile with the adult dictionaries in the "semi-unabridged" section of the *Buying Guide.*

Webster's New World Dictionary (Students Edition)

Descriptive Information

Full Title: **Webster's New World Dictionary of the American Language: Students Edition.** *Editor:* David B. Guralnik, Editor in Chief. *Publisher:* Collins+World. *Edition Reviewed:* Students Edition, 1977.

Classification: School & Children—Secondary School. *Grade Suitability:* Grade 9 through 12. *Pages:* 1152. *Total Entries:* 108,000. *Graphics:* 1,500. *Physical Size:* 7½ by 9¾ in.; 25 cm. *Lowest Retail Price:* $8.95.

Comments

As the *Buying Guide* was going to press, Collins+World reported that a Students Edition of *Webster's New World Dictionary* would be published in the fall of 1977. The Students Edition, which has not been seen by the *Buying Guide*, is said to contain 108,000 entries derived from the larger Second College Edition of *Webster's New World Dictionary*. It is also advertised as being up-to-date, including such recent terms as *citizens' band*, *conflict of interest*, *no-fault*, and *Richter scale*. The Students Edition will be available only in an unindexed trade edition at $8.95.

World Book Dictionary

Descriptive Information

Full Title: **The World Book Dictionary.** *Editors:* Clarence L. Barnhart and Robert K. Barnhart. *Publisher:* Field Enterprises Educational Corp. Former title: *The World Book Encyclopedia Dictionary.* *Edition Reviewed:* 1977.

Classification: School & Children—Secondary School. *Grade Suitability:* Grade 7 through 12. *Volumes:* 2. *Pages:* 124 (colored paper), 2430. *Total Entries:* 225,000. *Graphics:* 3,000. *Physical Size:* 8¾ by 11¼ in.; 29 cm. *LC:* 76-23524. *ISBN:* 0-7166-0277-6. *Lowest Retail Price:* $59.00 the set.

Consumer Note

The World Book Dictionary is the largest dictionary prepared by Clarence L. Barnhart and his staff. Although the dictionary complements *The World Book Encyclopedia*, it is considered part of the Thorndike-Barnhart line of school dictionaries. Its school use, however, is normally restricted to the library, where the large (and heavy) two-volume set can be more conveniently consulted than in individual classrooms. In addition, *The World Book Dictionary*, because it is sold in combination with *The World Book Encyclopedia*, is often acquired for use in the home by the entire family. Because of the dictionary's size (225,000 entries) and its broad range of potential users, the *Buying Guide* has treated *The World Book Dictionary* as an adult dictionary in the semi-unabridged class. One fact is quite clear: this dictionary is an outstanding work, whether used by students or adults in the home, library, or school. For further information about *The World Book Dictionary*, see the profile in the "semi-unabridged" section of Adult Dictionaries.

MIDDLE SCHOOL DICTIONARIES

American Heritage School Dictionary

Descriptive Information

Full Title: **The American Heritage School Dictionary.** *Editor:* American Heritage Dictionary Staff. *Publisher:* Houghton Mifflin Co. *Edition Reviewed:* 1972.

Classification: School & Children—Middle School. *Grade Suitability:* Grade 6 through 10. *Pages:* xxxii, 992. *Total Entries:* 55,000. *Graphics:* 1,500. *Physical Size:* 8½ by 9½ in.; 24 cm. *LC:* 72-75557. *ISBN:* 0-395-13850-7. *Lowest Retail Price:* $8.95; to schools & libraries, $5.10.

Comments

The American Heritage School Dictionary contains "about 35,000 main entries, which amount to about 55,000 different words if inflected forms are counted, and about 70,000 separately defined meanings and uses." The vocabulary, which is generally up-to-date but somewhat sanitized, is based on a computer analysis of a thousand books used in grades 3 through 9 containing some five million words. "The computer counted all the words in the five million and found that there were 87,000 *different* words, starting with *the, of, and,* and all the common words." The editors further state that "Most of our 35,000 'main entries' and 50,000 'forms' come from a list that emerged from the computer." The definitions are usually quite concise and do not always adequately define the term, e.g., the current meanings of *gay, impressionist,* and *mace* are not given. Also such words as *funky, groupie,* and *Orwellian* are completely omitted. Illustrative examples are provided but there are few etymologies and no synonym studies. A useful feature is the identification of homonyms, e.g., the entry *canvas* ends with the note "These sound alike *canvas, canvass.*" Like the parent *American Heritage Dictionary of the English Language,* the book is very attractively put together. A two-inch yellow column runs through the center of each page. The column contains graphics, which are usually instructive, and sometimes additional tidbits of information about words on that page. A teacher's guide and student activities book are also available. *The American Heritage School Dictionary* will meet the vocabulary needs of junior high school students, as well as advanced upper elementary youngsters. It compares favorably with the other outstanding dictionaries in the middle school category: the *Macmillan School Dictionary, The Random House Dictionary* (School Edition), the *Thorndike-Barnhart Intermediate Dictionary,* and *Webster's Intermediate Dictionary.*

Other Critical Opinions

American Reference Books Annual 1973 (review by Christine L. Wynar), pp. 449–450.

Harcourt Brace Intermediate Dictionary

Descriptive Information

Full Title: **The Harcourt Brace Intermediate Dictionary.** *Editor:* Harrison Gray Platt, Editor in Chief. *Publisher:* Harcourt Brace Jovanovich. Alternate title: *The HBJ School Dictionary* (Text Edition). *Edition Reviewed:* Trade Edition, 1968.

Classification: School & Children—Middle School. *Grade Suitability:* Grade 6 through 10. *Pages:* 64, 895. *Total Entries:* 46,000. *Graphics:* 1,300. *Physical Size:* 7¼ by 9½ in.; 24 cm. *LC:* 68-1860. *Lowest Retail Price:* $5.97.

Consumer Note

The Harcourt Brace Intermediate Dictionary, first published in 1968 and not since revised, is the trade edition of *The HBJ School Dictionary*, the text edition which indicates 1977 as its latest copyright date. In almost every respect, however, the two titles are the same. Certainly the vocabulary portion (pages 1–864 in both dictionaries) is practically identical in both dictionaries. For further information, see the profile of *The HBJ School Dictionary* which immediately follows.

HBJ School Dictionary

Descriptive Information

Full Title: **The HBJ School Dictionary.** *Editor:* Harrison Gray Platt, Editor in Chief. *Publisher:* Harcourt Brace Jovanovich. Alternate title. *The Harcourt Brace Intermediate Dictionary* (Trade Edition). Former title: *The Harcourt Brace School Dictionary* (1968). *Edition Reviewed:* Text Edition, 1977.

Classification: School & Children—Middle School. *Grade Suitability:* Grade 6 through 10. *Pages:* 64, 896. *Total Entries:* 46,000. *Graphics:* 1,300. *Physical Size:* 7½ by 9½ in.; 24 cm. *ISBN:* 0-15-321142-3. *School Price:* $5.97.

Comments

The HBJ School Dictionary is practically the same dictionary as *The Harcourt Brace School Dictionary*, published in 1968. The only differences between the two titles are that *HBJ School* appends 32 pages of encyclopedic information not included in *Harcourt Brace School*, that a few new words like *Chicano* have been squeezed into *HBJ School*, that *HBJ School* has a slightly reworded introduction, and of course the titles vary. Note also that *HBJ School*, although it sports a 1977 copyright, is almost identical in its vocabulary contents to the 1968 trade edition entitled *The Harcourt Brace Intermediate Dictionary*, which is still in print. (For further information about *Harcourt Brace Intermediate*, see the Consumer Note immediately preceding.)

Although *HBJ School* has a recent copyright, its vocabulary is actually over ten years old. At the time of the dictionary's compilation in the mid-1960s, the vocabulary was selected from lists prepared by seven curriculum specialists. In addition, the editorial staff searched "scores of textbooks published within the last five or six years and other scores of juvenile books widely used today for supplementary or enrichment reading" for potential vocabulary entries. The basic word stock includes common terms, some of them labeled "slang" or "informal," e.g., *chicken* meaning cowardly is labeled "slang." Like almost all school dictionaries, biographical and geographical entries are included in the main A–Z sequence, as are abbreviations and selected proper nouns (e.g., *Day of Atonement*). Many new but quite common words and phrases are omitted (e.g., *data bank*, *détente*, *funky*, *groupie*, *minibike*, and *spaced-out*) as are new meanings of older words (e.g., *busing* or *bussing*). The dictionary also provides some illustrative phrases, but they are not always helpful. Example: The two phrases given for the adjective *aesthetic* are "an *aesthetic* view" and "an *aesthetic* person." The definitions are reasonably full, considering the intended usership, and there are numerous helpful usage notes. The dictionary is attractively printed and well bound. Harrison Gray Platt is editor in chief and Sidney I. Landau, a well-known lexicographer, is listed as managing editor. There is also an impressive board of supervising editors, which includes Albert H. Marckwardt (chairman), Frederic G. Cassidy, and S. I. Hayakawa. Overall, *HBJ School* is a reasonably good middle-level school dictionary, but it hardly compares with *The American Heritage School Dictionary*, the *Macmillan School Dictionary*, the *Thorndike-Barnhart Intermediate Dictionary*, and *Webster's Intermediate Dictionary*.

Holt Intermediate Dictionary

Descriptive Information

Full Title: **The Holt Intermediate Dictionary of American English.** *Editor:* Morgan L. Walters, Editor in Chief. *Publisher:* Holt, Rinehart & Winston. *Edition Reviewed:* Text Edition, 1967.

Classification: School & Children—Middle School. *Grade Suitability:* Grade 6 through 10. *Pages:* 28A, 995. *Total Entries:* 65,000. *Graphics:* 1,500. *Physical Size:* 7½ by 9½ in.; 24 cm. *LC:* 66-13853. *ISBN:* 0-03-067320-8. *School Price:* $9.84.

Comments

The Holt Intermediate Dictionary of American English was first published in 1966. At the time it was called "a completely new work in a new series, the Holt Dictionaries," but to the best of the *Buying Guide*'s knowledge, the Holt dictionary series failed to materialize. (In 1966, Holt did add its name to the *Basic Dictionary of American English*, an elementary school dictionary published in 1962 but now out of print.) Moreover, *Holt Intermediate* has not been revised since its initial publication. The dictionary contains about 40,000 main entries and 65,000 total entries. The vocabulary includes the common terms which comprise the basic English language word stock, as well as abbreviations and some proper names (e.g., *World Court*). Biographical and geographical entries, however, are listed separately in the back, along with brief material on the metric system, weights and measures, signs and symbols, the American presidents (up to Lyndon Johnson), the states, etc. Definitions tend to be clear and precise. Illustrative examples are copiously provided, as are simple etymologies. The graphics and physical format are unexceptional. The dictionary's gravest defect is its age. With so many fine school dictionaries available in the middle school category (*The American Heritage School Dictionary*, the *Macmillan School Dictionary*, the *Thorndike-Barnhart Intermediate Dictionary*, and *Webster's Intermediate Dictionary*), *The Holt Intermediate Dictionary* is hopelessly outclassed.

Macmillan School Dictionary

Descriptive Information

Full Title: **Macmillan School Dictionary**. *Editors:* William D. Halsey, Editorial Director; Christopher G. Morris, Managing Editor. *Publisher:* Macmillan Publishing Co. *Edition Reviewed:* Text Edition, 1974.

Classification: School & Children—Middle School. *Grade Suitability:* Grade 6 through 10. *Pages:* G40, 1064. *Total Entries:* 65,000. *Graphics:* 1,500. *Physical Size:* 8¼ by 10¼ in.; 26 cm. *LC:* 73-15248. *Lowest Retail Price:* $9.32; to schools & libraries, $5.25.

Comments

The *Macmillan School Dictionary* is an abridged version of the *Macmillan Dictionary* which contains some 90,000 entries and is designed for use by high school students. The *Macmillan School Dictionary* is most appropriate for junior high school use. Like the larger dictionary, its vocabulary covers words and phrases likely to be encountered by students in their studies and recreational reading. According to the editors, the definitions have been written to grade level—that is, "the simplest and most common words have the simplest treatment. More complex terms are defined in a slightly more sophisticated way." The editors also indicate that vocabulary selection has been based on "a thorough and systematic examination of . . . the current textbooks of all major publishers," on literary works read by middle school students, on current magazines and newspapers, and on "everyday conversation."

The definitions are relatively thorough and, like the *Macmillan Dictionary*, numerous illustrative examples show the use of words in context. The synonym studies found in the larger dictionary have been omitted in *Macmillan School*, but the latter does include a number of unique and very useful "language study essays," i.e., concise discussions of such terms as *alphabet*, *American English*, *analogy*, *antonym*, *etymology*, *euphemism*, and *figure of speech*. Etymologies have been eliminated from *Macmillan School*. Like the larger dictionary, however, many geographical and biographical entries are included in the single alphabet. The graphics are the same as those found in the *Macmillan Dictionary*. The same two-color combinations (green or orange and white) are used in both dictionaries. The Macmillan series of school dictionaries—the *Macmillan Dictionary* (high school), *Macmillan School* (middle school), and the *Macmillan Dictionary for Children* (elementary school)—is authoritative, up-to-date, and carefully prepared. It compares favorably with the two other fine school series (Thorndike-Barnhart and Merriam-Webster).

Other Critical Opinions

Booklist, June 15, 1975, pp. 1086–1087.

Oxford School Dictionary

Descriptive Information

Full Title: **The Oxford School Dictionary.** *Editors:* Dorothy C. Mackenzie; Third Edition revised by Joan Pusey. *Publisher:* Oxford University Press. *Edition Reviewed:* Third Edition, 1974.

Classification: School & Children—Middle School. *Grade Suitability:* Grade 5 through 8. *Pages:* xii, 371. *Total Entries:* 30,000. *Graphics:* None. *Physical Size:* 5½ by 8¼ in.; 21 cm. *ISBN:* 0-19-910208-2. *Lowest Retail Price:* $3.00.

Comments

The Oxford School Dictionary, first published in 1957 and revised in 1960 and again in 1974, covers common vocabulary terms which may be encountered by "English-speaking pupils between the ages of 11 and 16." Biographical and geographical information is excluded. Vocabulary treatment is entirely British. Example: The word *bonnet* is defined as "hinged cover over engine of motor-vehicle." The word *center* is given as only *centre*. Definitions closely resemble those found in *The Little Oxford Dictionary* (Fourth Edition, 1969), an adult pocket dictionary of some 35,000 entries. Etymologies, which were included in previous editions, have been dropped. There are no illustrative examples, no synonym studies, and no graphics. *Oxford School Dictionary* will not be useful to American students at any level. Its British orientation militates against it but, more than that, *Oxford School Dictionary* is simply inferior in overall lexicographical design and treatment when compared with most American school dictionaries. It is almost as if the good people at Oxford University Press had never heard of E. L. Thorndike.

Random House Dictionary (School Edition)

Descriptive Information

Full Title: **The Random House Dictionary of the English Language: School Edition.** *Editors:* Stuart Berg Flexner, Editor in Chief; Eugene F. Shewmaker, Managing Editor. *Publisher:* Random House. *Edition Reviewed:* School Edition, 1973.

Classification: School & Children—Middle School. *Grade Suitability:* Grade 6 through 10. *Pages:* x, 950. *Total Entries:* 45,000. *Graphics:* 1,200. *Physical Size:* 7¼ by 9¾ in.; 25 cm. *LC:* 79-94094. *ISBN:* 0-394-01951-2. *School Price:* $6.50.

Comments

The Random House Dictionary (School Edition) bases its vocabulary treatment on the lexicographical files and authority established for the larger *Random House Dictionary* (Unabridged Edition) and *The Random House College Dictionary*. But the School Edition's vocabulary selection has been based on word frequency studies involving textbooks, standard school literature, popular magazines and newspapers likely to be read by young people, and everyday conversational English. The vocabulary includes common words, brief biographical and geographical entries, abbreviations, terms from mythology, and idiomatic expressions. A 16-page color atlas is appended in the back. The definitions are reasonably clear and full. Many illustrative examples are included to clarify meanings in context. Usage notes and labels are fairly generously provided, as are synonyms. The latter, which are included as part of the definition, are not discriminated. A 41-page "Student's Guide to the Dictionary," located in the front of the book, is an outstanding feature. The discussion of how dictionaries are made and their various components is very informative. Teachers will find it useful as an introduction to word and dictionary studies. *Random House Dictionary* (School Edition) has a clear and attractive format. The dictionary compares favorably with the other better dictionaries in the middle school category, namely, *The American Heritage School Dictionary*, the *Macmillan School Dictionary*, the *Thorndike-Barnhart Intermediate Dictionary*, and *Webster's Intermediate Dictionary*.

Thorndike-Barnhart Advanced Junior Dictionary

Descriptive Information

Full Title: **Thorndike-Barnhart Advanced Junior Dictionary**. *Editor:* Clarence L. Barnhart. *Publishers:* Doubleday & Co. (Trade Edition); Scott, Foresman & Co. (Text Edition). *Edition Reviewed:* Fourth (Trade) Edition, 1968.

Classification: School & Children—Middle School. *Grade Suitability:* Grade 7 through 10. *Pages:* xxxvi, 946. *Total Entries:* 65,000. *Graphics:* 1,850. *Physical Size:* 7½ by 9¾ in.; 25 cm. *ISBN:* 0-385-02812-1 (trade). *Lowest Retail Price:* $9.50; to schools & libraries, $7.14.

Consumer Note

Although the *Thorndike-Barnhart Advanced Junior Dictionary* remains in print, it has been superseded by the *Thorndike-Barnhart Intermediate Dictionary* and to some extent by the *Thorndike-Barnhart Advanced Dictionary*. Previously, the Thorndike-Barnhart series comprised four titles: *Thorndike-Barnhart High School Dictionary* (1952–1972), *Thorndike-Barnhart Advanced Junior Dictionary* (1957–1968), *Thorndike-Barnhart Junior Dictionary* (1957–1968), and *Thorndike-Barnhart Beginning Dictionary* (1952–1974). In the graded scheme of things, the *Advanced Junior* stood between *Junior* and *High School*. Among these four titles, only *Advanced Junior* and *Beginning* remain in print. The current Thorndike-Barnhart school series is made up of three titles: *Thorndike-Barnhart Advanced*

Dictionary (first published in 1973 and designed to serve high school students), *Thorndike-Barnhart Intermediate Dictionary* (first published in 1971 for middle school students), and the *Scott, Foresman Beginning Dictionary* (first published in 1976 as a revision of *Thorndike-Barnhart Beginning Dictionary* and designed for elementary school students). With this history in mind, dictionary consumers are advised not to buy the *Thorndike-Barnhart Advanced Junior Dictionary*, which has not been revised for ten years and presumably will be phased out in the near future.

Thorndike-Barnhart Intermediate Dictionary

Descriptive Information

Full Title: **Thorndike-Barnhart Intermediate Dictionary.** *Editor:* Clarence L. Barnhart. *Publishers:* Doubleday & Co. (Trade Edition); Scott, Foresman & Co. (Text Edition). Former titles: *Thorndike-Barnhart Junior Dictionary* (1952–1970); *Thorndike-Barnhart Advanced Junior Dictionary* (1957–1968); *Thorndike-Century Junior Dictionary* (1935–1951). *Edition Reviewed:* Second (Trade) Edition, 1974.

Classification: School & Children—Middle School. *Grade Suitability:* Grade 5 through 8. *Pages:* 38, 985. *Total Entries:* 57,000. *Graphics:* 1,300. *Physical Size:* 8 by 9½ in.; 24 cm. *ISBN:* 0-673-04800-4 (trade). *Lowest Retail Price:* $9.50; to schools & libraries, $7.14.

Comments

The *Thorndike-Barnhart Intermediate Dictionary*, initially published in 1971 and revised in 1974, is the middle dictionary in the Thorndike-Barnhart graded series. The other two titles are the *Thorndike-Barnhart Advanced Dictionary* (for high school students) and the *Scott, Foresman Beginning Dictionary* (a recent revision of the *Thorndike-Barnhart Beginning Dictionary* designed to serve elementary school students). The Thorndike-Barnhart imprint also appears on the 225,000-entry (semi-unabridged) *World Book Dictionary*. This entire line of dictionaries is authoritative and reasonably up-to-date. The *Intermediate* includes common words, names of people and places, abbreviations, and scientific and technical terms in a single alphabet. The definitions are crisp and clear, enhanced by numerous well-chosen illustrative sentences and phrases, a feature introduced into school dictionaries by E. L. Thorndike in the 1930s. Another distinctive feature of the series is the legible print and clean, uncluttered page layout. Other school dictionaries in the middle school category, however, have imitated the pioneering Thorndike-Barnhart series and some are worthy competitors. Among the best are *The American Heritage School Dictionary*, the *Macmillan School Dictionary*, and *The Random House Dictionary* (School Edition).

Other Critical Opinions

American Reference Books Annual 1976 (review by Robert Parslow), p. 542.
Katz, William A. *Basic Information Sources.* Vol. 1 of *Introduction to Reference Work*, 2nd ed. (New York: McGraw-Hill, 1974), pp. 271–272.

Webster's Intermediate Dictionary

Descriptive Information

Full Title: **Webster's Intermediate Dictionary: A New School Dictionary.** *Editor:* Merriam-Webster Staff. *Publishers:* G. & C. Merriam Co. (Trade Edition); American Book Co. (Text Edition). *Edition Reviewed:* Trade Edition, 1972.

Classification: School & Children—Middle School. *Grade Suitability:* Grade 6 through 10. *Pages:* 24a, 910. *Total Entries:* 57,000. *Graphics:* 700. *Physical Size:* 6¾ by 9½ in.; 24 cm. *LC:* 70-38974. *ISBN:* 0-87779-179-1 (trade). *Lowest Retail Price:* $7.50; to schools, $6.81.

Comments

Webster's Intermediate Dictionary is the middle dictionary in Merriam-Webster's school line. *Webster's New Students Dictionary* (for high school use) and *Webster's New Elementary Dictionary* (for elementary school use) are the other titles in the series. *Webster's Intermediate*, which claims over 57,000 entries and 70,000 definitions, covers common words and phrases "selected chiefly on the basis of their occurrence in textbooks and supplementary reading in all subjects of the school curriculum." Unlike most dictionaries in the middle school category, *Webster's Intermediate* does not include biographical and geographical entries, although the American presidents and vice-presidents are listed in the back, along with the nations of the world and the U.S. states. Vocabulary treatment also differs somewhat from that in the better dictionaries in this class. Although the definitions are full and authoritative, relatively few illustrative examples are given. On the other hand, numerous synonym studies as well as etymologies are included. A substantial dictionary for junior high school students, but overall the Merriam-Webster school series is no match for the excellent Thorndike-Barnhart dictionaries or the fine new Macmillan series.

Other Critical Opinions

American Reference Books Annual 1974 (review by Francis J. Witty), p. 455.
Wilson Library Bulletin (review by Charles A. Bunge), September 1972, p. 91.

Webster's Scholastic Dictionary

Descriptive Information

Full Title: **Webster's Scholastic Dictionary.** *Editor:* Staff produced. *Publisher:* Airmont Publishing Co. *Edition Reviewed:* New Edition, 1976.

Classification: School & Children—Middle School. *Grade Suitability:* Grade 6 through 10. *Pages:* 416. *Total Entries:* 30,000. *Graphics:* 50. *Physical Size:* 4¼ by 7 in.; 18 cm. *Lowest Retail Price:* $1.50 paper.

Comments

Webster's Scholastic Dictionary, a paperback work first copyrighted in 1966, is said to be "designed for the use of the pupil in schools, but it can be of equal value for everyone for general use." How the vocabulary was selected is not indicated but, despite the recent copyright (1976), the dictionary is considerably out-of-date. For instance, the following words and phrases are not included: *data bank, funky, gene, minibike,* and *spaced-out.* Nor is most recent meaning given for such terms as *gay* and *mace.* The word *busing* (or *bussing*) does not appear in *Webster's Scholastic.* In fact the definition provided for *bus* is simply "an omnibus." Aside from definitions, the dictionary offers only spelling and parts of speech. Entries are not even syllabified. The graphics, print, and paper are of inferior quality. Definitely not recommended for either student or family use.

Winston Dictionary for Schools

Descriptive Information

Full Title: **The Winston Dictionary for Schools.** *Editor:* Morgan L. Walters. *Publisher:* Holt, Rinehart & Winston. Former title: *The New Winston Simplified Dictionary for Young People* (1936). *Edition Reviewed:* Text Edition, 1967.

Classification: School & Children—Middle School. *Grade Suitability:* Grade 6 through 10. *Pages:* x, 950. *Total Entries;* 46,000. *Graphics:* 1,725. *Physical Size:* 6¼ by 8¾ in.; 22 cm. *LC:* 36-17418. *ISBN:* 0-03-063485-7. *School Price:* $5.36.

Consumer Note

At one time there was a whole line of Winston dictionaries, including the 100,000-entry *Winston Dictionary,* the slightly reduced *Winston Home, School and Office Dictionary,* *The Winston Dictionary for Children* (30,000 entries), and the "New Winston Simplified" series from which *The Winston Dictionary for School* derives. All dictionaries bearing the Winston name are currently out-of-print except for *The Winston Dictionary for Schools,* which was last revised in 1967. The dictionary is woefully out-of-date and, according to the publisher, there are no plans to revise or reissue it. Dictionary consumers are advised to avoid *The Winston Dictionary for Schools.* Note that, as the *Buying Guide* was going to press, the publisher reported the dictionary out of stock.

ELEMENTARY SCHOOL DICTIONARIES

Charlie Brown Dictionary

Descriptive Information

Full Title: **The Charlie Brown Dictionary.** *Author:* Charles M. Schulz. *Publishers:* Random House (hardcover); Scholastic Paperbacks (paper). *Based on:* *The Rainbow Dictionary* by Wendell W. Wright. *Edition Reviewed:* 1973.

Classification: School & Children—Elementary School. *Grade Suitability:* Kindergarten through Grade 3. *Pages:* 399. *Total Entries:* 2,400. *Graphics:* 580. *Physical Size:* 8½ by 11 in.; 28 cm. (hardcover). *LC:* 72-12135. *ISBN:* 0-394-83041-5 (hardcover). *Lowest Retail Price:* $7.95; also $5.95 paper.

Comments

The Charlie Brown Dictionary covers the basic words which "children use in speaking, hear on television and recognize when reading." The vocabulary is based on word frequency studies involving youngsters from five to eight years old. Essentially the vocabulary selection and treatment are modeled on the popular *Rainbow Dictionary*, originally published in 1947, revised in 1959, and to be revised in 1978 (see Appendix A for a brief description). The illustrations, however, now feature the familiar Schulz characters of Snoopy, Charlie Brown, Lucy, Linus, et al. The definitional style is quite simple but effective. Example: The word *guest* has an illustration showing a little girl greeting two boys with presents. The text reads: "Pig-Pen is Violet's *guest.* Pig-Pen is visiting Violet at her home. Charlie Brown is another *guest.* He is also a *visitor.*" *The Charlie Brown Dictionary* is an appealing, colorful dictionary for young children. It compares favorably with the expensive and original *Troll Talking Picture Dictionary* (which comprises both printed text and cassette tapes), *The Weekly Reader Beginning Dictionary*, and the smaller *Words to Know.*

Other Critical Opinions

American Reference Books Annual 1974 (review by Christine L. Wynar), pp. 454–455.
Booklist (review by Lucile Hatch), November 1, 1974, pp. 297–298.

Children's Dictionary

Descriptive Information

Full Title: **The Children's Dictionary.** *Editor:* Staff produced. *Publisher:* A. Wheaton & Co. *Distributor:* British Book Centre. *Edition Reviewed:* New & Revised Edition, 1970.
Classification: School & Children—Elementary School. *Grade Suitability:* Grade 3 through 6. *Pages:* viii, 478. *Total Entries:* 10,000. *Graphics:* None. *Physical Size:* 5 by 7¼ in.; 19 cm. *ISBN:* 0-08-006657-7. *Lowest Retail Price:* $3.25.

Comments

The Children's Dictionary is a British production which includes "those words which would come within the scope of the conversation of normal boys and girls or be found in children's story books." The dictionary deliberately omits "words so simple that every child knows their meaning, likewise words so rare that a child is never likely to meet them." For instance, *and, from,* and *if* are not included. The definitions are quite brief. Aside from spelling and pronunciations, no other information is given, not even the part of speech. The dictionary is strictly British. For instance, *bonnet* is defined as "a covering for machinery such as the engine of a motorcar." The only spelling given for *center* is *centre*. Whatever its merits might be for English children, *The Children's Dictionary* is not recommended for American boys and girls.

Courtis-Watters Illustrated Golden Dictionary

Descriptive Information

Full Title: **The Courtis-Watters Illustrated Golden Dictionary for Young Readers.** *Editors:* Stuart A. Courtis and Garnette Watters. *Illustrators:* Beth Krush and Joe Krush. *Publisher:* Western Publishing Co. Alternate title: *Golden Book Dictionary. Edition Reviewed:* Revised & Expanded Edition, 1965.

Classification: School & Children—Elementary School. *Grade Suitability:* Grade 3 through 6. *Pages:* 668. *Total Entries:* 10,000. *Graphics:* 3,000. *Physical Size:* 7¼ by 10¼ in.; 26 cm. *LC:* 65-18917. *ISBN:* 0-307-66544-5. *Lowest Retail Price:* $7.95.

Comments

The Courtis-Watters Illustrated Golden Dictionary for Young Readers, first published in 1951 and modestly revised in 1965, bases its vocabulary on various standard word lists as well as some 80 elementary school texts and readers. For a time, a six-volume edition entitled the *Golden Book Dictionary* was sold in supermarkets. Although the dictionary is now essentially more than 25 years old, it is still useful as a beginning work. The pronunciations, prepared under the direction of Allen Walker Read, are simple and clear. The definitions are likewise lucid. Over 20,000 illustrative sentences contribute to definitional clarity. As a rule, the dictionary contains few idioms and slang meanings. Example: Colloquial usages of *creep, grind,* and *moon* are not given, nor are such idiomatic expressions as *lay aside, lay away, lay off,* and *lay out.* The graphics consist of small black-and-white line drawings of unexceptional quality. There are also eight pages of color plates in the middle of the dictionary depicting military uniforms, national flags, animals, birds, etc. Although they are somewhat larger in terms of number of entries, the *Macmillan Dictionary for Children* (same as the *Macmillan Beginning Dictionary*) and the *Scott, Foresman Beginning Dictionary* (a revision of the *Thorndike-Barnhart Beginning Dictionary*) are comparable and preferable to *Courtis-Watters Illustrated.* Not only are the Macmillan and Scott, Foresman dictionaries much more up-to-date but they are better designed and provide more thorough treatment of vocabulary.

Dictionary of Basic Words

Descriptive Information

Full Title: **Dictionary of Basic Words.** *Editor:* Day A. Perry. *Publisher:* Childrens Press. *Edition Reviewed:* 1969.

Classification: School & Children—Elementary School. *Grade Suitability:* Grade 2 through 8. *Pages:* xxiii, 614. *Total Entries:* 21,000. *Graphics:* 2,000.

Physical Size: 8¾ by 11¼ in.; 29 cm. *LC:* 73-86343. *Lowest Retail Price:* $14.95.

Comments

The *Dictionary of Basic Words* has been compiled to serve "the basic vocabulary needs of those who have outgrown a beginning dictionary but do not want or cannot use the usual intermediate dictionary containing 40,000 or more words." The vocabulary is based on the Wolfe High Correlation Word List compiled by Dr. Josephine B. Wolfe, a well-known children's educator and textbook author. The dictionary includes standard core words as well as numerous idioms (e.g., under *short* the user finds *cut short, fall short of*, and *in short*) and colloquial meanings (e.g., *dope* has five meanings, one of which is "a stupid person"). The definitions are reasonably clear and detailed enough for elementary school pupils. Like almost all school dictionaries currently available, definitions are augmented by many illustrative examples which help clarify the connotations of words. The graphics, all in pastel color, are usually instructive though not always sufficiently detailed. Example: The two illustrations accompanying *printing press* merely convey the overall impression of two types of presses, but neither is captioned to show how the press works, the names of its various parts, etc. Also, some of the illustrations are blurred. The somewhat larger and newer *Macmillan Dictionary for Children* (same as the *Macmillan Beginning Dictionary;* 30,000 entries, 1975) and *Scott, Foresman Beginning Dictionary* (25,000 entries, 1976) are both preferable to the *Dictionary of Basic Words* purely on the basis of quality. In addition, the Macmillan and Scott, Foresman dictionaries are less expensive.

Other Critical Opinions

American Reference Books Annual 1970, p. 50 (in Vol. 2).

General Basic English Dictionary

Descriptive Information

Full Title: **The General Basic English Dictionary.** *Editor:* C. K. Ogden. *Publisher:* Evans Brothers, Ltd. *Distributor:* Rowman & Littlefield. *Edition Reviewed:* 1940.

Classification: School & Children—Elementary School. *Grade Suitability:* Grade 3 through 8. *Pages:* x, 438. *Total Entries:* 20,000. *Graphics:* 250. *Physical Size:* 5 by 7½ in.; 19 cm. *Lowest Retail Price:* $5.00.

Comments

The *General Basic English Dictionary* is a work of British origin first published in 1940. There is also apparently a 1942 revised edition. Rowman & Littlefield, however, distributes only the original edition. The dictionary provides "more than 40,000 senses of over 20,000 words" defined in what the editor calls 850 basic words, along with "the 50 international words which go with them." Numerous idioms are also defined, e.g., under *come* the user finds such expressions as *come of age, come off well, come out, come round*, and *come to light.* Because the definitions are limited to about 900 essential words, they are quite clear. Meanings, however, are strictly British (e.g., *bonnet* is "part covering engine of automobile") as are spellings (e.g., *labour*). In addition, pronunciations are those "common in the south of England among persons of good education." *The General Basic English Dictionary,* now nearly 40 years old, has minimal value for American users, not only because of its British orientation but its advanced age. The dictionary nevertheless still might be of limited value as a supplementary text in the teaching of English as a second or foreign language.

Ginn Beginning Dictionary

Descriptive Information

Full Title: **The Ginn Beginning Dictionary.** *Editor:* William Morris, Editor in Chief. *Publisher:* Ginn & Co. Alternate title: *The Weekly Reader Beginning Dictionary* (Trade Edition). *Edition Reviewed:* Text Edition, 1973.

Classification: School & Children—Elementary School. *Grade Suitability:* Grade 2 through 4. *Pages:* 352. *Total Entries:* 5,000. *Graphics:* 600. *Physical Size:* 8 by 11¼ in.; 29 cm. *School Price:* $4.65.

Consumer Note

The *Ginn Beginning Dictionary* has exactly the same contents as *The Weekly Reader Beginning Dictionary,* a trade dictionary for children published by Grosset & Dunlap. See the profile of *The Weekly Reader Beginning Dictionary* which follows in this section of the *Buying Guide* for further information.

Ginn Intermediate Dictionary

Descriptive Information

Full Title: **The Ginn Intermediate Dictionary.** *Editor:* William Morris, Editor in Chief. *Publisher:* Ginn & Co. Alternate title: *The Xerox Intermediate Dictionary* (Trade Edition). *Edition Reviewed:* Text Edition, 1974.

Classification: School & Children—Elementary School. *Grade Suitability:* Grade 3 through 8. *Pages:* 800. *Total Entries:* 34,000. *Graphics:* 1,400. *Physical Size:* 8 by 11¼ in.; 29 cm. *School Price:* $6.95.

Consumer Note

The *Ginn Intermediate Dictionary* is exactly the same work as *The Xerox Intermediate Dictionary,* a trade dictionary for upper elementary children published by Xerox Education Publications and distributed by Grosset & Dunlap. *Ginn Intermediate* is accompanied by a teacher's manual available for an additional $1.50. For further information, see the profile of *The Xerox Intermediate Dictionary* which follows in this section of the *Buying Guide.*

Macmillan Beginning Dictionary

Descriptive Information

Full Title: **Macmillan Beginning Dictionary.** *Editors:* William D. Halsey, Editorial Director; Christopher G. Morris, Editor. *Publisher:* Macmillan Publishing Co. Alternate title: *Macmillan Dictionary for Children* (Trade Edition). *Edition Reviewed:* Text Edition, 1976.

Classification: School & Children—Elementary School. *Grade Suitability:* Grade 3 through 8. *Pages:* xii, 724. *Total Entries:* 30,000. *Graphics:* 1,200. *Physical Size:* 8¼ by 10¼ in.; 26 cm. *School Price:* $9.84.

Consumer Note

The *Macmillan Beginning Dictionary* is the text edition of the *Macmillan Dictionary for Children*. The contents of the two dictionaries are identical except for somewhat different introductions. For further information see the profile of the *Macmillan Dictionary for Children* immediately following.

Macmillan Dictionary for Children

Descriptive Information

Full Title: **Macmillan Dictionary for Children.** *Editors:* William D. Halsey, Editorial Director; Christopher G. Morris, Editor. *Publisher:* Macmillan Publishing Co. Alternate title: *Macmillan Beginning Dictionary* (Text Edition). *Edition Reviewed:* Trade Edition, 1976.

Classification: School & Children—Elementary School. *Grade Suitability:* Grade 3 through 8. *Pages:* xii, 724. *Total Entries:* 30,000. *Graphics:* 1,200. *Physical Size:* 8¼ by 10¼ in.; 26 cm. *LC:* 74-24661. *Lowest Retail Price:* $10.95.

Comments

The *Macmillan Dictionary for Children* is the elementary work in the new Macmillan school dictionary series. The other titles are the *Macmillan School Dictionary* (for junior high school students) and the *Macmillan Dictionary* (for senior high school students). The *Macmillan Dictionary for Children* (a trade edition) is also published with a slightly modified introduction under the title *Macmillan Beginning Dictionary* (a text edition). Like the other Macmillan dictionaries, the *Macmillan Dictionary for Children* is a carefully designed, authoritatively produced dictionary. The vocabulary represents those words and phrases young people commonly encounter in their reading, everyday conversation, and viewing. Unfortunately, however, idioms (e.g., *by all means*) are not included. The definitions are clear and contain numerous illustrative examples which aid definitional clarity. The dictionary deliberately omits syllabication and diacritical marks in the main entry so that the child will see each word "exactly the way it would look in any book, magazine or newspaper you may be reading." Syllabication and pronunciations are given, however, at the end of the entry. Some simple etymologies are also included, along with various usage notes. The colorful illustrations and appealing format are outstanding features. Not only will they attract and hold the child's attention but they help clarify or enhance the written definition. Without doubt, the two best elementary school dictionaries on the American market today are the *Macmillan Dictionary for Children* and *Scott, Foresman Beginning Dictionary* (a recent revision of the *Thorndike-Barnhart Beginning Dictionary*), with the edge going to the latter which includes idioms and is graphically superior.

Other Critical Opinions

American Reference Books Annual 1976 (review by Eleanor Elving Schwartz), pp. 541–542.
Booklist, October 1, 1975, pp. 261–262.

New Horizon Ladder Dictionary

Descriptive Information

Full Title: **The New Horizon Ladder Dictionary of the English Language.** *Editors:* John Robert Shaw and Janet Shaw. *Publisher:* New American Library. *Edition Reviewed:* Revised Edition, 1970.

Classification: School & Children—Elementary School. *Grade Suitability:* Grade 2 through 6. *Pages:* xviii, 686. *Total Entries:* 9,500. *Graphics:* 400. *Physical Size:* 4 by 7 in.; 18 cm. *Lowest Retail Price:* $0.95 paper.

Comments

The New Horizon Ladder Dictionary of the English Language is a paperback dictionary "based on 5,000 of the most frequently used words in written English—words a person will most often see and need to know in reading general English literature." First published in 1969 and revised the next year, *New Horizon Ladder* was prepared under the auspices of the United States Information Agency which, according to the acknowledgments, "wanted a dictionary in simple English for use in its overseas program among foreign readers of English as a second language." The vocabulary, based on word frequency counts and basic English word lists, is "divided into five levels or ladder rungs of approximately one thousand words each, according to the frequency of their use." After each main entry there is a number (in parentheses) from one to five indicating frequency of use. Example: The adjective *capable* has the number three (3) following the boldfaced entry. The noun *cell* is followed by the number two (2). Note, however, that different meanings of the same word (e.g., *cell* is defined as both a small room and a basic part of the structure of all living matter) are not numerically differentiated. Definitions are quite simple but usually detailed enough for the dictionary's intended usership. Like almost all school dictionaries, *New Horizon Ladder* includes many illustrative examples.

Although compiled for an American propaganda agency, no discernible political bias appears in the definitions of such words as *capitalism, communism, dictator, freedom,* and *liberty.* The graphics are very small black-and-white line drawings, usually of common objects like celery, a hammer, and pants. The relatively large type and single-column page render this one of the more readable paperback dictionaries available. *New Horizon Ladder* lacks the overall excellence of such larger elementary school dictionaries as the *Macmillan Dictionary for Children* and the *Scott, Foresman Beginning Dictionary*, but its respectable level of quality, inexpensive price, and paperbound format make it an attractive dictionary for young children either in the home or classroom where cost is a principal concern. Also, because of its "ladder" approach to basic English vocabulary, *New Horizon Ladder* is useful for remedial reading students and those studying English as a second language.

Other Critical Opinions

American Reference Books Annual 1972, pp. 466–467.

Oxford Children's Dictionary in Colour

Descriptive Information

Full Title: **The Oxford Children's Dictionary in Colour.** *Editors:* John Weston and Alan Spooner. *Publisher:* Oxford University Press. *Edition Reviewed:* 1976.

Classification: School & Children—Elementary School. *Grade Suitability:* Grade 1 through 3. *Pages:* 320. *Total Entries:* 15,000. *Graphics:* 227. *Physical Size:* 6 by 7¾ in.; 20 cm. *ISBN:* 0-19-910209-0. *Lowest Retail Price:* $6.00.

Comments

The Oxford Children's Dictionary in Colour is a simple listing of about 11,500 main entries, plus 3,500 subentries. The vocabulary is very basic but British in orientation. For instance, *public school* is defined as "a kind of secondary school where fees are charged." Spellings are also entirely British, as the title suggests. Pronunciations, etymologies, parts of speech, etc. are not given. Some illustrative examples are provided but relatively few when compared with most American school dictionaries. The main entry word or phrase is printed in red, as are the guide words at the top of each page. The illustrations, which average less than one per page, are attractive and they usually help clarify or augment the simple definitions. Although the dictionary is appealing to the eye, its contents are too limited and too British for American users, no matter how young. *The Oxford Children's Dictionary in Colour* simply cannot compete with the better American elementary school dictionaries, such as the *Macmillan Dictionary for Children* and the *Scott, Foresman Beginning Dictionary*.

Other Critical Opinions

American Reference Books Annual 1977 (review by Carolyn J. Henderson), pp. 523–524.
Booklist, January 15, 1977, pp. 747–748.

Picture Dictionary for Children

Descriptive Information

Full Title: **The Picture Dictionary for Children.** *Editors:* Garnette Watters and Stuart A. Courtis. *Publisher:* Grosset & Dunlap. *Edition Reviewed:* Revised Edition, 1977.

Classification: School & Children—Elementary School. *Grade Suitability:* Kindergarten through Grade 3. *Pages:* 384. *Total Entries:* 5,000. *Graphics:* 1,450. *Lowest Retail Price:* $3.95 paper.

Comments

The Picture Dictionary for Children, originally published in 1938, is a smaller and earlier version of *The Courtis-Watters Illustrated Golden Dictionary for Young Readers,* a dictionary aimed at upper elementary school youngsters. The dictionary was revised in 1948 and again in 1977, when it was newly illustrated and issued in a paperback edition. The vocabulary is very basic and the treatment limited to simple definitions, spellings, and illustrative sentences. There are no synonyms, etymologies, parts of speech, or the like. The graphics are small drawings in color which are placed near the word being defined. The dictionary compares favorably with *The Weekly Reader Beginning Dictionary* (also titled *The Ginn Beginning Dictionary*) and *The Charlie Brown Dictionary,* both of which are appealing works for very young readers. *The Picture Dictionary for Children* will be especially useful for slow readers.

Scott, Foresman Beginning Dictionary

Descriptive Information

Full Title: **Scott, Foresman Beginning Dictionary.** *Editor:* Clarence L. Barnhart. *Publishers:* Doubleday & Co. (Trade Edition); Scott, Foresman & Co. (Text Edition). Former titles: *Thorndike-Barnhart Beginning Dictionary* (1952–1974); *Thorndike-Century Beginning Dictionary* (1945–1951). *Edition Reviewed:* Text Edition, 1976.

Classification: School & Children—Elementary School. *Grade Suitability:* Grade 3 through 8. *Pages:* 49, 718. *Total Entries:* 25,000. *Graphics:* 1,000. *Physical Size:* 8¼ by 10¼ in.; 26 cm. *ISBN:* 0-673-4756 (text). *Lowest Retail Price:* $10.95; to schools & libraries, $7.50.

Comments

The *Scott, Foresman Beginning Dictionary* is the successor to the popular and authoritative *Thorndike-Barnhart Beginning Dictionary* (which remains in print). Note that the dictionary is still prepared and edited by Clarence L. Barnhart and adheres to the lexicographical principles established by E. L. Thorndike almost four decades ago. Note also that Thorndike and Barnhart are the preeminent names associated with American school dictionaries. The *Scott, Foresman Beginning Dictionary* provides 25,220 main entries, 32,365 individual definitions, nearly 23,000 illustrative sentences and phrases, and some 300 etymologies. The vocabulary, which includes many idiomatic expressions, was selected on the basis of recent word frequency counts and treatment derives from a citation file of over one million examples. As a result, the definitions are clear, precise, and informative. The excellent Thorndike-Barnhart pronunciation system is used.

The most striking feature of the dictionary, however, is its innovative use of graphics and improved format design. According to the editors' introduction, "The purpose of the improved format is to stimulate young people to notice and retain interesting facts and impressions about words." This is not an empty or self-serving statement. Indeed, the *Scott, Foresman Beginning Dictionary* has the most impressive illustrations and design of any dictionary currently on the American market, including the handsomely illustrated *American Heritage Dictionary*. The pictorial illustrations in *Scott, Foresman* include color and black-and-white photographs, drawings, art reproductions, cartoons, movie stills, and collages. Even more exciting, the graphics depict such abstract concepts as *inedible*, *indiscreet*, and *infancy*. The editors point out that "Words that express feelings, ideas, and actions deserve to be illustrated as much as words for things. Art can be very effective when called on to express melancholy, gleeful, affection, blacken, breathtaking, and similar words. Dramatizing such words broadens and deepens young people's conversational and written vocabulary. This new approach to dictionary illustration is pioneered in the Beginning Dictionary." The *Scott, Foresman Beginning Dictionary* is currently the most authoritative, up-to-date, and best illustrated elementary school dictionary available.

Other Critical Opinions

American Reference Books Annual 1977 (review by Evelyn F. Searls), p. 523.

Thorndike-Barnhart Beginning Dictionary

Descriptive Information

Full Title: **Thorndike-Barnhart Beginning Dictionary**. *Editor:* Clarence L. Barnhart. *Publishers:* Doubleday & Co. (Trade Edition); Scott, Foresman & Co. (Text Edition). Former title: *Thorndike-Century Beginning Dictionary* (1945–1951). *Edition Reviewed:* Eighth (Trade) Edition, 1974.

Classification: School & Children—Elementary School. *Grade Suitability:* Grade 3 through 8. *Pages:* 49, 718. *Total Entries:* 26,000. *Graphics:* 1,300. *Physical Size:* 7 by 9½ in.; 24 cm. *Lowest Retail Price:* $8.50; to schools & libraries, $5.97.

Consumer Note

The *Thorndike-Barnhart Beginning Dictionary*, originally published in 1952 as a revision of the *Thorndike-Century Beginning Dictionary*, has been superseded by the *Scott, Foresman Beginning Dictionary* (1976), an outstanding work for elementary school students. Consumers are advised that, although the *Thorndike-Barnhart Beginning Dictionary* (Eighth Edition, 1974) remains relatively up-to-date and is certainly an authoritative dictionary, the *Scott, Foresman Beginning Dictionary* is by far the better buy. Not only does the *Scott, Foresman Beginning Dictionary* incorporate the latest vocabulary information but it represents a dramatic advance in the area of pictorial illustrations among school and general dictionaries. For further information, see the profile of the *Scott, Foresman Beginning Dictionary* immediately preceding this note.

Troll Talking Picture Dictionary

Descriptive Information

Full Title: **Troll Talking Picture Dictionary.** *Authors:* Text by Robyn Supraner; Pictures by Paul Mauk. *Publisher:* Troll Associates. *Edition Reviewed:* 1974.

Classification: School & Children—Elementary School. *Grade Suitability:* Kindergarten through Grade 3. *Contents:* 16 cassette tapes; 64 paperback books (16 separate volumes, 4 copies each); and a teacher's classroom guide—all in a display box. *Cassette Length:* 15 minutes each side (8 hours total listening). *Pages:* 48 pages each book (3,072 pages the set). *Total Entries:* 1,400. *Graphics:* 1,600. *Physical Size:* Each booklet is 5½ by 8 in. (20 cm.); display box is 11 by 12 by 8¾ in. (28 cm.). *School & Library Price:* $145.00.

Comments

The *Troll Talking Picture Dictionary* is a read-along dictionary which consists of 16 cassette tapes and 16 individual *Let's Discover Words* booklets, covering the alphabet from *A* to *Z*. Four copies of each booklet are provided. The vocabulary covered includes basic words likely to be encountered by very young children. For instance, the *Let's Discover M Words* booklet covers *machine, magic, magnet, mail, mailman, make, make-believe, man, many, map, maple, march, March, marigold, marionette, market, mask, match, may, May, meal,* and about 60 more similar words. The text accompanying each entry ranges from two to six lines and is written to instruct as well as interest the young child. Example: The word *museum* is "a place where you can go to see beautiful pictures, or pots and beads and costumes that were used long, long ago. Marjorie is looking at the skeleton of a dinosaur in this museum." The colorful illustrations which complement each word feature various animals which will delight most children. The cassettes (the talking part of *Troll*) are keyed to the *Let's Discover Words* booklets. The audio quality, oral interpretation, and sound effects (including background music) are all excellent. Librarians and teachers have come to know Troll Associates as a publisher of high quality read-along materials which are enthusiastically received by children. The *Troll Talking Picture Dictionary*, though expensive, is a unique elementary school dictionary which will be useful in the classroom, both for normal and remedial instruction.

Other Critical Opinions

Booklist, June 15, 1975, p. 1067.

Webster's New Elementary Dictionary

Descriptive Information

Full Title: **Webster's New Elementary Dictionary.** *Editor:* Merriam-Webster Staff. *Publishers:* G. & C. Merriam Co. (Trade Edition); American Book Co. (Text Edition). Former title: *Webster's Elementary Dictionary.* *Edition Reviewed:* Trade Edition, 1975.

Classification: School & Children—Elementary School. *Grade Suitability:* Grade 3 through 8. *Pages:* 16a, 607. *Total Entries:* 32,000. *Graphics:* 1,200. *Physical Size:* 6¾ by 9½ in.; 24 cm. *ISBN:* 0-87779-275-5 (trade). *Lowest Retail Price:* $5.95; to schools, $6.27.

Comments

Webster's New Elementary Dictionary first appeared in 1965, replacing *Webster's Elementary Dictionary,* a 38,000-entry beginning dictionary originally published in the early 1940s. *Webster's New Elementary* is the smallest, most rudimentary of Merriam-Webster's school dictionary series. The other titles in the series are *Webster's New Students Dictionary* (for high school use) and *Webster's Intermediate Dictionary* (for middle school use). As is the case with all the titles in the series, vocabulary selection is based on word frequency studies and treatment on the extensive citation file maintained by the publisher. The definitions tend to be thorough, considering the intended usership. They are also clearly written and sometimes clarified or enhanced by illustrative phrases. There are also some 200 etymologies, numerous small black-and-white line drawings, and several typical supplements in the back (abbreviations, lists of presidents and vice-presidents, countries, etc.).

Although *Webster's New Elementary* is an authoritative, up-to-date, lucid, and clearly printed dictionary, it is not as impressive as the comparable sized *Macmillan Dictionary for Children* and *Scott, Foresman Beginning Dictionary,* both of which provide many more illustrative examples and pictorial illustrations. In addition, the latter two dictionaries each have a more inviting layout and design. Looking at a page in *Webster's New Elementary* and then one in the *Scott, Foresman Beginning Dictionary* is like going from a newspaper to a glossy magazine.

Other Critical Opinions

American Reference Books Annual 1976 (review by Christine L. Wynar), pp. 542–543.

Webster's New World Dictionary for Young Readers

Descriptive Information

Full Title: **Webster's New World Dictionary for Young Readers.** *Editor:* David B. Guralnik, Editor in Chief. *Publisher:* Collins+World. Former title: *Webster's New World Dictionary: Elementary Edition.* *Edition Reviewed:* 1976.

Classification: School & Children—Elementary School. *Grade Suitability:* Grade 3 through 8. *Pages:* v, 826. *Total Entries:* 44,000. *Graphics:* 1,700. *Physical Size:* 7 by 10 in.; 25 cm. *LC:* 76-7332. *ISBN:* 0-529-04509-5. *Lowest Retail Price:* $7.95.

Comments

Webster's New World Dictionary for Young Readers, a revision of the publisher's earlier Elementary Edition of *Webster's New World Dictionary*, bases its vocabulary on word lists geared to grades 4 through 8 as well as on an examination of recent textbooks covering those grades and on the advice of teachers and educators around the country. The vocabulary includes common words and idioms, abbreviations, and biographical and geographical entries. Definitions are brief but clear and precise. Illustrative sentences and phrases are sometimes provided to clarify meanings in context. Occasionally usage notes accompany the definitions. Example: The noun *funk* is defined as "the condition of being afraid or in a panic, because of cowardliness." The definition is followed by the note, "*used only in everyday talk*." The graphics are typical, small line drawings, usually sepia colored. They are helpful as definitional aids but unexceptional in quality. The guide words at the top of each page are also printed in sepia, giving the dictionary a touch of color. *Webster's New World Dictionary for Young Readers* is up-to-date, authoritative, and fairly attractively printed and designed. But like *Webster's New Elementary Dictionary* (which it closely resembles), it cannot match the overall quality of the two best dictionaries in the elementary school category, namely, the *Macmillan Dictionary for Children* and the *Scott, Foresman Beginning Dictionary* (a revision of the *Thorndike-Barnhart Beginning Dictionary*).

Weekly Reader Beginning Dictionary

Descriptive Information

Full Title: **The Weekly Reader Beginning Dictionary.** *Editor:* William Morris, Editor in Chief. *Publisher:* Grosset & Dunlap. Alternate title: *The Ginn Beginning Dictionary* (Text Edition). *Edition Reviewed:* Trade Edition, 1973.

Classification: School & Children—Elementary School. *Grade Suitability:* Grade 2 through 4. *Pages:* 352. *Total Entries:* 5,000. *Graphics:* 600. *Physical Size:* 8 by 11¼ in.; 29 cm. *LC:* 73-86458. *ISBN:* 0-448-11569-7. *Lowest Retail Price:* $6.95.

Comments

The Weekly Reader Beginning Dictionary, a trade dictionary, is also published in a text edition under the title *The Ginn Beginning Dictionary*. The dictionary is very simple, covering the basic vocabulary beginning readers will encounter in textbooks and more informal sources. Vocabulary treatment is also quite rudimentary. Ordinarily all that is given is a brief definition followed by a short sentence illustrating use of the word in context. Example: The entry *lift* is as follows: "To raise to a higher place or position. *Lift* the box onto the table." Also the past tense and present participle (*lifted* and *lifting*) are listed with the main entry. The graphics are colorful illustrations placed in the wide outer margins. The print is large and clear and the layout appealing. *The Weekly Reader Beginning Dictionary* is quite similar in scope and purpose to *The Charlie Brown Dictionary*, *The Picture Dictionary for Children*, the *Word Wonder Dictionary*, and, as far as vocabulary coverage is concerned, the *Troll Talking Picture Dictionary* (a unique read-along dictionary which comprises both printed text and cassette tapes).

Other Critical Opinions

Booklist, December 15, 1974, pp. 430–431.

Word Wonder Dictionary

Descriptive Information

Full Title: **Word Wonder Dictionary**. *Author:* Doris Whitman. *Publisher:* Holt, Rinehart & Winston. *Edition Reviewed:* Text Edition, 1966.

Classification: School & Children—Elementary School. *Grade Suitability:* Grade 2 through 4. *Pages:* 377. *Total Entries:* 1,500. *Graphics:* 500. *Physical Size:* 8 by 9½ in.; 24 cm. *LC:* 66-10828. *ISBN:* 0-03-047750-6. *School & Library Price:* $5.64.

Comments

Word Wonder Dictionary is limited to the most basic words for beginning readers, such as *brush, bud, build, building, bunch, bug, burn,* and *bus*. Words of more than one syllable are syllabified and accent marks indicated. Entries are defined only by illustrative quotations and sentences. A sentence illustration is provided for each meaning of a word. Example: The word *post* has four verbal illustrations, showing how *post* is used as a noun (e.g., an iron *post*), verb (to *post* a letter), etc. Following the illustrative sentences, various derivatives of the main entry are indicated, again through sentence illustrations, e.g., "Indians used to get supplies at the *trading post*." Pictorial illustrations (black-and-white drawings with light blue shading) appear in the outer margins. They complement the entries but are usually more decorative than instructional. A drawing of a post card, for instance, accompanies the entry *post*. There are also some useful appendixes dealing with synonyms, rhyming words, colors, numbers, and letter writing. *Word Wonder Dictionary* is attractively printed and designed. It will appeal to the same audience as *The Charlie Brown Dictionary*, *The Picture Dictionary for Children*, *The Weekly Reader Beginning Dictionary*, and the *Troll Talking Picture Dictionary*. Note that, as the *Buying Guide* was going to press, the publisher reported *Word Wonder Dictionary* out of stock.

Words to Know

Descriptive Information

Full Title: **Words to Know.** *Authors:* Harry Bricker, Yvonne Beckwith, and the Editors of the *New Standard Encyclopedia. Publisher:* Standard Educational Corp. *Edition Reviewed:* 1969.

Classification: School & Children—Elementary School. *Grade Suitability:* Kindergarten through Grade 3. *Pages:* 215. *Total Entries:* 1,200. *Graphics:* 1,200. *Physical Size:* 7¼ by 10¼ in.; 26 cm. *LC:* 68-54585. *ISBN:* 0-87392-001-5. *Lowest Retail Price:* $5.95.

Comments

Words to Know, according to the authors' foreword, is "a beginning word book for young children at various stages of reading development." Colorful drawings accompany each entry which merely consists of the entry word and a sentence or two illustrating its use in context. Example: The word *play* is "defined" by these sentences: "Pam is in a school play. She is the princess in the play." A large drawing shows Pam on stage. In the back of the book there is an alphabetical list of all the words used in the dictionary. The list can be used as an index to the main *A–Z* portion or, as the authors note, "it may be used to discover which words the child is able to recognize without the pictorial clues and which words he has not yet mastered." *Words to Know* is a fairly appealing introduction to some 1,200 basic words. Unfortunately, the drawings and illustrative examples show evidence of sex role stereotyping. Example: On page 52 the reader encounters the word *doctor* which is illustrated by a man ministering to a sick child. On page 132 *nurse* shows a woman with the sentence "Nancy wants to be a nurse someday." *Words to Know,* which is part of the publisher's *Child Horizons* series (a seven-volume collection of books for young children), is now ten years old and in need of revision. It does not compare well with such similar titles as *The Charlie Brown Dictionary* and *The Weekly Reader Beginning Dictionary.*

Other Critical Opinions

American Reference Books Annual 1970, p. 49 (in Vol. 2).

Xerox Intermediate Dictionary

Descriptive Information

Full Title: **The Xerox Intermediate Dictionary.** *Editor:* William Morris, Editor in Chief. *Publisher:* Xerox Family Education Services. *Distributor:* Grosset & Dunlap. Alternate title: *The Ginn Intermediate Dictionary* (Text Edition). *Edition Reviewed:* Trade Edition, 1974.

Classification: School & Children—Elementary School. *Grade Suitability:* Grade 3 through 6. *Pages:* 800. *Total Entries:* 34,000. *Graphics:* 1,400. *Physical Size:* 8 by 11¼ in.; 29 cm. *LC:* 73-75574. *ISBN:* 0-88375-0101. *Lowest Retail Price:* $8.95.

Comments

The Xerox Intermediate Dictionary covers the basic vocabulary likely to be encountered by upper elementary and middle school students. The dictionary also includes some standard abbreviations (e.g., *M.D.*), entries for each American state (e.g., *Florida*), and numerous colloquial and slang terms (e.g., *hoagie, loser,* and *pot shot*). According to the editor's introduction, "many hundreds of young people helped to choose the words" included in *Xerox Intermediate.* The inclusion of such words as *doodle, grippe, nitty-gritty, pimple,* and *pot* (meaning marijuana) reflects this procedure. Biographical and geographical terms (except for U.S. states) are not included, however. Nor are foreign words and phrases. Vocabulary treatment is relatively thorough, considering the intended audience. Definitions tend to be concise but clear and accurate. They are frequently supplemented by illustrative examples. The pronunciation system is simple and reasonably easy to understand. There are no etymologies or synonym studies.

The graphics show the hand of William Morris, who has also edited *The American Heritage Dictionary,* an adult dictionary which has been praised for its creative use of pictorial illustrations. In *Xerox Intermediate* Morris also uses photographs and drawings in wide outer margins while leaving considerable white space "so that there is plenty of room to give you a clear picture of every creature or object that we have illustrated." The illustrations are either in black-and-white or in sienna brown and white. Overall, *Xerox Intermediate* is an authoritative, quite contemporary dictionary which is preferable to the relatively stodgy *Webster's New Elementary Dictionary* and *Webster's New World Dictionary for Young Readers,* both of which are comparable in terms of size and intended usership. On the other hand, *Xerox Intermediate* lacks the all-around depth of treatment and excellent design which characterize the *Scott, Foresman Beginning Dictionary* (a revision of the *Thorndike-Barnhart Beginning Dictionary*) and the *Macmillan Dictionary for Children,* the two best elementary school dictionaries currently on the American market.

Note that *Xerox Intermediate* is also published in a text edition under the title *The Ginn Intermediate Dictionary.* Consumers should also be aware that a two-volume edition of *Xerox Intermediate* accompanies the *Young Students Encyclopedia,* a 15-volume general encyclopedia for elementary school students published by Xerox Education Publications.

Other Critical Opinions

Booklist, June 15, 1974, pp. 1114–1115.

PRESCHOOL DICTIONARIES

Cat in the Hat Beginner Book Dictionary

Descriptive Information

Full Title: **The Cat in the Hat Beginner Book Dictionary.** *Authors:* Dr. Seuss and P. D. Eastman. *Publisher:* Beginner Books, a division of Random House. *Edition Reviewed:* 1964.

Classification: School & Children—Preschool. *Grade Suitability:* Kindergarten through Grade 1. *Pages:* 133. *Total Entries:* 1,350. *Graphics:* Drawings on every page. *Physical Size:* 8¼ by 11¼ in.; 29 cm. *LC:* 64-11457. *ISBN:* 0-394-81009-0; 0-394-91009-5 (Library Edition). *Lowest Retail Price:* $4.95.

Comments

The *Cat in the Hat Beginner Book Dictionary* is an amusing picture dictionary "full of ridiculous alligators, foolish bears and giraffes' uncles, all racing around and getting involved in nonsensical adventures." The goal is to help the preschool child "recognize, remember, *and really enjoy* a basic elementary vocabulary of 1,350 words." Most of the drawings are captioned. Example: The entry *puzzle* shows an alligator putting together a jigsaw puzzle. The caption is *"Puzzled* by a *puzzle."* A longtime favorite.

Follett Beginning-to-Read Picture Dictionary

Descriptive Information

Full Title: **Follett Beginning-to-Read Picture Dictionary.** *Author:* Alta McIntire. *Illustrator:* Janet LaSalle. *Publisher:* Follett Publishing Co. *Edition Reviewed:* 1959.

Classification: School & Children—Preschool. *Grade Suitability:* Kindergarten through Grade 1. *Pages:* 32. *Total Entries:* 180. *Graphics:* Drawings on every page. *Physical Size:* 6½ by 8¼ in.; 21 cm. *LC:* 59-13400. *ISBN:* 0-695-86989-2; 0-695-46989-4 (Library Edition). *Lowest Retail Price:* $2.50.

Comments

The *Follett Beginning-to-Read Picture Dictionary* simply lists and colorfully illustrates 180 words "chosen because of their importance in daily living as well as their usefulness in written and spoken language and their familiarity to the child." Two pages of sample sentences using the words in the dictionary are in the back. Unexceptional.

Golden Picture Dictionary

Descriptive Information

Full Title: **The Golden Picture Dictionary.** *Authors:* Lucille Ogle and Tina Thoburn. *Illustrator:* Hilary Knight. *Publisher:* Western Publishing Co. *Edition Reviewed:* 1976.

Classification: School & Children—Preschool. *Grade Suitability:* Kindergarten through Grade 1. *Pages:* 160. *Total Entries:* 2,500. *Graphics:* 3,000. *Physical Size:* 8½ by 11¼ in.; 29 cm. *LC:* 76-4596. *ISBN:* 0-307-67861-X (Library Edition). *School & Library Price:* $7.95.

Comments

The *Golden Picture Dictionary* is a large, splashy word-and-picture book which devotes one- and two-page spreads to such elementary terms as *ma-*

chines, plants, and *school.* Within each spread are captioned drawings, e.g., *pupils, playground, globe, teacher, clay, book,* and *crayons.* Usually the user of the dictionary is asked to identify, match, classify, or compare various terms. The letters of the alphabet are similarly introduced. An alphabetical list of all words covered appears in the back of the dictionary. The drawings are lively but perhaps too busy, too small, and too crowded together. Also, the color printing is not always well aligned. But whatever the visual limitations of the book might be, *The Golden Picture Dictionary* accomplishes its goal of helping very young children "associate words with their meanings" through pictorial illustrations. Note that Lucille Ogle edited a small work called the *Golden Picture Dictionary* which appeared in 1954 and is now out of print. It contained only 800 entries and 77 pages. Although the titles are the same, the two dictionaries are apparently not related.

Other Critical Opinions

New York Times Book Review (review by Anne Boes), February 13, 1977, p. 25.

Grosset Starter Picture Dictionary

Descriptive Information

Full Title: **Grosset Starter Picture Dictionary.** *Publisher:* Grosset & Dunlap. *Edition Reviewed:* 1976.
Classification: School & Children—Preschool. *Grade Suitability:* Kindergarten through Grade 1. *Pages:* 92. *Total Entries:* 200. *Graphics:* Drawings on every page. *Physical Size:* 6¼ by 8¼ in.; 21 cm. *LC:* 74-27939. *ISBN:* 0-448-11980-3; 0-448-03277-X (Library Edition). *Lowest Retail Price:* $1.95; to schools & libraries, $3.95 (Library Edition).

Comments

The *Grosset Starter Picture Dictionary* is a typical picture dictionary. Color drawings illustrate the very simple entries, e.g., *bird, bottle, saw.* The entries are captioned and sometimes cover a whole page with related objects depicted. Some entries are extended whereas others are nothing more than a word and a simple drawing. Undistinguished.

Other Critical Opinions

American Reference Books Annual 1977 (review by Ann J. Harwell), p. 522.

International Visual Dictionary

Descriptive Information

Full Title: **International Visual Dictionary.** *Editor:* Leo F. Daniels. *Publisher:* Clute International Institute. *Distributor:* Carroll Book Service. *Edition Reviewed:* 1973.

Classification: School & Children—Preschool. *Grade Suitability:* Kindergarten through Grade 1. *Pages:* ix, 710. *Total Entries:* 3,000. *Graphics:* Drawings on every page. *Physical Size:* 8¼ by 11½ in.; 29 cm. *ISBN:* 0-88217-001-5. *Lowest Retail Price:* $19.95; to schools & libraries, $9.95.

Comments

The *International Visual Dictionary* defines its basic vocabulary terms principally through color drawings. In some instances, entries are defined briefly or their meanings conveyed in illustrative sentences. Moreover, entries are frequently accompanied by nursery rhymes and assorted problems the user is asked to solve. Essentially the dictionary is poorly produced. The color reproduction tends to be blurry, the definitions are sometimes confusing or inappropriate, and, despite the word "International" in the title, the dictionary is American in orientation and content. An overpriced work of poor quality.

Other Critical Opinions

Booklist (review by Margaret R. Sheviak), February 15, 1974, pp. 608–609.

Little Golden Picture Dictionary

Descriptive Information

Full Title: **Little Golden Picture Dictionary.** *Author:* Nancy F. Hulick. *Illustrator:* Tibor Gergely. *Publisher:* Western Publishing Co. *Edition Reviewed:* 1959.
Classification: School & Children—Preschool. *Grade Suitability:* Kindergarten through Grade 1. *Pages:* 24. *Total Entries:* 150. *Graphics:* Drawings on every page. *Physical Size:* 6½ by 8 in.; 21 cm. *ISBN:* 0-307-60369-5. *School & Library Price:* $2.75.

Comments

The *Little Golden Picture Dictionary* very briefly defines basic words by using them in sample sentences. Similar in concept and execution to the *Follett Beginning-to-Read Picture Dictionary* and the *Picture Book Dictionary.*

My First Dictionary

Descriptive Information

Full Title: **My First Dictionary: The Beginner's Word Book.** *Authors:* Laura Oftedal and Nina Jacob. *Illustrator:* Pelagie Doane. *Publisher:* Grosset & Dunlap. *Edition Reviewed:* 1948.
Classification: School & Children—Preschool. *Grade Suitability:* Kindergarten through Grade 1. *Pages:* 140. *Total Entries:* 650. *Graphics:* Drawings on every page. *Physical Size:* 7 by 9¼ in.; 24 cm. *Lowest Retail Price:* $3.50.

Comments

My First Dictionary is limited to simple words which can be readily depicted by pictorial illustrations, like *clown, coach, coal, coat, coat hanger, cobweb,* and *colors*. In addition to a color drawing, each entry has an illustrative sentence, e.g., "The clown made me laugh." A new cover was added in 1976, but the contents remain the same as when first published in 1948.

My First Golden Dictionary

Descriptive Information

Full Title: **My First Golden Dictionary.** *Authors:* Mary Reed and Edith Osswald. *Illustrator:* Richard Scarry. *Publisher:* Western Publishing Co. *Edition Reviewed:* 1957.

Classification: School & Children—Preschool. *Grade Suitability:* Kindergarten through Grade 1. *Pages:* 48. *Total Entries:* 270. *Graphics:* Drawings on every page. *Physical Size:* 8¼ by 11¼ in.; 29 cm. *ISBN:* 0-307-68004-5. *School & Library Price:* $4.95.

Comments

My First Golden Dictionary, illustrated by the distinctive drawings of Richard Scarry, provides about 270 basic words (e.g., *cooky, corn, cow, cowboy*) printed in large, clear type and accompanied by an illustrative sentence or two. In other words, a typical picture dictionary. A cheaper edition is sometimes merchandised in supermarkets. First published in 1949.

My First Picture Dictionary

Descriptive Information

Full Title: **My First Picture Dictionary.** *Authors:* William A. Jenkins and Andrew Schiller. *Publishers:* Lothrop, Lee & Shepard Co. (Library Edition); Scott, Foresman & Co. (Text Edition). *Edition Reviewed:* Revised (Library) Edition, 1977.

Classification: School & Children—Preschool. *Grade Suitability:* Kindergarten through Grade 1. *Pages:* 192. *Total Entries:* 800. *Graphics:* Drawings on every page. *Physical Size:* 7¾ by 9½ in.; 24 cm. *LC:* 76-42108. *ISBN:* 0-688-51786-2 (Library Edition). *Lowest Retail Price:* $6.94; to schools, $3.99.

Comments

My First Picture Dictionary, first published in 1970 and revised in 1977, includes about 800 entries, each with a color drawing and an illustrative sentence or two. The entries are arranged alphabetically in seven categories: people, animals, storybook characters, what we do, things, places, and words that help. There is an index listing all the words contained in the dictionary. An effort has been made to eliminate sexist and racist insinuations in the drawings and text. An appealing and up-to-date picture dictionary. Note that *My Pictionary* (see following profile) is a reduced version of *My First Picture Dictionary* (1970 edition) and that *My Second Picture Dictionary* (see profile following in this section) is the most advanced title in the series.

Other Critical Opinions

American Reference Books Annual 1971, pp. 420–421.

My Pictionary

Descriptive Information

Full Title: **My Pictionary.** *Authors:* W. Cabell Greet, William A. Jenkins, and Andrew Schiller. *Publishers:* Lothrop, Lee & Shepard Co. (Library Edition); Scott, Foresman & Co. (Text Edition). *Edition Reviewed:* Library Edition, 1970.

Classification: School & Children—Preschool. *Grade Suitability:* Kindergarten through Grade 1. *Pages:* 95. *Total Entries:* 535. *Graphics:* Drawings on every page. *Physical Size:* 7¾ by 9½ in.; 24 cm. *LC:* 74-132647. *Lowest Retail Price:* $4.59; to schools, $2.76.

Comments

My Pictionary is an abridged version of *My First Picture Dictionary* (see profile immediately preceding). The vocabulary is carefully chosen for preschoolers and each entry is explained by means of a color drawing and an illustrative sentence. *My Second Picture Dictionary* (see next profile) completes this fine series.

Other Critical Opinions

American Reference Books Annual 1971, pp. 420–421.

My Second Picture Dictionary

Descriptive Information

Full Title: **My Second Picture Dictionary.** *Authors:* W. Cabell Greet, William A. Jenkins, and Andrew Schiller. *Illustrator:* Jack White Graphics. *Publishers:* Lothrop, Lee & Shepard Co. (Library Edition); Scott, Foresman & Co. (Text Edition). *Edition Reviewed:* Library Edition, 1971.

Classification: School & Children—Preschool. *Grade Suitability:* Kindergarten through Grade 3. *Pages:* 384. *Total Entries:* 4,000. *Graphics:* Drawings on every page. *Physical Size:* 7¾ by 9½ in.; 24 cm. *LC:* 71-156919. *Lowest Retail Price:* $7.17; to schools, $5.40.

Comments

My Second Picture Dictionary is the most advanced work in the preschool series which also includes *My Pictionary* and *My First Picture Dictionary*. *My Second Picture Dictionary* bases its vocabulary selection and treatment on the Sixth Edition (1968) of the *Thorndike-Barnhart Beginning Dictionary*. Entries are briefly defined and syllabified but not pronounced. Illustrative sentences are usually provided and plurals and verb tenses are indicated at the end of the entries. The final 60 pages are devoted to geographical information about the U.S. states, the North American continent, etc. Excellent nonsexist illustrations appear in the ample outer margins of each page. *My Pictionary*, *My First Picture Dictionary*, and *My Second Picture Dictionary* form an outstanding graduated series for the child who is beginning to read.

New Golden Dictionary

Descriptive Information

Full Title: **The New Golden Dictionary.** *Author:* Bertha Morris Parker. *Illustrator:* Aurelius Battaglia. *Publisher:* Western Publishing Co. Former Title: *The Golden Dictionary.* *Edition Reviewed:* 1972.

Classification: School & Children—Preschool. *Grade Suitability:* Kindergarten through Grade 1. *Pages:* 118. *Total Entries:* 2,000. *Graphics:* Drawings on every page. *Physical Size:* 10¼ by 12 in.; 30 cm. *LC:* 72-76778. *ISBN:* 0-307-66837-1. *Lowest Retail Price:* $5.95.

Comments

The New Golden Dictionary, a revision of *The Golden Dictionary* (1944), is typical of the "Golden Press" line, which also includes *The Golden Picture Dictionary* and *My First Golden Dictionary*. Basic vocabulary entries are illustrated with colorful drawings as well as sample sentences showing how the words are used in context. The dictionary is attractively designed and produced. It is significantly larger than its predecessor, *The Golden Dictionary*.

Other Critical Opinions

American Reference Books Annual 1974 (review by Christine L. Wynar), p. 454.

Picture Book Dictionary

Descriptive Information

Full Title: **Picture Book Dictionary with a Picture Story.** *Author:* Dilla MacBean. *Illustrator:* Pauline Adams. *Publisher:* Childrens Press. *Edition Reviewed:* New Edition, 1962.

Classification: School & Children—Preschool. *Grade Suitability:* Kindergarten through Grade 1. *Pages:* 48. *Total Entries:* 166. *Graphics:* Drawings on every page. *Physical Size:* 7½ by 8½ in.; 22 cm. *Lowest Retail Price:* $4.50.

Comments

The Picture Book Dictionary simply lists 166 main entries in large (30 point) type and provides a simple sentence using the word. Example: The entry *hat* is accompanied by the sentence "My *hat* is blue." The sentences are also printed in large (24 point) type. There is a color drawing for each word. The drawings are more decorative than instructive. As the subtitle indicates, there is an illustrated story (five pages long) at the end of the book. All key words used in the story and the illustrative sentences are found in the dictionary. A satisfactory starter dictionary, but overpriced.

Storybook Dictionary

Descriptive Information

Full Title: **Storybook Dictionary.** *Author & Illustrator:* Richard Scarry. *Publisher:* Western Publishing Co. Alternate Title: *Richard Scarry's Storybook Dictionary. Edition Reviewed:* 1966.

Classification: School & Children—Preschool. *Grade Suitability:* Kindergarten through Grade 3. *Pages:* 128. *Total Entries:* 2,500. *Graphics:* 1,000. *Physical Size:* 10¼ by 12 in.; 31 cm. *ISBN:* 0-307-65548-2. *School & Library Price:* $6.95.

Comments

Approximately 700 entries cover a total of 2,500 words. Each entry is illustrated or enhanced by a story or verse. Scarry's illustrations featuring animal characters are captivating. The *Storybook Dictionary*, though unrevised since its original publication in 1966, compares well with such similar books as *The Golden Picture Dictionary* and *The New Golden Dictionary*.

Strawberry Picture Dictionary

Descriptive Information

Full Title: **The Strawberry Picture Dictionary.** *Author:* Richard Hefter. *Publisher:* Strawberry Books. *Distributor:* Larousse & Co. *Edition Reviewed:* Trade Edition, 1974.

Classification: School & Children—Preschool. *Grade Suitability:* Kindergarten through Grade 1. *Pages:* 30. *Total Entries:* 375. *Graphics:* Drawings on every page. *Physical Size:* 8¼ by 9¼ in.; 24 cm. *LC:* 74-81375. *ISBN:* 0-88470-010-0 (Trade Edition); 0-88470-011-9 (Library Edition). *Lowest Retail Price:* $3.50.

Comments

The Strawberry Picture Dictionary provides very basic vocabulary terms like *barn, basket, bath, bed, beside,* and *between* with illustrative sentences, e.g., "A bear *between* two boxes." Clever, colorful drawings complete the entries. The drawings usually feature animals (bears, elephants, moose, etc.) which will delight preschoolers. Excellent.

Two Thousand Plus Index & Glossary

Descriptive Information

Full Title: **Two Thousand Plus Index & Glossary.** *Editors:* Margaret Reuter, Jan Celba, Richard Hagle, and Georgianne Heymann. *Publisher:* Raintree Publishers, Ltd. *Distributor:* Macdonald-Raintree. *Edition Reviewed:* 1977.

Classification: School & Children—Preschool. *Grade Suitability:* Kindergarten through Grade 3. *Pages:* 120. *Total Entries:* 2,000. *Graphics:* None. *Physical Size:* 6¼ by 7¼ in.; 19 cm. *ISBN:* 0-8172-1025-3. *Lowest Retail Price:* $4.95.

Comments

Two Thousand Plus Index & Glossary very simply defines 2,000 or so basic words found in the "Macdonald First Reference Library" series, a 50-volume set of heavily illustrated books of 38 pages each on various topics of interest to young children (e.g., rivers, snakes, trees, cowboys). *Two Thousand Plus* also provides page-volume index references to the words in the book series. References to illustrations are likewise given. *Two Thousand Plus* obviously is most useful to those with access to the "Macdonald First Reference Library" series but it can be used separately for simple definitions.

ENGLISH AS A FOREIGN LANGUAGE DICTIONARIES

Naturally those studying English as a foreign language will need constant access to a good current bilingual dictionary published by Cassell's, Scribners, or the like. Eugene P. Sheehy's *Guide to Reference Books* (Ninth Edition, American Library Association, 1976) lists the better known bilingual dictionaries, e.g., Martin, Lee, and Chang's *Korean-English Dictionary.*

Students and teachers of English as a foreign language also use English-language dictionaries in their work. Such dictionaries should be up-to-date, provide clear and simple definitions with illustrative examples, and include a fair selection of common English idioms, such as *come across, go to pieces,* and *shoot the breeze.* Some of the better school and children's dictionaries— the *Scott, Foresman Beginning Dictionary,* for instance—will be useful in this regard, not only because they are up-to-date and cover idioms but because they include numerous illustrative examples showing precisely how a word or phrase is used in context. A few English-language dictionaries have been developed, however, especially for use by students and teachers of English as a foreign language. These dictionaries are described in the following portion of the *Buying Guide*. As might be expected, British publishers like Oxford University Press have been most active in this area since British English is used and studied in so many countries of the world (India, South Africa, Jamaica, etc.).

English-Reader's Dictionary

Descriptive Information

Full Title: **An English-Reader's Dictionary.** *Editors:* A. S. Hornby and E. C. Parnwell. *Publisher:* Oxford University Press. *Edition Reviewed:* Second Edition, 1969.

Classification: School & Children—English as a Foreign Language. *Pages:* viii, 631. *Total Entries:* 25,000. *Graphics:* 300. *Physical Size:* 4 by 6½ in.; 17 cm. *ISBN:* 0-19-431116-3. *Lowest Retail Price:* $2.50 paper.

Comments

An English-Reader's Dictionary, first published in 1952 and thoroughly revised in 1969, is for students and teachers of English as a foreign language at the intermediate level. Specifically, this paperbound dictionary "sets out to help students who have completed an elementary course to read books written in everyday English, to write straightforward, idiomatic compositions, and to converse naturally." It stands between the elementary *Progressive English Dictionary* and the *Oxford Advanced Learner's Dictionary* in the Oxford teaching of English series. British English is emphasized in the vocabulary selection, definitions, and examples. Pronunciations and spellings are also British.

General Basic English Dictionary

Descriptive Information

Full Title: **The General Basic English Dictionary.** *Editor:* C. K. Ogden. *Publisher:* Evans Brothers, Ltd. *Distributor:* Rowman & Littlefield. *Edition Reviewed:* 1940.

Classification: School & Children—English as a Foreign Language. *Pages:* x, 438. *Total Entries:* 20,000. *Graphics:* 250. *Physical Size:* 5 by 7½ in.; 19 cm. *Lowest Retail Price:* $5.00.

Consumer Note

The General Basic English Dictionary, an elementary work of British origin, is described more fully in the section "Elementary School Dictionaries." It is listed here, however, because of its potential usefulness in the teaching of English as a foreign language. Especially noteworthy is the dictionary's inclusion of many idioms as well as its clear and simple definitions, written with the use of less than a thousand basic words. But the dictionary is now very dated and most users will find the recently revised *International Reader's Dictionary* or Oxford's *English-Reader's Dictionary* preferable.

International Reader's Dictionary

Descriptive Information

Full Title: **An International Reader's Dictionary.** *Editor:* Michael West. *Publisher:* Longman. *Edition Reviewed:* New Edition, 1977.
Classification: School & Children—English as a Foreign Language. *Pages:* 320. *Total Entries:* 24,000. *Physical Size:* 5 by 7¼ in.; 19 cm. *Lowest Retail Price:* $2.50.

Comments

An International Reader's Dictionary was initially published in 1965 and substantially revised in 1977. Among the 24,000 terms defined are approximately 6,000 idioms. Although a British production, an effort has been made to include American expressions and meanings. All entries are defined using some 1,500 basic words. These words are listed separately in the back of the dictionary. Designed to meet the vocabulary needs of students and teachers of English as a foreign language at the intermediate level, *An International Reader's Dictionary* compares favorably with Oxford University's *English-Reader's Dictionary*, which is similar in size and purpose. Note that, as the *Buying Guide* was going to press, Longman reported that *An International Reader's Dictionary* is not stocked in the U.S., although it is available in Great Britain.

International Visual Dictionary

Descriptive Information

Full Title: **International Visual Dictionary.** *Editor:* Leo F. Daniels. *Publisher:* Clute International Institute. *Distributor:* Carroll Book Service. *Edition Reviewed:* 1973.
Classification: School & Children—English as a Foreign Language. *Pages:* ix, 710. *Total Entries:* 3,000. *Graphics:* Drawings on every page. *Physical Size:* 8¼ by 11½ in.; 29 cm. *ISBN:* 0-88217-001-5. *Lowest Retail Price:* $19.95; to schools and libraries, $9.95.

Consumer Note

The *International Visual Dictionary*, which is more fully described in the section "Preschool Dictionaries," claims to be a "tool for learning the English language," particularly designed for "children in the early grades of elementary school and for adults learning English," including the "foreign born."

New Horizon Ladder Dictionary

Descriptive Information

Full Title: **The New Horizon Ladder Dictionary of the English Language.** *Editors:* John Robert Shaw and Janet Shaw. *Publisher:* New American Library. *Edition Reviewed:* Revised Edition, 1970.

Classification: School & Children—English as a Foreign Language. *Pages:* xviii, 686. *Total Entries:* 9,500. *Graphics:* 400. *Physical Size:* 4ʹby 7 in.; 18 cm. *Lowest Retail Price:* $0.95 paper.

Consumer Note

The New Horizon Ladder Dictionary, a paperbound dictionary developed for the United States Information Agency, is based on 5,000 frequently used words in written English. The agency commissioned the project so that there would be "a dictionary in simple English for use in its overseas program among foreign readers of English as a second language." A good, inexpensive work for those studying or teaching American English as a foreign language. For further information, see the profile of *New Horizon Ladder* in the section "Elementary School Dictionaries."

Oxford Advanced Learner's Dictionary

Descriptive Information

Full Title: **Oxford Advanced Learner's Dictionary of Current English.** *Editors:* A. S. Hornby with the assistance of A. P. Cowie and J. Windsor Lewis. *Publisher:* Oxford University Press. Former titles: *Idiomatic and Syntactic English Dictionary* (1942); *A Learner's Dictionary of Current English* (1948). *Edition Reviewed:* Third Edition, 1974.

Classification: School & Children—English as a Foreign Language. *Pages:* xxvii, 1055. *Total Entries:* 60,000. *Graphics:* 1,000. *Physical Size:* 5½ by 8¾ in.; 23 cm. *ISBN:* 0-19-431101-5. *Lowest Retail Price:* $10.95.

Comments

The *Oxford Advanced Learner's Dictionary*, first published in Tokyo in 1942 and reprinted as *A Learner's Dictionary of Current English* in 1948, is now in its third and largest edition. It is the most advanced work in the publisher's dictionary series on English for foreigners. The intermediate work in the series is *An English-Reader's Dictionary* with *The Progressive English Dictionary* for beginners. *Oxford Advanced* includes some 11,000 idioms among its 60,000 total entries. The definitions are written in a clear, simple style and meanings are clarified by 50,000 illustrative phrases and sentences. The vocabulary includes numerous Americanisms (labeled "US"). Also, "When the word or phrase is British English and rarely used in American English, (GB) is placed before the definition." Obscene words and idioms (e.g., *fuck off*) are also defined. *Oxford Advanced* provides especially good coverage and treatment of English verb forms and patterns. Instructional material is included in the front matter on proper English syntax—that is, grammatical construction. In addition, the appendixes provide lists of irregular verbs as well as other useful information for the foreign student, such as common affixes, abbreviations, numbers, and weights and measures. The graphics include both drawings and photographs. Overall, an excellent dictionary for advanced students of English as a foreign or second language.

Other Critical Opinions

Booklist, July 15, 1975, pp. 1209–1210.

Progressive English Dictionary

Descriptive Information

Full Title: **The Progressive English Dictionary.** *Editors:* A. S. Hornby and E. C. Parnwell. *Publisher:* Oxford University Press. *Edition Reviewed:* Second Edition, 1972.

Classification: School & Children—English as a Foreign Language. *Pages:* 345. *Total Entries:* 10,000. *Graphics:* 100. *Physical Size:* 4 by 6½ in.; 17 cm. *ISBN:* 0-19-431120-1. *Lowest Retail Price:* $1.50 paper.

Comments

The Progressive English Dictionary, initially published in 1952 and revised in 1972, is the simplest dictionary in the Oxford series designed for students and teachers of English as a foreign language. Other titles in the series are the intermediate *English-Reader's Dictionary* and the larger *Oxford Advanced Learner's Dictionary of Current English. The Progressive English Dictionary*, available only in a paper edition, includes many idioms and emphasizes irregular construction of verbs and plural nouns. The definitions are brief but precise. Unfortunately, like *An English-Reader's Dictionary*, the dictionary's orientation is entirely British. American meanings and expressions, as well as spellings and pronunciations, are not given. Also, the small print and rather crowded page will not appeal to students of English, whether they are children, young adults, or adults.

SPECIAL-PURPOSE DICTIONARIES AND WORDBOOKS

Except for the smallest titles, general English-language dictionaries usually provide at least some information about new words, etymologies, proper usage, idioms, slang and colloquialisms, synonyms and antonyms, spelling, pronunciation, abbreviations, and the like. Understandably, however, general dictionaries rarely offer extended coverage or treatment of any of these specialized areas, except perhaps spelling and pronunciation. Dictionary consumers should be aware, therefore, that numerous special-purpose dictionaries and wordbooks are available which devote themselves entirely to such specialized concerns as etymology, slang, and usage. Students, teachers, and writers, for instance, will find a good synonym dictionary or thesaurus an indispensable complement to the general dictionary, no matter what its size or quality.

The following portion of the *Buying Guide* briefly describes and annotates special-purpose dictionaries and wordbooks currently in print. The categories covered are New Words; Etymology and History of Words; Usage and Idioms; Usage: Style Manuals; Usage: Secretarial Handbooks; Slang and Dialect; Synonyms, Antonyms, and Homonyms; Crossword Puzzles and Word Games; Rhymes; Spelling and Syllabication; Pronunciation; Abbreviations and Acronyms; Signs and Symbols; and Foreign Words and Phrases Commonly Used in English. Titles are arranged alphabetically within each category. For example, *Webster's Collegiate Thesaurus* is entered before *Webster's New Dictionary of Synonyms* in the section "Synonyms, Antonyms, and Homonyms." When looking for a specific title, consult the index at the back of the *Buying Guide*.

NEW WORDS

New words and meanings, of course, are included in the regularly revised general dictionaries like *Webster's New Collegiate Dictionary*, *The American Heritage Dictionary*, and *Webster's New World Dictionary*. Indeed, sometimes these and similar dictionaries appear to be in a frantic race to see which title can include the latest neologisms—that is, new coinages. Apparently dictionary promoters have learned that it is good business to claim more new words and newer new words than one's rivals. Be that as it may, the continuously revised general dictionaries are a good source for new vocabulary. Two other sources are almanacs and yearbooks like *Information Please Almanac* and encyclopedia annuals like *The World Book Year Book* or *The*

Americana Annual. Practically all of these annually revised reference books include a section on new words and meanings which have entered the language during the year covered. Unfortunately, Kenneth Versand's *Polyglot's Lexicon, 1943–1966* (Link Books, 1973), a work which brought together new words and meanings which entered the English language between 1943 and 1966, is no longer in print. There are, however, two excellent separately published wordbooks currently available which deal exclusively with new vocabulary which, according to the citational evidence, is now firmly established in the language. These books are *The Barnhart Dictionary of New English since 1963* and Merriam-Webster's *6,000 Words.*

Barnhart Dictionary of New English since 1963

Descriptive Information

Full Title: **The Barnhart Dictionary of New English since 1963.** *Editors:* Clarence L. Barnhart, Sol Steinmetz, and Robert K. Barnhart. *Publisher:* Barnhart/Harper & Row. *Distributor:* Harper & Row. *Edition Reviewed:* 1973.

Classification: Special-Purpose—New Words. *Pages:* 512. *Total Entries:* 5,000. *Physical Size:* 7 by 9½ in.; 24 cm. *LC:* 73-712. *ISBN:* 0-06-010223-3. *Lowest Retail Price:* $12.95.

Comments

The Barnhart Dictionary of New English since 1963 fully defines some 5,000 new terms and meanings "which have come into the common or working vocabulary of the English-speaking world during the period from 1963 to 1972." Quotations from the international citation files maintained by Clarence L. Barnhart, Inc. are included for each entry, along with etymological notes. The author, source, and date of each quotation are cited. A useful, authoritative supplement to the larger general dictionaries.

Other Critical Opinions

American Reference Books Annual 1974, p. 457.
Booklist, May 15, 1974, pp. 1011–1012.
Library Journal (review by B. Hunter Smeaton), September 15, 1973, p. 2537.

6,000 Words

Descriptive Information

Full Title: **6,000 Words: A Supplement to Webster's Third New International Dictionary.** *Editor:* Merriam-Webster Staff. *Publisher:* G. & C. Merriam Co. *Edition Reviewed:* 1976.

Classification: Special-Purpose—New Words. *Pages:* 20a, 220. *Total Entries:* 6,000. *Physical Size:* 6¼ by 9¼ in.; 24 cm. *LC:* 75-45056. *ISBN:* 0-87779-007-8. *Lowest Retail Price:* $8.50.

Comments

6,000 Words covers new words and meanings which have entered the language since publication of the unabridged *Webster's Third New International Dictionary* in 1961. The supplement includes many new abbreviations and technical terms. New meanings of established words are signified by means of an asterisk, e.g., the slang meaning of *crash**. Illustrative quotations are provided but not fully cited. Indispensable for owners of *Webster's Third*.

Other Critical Opinions

American Reference Books Annual 1977 (review by Francis J. Witty), p. 518.

ETYMOLOGY AND HISTORY OF WORDS

Etymology is the study of word origin and development. A specialized branch of linguistic science, etymology concerns itself not only with discovering the earliest roots of words but how words have evolved into their present forms and meanings. Etymologists are also concerned with cognates—words which have common roots. For instance, the word *mother* derives from the Anglo-Saxon *modor* which in turn is related to the German *mutter*, the Swedish and Danish *moder*, the French *mère*, the Italian *madre*, the Old Irish *mathir*, and the Latin *mater*. Knowledge of a word's history can provide greater insight into its innate or truest character. We understand the word *nausea*, for example, just that much better by knowing that it derives from the Greek *nautia* meaning seasickness and ultimately *naus* meaning ship. Or consider *ecology* which entered our vocabulary in the nineteenth century via the German cognate *Ökologie* which in turn came from the Greek *oikos* meaning home or habitat.

Word histories can be instructive, fascinating, complicated—and frustrating. Etymologists know, for instance, the origin of the word *hip* as part of the body, but they are not sure about the modern meaning of *hip* (to be knowledgeable, fashionable, with-it) or its famous derivative *hippie*. There are a number of outstanding, popular reference works on etymology which make the history of words come alive. Among the best are Stuart Berg Flexner's recent *I Hear America Talking*, William and Mary Morris's three-volume *Dictionary of Word and Phrase Origins*, and the series of little books by Charles Earle Funk which includes *Heavens to Betsy!* and *A Hog on Ice*. These and similar wordbooks are described in this section of the *Buying Guide*.

For linguists, lexicographers, and serious students of the English language, there are scholarly historical or etymological dictionaries available. Foremost among them, of course, is the monumental *Oxford English Dictionary* and its current supplements, the most complete and erudite record ever compiled of the development of the English language. In most instances, it is the final authority on English-language etymology. Following in the footsteps of the *Oxford English Dictionary* are four research dictionaries which provide etymological information restricted to particular time periods and geographical areas not fully covered by the *OED*. They are the *Middle English Dictionary*, *A Dictionary of the Older Scottish Tongue*, *The Scottish National Dictionary*, and *A Dictionary of American English on Historical Principles*. More restricted but also important are *A Dictionary of Americanisms on Historical Principles* and *A Dictionary of Canadianisms on Historical Principles*. The generally most useful historical dictionaries currently in print are described in the following pages.

The American Language

Descriptive Information

Full Title: **The American Language: An Inquiry into the Development of English in the United States.** *Author:* Henry Louis Mencken. *Publisher:* Knopf. *Edition Reviewed:* Fourth Edition (corrected, enlarged and rewritten), 1936; Supplements One and Two, 1945–1948.

Classification: Special-Purpose—Etymology. *Volumes:* One plus two supplements. *Pages:* 796 plus two supplements. *Lowest Retail Price:* $20.00 basic volume; $25.00 Supplement I; $17.50 Supplement II.

Comments

The American Language, a now classic work on the history of American English by the Baltimore journalist and sage H. L. Mencken, deals with word origins, the development of American slang and dialect, and variations between British and American usage and pronunciations. The volumes are not arranged in dictionary fashion but individual words and phrases can be located through a detailed index in each volume. The set also contains excellent material on the origin of American proper names. Note that a one-volume abridgment of *The American Language* (Fourth Edition), edited by Raven I. McDavid and published by Knopf in 1963, is available at $15.00. In 1977, Knopf published the McDavid abridgment in paperback for $7.95.

American Words

Descriptive Information

Full Title: **American Words.** *Editor:* Mitford M. Mathews. *Illustrator:* Lorence Bjorklund. *Publisher:* Collins+World. *Edition Reviewed:* Revised Edition, 1976.

Classification: Special-Purpose—Etymology. *Pages:* 266. *LC:* 76-20613. *ISBN:* 0-529-03550-2. *Lowest Retail Price:* $6.95.

Comments

American Words, first published in 1959, is a delightful introduction to etymology by Mitford Mathews, editor of the *Dictionary of Americanisms on Historical Principles*. *American Words* covers such terms as *RH factor*, *tea bag*, and *wooden Indian*. For junior and senior high school students.

Other Critical Opinions

Booklist, February 15, 1977, p. 891.

Americanisms

Descriptive Information

Full Title: **Americanisms: A Dictionary of Selected Americanisms on Historical Principles.** *Editor:* Mitford M. Mathews. *Publisher:* University of Chicago Press. *Edition Reviewed:* Phoenix Edition, 1966.

Classification: Special-Purpose—Etymology. *Pages:* xii, 304. *Total Entries:* 1,500. *Physical Size:* 5¼ by 8 in.; 21 cm. *Lowest Retail Price:* $1.95 paper.

Comments

Americanisms comprises approximately 1,500 entries selected from Mathews' scholarly *Dictionary of Americanisms on Historical Principles* published in 1951. The selected entries are reprinted in full from the larger dictionary. In the words of the publisher, this paperbound abridgment puts the lie to the "view that Americans have only burdened the language with vulgarisms and slang."

Brewer's Dictionary of Phrase and Fable

Descriptive Information

Full Title: **Brewer's Dictionary of Phrase and Fable.** *Authors:* E. Cobham Brewer; Revised by Ivor H. Evans. *Publisher:* Harper & Row. *Edition Reviewed:* Centenary Edition, 1970.

Classification: Special-Purpose—Etymology. *Pages:* xvi, 1175. *Total Entries:* 30,000. *Physical Size:* 5¾ by 8¾ in.; 22 cm. *LC:* 79-107024. *ISBN:* 0-06-010466-X. *Lowest Retail Price:* $15.00.

Comments

Brewer's Dictionary of Phrase and Fable, originally published in 1870 and revised many times since, is not a typical etymological dictionary. The founding author, an Englishman named Dr. Ebenezer Cobham Brewer who died in 1897, called the dictionary an "alms-basket of words" and subtitled the work as "giving the Derivation, Source, or Origin of Common Phrases, Allusions, and Words that have a Tale to Tell." Over the years successive editors have eliminated most of the common words and phrases while adding to those with a "tale to tell." In *Brewer*, for instance, the reader can learn the meaning and origin of *bared-faced*, *to conk out*, the American game *craps*, *dog-days*, *hob-nob*, *layman*, *to pour oil on troubled waters*, *Prussian blue*, and *simon pure*. A delightful book for browsing and reference.

Other Critical Opinions

Library Journal (review by B. Hunter Smeaton), March 15, 1972, p. 1002.

Chambers Etymological English Dictionary

Descriptive Information

Full Title: **Chambers Etymological English Dictionary.** *Editor:* A. M. Macdonald. *Publishers:* Littlefield, Adams; also Pyramid Publications. Alternate title: *Webster's Dictionary. Edition Reviewed:* New Edition, 1966. *Classification:* Special-Purpose—Etymology. *Pages:* 640. *Total Entries:* 85,000. *Physical Size:* 4¼ by 7 in.; 18 cm. *Lowest Retail Price:* $0.95 paper.

Comments

Chambers Etymological English Dictionary was first published at the beginning of the century, revised and enlarged in 1912, and thoroughly overhauled in the 1960s by A. M. Macdonald. Published in Great Britain by W. & R. Chambers, Ltd., the dictionary is available from two American publishers—Littlefield, Adams and Pyramid Publications—in reprinted paperback editions under the title *Chambers Etymological English Dictionary.* The Littlefield, Adams edition, which sells for $2.95 and carries a 1964 imprint date, adds an apostrophe to *Chambers'.* Both editions have the same contents, however. In addition, the dictionary is published under the imprint of the Banner Press and distributed by Hippocrene Press under the misleading title *Webster's Dictionary* (Special School and Reference Edition). As an etymological dictionary, *Chambers* is adequate but cannot compete with the better scholarly works such as Klein's *Comprehensive Etymological Dictionary of the English Language* and *The Oxford Dictionary of English Etymology.*

Comprehensive Etymological Dictionary

Descriptive Information

Full Title: **A Comprehensive Etymological Dictionary of the English Language: Dealing with the Origin of Words and Their Sense Development thus Illustrating the History of Civilization and Culture.** *Editor:* Ernest Klein. *Publisher:* Elsevier Publishing Co. *Distributor:* Elsevier North-Holland. *Edition Reviewed:* Unabridged One-Volume Edition, 1971.

Classification: Special-Purpose—Etymology. *Pages:* xxv, 844. *Total Entries:* 45,000. *Physical Size:* 8 by 11½ in.; 29 cm. *LC:* 73-172090. *ISBN:* 0-444-40930-0. *Lowest Retail Price:* $50.95.

Comments

A Comprehensive Etymological Dictionary of the English Language by Dr. Ernest Klein is an outstanding work of etymological scholarship. Originally published in two volumes in 1966–1967, it has more entries than Skeat's *Etymological Dictionary* or Onions' *Oxford Dictionary of English Etymology.* Moreover, Klein's work traces the origin of more scientific terms than does the work by Skeat or Onions and includes numerous proper names from mythology, etc. Dr. Klein, a rabbi and German concentration camp survivor, provides exact transliteration of Hebrew and Aramaic words. His knowledge of the Semitic languages and their development enhances his etymological descriptions. Along with Onions' dictionary, Klein's work is the best and most up-to-date etymological supplement to the *Oxford English Dictionary*.

Other Critical Opinions

American Reference Books Annual 1973, p. 449.
Katz, William A. *Basic Information Sources*. Vol. 1 of *Introduction to Reference Work*, 2nd ed. (New York: McGraw-Hill, 1974), pp. 274–275.

Concise Etymological Dictionary

Descriptive Information

Full Title: **A Concise Etymological Dictionary of the English Language.** *Editor:* Walter W. Skeat. *Publisher:* Oxford University Press. *Edition Reviewed:* 1911.
    Classification: Special-Purpose—Etymology. *Pages:* xv, 664. *Total Entries:* 14,000. *Physical Size:* 5 by 7½ in.; 19 cm. *ISBN:* 0-19-863105-7. *Lowest Retail Price:* $11.00.

Comments

A *Concise Etymological Dictionary of the English Language*, long an etymological classic, is still useful though it has been largely superseded by Onions' *Oxford Dictionary of English Etymology*. Skeat's work is especially valuable for its coverage of literary allusions, particularly those in the Bible and Shakespeare. The concise edition, published initially in 1882 and revised several times, is a condensation of the author's *Etymological Dictionary of the English Language* which remains in print. The concise version covers much the same vocabulary but omits some of the etymological history given in the unabridged edition.

Dictionary of American English

Descriptive Information

Full Title: **A Dictionary of American English on Historical Principles.** *Editors:* Sir William A. Craigie and James R. Hulbert. *Publisher:* University of Chicago Press. *Edition Reviewed:* 1936–1944.
    Classification: Special-Purpose—Etymology. *Volumes:* 4. *Pages:* xii, 2552. *Total Entries:* 50,000. *Physical Size:* 8¾ by 11¼ in.; 29 cm. *LC:* 36-21500. *ISBN:* 0-226-11737-5 (vol. 1); 0-226-11738-3 (vol. 2); 0-226-11739-1 (vol. 3); 0-226-11740-5 (vol. 4). *Lowest Retail Price:* $30.00 per volume; $120.00 the set.

Comments

Craigie and Hulbert's *Dictionary of American English on Historical Principles* is a research dictionary modeled after the famous *Oxford English*

Dictionary. Known as the *DAE*, it covers words and meanings which developed in the American colonies and later the United States through the end of the nineteenth century. As such, it is the most extensive etymological dictionary of American English. The *DAE* does not, however, attempt to include every word ever used by Americans; rather, the dictionary confines itself to "words and phrases which are clearly or apparently of American origin, or have greater currency here than elsewhere, but also every word denoting something which has a real connection with the development of the country and the history of its people." Like the *OED*, the *DAE* provides numerous illustrative quotations (dated with full citations) although, unlike the *OED*, it includes relatively little information about pronunciation. Slang and regionalisms are not fully covered, nor are technical terms. Words of American origin are denoted by a plus (+) sign whereas those of English origin, but with American meanings, are indicated by an asterisk (*). In addition to being an indispensable source for information about word development in this country prior to 1900, the *DAE* is a storehouse of historical material on the making of the American nation. Mitford Mathews' *Dictionary of Americanisms* supplements the *DAE* by extending the history of American English into the twentieth century.

Other Critical Opinions

Katz, William A. *Basic Information Sources.* Vol. 1 of *Introduction to Reference Work,* 2nd ed. (New York: McGraw-Hill, 1974), p. 275.

Dictionary of Americanisms

Descriptive Information

Full Title: **A Dictionary of Americanisms on Historical Principles.** *Editor:* Mitford M. Mathews. *Publisher:* University of Chicago Press. *Edition Reviewed:* 1951.

Classification: Special-Purpose—Etymology. *Pages:* xvi, 1946. *Total Entries:* 50,000. *Physical Size:* 8¾ by 11¼ in.; 29 cm. *ISBN:* 0-226-51011-5. *Lowest Retail Price:* $27.50.

Comments

Mathews' *Dictionary of Americanisms on Historical Principles,* originally published in 1951 in two volumes and more recently reprinted in a one-volume edition, is limited to words and expressions which originated in the United States, such as *appendicitis, hydrant, campus,* and *gorilla.* Whereas the four-volume *Dictionary of American English* covers American English only up to 1900, Mathews' dictionary extends coverage to the mid-twentieth century. Mathews also includes proportionately more slang and regional dialect, but many of the illustrative quotations are the same as those found in the *DAE.* A *Dictionary of Americanisms* neatly complements the larger *DAE.*

Other Critical Opinions

Katz, William A. *Basic Information Sources.* Vol. 1 of *Introduction to Reference Work,* 2nd ed. (New York: McGraw-Hill, 1974), pp. 275–276.

Dictionary of English Word-Roots

Descriptive Information

Full Title: **Dictionary of English Word-Roots: English-Roots and Roots-English.** *Compiler:* Robert W. L. Smith. *Publisher:* Littlefield, Adams. *Edition Reviewed:* 1966.

Classification: Special-Purpose—Etymology. *Pages:* 373. *Total Entries:* 6,000. *Physical Size:* 5 by 8 in.; 20 cm. *LC:* 66-18141. *Lowest Retail Price:* $3.95 paper.

Comments

Smith's *Dictionary of English Word-Roots* is not an etymological dictionary in the usual sense although it does deal with word origins and hence is included here. The first section, "Roots-to-English," lists common word bases (prefixes, suffixes, Latin and Greek roots, etc.) like *phil* and then indicates the meaning (*phil = to love*) and provides several examples (*philanthropist, philosopher, Philadelphia*). The second section, "English-to-Roots," lists common words (*love* and *to love*) and then notes their various bases or roots (e.g., *agap, am, ero, fre,* and *phil*). Exercises and a bibliography complete the book, which is intended for both classroom and reference use. Useful for understanding how English words and meanings have evolved from their Indo-European roots.

Other Critical Opinions

American Reference Books Annual 1977, p. 526.

Dictionary of Word and Phrase Origins

Descriptive Information

Full Title: **Dictionary of Word and Phrase Origins.** *Editors:* William Morris and Mary Morris. *Publisher:* Harper & Row. *Edition Reviewed:* 1962, 1967, and 1971.

Classification: Special-Purpose—Etymology. *Volumes:* 3. *Total Entries:* 8,000. *Physical Size:* 6½ by 9½ in.; 24 cm. *Lowest Retail Price:* $12.95 each volume.

Comments

The three volumes which make up the *Dictionary of Word and Phrase Origins* have appeared on a fairly regular basis since the early 1960s. Written in a popular, readable style, the word and phrase histories average from four or five lines to a page or so. Typical entries are *Devil, speak of the; Elgin marbles; ghetto; GI; like Caesar's wife, above suspicion; overpaid, oversexed and over here;* and *shucks.* The Morrises, who also co-authored the *Harper Dictionary of Contemporary Usage* (see profile in "Usage and Idioms" section), are well qualified to write these amusing and informative word histories. A new revised volume of the *Dictionary of Word and Phrase Origins* is planned for late 1977. Entitled *Morris Dictionary of Word and Phrase Origins*, it is an abridgment of the three previous volumes.

Other Critical Opinions

American Reference Books Annual 1970, p. 50 (in Vol. 2); also *American Reference Books Annual* 1972, p. 468.

Dictionary of Word Origins

Descriptive Information

Full Title: **Dictionary of Word Origins.** *Editor:* Joseph T. Shipley. *Publisher:* Littlefield, Adams. *Edition Reviewed:* 1945.
Classification: Special-Purpose—Etymology. *Pages:* x, 430. *Total Entries:* 10,000. *Physical Size:* 5½ by 8¼ in.; 21 cm. *Lowest Retail Price:* $4.50 paper.

Comments

Shipley's little dictionary is available in a number of editions. Philosophical Library holds the original 1945 copyright. The Littlefield, Adams edition (in paperback) is dated 1967, but is essentially the same as the 1945 edition. There is also a Greenwood Press edition, which sells for $25.50. The dictionary's coverage is popular though the style tends to be dry and academic. Entries include such terms as *gaga, galligaskins, gallop, gallows, galore,* and *gangster.* Obviously, words which have entered the language over the past 35 years or so are not covered.

Other Critical Opinions

American Reference Books Annual 1972, p. 469.

English Language in America

Descriptive Information

Full Title: **The English Language in America.** *Author:* George Philip Krapp. *Publisher:* Frederick Ungar Publishing Co. *Edition Reviewed:* 1960.
Classification: Special-Purpose—Etymology. *Volumes:* 2. *Physical Size:* 6½ by 9½ in.; 24 cm. *LC:* 60-9103. *Lowest Retail Price:* $20.00 the set.

Comments

The English Language in America, a scholarly history of the development of American English, first appeared in 1925 under the imprint of the Modern Language Association of America. The original publication was reissued in 1960 by Ungar. The work is not a dictionary but does cover the history of over 5,000 American terms, all of which are listed in the detailed index in Volume 2. Not as famous or readable as Mencken's *American Language* but useful in the same manner.

Eponyms Dictionaries Index

Descriptive Information

Full Title: **Eponyms Dictionaries Index: A Reference Guide to Persons, Both Real and Imaginary, and the Terms Derived from Their Names.** *Editor:* James A. Ruffner. *Publisher:* Gale Research Co. *Edition Reviewed:* 1977. *Classification:* Special-Purpose—Etymology. *Pages:* 730. *Total Entries:* 33,000. *LC:* 76-20341. *ISBN:* 0-8103-0688-3. *Lowest Retail Price:* $45.00.

Comments

Ruffner's *Eponyms Dictionaries Index* is a new source of information about people whose names have entered the common vocabulary. The word *lynch*, for instance, derives from a Judge Lynch (but which one etymologists are not sure). This work identifies over 30,000 eponyms (e.g., Cyril Northcote Parkinson who has given his name to *Parkinson's Law*) and refers the user to various biographical dictionaries where additional information can be found—hence the title *Eponyms Dictionaries Index*. People who have lent their names to inventions, mechanical devices, diseases, and drugs are especially well covered. Expensive but useful. Compare with Hendrickson's *Human Words* and Partridge's *Name into Word.*

Other Critical Opinions

Library Journal (review by John D. Campbell), May 15, 1977, p. 1169.

Etymological Dictionary of Modern English

Descriptive Information

Full Title: **An Etymological Dictionary of Modern English.** *Editor:* Ernest Weekley. *Publisher:* Dover Publications. *Edition Reviewed:* 1967. *Classification:* Special-Purpose—Etymology. *Volumes:* 2. *Pages:* xx, 1659. *Total Entries:* 40,000. *Physical Size:* 6½ by 9¾ in.; 23 cm. *LC:* 67-26968. *ISBN:* 0-486-21873-2. *Lowest Retail Price:* $5.00 each volume (paper).

Comments

Ernest Weekley's *Etymological Dictionary of Modern English*, first published in Great Britain in 1921 and reprinted here with a biographical note on Weekley by his son Montague Weekley, is for those who "have an educated interest in words and an intelligent curiosity as to their origins and earlier senses." The style is fairly simple and the coverage quite broad, except for scientific terms which are usually omitted. Comparable to, but not as scholarly as, Skeat's *Etymological Dictionary of the English Language* (1910). The works by Skeat and Weekley, however, have seen their day and have been replaced by such new etymological works as C. T. Onions' *Oxford Dictionary of English Etymology* and Klein's *Comprehensive Etymological Dictionary.* A concise edition of Weekley's dictionary containing about 27,000 entries appeared in 1952, but it is no longer in print.

Etymological Dictionary of the English Language

Descriptive Information

Full Title: **An Etymological Dictionary of the English Language.** *Editor:* Walter W. Skeat. *Publisher:* Oxford University Press. *Edition Reviewed:* New (Fourth) Edition, revised and enlarged, 1910.

Classification: Special-Purpose—Etymology. *Pages:* 824. *Total Entries:* 14,000. *Physical Size:* 9¾ by 12¼ in.; 31 cm. *ISBN:* 0-19-863104-9. *Lowest Retail Price:* $27.50.

Comments

Skeat's *Etymological Dictionary of the English Language* has achieved enduring fame as one of the most authoritative works of modern etymology. Unfortunately, the last edition appeared about 70 years ago and the dictionary has had its day. Fortunately, it has been replaced by the equally authoritative *Oxford Dictionary of English Etymology*, edited by C. T. Onions, who naturally drew upon the Skeat work in his research. A concise edition of Skeat's *Etymological Dictionary of the English Language* is also available from the publisher at a more modest $11.00.

Heavens to Betsy!

Descriptive Information

Full Title: **Heavens to Betsy! And Other Curious Sayings.** *Author:* Charles Earle Funk. *Illustrator:* Tom Funk. *Publishers:* Harper & Row (hardcover); Warner Books (paper). *Edition Reviewed:* 1955.

Classification: Special-Purpose—Etymology. *Pages:* xviii, 224. *Total Entries:* 500. *Graphics:* 50. *Physical Size:* 6 by 8½ in.; 22 cm (hardcover). *LC:* 55-8053. *ISBN:* 0-446-66958-X (paper). *Lowest Retail Price:* $9.95; also $1.25 paper.

Comments

Charles Earle Funk, who edited the Funk & Wagnalls Standard dictionary line until his retirement in 1947, has written a series of four little books which give brief and sometimes speculative histories of colorful and familiar expressions. *Heavens to Betsy!* is the second in the series and contains such items as *to pull up stakes*, *shiver my timbers*, and *scarcer than hen's teeth*. The Funk books can be read for pleasure or consulted for reference. The pen-and-ink drawings are by Dr. Funk's nephew, Tom. In 1972, *Heavens to Betsy!* was reissued as part of the Warner Paperback Library at $1.25.

Other Critical Opinions

American Reference Books Annual 1974 (review by Robert Parslow), p. 454.

Hog on Ice

Descriptive Information

Full Title: **A Hog on Ice and Other Curious Expressions.** *Author:* Charles Earle Funk. *Illustrator:* Tom Funk. *Publisher:* Harper & Row. *Edition Reviewed:* 1948.
Classification: Special-Purpose—Etymology. *Pages:* 214. *Total Entries:* 400. *Graphics:* 50. *Physical Size:* 6 by 8½ in.; 22 cm. *Lowest Retail Price:* $9.95.

Comments

Hog on Ice was the first of Dr. Funk's popular series on the origin of familiar sayings, such as *a wild-goose chase* and *to go berserk.* Other titles in the series are *Heavens to Betsy!*, *Horsefeathers*, and *Thereby Hangs a Tale.* Readable and informative.

Horsefeathers

Descriptive Information

Full Title: **Horsefeathers and Other Curious Words.** *Authors:* Charles Earle Funk and Charles Earle Funk, Jr. *Illustrator:* Tom Funk. *Publisher:* Harper & Row. *Edition Reviewed:* 1958.
Classification: Special-Purpose—Etymology. *Pages:* 240. *Total Entries:* 600. *Graphics:* 50. *Physical Size:* 6 by 8½ in.; 22 cm. *LC:* 58-8870. *Lowest Retail Price:* $9.95.

Comments

Horsefeathers was about 70 percent completed when Dr. Funk died in 1957 at age 76. He had edited the Funk & Wagnalls Standard dictionary line and in his retirement wrote a series of popular books on the origin of words and colloquial expressions, of which *Horsefeathers* is the last. His son completed the book. Other titles in the series are *Heavens to Betsy!*, *Hog on Ice*, and *Thereby Hangs a Tale.* The first two titles deal with familiar expressions like *to cry over spilt milk* whereas *Thereby Hangs a Tale* and *Horsefeathers* are limited to curious words (e.g., *rambunctious*) and compounds (e.g., *Sam Browne belt*). Popular lexicography.

Human Words

Descriptive Information

Full Title: **Human Words: The Complete Unexpurgated, Uncomputerized Human Wordbook.** *Editor:* Robert Hendrickson. *Publisher:* Chilton Book Co. *Edition Reviewed:* 1972.
Classification: Special-Purpose—Etymology. *Pages:* 342. *Total Entries:* 3,500. *Physical Size:* 6½ by 9½ in.; 25 cm. *LC:* 72-6492. *ISBN:* 0-8019-5697-8. *Lowest Retail Price:* $9.95.

Comments

Human Words is described as "Containing herein the true unadulterated stories of more than 3,500 unique and remarkably eponymous personalities: saints and sinners, losers and winners, lovers and hate-mongers, murderers and masochists, scoundrels and scalawags and saviors . . . that have given their names to the language." Thus, the user finds such entries as *Jim Crow, Lazy Susan, Mata Hari, Pap test,* and *Sten gun.* A paragraph or two is devoted to each term and the person from whom it derived. Compare with the *Eponyms Dictionaries Index* and Partridge's *Name into Word.*

Other Critical Opinions

American Reference Books Annual 1973 (review by P. William Filby), pp. 182–183.
Library Journal, February 1, 1973, p. 408.
RQ, Summer 1973, p. 406.

I Hear America Talking

Descriptive Information

Full Title: **I Hear America Talking: An Illustrated Treasury of American Words and Phrases.** *Author:* Stuart Berg Flexner. *Publisher:* Van Nostrand Reinhold (A Hudson Group Book). *Edition Reviewed:* 1976.
Classification: Special-Purpose—Etymology. *Pages:* x, 505. *Total Entries:* 10,000. *Graphics:* 500. *Physical Size:* 8¾ by 11¼ in.; 29 cm. *LC:* 76-42454. *ISBN:* 0-442-22413-3. *Lowest Retail Price:* $18.95.

Comments

I Hear America Talking is a handsomely designed, knowledgeably prepared, and popularly written study of American word origins. Flexner, a well-known lexicographer and language scholar, groups his interesting and readable etymologies under 157 topics such as "Where's the Bathroom?" (wherein terms like *toilet paper, bathtub,* and *wash rag* are discussed) and "Dashing Men" (which includes terms like *dude, lounge lizard, lover boy, stud,* and *wolf*). There is an alphabetical index of all words and phrases covered. Five hundred halftones and line illustrations enhance the book's visual appeal as well as its scholarly content. *I Hear America Talking* is an outstanding recent work of popular language history which also tells us much about American social and cultural development. For both browsing and research.

Other Critical Opinions

Library Journal (review by Catherine von Schon), January 1, 1977. p. 108.
New York Times Book Review (review by William Safire), December 12, 1976, pp. 8–12.
Wilson Library Bulletin (review by Charles A. Bunge), February 1977, p. 537.

Merriam-Webster Book of Word Histories

Descriptive Information

Full Title: **The Merriam-Webster Book of Word Histories.** *Editor:* Frederick C. Mish. *Publisher:* Pocket Books. *Edition Reviewed:* 1976. *Classification:* Special-Purpose—Etymology. *Pages:* xxiii, 277. *Total Entries:* 600. *Physical Size:* 4¼ by 7 in.; 18 cm. *LC:* 76-7339. *ISBN:* 0-671-80555-X. *Lowest Retail Price:* $1.95 paper.

Comments

The Merriam-Webster Book of Word Histories, published only in paperback, contains about 600 histories of selected words from *academy* to *marshal* to *zombie* and *zwieback*. Like Dr. Funk's books (*Heavens to Betsy!*, *Hog on Ice*, etc.), the Morrises' *Dictionary of Word and Phrase Origins*, and Stuart Flexner's *I Hear America Talking*, this book of popular etymology both instructs and amuses.

Other Critical Opinions

Booklist, July 1, 1976, p. 1507.
Library Journal, June 15, 1976, p. 1422.

Name into Word

Descriptive Information

Full Title: **Name into Word: Proper Names That Have Become Common Property; A Discursive Dictionary.** *Editor:* Eric Partridge. *Publisher:* Books for Libraries Press. *Distributor:* Arno Press. *Edition Reviewed:* Second Edition, revised and enlarged, 1950.
Classification: Special-Purpose—Etymology. *Pages:* xv, 648. *Total Entries:* 4,000. *Physical Size:* 5¾ by 8¾ in.; 22 cm. *LC:* 77-117906. *ISBN:* 0-8369-5361-4. *Lowest Retail Price:* $30.75.

Comments

Partridge's *Name into Word*, first published in Great Britain in 1949 and revised in 1950, was reprinted in the United States in 1970 by Books for Libraries Press. Partridge, the godfather of English slang and word oddities, is concerned here with proper names which have become common words. Examples include *cabana, doctrinaire, mauser, mayonnaise, scalawag,* and *uranium.* As might be expected, the book includes numerous eponyms—that is, people who have given their names to the common vocabulary. Compare Partridge's work with Hendrickson's *Human Words* and the *Eponyms Dictionaries Index.*

Origins

Descriptive Information

Full Title: **Origins: A Short Etymological Dictionary of Modern English.** *Editor:* Eric Partridge. *Publisher:* Macmillan Publishing Co. *Edition Reviewed:* Fourth Edition, 1966.
Classification: Special-Purpose—Etymology. *Pages:* xx, 972. *Total Entries:* 25,000. *Lowest Retail Price:* $25.00.

Comments

Partridge's *Origins*, first published in Great Britain in 1958 and revised several times, is a more appealing etymological dictionary for the layperson than, say, Skeat's *Etymological Dictionary of the English Language* or the more recent *Oxford Dictionary of English Etymology* by Onions or Klein's *Comprehensive Etymological Dictionary.* On the other hand, Partridge's dictionary is not as thorough or as conveniently arranged for reference purposes. Partridge groups his entries by related or cognate words. This arrangement does, however, allow the user to see word relationships that the works by Skeat, Onions, and Klein (which are strictly alphabetical) do not permit. Partridge's style is also livelier than the others.

Oxford Dictionary of English Etymology

Descriptive Information

Full Title: **The Oxford Dictionary of English Etymology.** *Editors:* C. T. Onions with the assistance of G. W. S. Friedrichsen and R. W. Burchfield. *Publisher:* Oxford University Press. *Edition Reviewed:* 1966.
Classification: Special-Purpose—Etymology. *Pages:* xiv, 1024. *Total Entries:* 38,000. *Physical Size:* 6¼ by 9½ in.; 24 cm. *LC:* 66-71621. *ISBN:* 0-19-861112-9. *Lowest Retail Price:* $30.00.

Comments

The Oxford Dictionary of English Etymology is an authoritative work which traces the history of common English words back to their Indo-European roots. The dictionary complements and, in some instances, updates the *Oxford English Dictionary* and, for all practical purposes, replaces Skeat's classic *Etymological Dictionary of the English Language.* The publisher says *The Oxford Dictionary of English Etymology* is "the most complete and most reliable etymological dictionary of the English language ever published," a statement which has generally been accepted as accurate. Note, however, that Klein's *Comprehensive Etymological Dictionary*, published in 1966–1967, contains more entries and provides the origin of many more scientific terms than does the Onions dictionary. Without question, the works by Klein and Onions are the best scholarly one-volume etymological dictionaries currently available.

Other Critical Opinions

Booklist, November 1, 1966, pp. 273–274.
Katz, William A. *Basic Information Sources.* Vol. 1 of *Introduction to Reference Work*, 2nd ed. (New York: McGraw-Hill, 1974), p. 274.

Oxford English Dictionary

Descriptive Information

Full Title: **Oxford English Dictionary, Being a Corrected Reissue with an Introduction, Supplement and Bibliography, of A New English Dictionary on Historical Principles.** *Editors:* James A. H. Murray, Henry Bradley, W. A. Craigie, and C. T. Onions; R. W. Burchfield, Editor of the Supplements. *Publisher:* Oxford University Press. *Editions Reviewed:* 13-volume set, 1933; Supplement I (A–G), 1972; Supplement II (H–N), 1976; the Compact Edition (2 volumes), 1971.

Classification: Special-Purpose—Etymology. *Volumes:* 13 plus 4 supplements (in progress). *Pages:* 16,570 plus supplements. *Total Entries:* 414,825 plus supplements. *Physical Size:* 9¼ by 12 in.; 30 cm. *ISBN:* 0-19-861101-3; 0-19-861115-3 (Supplement I, A–G); 0-19-861123-4 (Supplement II, H–N); 0-19-861117-X (Compact Edition). *Lowest Retail Price:* $395.00 the 13-volume set; $65.00 Supplement I; $65.00 Supplement II; $95.00 the Compact Edition.

Comments

The *Oxford English Dictionary* (*OED*) is a work of staggering size and unimpeachable authority. The basic 13 volumes (a corrected reissue of Murray's *New English Dictionary on Historical Principles*) contain 240,165 main entries, a total vocabulary of 414,825 words, over 500,000 separate definitions, and nearly two million illustrative quotations. The aim of the *OED* is to cover all words and meanings introduced into the English language since 1150 and to trace their evolution through dated citations. Work on the main *OED* project consumed over 70 years, beginning with initial preparations by the (British) Philological Society in the late 1850s and culminating with the publication of 12 volumes between 1884 and 1928. A supplementary volume was added in 1933. And at the present time a 4-volume supplement currently in progress will add some 60,000 new words to the *OED* which have entered the language over the past four decades.

The *OED* is principally a historical dictionary most useful to those engaged in etymological and linguistic research, as well as writers and teachers who need accurate and detailed information about word origins, derivatives, and histories. The *OED*, despite its comprehensiveness, is not intended as a general dictionary. For instance, the entry for *set* covers 20 pages and has 150 main divisions. The dictionary is strictly British in its orientation and the most frequently expressed criticism of the *OED* is its lack of coverage and treatment of American words and meanings. The new 4-volume supplement, however, is attempting to rectify this situation. The new supplement also includes all the previously taboo four-letter words.

Interested consumers should note that in 1971 Oxford University Press issued the 13-volume *OED* in a Compact Edition comprising two hefty volumes and a magnifying glass. This edition photographically reduced the *OED* to microprint size, thus compressing 16,000 pages into 4,116. The quality of the micrographic reproduction is excellent but use, which requires the magnifying glass, is awkward. Only the most diligent word hound will use the Compact Edition. A compensating factor, however, is the price of the Compact Edition. It can be acquired from the publisher for $95.00 and the Book-of-the-Month Club offers it for $17.50 with a trial membership.

Other Critical Opinions

American Reference Books Annual 1973, p. 448 (Supplement I, A–G).
American Reference Books Annual 1977 (review by Koert C. Loomis, Jr.), pp. 520–521 (Supplement II, H–N).
American Reference Books Annual 1973, p. 448 (Compact Edition).
Booklist, May 1, 1973, pp. 818, 820 (Supplement I, A–G).
Booklist, May 15, 1977, p. 1455 (Supplement II, H–N).
Booklist, June 1, 1973, p. 916 (Compact Edition).
Katz, William A. *Basic Information Sources.* Vol. 1 of *Introduction to Reference Work*, 2nd ed. (New York: McGraw-Hill, 1974), pp. 272–274 (13-volume *OED*; Supplement I, A–G; & Compact Edition).
Library Journal (review by B. Hunter Smeaton), December 15, 1976, p. 2559 (Supplement II, H–N).
Library Journal (review by B. Hunter Smeaton), March 15, 1972, p. 1002 (Compact Edition).
New York Times (review by Christopher Lehmann-Haupt), October 13, 1971 (Compact Edition).
Newsweek, October 11, 1971, p. 102 (Compact Edition).
Time, January 24, 1977, p. 66 (Supplement II, H–N).

Oxford Universal Dictionary Illustrated

Descriptive Information

Full Title: **The Oxford Universal Dictionary Illustrated on Historical Principles.** *Editors:* William Little, H. W. Fowler, and Jessie Coulson; Revised by C. T. Onions. *Publisher:* Oxford University Press for the Caxton Publishing Co. *Distributor:* Macdonald-Raintree. *Edition Reviewed:* Third Edition, 1973.

Classification: Special-Purpose—Etymology. *Volumes:* 2. *Pages:* xxv, 2712. *Total Entries:* 205,000. *Graphics:* 226. *Physical Size:* 8 by 11 in.; 28 cm. *Lowest Retail Price:* $29.95 the set.

Consumer Note

The Oxford Universal Dictionary Illustrated is called a "special illustrated edition" of *The Shorter Oxford English Dictionary* which in turn is an abridgment of the 13-volume *Oxford English Dictionary*. Actually the only differences between *Oxford Universal* and *Shorter Oxford* are that the former appends a 40-page biographical supplement and interleaves a number of full-page pictorial illustrations. Unfortunately, the illustrations are completely unrelated to the text. For instance, a black-and-white plate of dog photographs is inserted after the entry *flinch*. Naturally, since the text is exactly the same as *Shorter Oxford*, there is no cross-reference from the entry *dog* to the plate. The bindings are also considerably different. Whereas *Shorter Oxford* is sturdily bound in a dark willow grain calf binding, *Oxford Universal* has a white leathercloth binding which will show every dirt and pencil mark and is not firmly secured to the book. Consumers who want an abridgment of the *Oxford English Dictionary* are advised to weigh *Shorter Oxford*'s superior binding against *Oxford Universal*'s lower price. Note that Macdonald-Raintree, distributor of *Oxford Universal*, deals principally with educational institutions but will accept orders from individuals. (See the comments about *Shorter Oxford* which follow below.)

Phrase and Word Origins

Descriptive Information

Full Title: **Phrase and Word Origins: A Study of Familiar Expressions.** *Editor:* Alfred H. Holt. *Publisher:* Dover Publications. Former title: *Phrase Origins. Edition Reviewed:* 1961.

Classification: Special-Purpose—Etymology. *Pages:* xi, 254. *Total Entries:* 2,500. *Physical Size:* 5¼ by 8 in.; 20 cm. *LC:* 61-2238. *ISBN:* 0-486-20758-7. *Lowest Retail Price:* $3.00 paper.

Comments

Phrase and Word Origins, published in 1961 by Dover in a quality soft-cover edition, is a revised and enlarged version of Holt's *Phrase Origins* published by T. Y. Crowell Company in 1936. The words and phrases covered have been chosen for their "picturesque interest." Typical entries, which range in length from two lines to half a page, are *carrot-top, carry the banner, cart before the horse, catawampus, catch a crab, caucus,* and *cauliflower ear.* Readable, popular etymology.

Shorter Oxford English Dictionary

Descriptive Information

Full Title: **The Shorter Oxford English Dictionary on Historical Principles.** *Editors:* William Little, H. W. Fowler, and Jessie Coulson; Revised by C. T. Onions. *Publisher:* Oxford University Press. *Edition Reviewed:* Third Edition, completely reset, 1973.

Classification: Special-Purpose—Etymology. *Volumes:* 2. *Pages:* xxv, 2672. *Total Entries:* 202,000. *Physical Size:* 8 by 11 in.; 28 cm. *ISBN:* 0-19-861126-9 (plain, 2-vol. ed.); 0-19-861127-7 (thumb-indexed, 2-vol. ed.); 0-19-861125-0 (thumb-indexed 1-vol. ed.). *Lowest Retail Price:* $60.00 (1-vol. ed.); $65.00 (2-vol. ed.).

Comments

The Shorter Oxford English Dictionary, first published in 1933 and revised in 1936 (Second Edition) and again in 1944 (Third Edition), is an abridgment of the 13-volume *Oxford English Dictionary*. It includes perhaps 40 percent of the words covered in the *OED* and, in order to conserve space, eliminates many of the illustrative quotations found in the larger work. *Shorter Oxford* also condenses the *OED*'s etymologies and employs numerous abbreviations not used in the *OED*. The 1973 reset version of the Third Edition of *Shorter Oxford* is distinguished by thoroughly revised etymologies and an extensive 74-page addendum covering new words and meanings which have entered the language since the *OED* first appeared. This material is based on the new supplements currently being prepared for the *OED*. Note that there is an illustrated edition of *Shorter Oxford* available under the title of *Oxford Universal Dictionary Illustrated*, distributed by Macdonald-Raintree in the U.S. (See the note preceding in this section of the *Buying Guide* for further details about the *Oxford Universal Dictionary Illustrated*.)

Other Critical Opinions

Booklist, November 1, 1974, pp. 298–299.
Katz, William A. *Basic Information Sources*. Vol. 1 of *Introduction to Reference Work*, 2nd ed. (New York: McGraw-Hill, 1974), p. 275.
Library Journal (review by B. Hunter Smeaton), February 1, 1974, p. 352.
Wilson Library Bulletin (review by Charles A. Bunge), February 1974, p. 508.

Thereby Hangs a Tale

Descriptive Information

Full Title: **Thereby Hangs a Tale: Stories of Curious Word Origins.** *Author:* Charles Earle Funk. *Publishers:* Harper & Row (hardcover); Warner Books (paper). *Edition Reviewed:* 1950.

Classification: Special-Purpose—Etymology. *Pages:* xii, 303. *Total Entries:* 800. *Physical Size:* 6 by 8½ in.; 22 cm. (hardcover). *ISBN:* 0-446-66957-1 (paper). *Lowest Retail Price:* $9.95; also $1.25 paper.

Comments

Another of Dr. Funk's entertaining books on word histories. This one covers such everyday terms as *fad*, *fake*, *fan*, *fanatic*, and *farce*. Other titles in the series are *Heavens to Betsy!*, *Hog on Ice*, and *Horsefeathers*.

Wordpower

Descriptive Information

Full Title: **Wordpower: An Illustrated Dictionary of Concepts.** *Author:* Edward de Bono. *Publisher:* Harper & Row. *Edition Reviewed:* 1977.

Classification: Special-Purpose—Etymology. *Total Entries:* 330. *ISBN:* 0-06-090568-9. *Lowest Retail Price:* $12.50; also $4.95 paper.

Comments

Wordpower, an original paperback published in 1977, discusses the origins and meanings of selected terms which derive from modern business, medicine, and psychology. Dr. de Bono, an English psychologist who originated the idea of lateral thinking, believes that such words as *cybernetics* and *cloning* convey difficult scientific concepts in manageable "thinking chunks." A readable, often stimulating investigation into some key contemporary words, but its selectivity limits its reference value.

Words and Phrases Index

Descriptive Information

Full Title: **Words and Phrases Index: A Guide to Antedatings, New Words, New Compounds, New Meanings, and Other Published Scholarship Supplementing the Oxford English Dictionary, Dictionary of American English and other Major Dictionaries of the English Language.** *Compilers:* C. Edward Wall and Edward Przebienda. *Publisher:* Pierian Press. *Edition Reviewed:* 1968–1970 (4 volumes).

Classification: Special-Purpose—Etymology. *Volumes:* 4. *Total Entries:* 200,000. *LC:* 68-68874. *ISBN:* 0-87650-001-7. *Lowest Retail Price:* $19.95 each volume; $75.00 the set.

Comments

Words and Phrases Index is a computer-produced index to material on word histories and meanings in such serial sources as *American Notes and Queries, American Speech, Notes and Queries, College English, Dialect Notes,* and *Publications of the American Dialect Society.* Essentially a time-saver for lexicographers and linguists, this set will most likely be only acquired by large public and academic libraries.

Other Critical Opinions

American Reference Books Annual 1971, pp. 422–423.

USAGE AND IDIOMS

General dictionaries often include usage notes which advise on such matters as the use of the plural *data* as a singular noun (e.g., the *data* is inconclusive), the acceptability or unacceptability of *irregardless,* and the subtle and apparently fading distinction between *infer* and *imply.* For perfectionists, purists, English teachers, snobs, grammatical worrywarts, and others who want to use the language properly or desire more detailed information about points of questionable usage, there are a number of dictionaries and wordbooks devoted to the subject. These works tend to be quite personal, didactic, and sometimes idiosyncratic, the degree of each depending on the particular personality and peeves of the author. Among the best known usage dictionaries are H. W. Fowler's *Dictionary of Modern English Usage* and Margaret Nicholson's *Dictionary of American-English Usage.* Also covered in this section of the *Buying Guide* are dictionaries of idioms, difficult or odd words, and a couple of titles devoted to clarifying the differences between English and American usage. Style manuals, which deal with a specialized and quite restricted area of usage, are covered next, followed by a section on in-print secretarial handbooks.

British Self-Taught: With Comments in American

Descriptive Information

Full Title: **British Self-Taught: With Comments in American.** *Editor:* Norman W. Schur. *Publisher:* Macmillan Publishing Co. *Edition Reviewed:* 1973.

Classification: Special-Purpose—Usage & Idioms. *Pages:* xxxi, 438. *Total Entries:* 3,000. *Physical Size:* 5¾ by 8½ in.; 22 cm. *LC:* 70-127941. *Lowest Retail Price:* $6.95.

Comments

Schur's dictionary enters the British word, phrase, or idiom in the left-hand column and gives the American equivalent directly opposite in the right-hand column. For instance, *loo* (British) and *john* (American) are so entered. A brief discussion follows, noting that these colloquial terms refer to the *bathroom, lavatory, washroom, water closet,* etc. Schur also explains the origin of *loo.* The dictionary contains an informative introduction to British English, many slang and idiomatic terms, and a few amusing cartoons. Compare with Norman Moss's *What's the Difference? A British/ American Dictionary.*

Other Critical Opinions

American Reference Books Annual 1974 (review by Robert Parslow), pp. 457–458.
Library Journal (review by B. Hunter Smeaton), October 1, 1972, p. 3138.

The Careful Writer

Descriptive Information

Full Title: **The Careful Writer: A Modern Guide to English Usage.** *Author:* Theodore M. Bernstein. *Publisher:* Atheneum. *Edition Reviewed:* 1965.

Classification: Special-Purpose—Usage & Idioms. *Lowest Retail Price:* $12.95.

Comments

The longtime usage authority for the *New York Times*, Theodore Bernstein, offers his firm but reasonable opinions on disputed or questionable language constructions, abused and overused words and phrases, and how to write more efficiently and effectively. Bernstein, who has provided usage notes for *The Random House Dictionary*, is the author of other usage guides, including *Watch Your Language* and the more recent *Dos, Don'ts and Maybes of English Usage*.

Collins Gem Dictionary of American Usage

Descriptive Information

Full Title: **Collins Gem Dictionary of American Usage.** *Editors:* Margot Butt and Linda Lane. *Publisher:* Collins+World. *Edition Reviewed:* 1973.

Classification: Special-Purpose—Usage & Idioms. *Pages:* xxv, 454. *Total Entries:* 1,500. *Physical Size:* 3¼ by 4½ in.; 12 cm. *ISBN:* 0-00-458736-7. *Lowest Retail Price:* $2.45 paper (Leatheroid).

Comments

Butt and Lane's little usage guide is based on *Collins Gem Dictionary of English Usage* (1970). According to the editors' introduction, the dictionary "is designed not to give a cut and dried set of rules but to indicate what are the most accepted forms and uses of troublesome words and phrases." There are about 75 pages of supplementary material, including a vocabulary list showing differences between British and American English, commonly used foreign expressions, forms of address, and proofreading symbols. The Collins Gem series is well known for its reliable pocket reference works. This dictionary of American usage enhances the series' good reputation.

Concise Dictionary of English Idioms

Descriptive Information

Full Title: **A Concise Dictionary of English Idioms.** *Editors:* William Freeman; Revised by Brian Phythian. *Publisher:* The Writer, Inc. *Edition Reviewed:* Third Edition, 1973.

Classification: Special-Purpose—Usage & Idioms. *Pages:* 215. *Total Entries:* 4,000. *Physical Size:* 5¼ by 8½ in.; 22 cm. *LC:* 75-29029. *ISBN:* 0-87116-094-3. *Lowest Retail Price:* $4.95 paper.

Comments

A Concise Dictionary of English Idioms was initially published in 1951, revised the next year, and then totally reworked by Brian Phythian in a Third Edition 20 years later. The purpose is "to furnish both the native or the foreign reader with a simple and practical guide to the most frequently used idiomatic expressions in English." The idioms are grouped under key words (e.g., under *hang* the user finds *hang fire, get the hang of, hang in the balance, hang on, hang out,* etc.), but there are no cross-references or index entries for such key words as *fire* and *balance*. Each idiom is briefly defined, followed by an illustrative sentence. Includes both British and American idioms.

Other Critical Opinions

American Reference Books Annual 1977 (review by Francis J. Witty), p. 519.

Concise Usage and Abusage

Descriptive Information

Full Title: **The Concise Usage and Abusage: A Modern Guide to Good English.** *Editor:* Eric Partridge. *Publisher:* Greenwood Press. *Edition Reviewed:* 1955.

Classification: Special-Purpose—Usage & Idioms. *Pages:* ix, 219. *Total Entries:* 2,500. *Physical Size:* 5¾ by 8¾ in.; 23 cm. *ISBN:* 0-8371-2466-2. *Lowest Retail Price:* $12.00.

Comments

This guide by the indefatigable word-sleuth Eric Partridge is an abridgment of his *Usage and Abusage,* now in its Sixth Edition (1965) although the *Concise* is based on the Fourth Edition (1953). Partridge calls the *Concise* "a drastically shortened and mildly simplified" version of *Usage and Abusage*. The *Concise* omits many entries that appear in the larger work and also drops the American notes by W. Cabell Greet. Although Partridge is authoritative and always worth studying, consumers are advised to avoid this book, which is both dated and overpriced. The more recent and larger *Usage and Abusage* is available from the British Book Centre for $17.50.

Current American Usage

Descriptive Information

Full Title: **Current American Usage.** *Editor:* Margaret M. Bryant. *Publisher:* Funk & Wagnalls. *Distributor:* T. Y. Crowell Co. *Edition Reviewed:* 1962.

Classification: Special-Purpose—Usage & Idioms. *Pages:* xxiv, 290. *Total Entries:* 240. *Physical Size:* 6 by 8½ in.; 22 cm. *LC:* 62-9735. *Lowest Retail Price:* $5.00.

Comments

The editor's introduction states that "This book attempts to bring together the most recent information about frequently debated points of usage in English speech and writing." The book grew out of work done by a committee of the National Council of Teachers of English and covers such usage problems as *dreamed* vs. *dreamt*, the usage of *either* and *neither* with more than two items, and the frequently misused *sit* and *set*. Many authoritative sources are cited throughout but, unfortunately, *Current American Usage* is no longer current. Similar but more up-to-date guides include the Morrises' *Harper Dictionary of Contemporary Usage* and Perrin's *Reference Handbook of Grammar & Usage*.

Dictionary of American-English Usage

Descriptive Information

Full Title: **A Dictionary of American-English Usage: Based on Fowler's Modern English Usage.** *Editor:* Margaret Nicholson. *Publisher:* New American Library. *Edition Reviewed:* 1957.

Classification: Special-Purpose—Usage & Idioms. *Pages:* xii, 671. *Total Entries:* 7,500. *Physical Size:* 4¼ by 7 in.; 18 cm. *Lowest Retail Price:* $1.50 paper.

Comments

In her preface, Nicholson says "*American-English Usage* is an adaptation of *MEU* [Fowler's *Dictionary of Modern English Usage*], not a replacement. *AEU* is a simplified *MEU*, with American variations, retaining as much of the original as space allowed." Nicholson also updates *Fowler*, which first appeared in 1926. Both titles, however, are beginning to show their age. For instance, Nicholson's entry *female, feminine, womanly, womanish* has a somewhat antique ring to it. The same is true of the next entry, *feminine designations.* Now only available in a paperback edition (an unabridged reprint of the now out-of-print Oxford University Press edition published in 1957), *A Dictionary of American-English Usage* is still useful for its literate, authoritative notes on correct usage—or what once was correct.

Dictionary of American Idioms

Descriptive Information

Full Title: **A Dictionary of American Idioms.** *Editors:* Maxine Tull Boatner and John Edward Gates; Revised by Adam Makkai. *Publisher:* Barron's Educational Series. Former title: *A Dictionary of Idioms for the Deaf. Edition Reviewed:* 1975.

Classification: Special-Purpose—Usage & Idioms. *Pages:* xiii, 392. *Total Entries:* 4,000. *Physical Size:* 6 by 9 in.; 23 cm. *LC:* 75-42110. *ISBN:* 0-8120-0612-7. *Lowest Retail Price:* $5.95 paper.

Comments

Originally published in the 1960s by the American School of the Deaf in West Hartford (Conn.), the dictionary was revised, updated, enlarged, and retitled in 1975. The book is reasonably current and quite detailed. Each idiom is defined and its use illustrated by a sample sentence. Cross-references are provided, e.g., under *finger* is a cross-reference to *keep one's fingers crossed, slip through one's fingers, sticky fingers,* etc. Better in terms of both coverage and treatment than Phythian's *Concise Dictionary of English Idioms.*

Dictionary of Clichés

Descriptive Information

Full Title: **A Dictionary of Clichés: With an Introductory Essay.** *Editor:* Eric Partridge. *Publisher:* Macmillan Publishing Co. *Edition Reviewed:* Fourth Edition, 1950.

Classification: Special-Purpose—Usage & Idioms. *Pages:* 259. *Total Entries:* 2,500. *Lowest Retail Price:* $4.50.

Comments

The cliché or trite expression is a form of idiomatic phrase in many instances. Partridge groups his 2,500 "wornout commonplaces" in four categories: (1) Idioms that have become hackneyed through overuse, e.g., *safe and sound;* (2) Other trite phrases, e.g., *add insult to injury;* (3) Stock phrases and quotations from foreign languages, e.g., *cherchez la femme;* and (4) Quotations from English literature, e.g., *"Their name is legion."* Partridge, bless him, even stars the most objectionable clichés, e.g., *in the last resort. A Dictionary of Clichés* was first published in 1940.

Dictionary of Collective Nouns

Descriptive Information

Full Title: **A Dictionary of Collective Nouns and Group Terms.** *Editor:* Ivan G. Sparkes. *Publisher:* Gale Research Co. *Edition Reviewed:* 1975.

Classification: Special-Purpose—Usage & Idioms. *Pages:* 191. *Total Entries:* 1,000. *Physical Size:* 5¼ by 8 in.; 21 cm. *LC:* 75-4117. *ISBN:* 0-8103-2016-9. *Lowest Retail Price:* $15.00.

Comments

This unique lexicon identifies and briefly defines over 1,000 collective nouns such as *colony* (of ants, etc.), *gaggle* (of geese), *giggle* (of girls), *nest* (of rabbits, robbers, etc.), and *school* (of dolphins, fish, etc.). The dictionary also contains a separate list of subjects so the reader can look under, say, *geese* and find appropriate collective terms (such as *clutch, flock, gaggle, nide,* or *skein*). The dictionary has limited reference use but it's fun to browse in. Also useful for crossword puzzle addicts.

Other Critical Opinions

American Reference Books Annual 1976 (review by Richard A. Gray), pp. 547–548.

Wilson Library Bulletin (review by Charles A. Bunge), May 1976, p. 747.

Dictionary of Contemporary American Usage

Descriptive Information

Full Title: **A Dictionary of Contemporary American Usage.** *Authors:* Bergen Evans and Cornelia Evans. *Publisher:* Random House. *Edition Reviewed:* 1957.

Classification: Special-Purpose—Usage & Idioms. *Pages:* viii, 567. *Total Entries:* 8,000. *Physical Size:* 7 by 10 in.; 25 cm. *LC:* 57-5379. *ISBN:* 0-394-40085-2. *Lowest Retail Price:* $7.95.

Comments

The Evanses' dictionary deals not only with troublesome words and phrases which are often misused or confused (e.g., *oblige/obligate*) but also questions of grammar, style, and punctuation. Numerous idioms are also covered, such as *make no bones about* and *make the best of a bad bargain.* Bergen Evans is a prominent language authority and teacher best known perhaps for his liberal (or permissive) stand on contemporary usage. This dictionary, however, adheres to and explains the rules of proper usage in an engaging, forthright manner.

Dictionary of Difficult Words

Descriptive Information

Full Title: **A Dictionary of Difficult Words.** *Editor:* Robert H. Hill. *Publisher:* New American Library. *Edition Reviewed:* 1971.

Classification: Special-Purpose—Usage & Idioms. *Pages:* 368. *Total Entries:* 15,000. *Physical Size:* 4¼ by 7 in.; 18 cm. *LC:* 79-140466. *Lowest Retail Price:* $1.95 paper.

Comments

This paperback edition of Hill's *Dictionary of Difficult Words* is a reprint of the hardcover edition (now out of print) published by the John Day Company in 1971. That edition in turn was reprinted from a revision of the dictionary published in Great Britain in 1969 by Hutchinson & Company. The cover proclaims *A Dictionary of Difficult Words* "The Essential Companion Volume to Every Abridged Dictionary," and indeed many strange or problem words are briefly defined, e.g., *heterotelic, heterotrichosis, heterotropia, heuristic, hetman, hexachord.* On the other hand, numerous recent scientific and technical terms are not included. Unfortunately, this paperback edition is poorly printed. Most useful for word buffs, Scrabble players, crossword puzzle fans, et al. Compare with *Mrs. Byrne's Dictionary of Unusual, Obscure, and Preposterous Words.*

Other Critical Opinions

American Reference Books Annual 1972 (review by Marjorie P. Holt), p. 474.

Dictionary of Do's and Don'ts

Descriptive Information

Full Title: **The Dictionary of Do's and Don'ts: A Guide for Writers and Speakers.** *Editor:* Harry G. Nickles. *Publisher:* McGraw-Hill. *Edition Reviewed:* 1974.

   Classification: Special-Purpose—Usage & Idioms. *Pages:* 288. *Lowest Retail Price:* $8.95.

Comments

On much the same order as Theodore Bernstein's *Miss Thistlebottom's Hobgoblins*, this usage guide emphasizes clichés and is distinguished by its rather cutesy headings, e.g., *messy possessives.* The Bernstein books, Rudolf Flesch's *Look It Up*, and Porter Perrin's *Reference Handbook of Grammar & Usage* are all preferable to *The Dictionary of Do's and Don'ts.*

Other Critical Opinions

Library Journal, October 1, 1974, p. 2478.

Dictionary of Modern American Usage

Descriptive Information

Full Title: **A Dictionary of Modern American Usage.** *Editor:* H. W. Horwill. *Publisher:* Oxford University Press. *Edition Reviewed:* Second Edition, 1944.

   Classification: Special-Purpose—Usage & Idioms. *Pages:* xxxi, 360. *Total Entries:* 2,000. *Physical Size:* 5 by 7½ in.; 19 cm. *ISBN:* 0-19-869109-2. *Lowest Retail Price:* $13.00.

Comments

A Dictionary of Modern American Usage first appeared in 1935 and was substantially revised in 1944. Its basic purpose is "to assist English people who visit the United States, or who meet American friends, or who read American books and magazines, or who listen to American 'talkies'." Thus, Horwill deals with terms which have a distinctive American origin or connotation. For instance, the word *lobby* and its derivative *lobbyist* originated in the U.S. and once had a uniquely American political meaning. Of course, the problem with Horwill's dictionary is that today *lobby* and similar terms are commonly recognized and used in both countries. But, though Horwill's work is out-of-date and no longer of much use to the average person as a guide to peculiar American usage, it remains interesting historically. More recent works of similar purpose are Schur's *British Self-Taught* and Moss's *What's the Difference? A British/American Dictionary.*

Dictionary of Modern English Usage

Descriptive Information

Full Title: **A Dictionary of Modern English Usage.** *Editor:* H. W. Fowler; Revised by Sir Ernest Gowers. *Publisher:* Oxford University Press. *Edition Reviewed:* Second Edition, 1965.

Classification: Special-Purpose—Usage & Idioms. *Pages:* xx, 725. *Total Entries:* 3,000. *Physical Size:* 5 by 7½ in.; 19 cm. *LC:* 65-24351. *ISBN:* 0-19-500153-2. *Lowest Retail Price:* $10.00.

Comments

A Dictionary of Modern English Usage by H. W. Fowler first appeared in 1926 and was revised 40 years later by Sir Ernest Gowers. Known to students of the English language simply as *Fowler*, this usage guide is the most famous work of its kind. The advice is authoritative, the style readable and to-the-point, the orientation British, and the tone prescriptive. Fowler (and his reviser) believed strongly in proper usage and rules strictly observed. Though cherished by many, *Fowler* is not really the best usage guide for most Americans. (Compare, for example, the Evanses' *Dictionary of Contemporary American Usage* or Wilson Follett's *Modern American Usage.*) Note also that Margaret Nicholson's *A Dictionary of American-English Usage* (1957) is based on the earlier edition of *Fowler.*

Other Critical Opinions

Katz, William A. *Basic Information Sources.* Vol. 1 of *Introduction to Reference Work,* 2nd ed. (New York: McGraw-Hill, 1974), pp. 280–281.

Dictionary of Problem Words and Expressions

Descriptive Information

Full Title: **Dictionary of Problem Words and Expressions.** *Editor:* Harry Shaw. *Publisher:* McGraw-Hill. *Edition Reviewed:* 1975.

Classification: Special-Purpose—Usage & Idioms. *Pages:* 261. *Total Entries:* 1,500. *Physical Size:* 6 by 9 in.; 23 cm. *LC:* 74-13722. *ISBN:* 0-07-056489-2. *Lowest Retail Price:* $10.95.

Comments

Shaw's *Dictionary of Problem Words and Expressions* aims "to alert you to faulty speech and writing habits you may have acquired and to confirm and strengthen you in good ones." Such problems as *will/shall, learn/teach,* and *plaintiff/defendant* are discussed knowledgeably and precisely. Shaw includes many examples of good and bad usage and there are numerous cross-references.

Other Critical Opinions

American Reference Books Annual 1976 (review by Francis J. Witty), p. 546.
Wilson Library Bulletin (review by Charles A. Bunge), October 1975, p. 121.

Dos, Don'ts and Maybes of English Usage

Descriptive Information

Full Title: **Dos, Don'ts and Maybes of English Usage.** *Author:* Theodore M. Bernstein. *Publisher:* Quadrangle. *Edition Reviewed:* 1977.

Classification: Special-Purpose—Usage & Idioms. *Pages:* 320. *LC:* 77-4293. *ISBN:* 0-8129-0695-0. *Lowest Retail Price:* $12.50.

Comments

Dos, Don'ts and Maybes of English Usage is the latest of Bernstein's books on proper usage. Others include *The Careful Writer, Miss Thistlebottom's Hobgoblins,* and *Watch Your Language. Dos, Don'ts and Maybes* is arranged alphabetically and covers such usage problems as differentiating between *bring* and *take* and *evoke* and *invoke.* Readable and authoritative.

Encyclopedic Dictionary of English Usage

Descriptive Information

Full Title: **Encyclopedic Dictionary of English Usage.** *Editors:* N. H. Mager and S. K. Mager. *Publisher:* Prentice-Hall. *Edition Reviewed:* 1974.

Classification: Special-Purpose—Usage & Idioms. *Pages:* x, 342. *Total Entries:* 15,000. *Physical Size:* 6¼ by 9½ in.; 24 cm. (hardcover). *LC:* 78-37656. *ISBN:* 0-13-275792-3 (hardcover). *Lowest Retail Price:* $10.95; also $3.95 paper.

Comments

The Magers' dictionary is a potpourri of usage questions "from many reference books, from clippings, and from original inquiry." The authors' preface continues: "It is more than a dictionary, more than a grammar, more than a manual of style—in many ways it serves the purposes of all three." You can find here the pronunciation of troublesome words, notes on punctuation, uncommon abbreviations, brief definitions of odd terms, etc. Possibly useful but not essential.

Other Critical Opinions

Booklist, July 1, 1975, p. 1136.
Library Journal, May 15, 1974, p. 1377.
Wilson Library Bulletin (review by Charles A. Bunge), September 1974, p. 94.

Harper Dictionary of Contemporary Usage

Descriptive Information

Full Title: **Harper Dictionary of Contemporary Usage.** *Editors:* William Morris and Mary Morris. *Publisher:* Harper & Row. *Edition Reviewed:* 1975.

Classification: Special-Purpose—Usage & Idioms. *Pages:* xx, 650. *Total Entries:* 3,500. *Physical Size:* 6¼ by 9½ in.; 24 cm. *LC:* 73-4112. *ISBN:* 0-06-013062-8. *Lowest Retail Price:* $15.00.

Comments

The *Harper Dictionary of Contemporary Usage* is an up-to-date, readable, and often laughably prescriptive usage guide. The Morrises, who also compiled the three-volume *Dictionary of Word and Phrase Origins*, cover such usage problems as using the word *author* as a verb (e.g., he *authored* the book), substituting *due to* for *because of*, distinguishing between *less* and *fewer*, and using *Ms.* as a title for women. Borrowing a page from *The American Heritage Dictionary* (which William Morris edited originally), the Morrises have a usage panel of 136 writers, editors, and public personalities who react to various usage questions, usually concerning words and phrases of current vintage. For instance, the panel is informed that *media* is a plural noun and then asked, "Would you accept 'The news *media* is to be commended'?" The Morrises tally the panel's votes (in the case of using *media* as a singular noun, the vote was 30 percent yes, 70 percent no) followed by a sampling of comments, e.g., Joseph A. Brandt sniffed that "Latin is too integrated in the language to be violated easily" and both Jean Stafford and S. I. Hayakawa cleverly said "Good God!" One reviewer put it just right: the *Harper Dictionary of Contemporary Usage* "equates change with corruption, and I cannot recommend it." Nonetheless, it's fun to browse in.

Other Critical Opinions

American Reference Books Annual 1976, pp. 545–546.
Booklist, December 15, 1976, p. 630.
Library Journal (review by B. Hunter Smeaton), September 15, 1975, p. 1618.
RQ (review by Raymond G. McInnis), Spring 1976, pp. 276–278.
Wilson Library Bulletin (review by Charles A. Bunge), March 1976, p. 557.

The King's English

Descriptive Information

Full Title: **The King's English.** *Editors:* H. W. Fowler and F. G. Fowler. *Publisher:* Oxford University Press. *Edition Reviewed:* Third Edition, 1931. *Classification:* Special-Purpose—Usage & Idioms. *Pages:* 383. *ISBN:* 0-19-869105-X (hardcover); 0-19-881330-9 (paper). *Lowest Retail Price:* $6.50; also $2.95 paper.

Comments

A forerunner of the Fowler brothers' famous *Dictionary of Modern English Usage*, this book on the rules of proper usage and common blunders was first published in 1906, revised the next year, and finally issued in its present edition in 1931. *The King's English* is not a dictionary but a wordbook which tells us what good usage was a generation or so ago.

Other Critical Opinions

American Reference Books Annual 1974, p. 471.

Look It Up

Descriptive Information

Full Title: **Look It Up: A Deskbook of American Spelling and Style.**
Editor: Rudolf Flesch. *Publisher:* Harper & Row. *Edition Reviewed:* 1977.
Classification: Special-Purpose—Usage & Idioms. *Pages:* x, 431. *Total
Entries:* 18,000. *Physical Size:* 5 by 7¼ in.; 18 cm. *LC:* 75-23880. *ISBN:* 0-06-
011292-1. *Lowest Retail Price:* $9.95.

Comments

Look It Up by Rudolf Flesch (who also wrote *Why Johnny Can't Read*
among other books) covers over 18,000 words which often pose problems in
everyday usage. Examples are *bejeweled* (Flesch simply comments "One *l*"),
conqueror ("ends in -*or*"), *inclement weather* ("Don't use this phrase when
stormy weather or *bad weather* will do"), *paper-thin* ("Hyphened"), and
stink ("Webster's lists *stink* in the sense of being very bad as standard usage").
Flesch consulted some 31 standard dictionaries when compiling *Look It Up*,
relying most heavily on the unabridged *Webster's Third New International
Dictionary. Look It Up* is a useful, authoritative, and up-to-date desk
companion. It will be especially helpful to secretaries and poor spellers.

Other Critical Opinions

Booklist, April 1, 1977, p. 1130.
Library Journal (review by David M. Hoffman), December 15, 1976, p. 2558.

Miss Thistlebottom's Hobgoblins

Descriptive Information

Full Title: **Miss Thistlebottom's Hobgoblins: The Careful Writer's Guide to
the Taboos, Bugbears and Outmoded Rules of English Usage.** *Author:*
Theodore M. Bernstein. *Publisher:* Farrar, Straus & Giroux. *Edition Reviewed:* 1971.
Classification: Special-Purpose—Usage & Idioms. *Pages:* 280. *LC:* 78-
143299. *Lowest Retail Price:* $2.95.

Comments

Theodore Bernstein, author of *The Careful Writer* and *Watch Your
Language*, is one of this country's leading authorities on English-language
usage. *Miss Thistlebottom's Hobgoblins* is another of Bernstein's excellent
books on the subject. This one is divided into four sections covering words,
syntax, idioms, and style. Such knotty problems as dangling participles, split

infinitives, and ending sentences with prepositions are clarified, often with good-humored examples. English teachers will find this manual especially helpful.

Other Critical Opinions

American Reference Books Annual 1972 (review by Marjorie P. Holt), p. 471.
Booklist, November 15, 1971, p. 261.
Library Journal, June 15, 1971, p. 2070.

Modern American Usage

Descriptive Information

Full Title: **Modern American Usage: A Guide.** *Author:* Wilson Follett. *Editors:* Jacques Barzun in collaboration with Carlos Baker, Frederick W. Dupee, Dudley Fitts, James D. Hart, Phyllis McGinley, and Lionel Trilling. *Publishers:* Hill & Wang (hardcover); Warner Books (paper). *Edition Reviewed:* 1966.

Classification: Special-Purpose—Usage & Idioms. *Pages:* 448. *ISBN:* 0-446-78119-3 (paper). *Lowest Retail Price:* $10.95; also $2.50 paper.

Comments

Wilson Follett, who died in 1963 before this book was completed, is perhaps the closest Americans have come to equaling the likes of H. W. Fowler, the great English usage authority. Indeed, Follett agreed with and emulated Fowler's position that there are few right ways and many wrong ways to use words and construct sentences. *Modern American Usage*, completed by seven literary notables under the general editorial direction of Jacques Barzun, represents Follett's accumulated wisdom on usage. The British novelist Kingsley Amis hailed *Modern American Usage* as having "an accuracy that, in my view, equals or surpasses Fowler's." And Bruce Catton, the American Civil War historian (writing in *American Heritage*, April 1967), said of Follett's book, "I wish that anyone who ever tries to write anything more consequential than a letter to his family might be required to read it, to reread it, and to meditate upon it. Here is a wise, effective, and pleasingly witty attack on sloppy writing and on the things that cause sloppy writing." But somewhat dated now.

Other Critical Opinions

American Reference Books Annual 1971 (review by John Phillip Immroth), p. 424.

Mrs. Byrne's Dictionary

Descriptive Information

Full Title: **Mrs. Byrne's Dictionary of Unusual, Obscure, and Preposterous Words: Gathered from Numerous and Diverse Authoritative Sources by Mrs.**

Byrne. *Author:* Josefa Heifetz Byrne. *Editor:* Robert Byrne. *Publisher:* University Books, distributed by Lyle Stuart (hardcover); Citadel Press (paper). *Edition Reviewed:* 1974.

Classification: Special-Purpose—Usage & Idioms. *Pages:* 242. *Total Entries:* 6,000. *Physical Size:* 6 by 9¼ in.; 24 cm. (paper). *ISBN:* 0-8216-0203-9 (hardcover); 0-8065-0498-6 (paper). *Lowest Retail Price:* $12.50; also $5.95 paper.

Comments

Josefa Heifetz Byrne, daughter of the famous violinist Jascha Heifetz, has according to the editor's introduction "managed to assemble the six thousand weirdest words in the English language." Example: *minimifidianism, furfuraceous, fizgig,* and *sthenobulia.* The definitions are brief and, thank heavens, pronunciations are given. Some 86 dictionaries and wordbooks were "thoroughly culled from *aasvogel* to *zzxjoanx*" in the course of compiling this interesting dictionary.

Other Critical Opinions

Booklist, October 1, 1974, p. 196.
Library Journal, June 1, 1974, pp. 1533–1534.

New York Times Everyday Reader's Dictionary

Descriptive Information

Full Title: **The New York Times Everyday Reader's Dictionary of Misunderstood, Misused, Mispronounced Words.** *Editor:* Laurence Urdang. *Publisher:* Quadrangle. *Edition Reviewed:* 1972.

Classification: Special-Purpose—Usage & Idioms. *Pages:* 377. *Total Entries:* 15,000. *Physical Size:* 5½ by 8¼ in.; 21 cm. (hardcover). *LC:* 74-184644. *ISBN:* 0-8129-0232-7 (hardcover); 0-8129-6244-3 (paper). *Lowest Retail Price:* $7.95; also $4.50 paper.

Comments

Urdang's dictionary of uncommon and/or troublesome words is a useful supplement to an abridged or pocket dictionary but most of the words (e.g., *fetid* or *foetid, fetiparous* or *foetiparous, fetor* or *foetor, fettle, feuilleton, fiacre, fiasco, fiat*) can be found in an unabridged dictionary. The definitions are concise and variant pronunciations are provided. Rudolf Flesch's *Look It Up* covers some of the same ground and is overall a more useful supplementary source.

Other Critical Opinions

American Reference Books Annual 1973, pp. 447–448.
Booklist, October 15, 1973, p. 186.
Library Journal, November 15, 1972, p. 3697.
Wilson Library Bulletin, October 1972, p. 199.

Oxford Dictionary of Current Idiomatic English

Descriptive Information

Full Title: **Oxford Dictionary of Current Idiomatic English. Volume 1: Verbs with Prepositions & Particles.** *Editors:* A. P. Cowie and R. Mackin. *Publisher:* Oxford University Press. *Edition Reviewed:* 1975.

Classification: Special-Purpose—Usage & Idioms. *Pages:* lxxxi, 396. *Total Entries:* 20,000. *Physical Size:* 5¾ by 8¾ in.; 22 cm. *ISBN:* 0-19-431145-7. *Lowest Retail Price:* $13.50.

Comments

The first of two volumes which will provide the most comprehensive source for English idioms, this dictionary concentrates on defining idiomatic expressions consisting of a verb and preposition, e.g., *back off, back on to, back up.* Volume 2, tentatively entitled *General Expressions,* will include more common idioms involving nouns, adjectives, adverbs, and proverbial sayings. The front matter of Volume 1 provides an informative and detailed 80-page discussion on the nature and formation of idioms. In the back there is a comprehensive index of nouns, adjectives, and adverbs which appear in the idioms. Despite its British orientation, this dictionary, when completed, will constitute the most significant source for idioms available.

Other Critical Opinions

American Reference Books Annual 1977 (review by Bohdan S. Wynar), p. 519.

RQ (review by Pamela C. Sieving), Summer 1976, pp. 352–353.

Reference Handbook of Grammar & Usage

Descriptive Information

Full Title: **Reference Handbook of Grammar & Usage: Derived from Writer's Guide and Index to English.** *Editor:* Porter G. Perrin. *Publisher:* William Morrow & Co. *Edition Reviewed:* 1972.

Classification: Special-Purpose—Usage & Idioms. *Pages:* 297. *Total Entries:* 900. *Physical Size:* 6¼ by 9¼ in.; 24 cm. *Lowest Retail Price:* $6.50.

Comments

The publisher says the *Reference Handbook of Grammar & Usage* is a new work but that the idea for it came from Perrin's successful *Writer's Guide and Index to English* (now in its Fifth Edition). The *Reference Handbook* covers such common usage problems as *can* vs. *may, lie* vs. *lay,* and *shall* vs. *will.* Much attention is also given to such terms as *comma, direct object, jargon, prefix, preposition, shifted construction,* and *spelling.* The entries, arranged A–Z, vary in length from a few lines to several pages. Perrin provides many helpful examples. In the back of the book there are 24 exercises. The material is clear, reliable, and up-to-date.

Other Critical Opinions

Booklist, December 15, 1972, p. 370.

Usage and Abusage

Descriptive Information

Full Title: **Usage and Abusage: A Guide to Good English.** *Editor:* Eric Partridge. *Publisher:* Hamish Hamilton. *Distributor:* British Book Centre. *Edition Reviewed:* Sixth Edition, 1965.
Classification: Special-Purpose—Usage & Idioms. *Pages:* 392. *Total Entries:* 5,000. *Physical Size:* 5½ by 8½ in.; 22 cm. *ISBN:* 0-241-90678-4. *Lowest Retail Price:* $17.50.

Comments

Usage and Abusage, according to Partridge, "is designed, not to compete with H. W. Fowler's *Modern English Usage* (that would be a fatuous attempt—and impossible), but to supplement it and to complement it, and yet to write a book that should be less Olympian and less austere." Hence Partridge's commentaries on questions of usage tend to be more informal and livelier than Fowler's. The book, first published in 1942, was substantially revised in 1957 (Fifth Edition) but only slightly so in 1965 (Sixth Edition). American users will be happy to note that *Usage and Abusage* has been annotated by W. Cabell Greet on points of American usage. An abridged version, *The Concise Usage and Abusage*, is also available.

Watch Your Language

Descriptive Information

Full Title: **Watch Your Language.** *Author:* Theodore M. Bernstein. *Publisher:* Atheneum. *Edition Reviewed:* 1965.
Classification: Special-Purpose—Usage & Idioms. *Lowest Retail Price:* $3.95 paper.

Comments

Watch Your Language, which contains a preface by Jacques Barzun, illuminates thorny questions of usage in a manner similar to Bernstein's other books on the subject, e.g., *The Careful Writer* and *Miss Thistlebottom's Hobgoblins*. Bernstein's style is readable and fresh, his approach reasonable.

What's the Difference? A British/American Dictionary

Descriptive Information

Full Title: **What's the Difference? A British/American Dictionary.** *Editor:* Norman Moss. *Publisher:* Harper & Row. *Edition Reviewed:* 1973.

Classification: Special-Purpose—Usage & Idioms. *Pages:* 138. *Total Entries:* 3,000. *Physical Size:* 5¾ by 8½ in.; 22 cm. *LC:* 72-9140. *ISBN:* 0-06-013096-2. *Lowest Retail Price:* $8.95.

Comments

Moss's little dictionary is set up in bilingual fashion with the first part British/American and the second American/British. In the British/American section there are such entries as *flea pit* (a shabby movie theater), *Fleet Street* (London's newspaper headquarters), *flog* (to sell), and *fridge* (short for refrigerator). Moss's definitions are brief but clear. Unfortunately, pronunciations are not given. The dictionary's rationale is "to help Britons and Americans understand and communicate better with one another." *What's the Difference?* achieves that purpose. In addition, it's rather fun to browse in. Compare Schur's *British Self-Taught*, a similar work.

Other Critical Opinions

American Reference Books Annual 1974, p. 457.
Library Journal (review by B. Hunter Smeaton), September 1, 1973, p. 2424.

Word Watcher's Handbook

Descriptive Information

Full Title: **Word Watcher's Handbook: Including a Deletionary of the Most Abused and Misused Words.** *Editor:* Phyllis Martin. *Publisher:* David McKay Co. *Edition Reviewed:* 1977.

Classification: Special-Purpose—Usage & Idioms. *Pages:* x, 81. *Total Entries:* 2,000. *Physical Size:* 5¾ by 8½ in.; 22 cm. (hardcover). *LC:* 76-12741. *ISBN:* 0-679-20354-0 (hardcover); 0-679-20369-9 (paper). *Lowest Retail Price:* $7.95; also $3.95 paper.

Comments

Martin is principally concerned about clichés and atrocious usage mistakes like saying *hunnert* for *hundred.* She claims, probably correctly, that such illiterate usage will cost white collar workers promotions and better jobs. As a former supervisor of women's employment for the Procter & Gamble Company, she speaks with some authority on that subject. The handbook has several sections: a deletionary (words and idioms which should be deleted from one's vocabulary, like *theirselves*), a list of "feeble phrases" (like *blushing bride*), a usage list (e.g., *drug* is "not the past tense of *drag*"), and "pronunciation pitfalls." Slight and somewhat repetitious but possibly useful for hardcore cases.

Other Critical Opinions

Library Journal, April 1, 1977, pp. 786–787.

USAGE: STYLE MANUALS

The Elements of Style

Descriptive Information

Full Title: **The Elements of Style.** *Authors:* William Strunk, Jr.; Revised by E. B. White. *Publisher:* Macmillan Publishing Co. *Edition Reviewed:* Second Edition, 1972.
Classification: Special-Purpose—Usage: Style Manuals. *Pages:* xiii, 78. *Physical Size:* 4¼ by 7 in.; 18 cm. (paper). *LC:* 75-188776. *ISBN:* 0-02-418270-2 (hardcover); 0-02-418260-5 (paper). *Lowest Retail Price:* $4.50; also $1.65 paper.

Comments

Not long after Jimmy Carter became president, someone accused him of making his speeches too simple. According to *Time* magazine, one of the president's speech writers retorted, "we are not writing down to people. If you follow Strunk and White's *Elements of Style*, you can meet his standard." The book, which provides many examples of correct usage, is very brief, very precise, and very popular. It dates back to 1918 and a Cornell professor named William Strunk, Jr. In 1959 and again in 1972, E. B. White revised this famous "little book," the only style manual ever to make the bestseller list.

Other Critical Opinions

Booklist, July 15, 1972, p. 986.
Katz, William A. *Basic Information Sources.* Vol. 1 of *Introduction to Reference Work*, 2nd ed. (New York: McGraw-Hill, 1974), pp. 280–281.

A Manual for Writers

Descriptive Information

Full Title: **A Manual for Writers of Term Papers, Theses, and Dissertations.** *Author:* Kate L. Turabian. *Publisher:* University of Chicago Press. *Edition Reviewed:* Fourth Edition, 1973.
Classification: Special-Purpose—Usage: Style Manuals. *Pages:* viii, 216. *Physical Size:* 5¼ by 8 in.; 21 cm. (paper). *LC:* 73-77792. *ISBN:* 0-226-81620-6 (hardcover); 0-226-81621-4 (paper). *Lowest Retail Price:* $8.50; also $3.45 paper.

Comments

This manual, based on the University of Chicago's indispensable *Manual of Style* (Twelfth Edition), provides detailed instructions for preparing formal papers. First published in 1937, *A Manual for Writers* was thoroughly revised in 1955, 1967, and most recently 1973. The current edition recommends that certain Latin abbreviations (such as *op. cit.* and *loc. cit.*) no longer be used in footnotes and there is an expanded section on punctuation.

Other Critical Opinions

American Reference Books Annual 1974, pp. 39–40.

A Manual of Style

Descriptive Information

Full Title: **A Manual of Style for Authors, Editors, and Copywriters.** *Author:* Editorial Staff of the University of Chicago Press. *Publisher:* University of Chicago Press. *Edition Reviewed:* Twelfth Edition, Revised, 1969.

Classification: Special-Purpose—Usage: Style Manuals. *Pages:* ix, 546. *Physical Size:* 6¼ by 9¼ in.; 24 cm. *LC:* 6-40582. *ISBN:* 0-226-77008-7. *Lowest Retail Price:* $12.50.

Comments

The famous and influential University of Chicago's *Manual of Style* first appeared in 1906 and has undergone numerous revisions, the latest in 1969. Along with the style manuals issued by the Government Printing Office and the *New York Times*, this manual is a final authority on questions involving punctuation, spelling, abbreviations, footnotes, etc. when preparing or editing manuscript material. There are also sections covering bookmaking, production, and printing.

The New York Times Manual of Style and Usage

Descriptive Information

Full Title: **The New York Times Manual of Style and Usage: A Desk Book of Guidelines for Writers and Editors.** *Editor:* Lewis Jordan. *Publisher:* Quadrangle. Former title: *The New York Times Style Book for Writers and Editors. Edition Reviewed:* Revised Edition, 1976.

Classification: Special-Purpose—Usage: Style Manuals. *Pages:* 231. *Total Entries:* 4,000. *Physical Size:* 6¾ by 9½ in.; 25 cm. *LC:* 75-8306. *ISBN:* 0-8129-0578-4. *Lowest Retail Price:* $10.00.

Comments

Not as extensive as the University of Chicago's *Manual of Style* or the Government Printing Office's *Style Manual,* the *New York Times'* manual nonetheless wields considerable influence. This revised edition has added the word *usage* to the title, reflecting the fact that the manual deals as much with questions of good usage as it does the mechanics of spelling, capitalization, punctuation, and abbreviation. Lewis Jordan is news editor of the *New York Times.*

Other Critical Opinions

American Reference Books Annual 1977 (review by Peggy M. Tozer), pp. 69–70.

Wilson Library Bulletin (review by Charles A. Bunge), May 1976, p. 747.

Preparation of Manuscripts

Descriptive Information

Full Title: **Preparation of Manuscripts and Correction of Proofs.** *Author:* Brooke Crutchley. *Publisher:* Cambridge University Press. *Edition Reviewed:* Sixth Edition, 1970.

Classification: Special-Purpose—Usage: Style Manuals. *Pages:* 20. *Physical Size:* 5½ by 8½ in.; 22 cm. *ISBN:* 0-521-07864-4. *Lowest Retail Price:* $1.75 paper.

Comments

Strunk and White's slim *Elements of Style* proves that a manual of style need not be overly long to be useful and even cherished. The Cambridge University Press's *Preparation of Manuscripts*, a concise papercover guide designed for the publisher's authors and printers, is hardly in the same category of usefulness and cherishedness as *The Elements of Style*. It is, however, an intelligently prepared guide which can be quickly digested.

Preparing the Manuscript

Descriptive Information

Full Title: **Preparing the Manuscript.** *Author:* Udia G. Olsen. *Publisher:* The Writer, Inc. *Edition Reviewed:* Eighth Edition, 1976.

Classification: Special-Purpose—Usage: Style Manuals. *Pages:* 154. *LC:* 75-42592. *ISBN:* 0-87116-097-8. *Lowest Retail Price:* $4.95.

Comments

This standard guide is directed mainly at authors, not students. Like Edward Seeber's *A Style Manual for Authors*, it provides basic information about typing the manuscript, punctuation and the mechanics of writing, proofreading, quoted matter in the text and copyright, and even a section on how to market the completed manuscript.

Other Critical Opinions

American Reference Books Annual 1977 (review by Ann J. Harwell), p. 70.

Student's Guide for Writing College Papers

Descriptive Information

Full Title: **Student's Guide for Writing College Papers.** *Author:* Kate L. Turabian. *Publisher:* University of Chicago Press. *Edition Reviewed:* Third Edition, 1976.
   Classification: Special-Purpose—Usage: Style Manuals. *Pages:* viii, 256. *Physical Size:* 5¼ by 8 in.; 21 cm. (paper). *LC:* 76-435. *ISBN:* 0-226-81622-2 (hardcover); 0-226-81623-0 (paper). *Lowest Retail Price:* $7.95; also $3.45 paper.

Comments

This well-known guide for secondary school and college students was first published in 1963 and revised in 1969 and most recently in 1976. The Third Edition has added sections on numbers and punctuation and greatly expanded the "Select List of Reference Works" found in Appendix B. The best work of its kind.

Style Manual (GPO)

Descriptive Information

Full Title: **Style Manual.** *Author:* U.S. Government Printing Office. *Publisher:* U. S. Government Printing Office. *Edition Reviewed:* 1973.
   Classification: Special-Purpose—Usage: Style Manuals. *Pages:* 548. *Lowest Retail Price:* $4.70.

Comments

This manual, issued by the U.S. Government Printing Office (GPO) as a style guide for government authors, covers basic rules of grammar, punctuation, spelling, abbreviation, type size, and other printing questions. The GPO *Style Manual* is one of the best known such guides, along with the University of Chicago's *Manual of Style* and *The New York Times Manual of Style and Usage.*

Other Critical Opinions

American Reference Books Annual 1974, p. 40.

Style Manual for Authors

Descriptive Information

Full Title: **A Style Manual for Authors.** *Author:* Edward D. Seeber. *Publisher:* Indiana University Press. *Edition Reviewed:* 1965.
   Classification: Special-Purpose—Usage: Style Manuals. *Pages:* 96. *Physical Size:* 5 by 8 in.; 20 cm. *LC:* 65-11798. *ISBN:* 0-253-20076-8. *Lowest Retail Price:* $1.25 paper.

Comments

About the same size as Strunk and White's excellent *Elements of Style*, Seeber's manual lacks the stylistic flair and pungent examples which characterize Strunk and White, but *A Style Manual for Authors* is clear and informative. It is, however, in need of some revision. For instance, *op. cit.* and other Latin abbreviations associated with footnote style are used less and less today.

Washington Post Deskbook on Style

Descriptive Information

Full Title: **The Washington Post Deskbook on Style.** *Editor:* Robert A. Webb. *Publisher:* McGraw-Hill. *Edition Reviewed:* 1978.

Classification: Special-Purpose—Usage: Style Manuals. *Pages:* 288. *Physical Size:* 5½ by 8 in.; 21 cm. (hardcover). *ISBN:* 0-07-068397-2 (hardcover); 0-07-068398-0 (paper). *Lowest Retail Price:* $10.00; also $4.95 paper.

Comments

The Washington Post Deskbook on Style, to appear in January 1978, includes the usual rules concerning the mechanics of punctuation, spelling, abbreviation, capitalization, etc. Common usage questions are also covered. In addition, the book provides information on such diverse subjects as recent language changes, the press and the First Amendment, and local and federal governmental agencies and officials. Compare with *The New York Times Manual of Style and Usage.*

Words into Type

Descriptive Information

Full Title: **Words into Type.** *Authors:* Marjorie E. Skillin and Robert M. Gay. *Publisher:* Prentice-Hall. *Edition Reviewed:* Third Edition, 1974.

Classification: Special-Purpose—Usage: Style Manuals. *Pages:* 585. *LC:* 73-21726. *ISBN:* 0-13-964262-5. *Lowest Retail Price:* $12.50.

Comments

Words into Type is principally for printers, designers, and production departments of publishers. It is considered the best typographic style manual available. The Third Edition has been heavily revised.

Other Critical Opinions

American Reference Books Annual 1975, p. 54.
Choice, December 1974, p. 1459.

Zondervan Manual of Style

Descriptive Information

Full Title: **The Zondervan Manual of Style for Authors, Editors, and Proofreaders.** *Author:* Editorial Staff of Zondervan Publishing House. *Publisher:* Zondervan Publishing House. *Edition Reviewed:* 1976.

Classification: Special-Purpose—Usage: Style Manuals. *Pages:* 48. *Physical Size:* 5½ by 8 in.; 21 cm. *Lowest Retail Price:* $1.95 paper.

Comments

The Zondervan Manual of Style is a small papercover manual which succinctly covers such mechanics as punctuation, numbers and abbreviations, capitalization, and proofreading. Because Zondervan is a religious book publisher, a list of specialized "Biblical and religious terms" which might pose problems is included. Most of the examples and the basic style, however, derive from the University of Chicago's *Manual of Style* (Twelfth Edition).

USAGE: SECRETARIAL HANDBOOKS

Complete Secretary's Handbook

Descriptive Information

Full Title: **Complete Secretary's Handbook.** *Authors:* Lillian Doris and Esse May Miller; Revised by Mary A. De Vries. *Publisher:* Prentice-Hall. *Edition Reviewed:* Fourth Edition, 1977.

Classification: Special-Purpose—Usage: Secretarial Handbooks. *Pages:* 555. *Physical Size:* 6¼ by 9¼ in.; 24 cm. *LC:* 76-40184. *ISBN:* 0-13-163402-X. *Lowest Retail Price:* $10.95.

Comments

This standard secretarial manual was initially published in 1951 and revised several times, most recently in 1977. Part 3 contains chapters on word usage, spelling and syllabication, punctuation, capitalization, and abbreviations. The material is clearly and simply presented, with many helpful examples. Also, Part 5 provides an annotated list of additional reference sources. One of the best works of its kind.

Follett Vest-Pocket Secretary's Handbook

Descriptive Information

Full Title: **Follett Vest-Pocket Secretary's Handbook.** *Authors:* Bradford Chambers and L. Barbara Tanner. *Publisher:* Follett Publishing Co. *Edition Reviewed:* 1965.

Classification: Special-Purpose—Usage: Secretarial Handbooks. *Pages:* xviii, 332. *Physical Size:* 3 by 5½ in.; 14 cm. *LC:* 65-16545. *ISBN:* 0-695-89068-9. *Lowest Retail Price:* $2.50 paper.

Comments

This small papercover handbook for secretaries includes standard proofreader's marks and a section on "Where to Look It Up" but little else on the mechanics of style and nothing on word usage.

Modern Secretary's Complete Guide

Descriptive Information

Full Title: **The Modern Secretary's Complete Guide.** *Author:* Twyla K. Schwieger. *Publisher:* Parker Publishing Co. *Distributor:* Prentice-Hall. *Edition Reviewed:* 1971.

Classification: Special-Purpose—Usage: Secretarial Handbooks. *Pages:* 286. *Physical Size:* 6¼ by 9¼ in.; 24 cm. *LC:* 72-150094. *ISBN:* 0-13-597591-3. *Lowest Retail Price:* $8.95.

Comments

Schwieger's guide includes a chapter on "Business Writing Made Easy" which covers punctuation, spelling, word division, capitalization, and abbreviations. The material is quite elementary compared with other secretarial manuals like the *Complete Secretary's Handbook*, the *New Standard Reference for Secretaries*, *The Secretary's Handbook*, and *Webster's Secretarial Handbook*.

New Standard Reference for Secretaries

Descriptive Information

Full Title: **New Standard Reference for Secretaries and Administrative Assistants.** *Authors:* J. Harold Janis and Margaret H. Thompson. *Publisher:* Macmillan Publishing Co. *Edition Reviewed:* 1972.

Classification: Special-Purpose—Usage: Secretarial Handbooks. *Pages:* xiv, 801. *Physical Size:* 6½ by 9½ in.; 24 cm. *LC:* 78-150074. *ISBN:* 0-02-360260-0. *Lowest Retail Price:* $12.95.

Comments

This excellent manual devotes well over 100 pages to correct usage, punctuation, and the mechanics of style. There is also a lengthy dictionary of business terms and a list of standard abbreviations toward the back of the book. Written by two business professors, the *New Standard Reference for Secretaries and Administrative Assistants* provides clear, detailed usage information which may be needed by modern secretaries.

Other Critical Opinions

American Reference Books Annual 1973, p. 346.
Booklist, October 15, 1972, p. 166.

The Secretary's Handbook

Descriptive Information

Full Title: **The Secretary's Handbook: A Manual of Correct Usage.**
Authors: Sarah Augusta Taintor and Kate M. Monro; Revised by Kate M.
Monro and Margaret D. Shertzer. *Publisher:* Macmillan Publishing Co.
Edition Reviewed: Ninth Edition, 1969.

Classification: Special-Purpose—Usage: Secretarial Handbooks. *Pages:*
xi, 530. *Physical Size:* 5¾ by 8½ in.; 22 cm. *LC:* 69-10466. *ISBN:* 0-02-
616230-X. *Lowest Retail Price:* $9.95.

Comments

The Secretary's Handbook has assisted secretaries and office workers for
50 years. Part I (the first 186 pages) deals with capitalization, punctuation,
word division, numbers, spelling, diction, pronunciation, abbreviations, and
concludes with a lengthy section called "Points of Grammar." Part II
contains useful material on manuscript preparation and report writing.
Provides fuller coverage of the mechanics of style than other secretarial
manuals. There should be a new edition soon.

Standard Handbook for Secretaries

Descriptive Information

Full Title: **Standard Handbook for Secretaries.** *Author:* Lois Hutchinson.
Publisher: McGraw-Hill. *Edition Reviewed:* Eighth Edition, 1969.

Classification: Special-Purpose—Usage: Secretarial Handbooks. *Pages:*
638. *LC:* 69-19201. *ISBN:* 0-07-031537-X. *Lowest Retail Price:* $7.95.

Comments

Designed as a complete office reference book, the *Standard Handbook for
Secretaries* includes information about the mechanics of style and usage. Not
as up-to-date, however, as the *Complete Secretary's Handbook* (Fourth
Edition, 1977) and *Webster's Secretarial Handbook* (1976).

Successful Secretary's Handbook

Descriptive Information

Full Title: **The Successful Secretary's Handbook.** *Authors:* Esther R.
Becker and Evelyn Anders. *Publisher:* Harper & Row. *Edition Reviewed:*
1971.

Classification: Special-Purpose—Usage: Secretarial Handbooks. *Pages:* xi, 418. *Physical Size:* 6½ by 9½ in.; 24 cm. *LC:* 70-83584. *Lowest Retail Price:* $10.95.

Comments

Becker and Anders' handbook devotes Part III (about 115 pages) to the basic mechanics of writing such as punctuation, grammar, and syntax. There is also information on abbreviations, capitalization, and spelling, including 500 frequently misspelled words. Part VI (about 70 pages) covers homonyms, usage problems and tips, and foreign expressions. A useful desk reference for simple questions of usage and style. The handbook was one of *Library Journal*'s best business books of 1971.

Other Critical Opinions

Library Journal, March 1, 1972, p. 843.

Webster's Secretarial Handbook

Descriptive Information

Full Title: **Webster's Secretarial Handbook.** *Editor:* Anna L. Eckersley-Johnson. *Publisher:* G. & C. Merriam Co. *Edition Reviewed:* 1976.

Classification: Special-Purpose—Usage: Secretarial Handbooks. *Pages:* 546. *Physical Size:* 7 by 10 in.; 25 cm. *LC:* 76-22498. *ISBN:* 0-87779-036-1. *Lowest Retail Price:* $8.95.

Comments

This up-to-date, well organized, authoritatively prepared manual deals with all matters secretarial, including effective business English. Specifically, Chapter 7 covers abbreviations, capitalization, italicization, numbers, punctuation, syllabication, grammar, and troublesome questions of style with sensible tips for effective writing. The approach is contemporary and there are numerous illustrative examples. Much useful information in tabular form.

Other Critical Opinions

Booklist, July 15, 1977, p. 1757.
Library Journal (review by John D. Campbell), February 1, 1977, p. 371.

SLANG AND DIALECT

Francis Grose, an eighteenth-century British lexicographer, called slang "A nasty name for a nasty thing." One of George Eliot's characters (young Fred Vincy) in *Middlemarch* remarks, "All choice of words is slang. It marks a class . . . . correct English is the slang of prigs who write history and essays. And the strongest slang of all is the slang of poets." And Eric Partridge, who has been called "the Godfather of slang," says that "Slang reveals men's urges, desires, their aspirations and what they detest." To most of us, however, slang simply means a word or phrase that is not accepted as standard English. Such terms may be widely known (e.g., *booze* meaning liquor) or their usage may be limited to a particular group (e.g., *duster* meaning a close pitch in baseball). Much slang originates in subcultures, such as racial, ethnic, social, and regional groups. For instance, the black subculture in America has produced a wealth of slang, as have the drug, homosexual, and criminal subcultures. One outstanding characteristic of slang is that it tends to come and go rather rapidly. Who, for example, says *sockdolager, cake-eater*, and *skiddoo* today? Yet, these words were widely used slang terms in the 1920s.

Slang dictionaries attempt to record this colorful and often fleeting vocabulary. The more substantial slang dictionaries provide detailed word histories and thus complement the etymological dictionaries. Also, because they identify and define various types of informal and sometimes offensive vocabulary (such as vulgarisms and epithets), slang dictionaries also serve as complements to usage dictionaries and manuals. This section of the *Buying Guide* covers three types of slang dictionaries: (1) General works like Wentworth and Flexner's indispensable *Dictionary of American Slang;* (2): Lists which deal with the vocabulary of a particular social or cultural group, such as *The Queens' Vernacular* (homosexual slang); and (3) Dictionaries of regional dialect, e.g., Gould's *Maine Lingo.*

Boontling

Descriptive Information

Full Title: **Boontling: An American Lingo.** *Compiler:* Charles C. Adams. *Publisher:* University of Texas Press. *Edition Reviewed:* 1971.
Classification: Special-Purpose—Slang. *Pages:* 272. *LC:* 77-147871. *ISBN:* 0-292-70082-2. *Lowest Retail Price:* $9.50.

Comments

Boontling is a local patois indigenous to the Boonville area of north central California which, prior to this book, had not been studied at any great length. Adams's book analyzes Boontling and provides an extensive vocabulary with etymological notes. Useful to linguists concerned with dialects.

Other Critical Opinions

American Reference Books Annual 1972 (review by Robert Parslow), pp. 470–471.

Concise Dictionary of English Slang

Descriptive Information

Full Title: **A Concise Dictionary of English Slang and Colloquialisms.** *Editor:* Brian A. Phythian. *Publisher:* The Writer, Inc. *Edition Reviewed:* Second Edition, 1976.

Classification: Special-Purpose—Slang. *Pages:* viii, 208. *Total Entries:* 6,500. *Physical Size:* 5¼ by 8½ in.; 22 cm. *LC:* 76-3524. *ISBN:* 0-87116-099-4. *Lowest Retail Price:* $4.95 paper.

Comments

Phythian says his work "began as a revision of William Freeman's *Concise Dictionary of Slang* [1955], but so little of this now remains in these pages that it would be wrong to hold him responsible for them." Phythian also revised Freeman's *Concise Dictionary of English Idioms.* Neither work is of any great consequence. The slang dictionary merely lists and very briefly defines nonstandard words and phrases not included in *The Concise Oxford Dictionary*, which Phythian adopted as "a generally handy guide to Standard English."

Dictionary of Afro-American Slang

Descriptive Information

Full Title: **Dictionary of Afro-American Slang.** *Editor:* Clarence Major. *Publisher:* International Publishers Co. *Edition Reviewed:* 1970.
Classification: Special-Purpose—Slang. *Pages:* 127. *Total Entries:* 2,500. *LC:* 74-130863. *Lowest Retail Price:* $5.95; also $1.95 paper.

Comments

Dictionary of Afro-American Slang is a slight work by a young black writer. It includes many terms derived from the jazz and drug subcultures. Larger than but similar to Roberts' *The Third Ear: A Black Glossary.*

Other Critical Opinions

Wilson Library Bulletin, February 1972, p. 544.

Dictionary of American Slang

Descriptive Information

Full Title: **Dictionary of American Slang: Second Supplemented Edition.** *Editors:* Harold Wentworth and Stuart Berg Flexner. *Publishers:* T. Y. Crowell Co. *Edition Reviewed:* Second Supplemented Edition, 1975.
Classification: Special-Purpose—Slang. *Pages:* xviii, 766. *Total Entries:* 22,000. *Physical Size:* 6¼ by 9¼ in.; 24 cm. *LC:* 75-8644. *ISBN:* 0-690-00670-5. *Lowest Retail Price:* $12.95.

Comments

The *Dictionary of American Slang* by Wentworth and Flexner was originally published in 1960. In 1967 the same work was reissued with a 48-page supplement by Flexner. And in 1975 the dictionary appeared with a new, much larger supplement which added about 1,500 entries plus those contained in the 1967 supplement. As such, the dictionary is the largest, most up-to-date, and authoritatively prepared list of contemporary American slang available. The late Harold Wentworth was a distinguished language scholar and Stuart Berg Flexner is a well-known, experienced lexicographer who has most recently published *I Hear America Talking*, an engaging work of popular etymology. The dictionary, which covers many taboo and/or vulgar terms, provides detailed definitions and numerous illustrative quotations (with full citations). Frequently the first known use of a word or phrase is indicated, thus making the *Dictionary of American Slang* an invaluable source of etymological information. All periods of American history are covered but the emphasis is on modern slang. The outstanding American slang dictionary. Note that there is an abridgment of the dictionary in paperback entitled *Pocket Dictionary of American Slang* (Pocket Books, $1.95).

Other Critical Opinions

American Reference Books Annual 1976 (review by Richard A. Gray), p. 545.
Booklist, June 15, 1976, pp. 1484–1485.
Katz, William A. *Basic Information Sources*. Vol. 1 of *Introduction to Reference Work*, 2nd ed. (New York: McGraw-Hill, 1974), pp. 276–277.
Library Journal, August 1975, p. 1404.

Dictionary of Contemporary and Colloquial Usage

Descriptive Information

Full Title: **A Dictionary of Contemporary and Colloquial Usage.** *Editor:* Helen Dahlskog. *Publisher:* English Language Institute of America. *Edition Reviewed:* 1972.
Classification: Special-Purpose—Slang. *Pages:* 32. *Total Entries:* 2,000.
Physical Size: 9 by 11 in.; 28 cm. *LC:* 77-38007. *ISBN:* 0-8326-0011-3.
Lowest Retail Price: $2.00 paper.

Comments

Dahlskog's slim paperbound list of recent slang terms "was prepared for use as a supplementary section in certain editions of *The Living Webster Encyclopedic Dictionary of the English Language*" (see profile in the "semi-unabridged" general dictionary section of the *Buying Guide*). For the most part, the Second Supplemented Edition of the *Dictionary of American Slang* (see profile immediately preceding) covers the same vocabulary as Dahlskog's lexicon. Unlike the *Dictionary of American Slang*, Dahlskog does not provide illustrative quotations or etymological information.

Other Critical Opinions

American Reference Books Annual 1973, p. 452.
Wilson Library Bulletin, November 1972, p. 292.

Dictionary of Rhyming Slang

Descriptive Information

Full Title: **A Dictionary of Rhyming Slang.** *Editor:* Julian Franklyn. *Publisher:* Routledge & Kegan Paul. *Edition Reviewed:* Second Edition, 1961.

Classification: Special-Purpose—Slang. *Pages:* xii, 202. *Total Entries:* 2,000. *Physical Size:* 5½ by 8¾ in.; 22 cm. (hardcover). *ISBN:* 0-7100-8051-4 (hardcover); 0-7100-8052-2 (paper). *Lowest Retail Price:* $11.95; also $4.80 paper.

Comments

In a long and informative essay which prefaces this dictionary, Franklyn comments that "Rhyming slang in England, more particularly in the South of England, and most particularly in London, is loved and enjoyed and, within the limits of their knowledge and ability, used by all classes of society: it is apparently not so loved and used in either Australia or America." With that in mind, Franklyn's dictionary includes about 2,000 examples of rhyming slang, e.g., *bit of blink* (meaning *drink*), *brass tacks* (meaning *facts*), and *Annie Laurie* (meaning *three-ton lorry*). Interesting to browse in but hardly essential.

Dictionary of Slang and Unconventional English

Descriptive Information

Full Title: **A Dictionary of Slang and Unconventional English: Colloquialisms and Catch-phrases, Solecisms and Catachreses, Nicknames, Vulgarisms and Such Americanisms as Have Been Naturalized.** *Editor:* Eric Partridge. *Publisher:* Macmillan Publishing Co. *Edition Reviewed:* Seventh Edition (two volumes in one: the dictionary and the supplement), 1970.

Classification: Special-Purpose—Slang. *Pages:* xiv, 1528. *Total Entries:* 65,000. *Physical Size:* 6½ by 9½ in.; 24 cm. *LC:* 79-136481. *ISBN:* 0-02-594970-5. *Lowest Retail Price:* $22.50.

Comments

First published in 1937 and subsequently revised a number of times, *A Dictionary of Slang and Unconventional English* (Seventh Edition) comprises the basic dictionary (974 pages) and a mammoth supplement (550 pages), all published in a large single volume. Eric Partridge is universally acknowledged as the foremost authority on English slang and this is his foremost work. *A Dictionary of Slang and Unconventional English* and its supplement cover over 65,000 terms, mostly of British origin. The intention is to include all slang and other informal words and phrases, including vulgarisms, in use since 1600. Partridge covers all such terms found in the *Oxford English Dictionary* plus numerous ones omitted from the famous historical dictionary. Partridge, like the *OED*, provides illustrative quotations with full citations. *The Dictionary of Slang and Unconventional English* is the largest and most scholarly work of its kind available. It includes, however, relatively little American slang. Fortunately, Wentworth and Flexner's *Dictionary of American Slang* (Second Supplemented Edition, 1975) nicely complements the Partridge dictionary.

Other Critical Opinions

Katz, William A. *Basic Information Sources.* Vol. 1 of *Introduction to Reference Work*, 2nd ed. (New York: McGraw-Hill, 1974), p. 277.

Dictionary of the Underworld, British and American

Descriptive Information

Full Title: **A Dictionary of the Underworld, British and American.** *Editor:* Eric Partridge. *Publisher:* Macmillan Publishing Co. *Edition Reviewed:* Third Edition, 1968.

Classification: Special-Purpose—Slang. *Pages:* 886. *Total Entries:* 25,000. *Lowest Retail Price:* $17.50.

Comments

First published in 1949 in Great Britain, revised in 1961, and greatly enlarged and updated in 1968, *A Dictionary of the Underworld, British and American* covers the "vocabularies of crooks, criminals, racketeers, beggars and tramps, convicts, the commercial underworld, the drug traffic, the white slave traffic, spivs," etc. It is more specialized than Partridge's basic *Dictionary of Slang and Unconventional English* and, although some modern terms are included, the emphasis is historical. An interesting sidelight is that Partridge verified his definitions through contacts in the underworld: "I was enabled, at no risk whatsoever, to establish contact with five or six crooks or knowledgeable near-crooks, and for a beer or two, a half-crown here and there, to obtain information I needed."

Other Critical Opinions

Katz, William A. *Basic Information Sources.* Vol. 1 of *Introduction to Reference Work*, 2nd ed. (New York: McGraw-Hill, 1974), pp. 276–277.

Dixie-Doodle Dictionary

Descriptive Information

Full Title: **The Dixie-Doodle Dictionary: How to Understand a Southerner.** *Author:* Jake Moon. *Publisher:* Two Continents. *Edition Reviewed:* 1977.

Classification: Special-Purpose—Slang. *Pages:* 128. *Total Entries:* 175. *Physical Size:* 5¼ by 8¼ in.; 21 cm. *ISBN:* 0-8467-0274-6. *Lowest Retail Price:* $2.95 paper.

Comments

The Dixie-Doodle Dictionary is not at all a serious dictionary but rather a bit of good-natured fun aimed at modern southern dialect. Examples include *enjawih* (enjoy), *hotail* (hotel), *purtneah* (pretty near), and *thang* (thing). Each entry is pronounced and used in an amusing illustrative example. Moon's pen-and-ink doodles appear throughout. Obviously inspired by Jimmy Carter of *Jawja* ("A state right next to *Alabayama*").

How to Speak Southern

Descriptive Information

Full Title: **How to Speak Southern.** *Author:* Steve Mitchell. *Illustrator:* Sam C. Rawls (SCRAWLS). *Publisher:* Bantam Books. *Edition Reviewed:* 1976.
Classification: Special-Purpose—Slang. *Pages:* 64. *Total Entries:* 250. *Physical Size:* 4¼ by 7 in.; 18 cm. *ISBN:* 0-553-10970-7. *Lowest Retail Price:* $1.25 paper.

Comments

Similar to Moon's *The Dixie-Doodle Dictionary*, this little dictionary is "dedicated to all Yankees in the hope that it will teach them how to talk right." Mitchell includes some regional idioms such as *give up to be* (i.e., "Generally conceded to be. 'He's *give up to be* the crookedest lawyer in the whole state'") and lots of slang corruptions like *heepa, jevver* (i.e., did you ever), *mah* (my), *Nyawlins* (New Orleans), *ratcheer* (right here), and *smore* (some more). SCRAWLS' wonderful drawings accompany the text.

Jazz Talk

Descriptive Information

Full Title: **Jazz Talk: A Dictionary of the Colorful Language that Has Emerged from America's Own Music.** *Editor:* Robert S. Gold. *Publisher:* Bobbs-Merrill Co. *Edition Reviewed:* 1975.
Classification: Special-Purpose—Slang. *Pages:* 400. *Total Entries:* 5,000. *Lowest Retail Price:* $10.00; also $5.95 paper.

Comments

Jazz Talk supersedes Gold's earlier *Jazz Lexicon* (Knopf, 1964), which is now out of print. The terms covered are defined and illustrated by examples taken from over 300 sources, including books, periodicals, and record jackets. Some definitions derive from other slang dictionaries, e.g., the *Dictionary of American Slang*. Includes both historical and contemporary terms.

Other Critical Opinions

Library Journal, May 15, 1975, p. 971.

Len Buckwalter's CB Channel Dictionary

Descriptive Information

Full Title: **Len Buckwalter's CB Channel Dictionary.** *Author:* Len Buckwalter. *Publisher:* Grosset & Dunlap/Today Press. *Edition Reviewed:* 1977.
Classification: Special-Purpose—Slang. *Lowest Retail Price:* $5.95.

Comments

Although not seen by the *Buying Guide*, *Publishers Weekly* (January 24, 1977, p. 285) reports that this dictionary "is a roadster's guide to contacting a variety of people and different services via citizens band radio. Listings include service stations, motels, restaurants and campgrounds." Similar to Lanie Dills' *'Official' CB Slanguage Language Dictionary*.

Macmillan Dictionary of Historical Slang

Descriptive Information

Full Title: **The Macmillan Dictionary of Historical Slang.** *Editors:* Eric Partridge; Abridged by Jacqueline Simpson. *Publisher:* Macmillan Publishing Co. Alternate titles: *A Dictionary of Historical Slang* (1972); *Routledge Dictionary of Historical Slang* (1973). *Edition Reviewed:* 1974.
Classification: Special-Purpose—Slang. *Pages:* 1065. *Total Entries:* 50,000. *Physical Size:* 6¼ by 9½ in.; 24 cm. *LC:* 74-10318. *ISBN:* 0-02-594950-0. *Lowest Retail Price:* $25.00.

Comments

First published in England in 1972 by Penguin Books in a paperback edition under the title *A Dictionary of Historical Slang* and the next year in hardcover as the *Routledge Dictionary of Historical Slang* (published by Routledge & Kegan Paul), *The Macmillan Dictionary of Historical Slang* is actually an abridgment of the Fifth Edition (1961) of Eric Partridge's *Dictionary of Slang and Unconventional English*. Specifically, *Macmillan Dictionary* is an abridgment in that it contains "only those words and expressions which were already in use before the First World War, and which may, therefore, be considered as historical, rather than modern, slang." Consumers should note that the Seventh Edition (1970) of Partridge's *Dictionary of Slang and Unconventional English* is available from Macmillan for $22.50. Since *A Dictionary of Slang and Unconventional English* contains everything included in *The Macmillan Dictionary of Historical Slang*, and much more, the latter is definitely not recommended. Consumers interested in Partridge's work on historical slang should acquire his *Dictionary of Slang and Unconventional English*, Seventh Edition, 1970.

Other Critical Opinions

American Reference Books Annual 1976 (review by Francis J. Witty), p. 545.
Booklist, May 1, 1975, p. 1926.

Library Journal, February 1, 1975, p. 281.
Wilson Library Bulletin (review by Charles A. Bunge), June 1975, p. 754.

Maine Lingo

Descriptive Information

Full Title: **Maine Lingo: Boiled Owls, Billdads & Wazzats.** *Editors:* John Gould; Written in collaboration with Lillian Ross and the Editors of *Down East* Magazine. *Publisher: Down East* Magazine. *Edition Reviewed:* 1975. *Classification:* Special-Purpose—Slang. *Pages:* xiv, 342. *Total Entries:* 1,700. *Graphics:* 70. *Physical Size:* 5½ by 8¾ in.; 22 cm. *LC:* 73-84185. *Lowest Retail Price:* $11.00.

Comments

This handsomely printed dictionary of words, phrases, and idioms indigenous to the state of Maine is useful as both a reference and an entertainment. There are about five entries per page, each defined and usually illustrated with a sample sentence. Examples are *come up all stavin'*, *ganging*, *oil up*, and *reg'lar-built*. The book is illustrated with some 70 black-and-white photographs showing Maine and its people—called *Maineiacs* (or *Mainiacs*) by some and *Mainers* by others.

Other Critical Opinions

Library Journal, August 1975, p. 1417.

Mountain-ese

Descriptive Information

Full Title: **Mountain-ese: Basic Grammar for Appalachia.** *Editor:* Aubrey Garber. *Publisher:* Commonwealth Press. *Edition Reviewed:* 1976. *Classification:* Special-Purpose—Slang. *Pages:* iv, 105. *Total Entries:* 2,000. *Physical Size:* 5¾ by 8¾ in.; 23 cm. *LC:* 76-3278. *ISBN:* 0-89227-004-7. *Lowest Retail Price:* $4.95.

Comments

Garber is an investment broker who grew up in Appalachia. His small book "is a glossary of words and phrases, used extensively by mountain and country folk, mainly in the rural sections of America called Appalachia." Each entry is briefly defined and then illustrated in a sample sentence. Example: The phrase *jump the broomstick* is simply defined as "marry" and illustrated by "Lucy and Bill have finally decided to jump the broomstick and settle down." Vulgarisms are not included, nor are pronunciations and etymologies.

'Official' CB Slanguage Language Dictionary

Descriptive Information

Full Title: The 'Official' CB Slanguage Language Dictionary, including Cross-reference. *Editors:* Lanie Dills; Revised by Dot Gilbertson and Joan Wheeler. *Publisher:* Lanie Dills. *Distributor:* Louis J. Martin Associates. *Edition Reviewed:* New Enlarged Fourth Edition, 1977.
  Classification: Special-Purpose—Slang. *Pages:* 245. *LC:* 76-43636. *ISBN:* 0-91644-01-9. *Lowest Retail Price:* $2.95 paper.

Comments

The best known, largest, and most up-to-date list of CB terms used by truck drivers and other folk throughout the U.S. Includes instructions on how to use both radio and CB code. Compare with *Len Buckwalter's CB Channel Dictionary*.

Playboy's Book of Forbidden Words

Descriptive Information

Full Title: Playboy's Book of Forbidden Words: A Liberated Dictionary of Improper English, Containing over 700 Uninhibited Definitions of Contemporary Erotic and Scatological Terms. *Editor:* Robert A. Wilson. *Publisher:* Playboy Press. *Edition Reviewed:* 1972.
  Classification: Special-Purpose—Slang. *Pages:* 302. *Total Entries:* 726. *LC:* 72-81109. *Lowest Retail Price:* $8.95; also $1.25 paper.

Comments

The dictionary provides clear and full discussions of over 700 dirty words, such as *hung* and *motherfucker*. The definitions are amply supported by illustrative quotations from modern writers like John O'Hara and William Burroughs as well as quotes from TV talk shows, contemporary films, and rock music lyrics. *Playboy's Book of Forbidden Words* has some small value as a complement to Wentworth and Flexner's scholarly *Dictionary of American Slang*, but titillation is its major achievement.

Other Critical Opinions

American Reference Books Annual 1974 (review by David W. Brunton), pp. 456–457.
Library Journal, October 15, 1972, pp. 3303–3304.
Wilson Library Bulletin, March 1973, p. 612.

The Queens' Vernacular

Descriptive Information

Full Title: The Queens' Vernacular: A Gay Lexicon. *Editor:* Bruce Rodgers. *Publisher:* Straight Arrow Books. *Edition Reviewed:* 1972.

Classification: Special-Purpose—Slang. *Pages:* 265. *Total Entries:* 12,000. *Physical Size:* 4½ by 8 in.; 20 cm. *LC:* 72-79023. *ISBN:* 0-87932-026-5. *Lowest Retail Price:* $3.50 paper.

Comments

The Queens' Vernacular "records, without meaning to shock or anger, over-heard pieces of living, fascinating slang." Indeed, the dictionary is very explicit. Practically all of the vocabulary involves sexuality and much of it the male sex organs. Words, phrases, and idiomatic expressions are included. The definitions are brief and to the point, often themselves in the vernacular. Because there are many subentries (e.g., *slob-job* is entered under *gum job*) Rodgers provides a useful alphabetical listing in the back. The largest collection of homosexual slang currently available.

Other Critical Opinions

American Reference Books Annual 1974 (review by David W. Brunton), p. 456.

Slang To-day and Yesterday

Descriptive Information

Full Title: **Slang To-day and Yesterday: With a Short Historical Sketch; and Vocabularies of English, American, and Australian Slang.** *Editor:* Eric Partridge. *Publisher:* Routledge & Kegan Paul. *Edition Reviewed:* Fourth Edition, 1970.

Classification: Special-Purpose—Slang. *Pages:* ix, 476. *Total Entries:* 6,500. *Physical Size:* 6½ by 9½ in.; 24 cm. *ISBN:* 0-7100-6922-7. *Lowest Retail Price:* $20.25.

Comments

Partridge's *Slang To-day and Yesterday* first appeared in 1933 and has been very modestly revised several times since. The bulk of the book (pages 1–348) is a treatise on the history and nature of slang, principally in Great Britain. The last part of the book, however, comprises lists of English, Australian, and American slang. Each entry is concisely defined and its initial appearance in the language dated. Unfortunately, these vocabularies have not been updated to any great extent since the book's first publication in 1933. Not an essential dictionary source but a useful complement to Partridge's *Dictionary of Slang and Unconventional English.*

Other Critical Opinions

American Reference Books Annual 1972 (review by Francis J. Witty), pp. 469–470.
Wilson Library Bulletin, March 1971, p. 695.

Smaller Slang Dictionary

Descriptive Information

Full Title: **Smaller Slang Dictionary.** *Editor:* Eric Partridge. *Publisher:* Routledge & Kegan Paul. *Edition Reviewed:* Second Edition, 1964.
Classification: Special-Purpose—Slang. *Pages:* ix, 204. *Total Entries:* 5,000. *Physical Size:* 5½ by 8¾ in.; 22 cm (hardcover). *ISBN:* 0-7100-1938-6 (hardcover); 0-7100-8331-9 (paper). *Lowest Retail Price:* $5.00; also $2.95 paper.

Comments

Smaller Slang Dictionary is a drastic abridgment of Partridge's major work, *A Dictionary of Slang and Unconventional English*, which contains over 60,000 entries in its current Seventh Edition (1970). The abridgment, first published in 1961, excludes all material obsolete by 1900, all underworld slang, and "all matter that could offend against propriety or even delicacy." Partridge says in his foreword that the "*Smaller Dictionary*, intended for general consumption, can therefore go into any home, any school, any library." Perhaps. But today serious American students will want the unabridged version, along with Wentworth and Flexner's *Dictionary of American Slang*.

The Third Ear

Descriptive Information

Full Title: **The Third Ear: A Black Glossary.** *Editor:* Hermese E. Roberts. *Publisher:* English Language Institute of America. *Edition Reviewed:* 1971.
Classification: Special-Purpose—Slang. *Pages:* 16. *Total Entries:* 400. *Physical Size:* 6 by 9 in.; 23 cm. *LC:* 78-143394. *ISBN:* 0-8326-2203-6. *Lowest Retail Price:* $1.00 paper.

Comments

"Why would anyone need a 'third ear'?" asks the author of this little glossary of black slang intended primarily for use in schools. "Could it be that we have used our two ears to listen to the communication-network variety of English for so long, we unconsciously have shut ourselves off from hearing, understanding, appreciating, and enjoying the colorful language varieties minted and used by specific groups of people." This then is your "third ear" for hearing, studying, and understanding the rich language used by American blacks. The list is expurgated (e.g., the sexual connotation of *ball* is excluded) and "makes no claim to being all-inclusive." A useful supplement to Wentworth and Flexner's *Dictionary of American Slang* and Major's *Dictionary of Afro-American Slang*.

Other Critical Opinions

American Reference Books Annual 1972, pp. 472–473.

Truck Talk

Descriptive Information

Full Title: **Truck Talk: The Language of the Open Road.** *Editor:* Montie Tak. *Publisher:* Chilton Book Co. *Edition Reviewed:* 1971.
Classification: Special-Purpose—Slang. *Pages:* xiv, 191. *Total Entries:* 1,200. *Physical Size:* 5¾ by 8¼ in.; 21 cm. *LC:* 72-169583. *ISBN:* 0-8019-5642-0. *Lowest Retail Price:* $5.95.

Comments

Although this dictionary of the cant of American truckers might now be somewhat dated due to the introduction and widespread use of CB communication on the road, it remains an informative and colorful work. Entries include synonyms and comparable terms. For instance, *mule* is "a small tractor used to relocate dollies in a terminal"; also given is *doodle-bug*, a synonym, and *yard bird* and *yard mule*, both comparable in meaning. Montie Tak has driven trucks coast-to-coast. She also writes poetry.

Other Critical Opinions

American Reference Books Annual 1972 (review by Robert Parslow), p. 473.

The Underground Dictionary

Descriptive Information

Full Title: **The Underground Dictionary.** *Editor:* Eugene E. Landy. *Publisher:* Simon & Schuster. *Edition Reviewed:* 1971.
Classification: Special-Purpose—Slang. *Pages:* 206. *Total Entries:* 2,000. *Physical Size:* 4½ by 7½ in.; 19 cm. *LC:* 73-139637. *ISBN:* 0-671-20803-9. *Lowest Retail Price:* $2.95 paper.

Comments

The Underground Dictionary, compiled by a clinical psychologist, is intended to provide a "much-needed communications bridge between the Establishment and the underground culture." Dr. Landy says that his work in treating young people in California allowed him to learn the lingo of "bikers, colors, connections, cons, dopers, fags, hippies, hookers, musicians, teenyboppers and yippies." Most of Landy's slang has been incorporated into Wentworth and Flexner's Second Supplemented Edition (1975) of *A Dictionary of American Slang*, although some specific drug terms are not found in the latter.

Other Critical Opinions

American Reference Books Annual 1973 (review by Richard Akeroyd), p. 454.

SYNONYMS, ANTONYMS, AND HOMONYMS

Synonyms are words which have similar or related meanings, like *flame* and *blaze*. Synonym dictionaries and thesauri group similar words together so that writers can, if they wish, vary or enliven their writing style or, more important, find a word which more closely expresses an intended meaning. Synonym dictionaries (as distinct from thesauri) are usually divided into two categories. First, there are those which discriminate (or differentiate) shades of meaning among similar words. For instance, *empty* and *hollow* are synonymous but *hollow* refers only to space. *Empty* and *inane* are also synonyms but *inane* applies only to a type of thought or action. Obviously, *empty* and *hollow* (and *empty* and *inane*) cannot be used interchangeably in every instance. The best synonym dictionaries, therefore, discriminate similar words and their meanings. The second type of synonym dictionary merely lists synonymous words (e.g., *empty*, *hollow*, *inane*, etc.) without discriminating their different connotations. This type of dictionary must be used with caution, especially if the user is not well versed in English.

Analogous to, but not the same as, a synonym dictionary is the thesaurus. The word *thesaurus* derives from the Greek *thēsauros* meaning a treasury or storehouse—in this case, a storehouse of words. Unlike the synonym dictionary, the thesaurus does not arrange its words alphabetically, but groups them topically by categories of ideas. Under the broad topic of "Affections," for example, there might be such subtopics as "Personal Affections," "Sympathetic Affections," "Moral Affections," and "Religious Affections." Under each subtopic are even more specific categories, e.g., under "Personal Affections" the user might find "Pleasure," "Pain," "Content," "Discontent," "Cheerfulness," "Dejection," etc. Within each of these categories synonymous words are listed, e.g., under "Dejection" such terms as *depression*, *mopishness*, *low spirits*, *gloom*, *weariness*, *broken heart*, *despair*. To locate specific terms in the thesaurus, there is an alphabetical index in the back which comprises about one-third of the entire book.

The thesaurus was "invented" by a British doctor, Peter Mark Roget, in the mid-nineteenth century. Roget, who died in 1869, saw his original *Thesaurus of English Words and Phrases* through 28 editions. His son, John L. Roget, added the alphabetical index in 1879. It should be pointed out that the thesaurus gives words for meanings whereas the dictionary gives meanings for words. The upshot is that the thesaurus cannot be used effectively unless the user is already familiar with the words contained therein. Those who lack a solid vocabulary and sound proficiency in the English language are advised to use a good synonym dictionary (like *Webster's New Dictionary of Synonyms*) which discriminates the meanings of similar words.

Today there is considerable confusion about the term *thesaurus*, in that publishers are now calling synonym dictionaries thesauri. Two recent examples are *Webster's Collegiate Thesaurus* and *The Doubleday Roget's Thesaurus of the American Language in Dictionary Form*. Neither is a thesaurus in the true sense though each uses the term. Professor George H. Douglas (English Department, University of Illinois, Urbana) has published an informative article entitled "What's Happened to the Thesaurus?" (*RQ*, Winter 1976, pp. 149–155) which discusses why "Lexicographers and editors of reference books appear to be privately of the opinion that the concept of the thesaurus in the original sense is strictly dead," yet continue to use the term. The consumer should note that, like *Webster*, the name *Roget* is out of copyright and may be used by any publisher who wishes to capitalize on its presumed sales value with the general public. Indeed, there are currently nine different books in print which use *Roget* in their titles. These include such works as *The Doubleday Roget's Thesaurus* which neither has anything to do with Roget nor is a thesaurus. The *Buying Guide* advises that the name *Roget* on a thesaurus or synonym dictionary is no mark of quality, one way or another.

This section of the *Buying Guide* also covers antonyms (words which mean the opposite, e.g., *sad* and *glad*) and homonyms. Homonyms are divided into two types: *homophones* (words pronounced the same but which have different spellings and meanings, e.g., *sweet* and *suite*) and *homographs* (words spelled the same but which have different pronunciations and meanings, e.g., *buffet* meaning to batter and *buffet* meaning an informal luncheon). At present no wordbook devoted exclusively to antonyms is available, but there are several works in print that deal with homonyms (e.g., *Encyclopedia of Homonyms*). Traditionally antonyms have been treated like poor relations in synonym dictionaries.

Allen's Synonyms and Antonyms

Descriptive Information

Full Title: **Allen's Synonyms and Antonyms.** *Compilers:* F. Sturges Allen; Revised and Edited by T. H. Vail Motter. *Publishers:* Harper & Row (hardcover); Barnes & Noble (paper). *Edition Reviewed:* Revised and Enlarged Edition, 1949.

Classification: Special-Purpose—Synonyms, Antonyms & Homonyms. *Pages:* x, 427. *Main Entries:* 20,000. *Physical Size:* 6¼ by 9 in.; 23 cm. (hardcover). *ISBN:* 0-06-463328-4 (paper). *Lowest Retail Price:* $12.50; also $2.95 paper.

Comments

Allen's Synonyms and Antonyms, first published in 1921 with about 10,000 main entries, underwent a revision by Dr. Motter in 1938 which doubled the number of entries, followed by a much more modest revision in 1949. The entries are arranged alphabetically and difficult terms are carefully discriminated. Helpful cross-references appear throughout. Another useful feature is the labeling of words which are archaic, bookish, colloquial, rare, slang, etc., by means of abbreviations, e.g., "(A)" means *archaic*. The paperbound edition appeared in 1972 but is simply a reprint of the 1949 version. Authoritative but now somewhat dated.

Other Critical Opinions

American Reference Books Annual 1973 (review by Charles D. Patterson), p. 455.

Bernstein's Reverse Dictionary

Descriptive Information

Full Title: **Bernstein's Reverse Dictionary.** *Editors:* Theodore M. Bernstein; With the collaboration of Jane Wagner. *Publisher:* Quadrangle. *Edition Reviewed:* 1975.

Classification: Special-Purpose—Synonyms, Antonyms & Homonyms. *Pages:* x, 276. *Main Entries:* 16,000. *Physical Size:* 6½ by 9½ in.; 24 cm. *LC:* 75-19178. *ISBN:* 0-8129-0566-0. *Lowest Retail Price:* $10.00.

Comments

Bernstein's Reverse Dictionary is for those people who know the word they want but can't think of it. For instance, there is a word meaning *false* and it's on the tip of your tongue. By looking in the reverse dictionary under *false*, you will find such "clues" as "*false, artificially invented, not real:* FICTITIOUS" along with "*false, fraudulently invented:* TRUMPED-UP and *false, not genuine:* SPURIOUS." The words in capitals are called "target words"; there are about 16,000 in the dictionary. Fun to browse in as well as a useful reference book.

Other Critical Opinions

American Reference Books Annual 1976 (review by Francis J. Witty), p. 74.
Library Journal, October 1, 1975, pp. 1809–1810.
RQ, Spring 1976, pp. 274–275.

Book of Synonyms

Descriptive Information

Full Title: **The Book of Synonyms.** *Compiler:* Oliver Stoner. *Publisher:* Citadel Press. *Distributor:* Lyle Stuart, Inc. Original title: *A First Book of Synonyms.* *Edition Reviewed:* First American Edition, 1966.

Classification: Special-Purpose—Synonyms, Antonyms & Homonyms. *Pages:* xvi, 144. *Total Entries:* 3,500. *Physical Size:* 5½ by 8 in.; 21 cm. *Lowest Retail Price:* $1.95 paper.

Comments

Stoner's little dictionary discriminates a total of 3,500 words within about 2,000 main entries (synonym paragraphs). For instance, the entry *fulsome* provides three synonyms: *oleaginous, oily,* and *unctuous.* Shades of meaning are indicated for each word. There is an alphabetical listing of all words covered in the back of the dictionary. First published in Great Britain in 1963 and not revised since, *The Book of Synonyms* is too selective to be of more than incidental reference value.

Clear and Simple Thesaurus Dictionary

Descriptive Information

Full Title: **The Clear and Simple Thesaurus Dictionary.** *Compilers:* Harriet Wittels and Joan Greisman. *Editor:* William Morris. *Publisher:*

Grosset & Dunlap. Former title: *The Young People's Thesaurus Dictionary.*
Edition Reviewed: 1971.

Classification: Special-Purpose—Synonyms, Antonyms & Homonyms.
Pages: 319. *Total Entries:* 5,000. *Physical Size:* 6¾ by 9¼ in.; 24 cm. *LC:* 70-158760. *ISBN:* 0-448-12198-0 (paper); 0-448-04286-X (library edition).
Lowest Retail Price: $4.95 paper.

Comments

Designed for young people in the elementary and middle school grades, *The Clear and Simple Thesaurus Dictionary* was originally issued as *The Young People's Thesaurus Dictionary* in 1971. It has not been revised, merely retitled. The arrangement is alphabetical and synonyms are not discriminated. Synonymic slang terms, however, are indicated and so labeled. Simpler but not as instructive as *In Other Words* (a two-volume synonym dictionary for young people which is described further on in this section of the *Buying Guide*).

Other Critical Opinions

American Reference Books Annual 1973 (review by Christine L. Wynar), p. 451.

Collins Gem Dictionary of Synonyms & Antonyms

Descriptive Information

Full Title: **Collins Gem Dictionary of Synonyms & Antonyms.** *Compiler:* A. H. Irvine. *Publisher:* Collins+World. *Edition Reviewed:* 1964.

Classification: Special-Purpose—Synonyms, Antonyms & Homonyms.
Pages: 447. *Main Entries:* 8,000. *Physical Size:* 3¼ by 4½ in.; 12 cm. *ISBN:* 0-00-458703-0. *Lowest Retail Price:* $2.45 paper (Leatheroid).

Comments

Irvine says in his foreword that "the synonyms in each main entry are arranged in alphabetical order, leaving the reader to choose the one which fits his context best." About 75,000 undiscriminated synonyms are provided in this dictionary. The work is of limited usefulness but in convenient pocket format.

Complete University Word Hunter

Descriptive Information

Full Title: **The Complete University Word Hunter.** *Compiler:* John T. Gause. *Publisher:* T. Y. Crowell Co. (Apollo Editions). Former title: *The Complete Word Hunter. Edition Reviewed:* Apollo Edition, 1967.

Classification: Special-Purpose—Synonyms, Antonyms & Homonyms.
Pages: viii, 497. *Main Entries:* 6,000. *Physical Size:* 5 by 7¾ in.; 20 cm. *LC:* 55-11106. *Lowest Retail Price:* $2.45 paper.

Comments

First published as *The Complete Word Hunter* in 1955 and reissued (but not revised) in the publisher's paperback Apollo series in 1967, *The Complete University Word Hunter* is arranged by 91 very broad subject categories (e.g., "Ailments," "Anger," "Animals," "Areas and Measurements") with an alphabetical index listing all words in the book. Example: Under the topic "Discourtesy" the user finds such synonyms as *acrimonious, bearish, biting, brash,* and *brusque.* Major synonyms like *brash* are discriminated. All terms are accessible via the index. Still useful but dated in certain areas, e.g., "Science," "Travel," and "Underworld."

Concept Dictionary of English

Descriptive Information

Full Title: **A Concept Dictionary of English.** *Compiler:* Julius Laffal. *Publisher:* Halsted Press. *Edition Reviewed:* 1973.

Classification: Special-Purpose—Synonyms, Antonyms & Homonyms. *Pages:* 305. *Total Entries:* 23,500. *LC:* 72-97927. *ISBN:* 0-470-51160-5. *Lowest Retail Price:* $13.50.

Comments

Laffal, a behavioral scientist, has grouped 23,500 words into 118 conceptual categories, e.g., the word *white* is placed in the category "COLR" (for color). The dictionary, which consists of two alphabetical lists, first "defines" the 23,500 words by their conceptual category and then lists the conceptual categories with specific words assigned to them. *A Concept Dictionary of English* is not intended as a general thesaurus, but as a professional tool for analyzing language development and structure. For behavioral and linguistic specialists.

Other Critical Opinions

American Reference Books Annual 1974 (review by Francis J. Witty), p. 460.

Dictionary of American Homophones and Homographs

Descriptive Information

Full Title: **A Dictionary of American Homophones and Homographs: With Illustrative Examples and Exercises.** *Compiler:* Harold C. Whitford. *Publisher:* Teachers College Press. *Edition Reviewed:* 1966.

Classification: Special-Purpose—Synonyms, Antonyms & Homonyms. *Pages:* vii, 83. *Total Entries:* 2,000. *Physical Size:* 5¼ by 8¼ in.; 21 cm. *LC:* 66-25461. *Lowest Retail Price:* $3.50 paper.

Comments

Whitford's small dictionary defines over 1,000 homophones in Part I. The homophones (pairs of words pronounced the same but different in meaning and spelling) are also clarified by illustrative sentences showing their use in context. Examples include *chic/sheik*, *Chile/chili/chilly*, *choir/quire*, and *choral/coral*. Parts II and III deal in similar fashion with homographs (pairs of words spelled the same but which differ in meaning and pronunciation). Examples include *August/august*, *commune/commune* and *sewer/sewer*. The final part consists of some 40 exercises. Compare with Newhouse's *Encyclopedia of Homonyms 'Sound-alikes,'* which covers only homophones.

Dictionary of English Synonyms

Descriptive Information

Full Title: **A Dictionary of English Synonyms and Synonymous Expressions.** *Compiler:* Richard Soule. *Editor:* Alfred Dwight Sheffield. *Publisher:* Bantam Books. Alternate title: *Soule's Dictionary of English Synonyms* (on cover and spine). *Edition Reviewed:* Revised Edition, 1959.

Classification: Special-Purpose—Synonyms, Antonyms & Homonyms. *Pages:* xvi, 528. *Main Entries:* 20,000. *Physical Size:* 4¼ by 7 in.; 18 cm. *ISBN:* 0-553-07883-125. *Lowest Retail Price:* $1.25 paper.

Comments

Soule's dictionary originally appeared in 1871 and has been revised several times. At present, only the Bantam paperback edition (a reprint of the 1959 Little, Brown hardcover edition) is in print. The dictionary merely lists synonyms without discriminating shades of meaning. Much better, more current works are available for roughly the same price, for instance, *The Merriam-Webster Pocket Dictionary of Synonyms.*

Dictionary of Synonyms and Antonyms

Descriptive Information

Full Title: **A Dictionary of Synonyms and Antonyms: With 5000 Words Most Often Mispronounced.** *Compiler:* Joseph Devlin. *Editor:* Jerome Fried. *Publisher:* Popular Library. *Edition Reviewed:* 1961.

Classification: Special-Purpose—Synonyms, Antonyms & Homonyms. *Pages:* 384. *Lowest Retail Price:* $1.50 paper.

Comments

Devlin's dictionary, first published in 1938, has been revised and enlarged by Jerome Fried. In addition to an alphabetical listing of undiscriminated synonyms and antonyms, there is a section on frequently mispronounced words. Of marginal reference value.

Other Critical Opinions

American Reference Books Annual 1971 (review by John Phillip Immroth), p. 423.

Doubleday Roget's Thesaurus

Descriptive Information

Full Title: **The Doubleday Roget's Thesaurus of the American Language in Dictionary Form.** *Editors:* Sidney I. Landau and Ronald J. Bogus. *Publisher:* Doubleday & Co. *Edition Reviewed:* 1977.

Classification: Special-Purpose—Synonyms, Antonyms & Homonyms. *Pages:* 804. *Main Entries:* 17,000. *LC:* 76-7696. *ISBN:* 0-385-01236-5 (plain); 0-385-12379-5 (thumb-indexed). *Lowest Retail Price:* $4.95.

Comments

Based on the vocabulary in the recently published *Doubleday Dictionary* (1975), an abridged adult dictionary of some 85,000 entries also edited by Landau and Bogus, *The Doubleday Roget's Thesaurus of the American Language in Dictionary Form* contains over 17,000 alphabetical entries, approximately 250,000 synonyms and antonyms, and many slang and colloquial terms. Note, however, that the dictionary is neither a thesaurus in the true sense nor has anything to do with "Roget." Like *Webster's Collegiate Thesaurus* (also not a true thesaurus), *The Doubleday Roget's Thesaurus* simply provides lists of synonymic terms for each entry, with the most common synonyms listed first and so on. Up-to-date.

Other Critical Opinions

Library Journal (review by B. Hunter Smeaton), May 1, 1977, pp. 1002–1003.

Encyclopedia of Homonyms

Descriptive Information

Full Title: **The Encyclopedia of Homonyms 'Sound-alikes': The Only Complete Comprehensive Collection of 'Sound-alike' Words Ever Published.** *Compiler:* Dora Newhouse. *Publisher:* Newhouse Press. *Edition Reviewed:* 1976.

Classification: Special-Purpose—Synonyms, Antonyms & Homonyms. *Pages:* 238. *Total Entries:* 8,000. *Physical Size:* 6¼ by 9¼ in.; 24 cm. *LC:* 76-27486. *ISBN:* 0-918050-01-4. *Lowest Retail Price:* $14.95.

Comments

There are some 3,500 groupings of "sound-alike" homonyms (or homophones) in this collection. Arranged A-to-Z, the book includes "some words that are obsolete or archaic; some that are colloquial or popular slang; some that are recorded in the English classics, the Bible or the literature of Scott and Burns; and some are informal and very up-to-date." Examples are *fret/frett/frette; friar/fryer;* and *froe/frow.* A list of the most commonly misspelled and misused homophones is found in the back of the book. An abridged version of the work is also available which omits the obsolete, archaic, and obscure entries. A Spanish-English edition of the abridged work is in progress. Compare with Whitford's *Dictionary of American Homophones and Homographs.*

Other Critical Opinions

Library Journal (review by Catherine von Schon), May 15, 1977, pp. 1170–1171.

Funk & Wagnalls Modern Guide to Synonyms

Descriptive Information

Full Title: **Funk & Wagnalls Modern Guide to Synonyms and Related Words.** *Editors:* S. I. Hayakawa and the Funk & Wagnalls Dictionary Staff. *Publisher:* Funk & Wagnalls. *Distributor:* T. Y. Crowell Co. *Edition Reviewed:* 1968.
Classification: Special-Purpose—Synonyms, Antonyms & Homonyms. *Pages:* x, 726. *Total Entries:* 6,000. *Physical Size:* 7¼ by 9½ in.; 24 cm. *LC:* 67-26446. *ISBN:* 0-308-40073-9. *Lowest Retail Price:* $9.95.

Comments

Although this guide is not as extensive as, say, the *Reader's Digest Family Word Finder, Webster's New Dictionary of Synonyms*, or the newer *Webster's Collegiate Thesaurus*, it does an outstanding job of discriminating meanings among synonymic words. Approximately 1,000 synonym studies cover some 6,000 words. For instance, under the entry *argue* four similar words are closely discriminated (*debate, discuss, dispute,* and *reason*). Illustrative examples show the use of each word in context. There are numerous cross-references as well as a comprehensive index of all words treated in the book. Note that Senator Hayakawa, prior to taking up politics, was a well-known semanticist. One of the best and most readable synonym studies available.

Other Critical Opinions

Katz, William A. *Basic Information Sources.* Vol. 1 of *Introduction to Reference Work*, 2nd ed. (New York: McGraw-Hill, 1974), pp. 278–279.

Funk & Wagnalls Standard Handbook of Synonyms

Descriptive Information

Full Title: **Funk & Wagnalls Standard Handbook of Synonyms, Antonyms, and Prepositions.** *Authors:* James Champlin; Revised by the Funk & Wagnalls Editorial Staff. *Publisher:* Funk & Wagnalls. *Distributor:* T. Y. Crowell Co. *Former title:* *English Synonyms and Antonyms* (1914). *Edition Reviewed:* Completely Revised Edition, 1947.
Classification: Special-Purpose—Synonyms, Antonyms & Homonyms. *Pages:* 515. *Total Entries:* 10,000. *LC:* 47-11924. *ISBN:* 0-308-40024-0. *Lowest Retail Price:* $9.95.

Comments

This work covers some 6,000 synonyms and 4,000 antonyms listed under key words. Words are discriminated and idiomatic changes in meaning brought about by prepositions are stressed, e.g., *do up, do in, come about, come on.* All words treated in the book are listed in an alphabetical index. Obviously in need of revision but still useful, especially for its treatment of idioms involving prepositions.

In Other Words I: A Beginning Thesaurus

Descriptive Information

Full Title: **In Other Words I: A Beginning Thesaurus.** *Authors:* William A. Jenkins and Andrew Schiller. *Publishers:* Lothrop, Lee & Shepard Co. (Library Edition); Scott, Foresman & Co. (Text Edition). *Edition Reviewed:* Revised Edition, 1977.

Classification: Special-Purpose—Synonyms, Antonyms & Homonyms. *Total Entries:* 1,200. *Physical Size:* 7¾ by 9½ in.; 24 cm. *ISBN:* 0-673-10263-7 (text). *School Price:* $4.50.

Comments

Aimed at grades three and four, *In Other Words I* was initially published in 1968 and substantially revised in 1977. The synonyms, arranged alphabetically, are illustrated with both sentence examples and pictures, all in color. The text of the 1977 edition has been simplified somewhat and the drawings are now captioned. Along with *In Other Words II: A Junior Thesaurus*, this is the most instructive synonym dictionary available for young people. Compare with *The Clear and Simple Thesaurus Dictionary.*

In Other Words II: A Junior Thesaurus

Descriptive Information

Full Title: **In Other Words II: A Junior Thesaurus.** *Authors:* William A. Jenkins and Andrew Schiller. *Publishers:* Lothrop, Lee & Shepard Co. (Library Edition); Scott, Foresman & Co. (Text Edition). *Edition Reviewed:* Revised Edition, 1977.

Classification: Special-Purpose—Synonyms, Antonyms & Homonyms. *Total Entries:* 2,500. *ISBN:* 0-673-10266-1 (text). *School Price:* $5.67.

Comments

A revision of the 1969 edition, *In Other Words II* is the second part of a two-volume synonym dictionary for elementary school students. Full-color illustrations accompany each entry. Words are defined and similar terms discriminated. The new edition includes numerous illustrative sentences and the drawings are captioned. The Text Edition comes with an exercise book ($1.08) and a teacher's answer key ($1.20). Along with its companion volume, *In Other Words I: A Beginning Thesaurus*, this is the outstanding synonym dictionary for children. Compare with *The Clear and Simple Thesaurus Dictionary.*

Other Critical Opinions

American Reference Books Annual 1971, p. 423.

Instant Synonyms and Antonyms

Descriptive Information

Full Title: **Instant Synonyms and Antonyms.** *Compilers:* Donald O. Bolander, Dolores D. Varner, and Elliott Pine. *Publisher:* Career Institute. *Distributor:* Franklin Watts, Inc. *Edition Reviewed:* 1970.

Classification: Special-Purpose—Synonyms, Antonyms & Homonyms. *Pages:* 314. *Main Entries:* 5,100. *Physical Size:* 4¼ by 6¼ in.; 16 cm. *LC:* 75-113518. *ISBN:* 0-911744-06-1. *Lowest Retail Price:* $2.95.

Comments

This little hardcover dictionary is part of the "Instant Reference Library" which includes such titles as *Instant Spelling Dictionary* (covered in the "Spelling and Syllabication" section of the *Buying Guide*), *Instant Quotation Dictionary*, and *Instant World Atlas*. It contains about 5,100 main entries, 52,000 synonyms, and 31,000 antonyms. There is no attempt to discriminate shades of meaning, nor are illustrative examples provided. Very elementary.

Other Critical Opinions

American Reference Books Annual 1971, p. 423.

Merriam-Webster Pocket Dictionary of Synonyms

Descriptive Information

Full Title: **The Merriam-Webster Pocket Dictionary of Synonyms.** *Editor:* Merriam-Webster Staff. *Publisher:* Pocket Books. *Edition Reviewed:* 1972.

Classification: Special-Purpose—Synonyms, Antonyms & Homonyms. *Pages:* 4a, 441. *Main Entries:* 10,000. *Physical Size:* 4 by 7 in.; 18 cm. *ISBN:* 0-671-80025-6. *Lowest Retail Price:* $2.45 paper.

Comments

The *Merriam-Webster Pocket Dictionary of Synonyms* is an abridgment of *Webster's New Dictionary of Synonyms*, one of the finest synonym dictionaries available. All words covered are listed in alphabetical order, though many entries are cross-references to lengthy synonym paragraphs where similar terms are carefully discriminated. An outstanding feature is the provision of numerous quotations from both modern and classical writers showing how particular words are used in context. Unquestionably the best paperbound synonym dictionary currently on the market.

New American Roget's College Thesaurus

Descriptive Information

Full Title: **The New American Roget's College Thesaurus in Dictionary Form.** *Editors:* Jack Luzzatto and Loy Morehead. *Publisher:* Grosset & Dunlap (hardcover); New American Library (paper). *Edition Reviewed:* 1958.

Classification: Special-Purpose—Synonyms, Antonyms & Homonyms. *Pages:* 440. *Physical Size:* 5¾ by 8¼ in.; 21 cm. (hardcover)*. ISBN:* 0-448-01605-2 (hardcover). *Lowest Retail Price:* $4.95; also $1.50 paper.

Comments

There are currently nine synonym dictionaries and thesauri in print which bear the name "Roget." *The New American Roget's College Thesaurus in Dictionary Form* is similar in arrangement to Norman Lewis's *New Roget's Thesaurus in Dictionary Form* and the more recent and preferable *Doubleday Roget's Thesaurus of the American Language in Dictionary Form.* These works, as their titles indicate, are arranged in A-to-Z fashion, not in logical categories as was Roget's original thesaurus. The *Doubleday Roget's Thesaurus,* based on the *Doubleday Dictionary,* is up-to-date whereas both *New American Roget's College Thesaurus* and Lewis's *New Roget's Thesaurus* are in need of updating.

New Roget's Thesaurus

Descriptive Information

Full Title: **The New Roget's Thesaurus of the English Language in Dictionary Form.** *Editor:* Norman Lewis. *Publishers:* Putnam (hardcover); Berkley Publishing Co. (paper). Original title: *Roget's Thesaurus of the English Language in Dictionary Form* (Revised Edition, 1936). *Edition Reviewed:* 1964.
Classification: Special-Purpose—Synonyms, Antonyms & Homonyms. *Pages:* 552. *Main Entries:* 17,000. *Physical Size:* 6¼ by 9¼ in.; 24 cm. (hardcover). *LC:* 65-20677. *ISBN:* 0-399-10579-4 (hardcover); 0-425-03176-4 (paper). *Lowest Retail Price:* $4.95; also $1.50 paper.

Comments

Back in the early 1920s, C. O. Sylvester Mawson contrived to arrange Peter Mark Roget's original thesaurus in alphabetical order in an effort to improve access and cut down on time expended referring back and forth between the main word list and the index. The result is essentially an undiscriminated synonym dictionary. The present edition, first published in 1961 and modestly revised in 1964, is quite dated. The more recent and similarly arranged *Doubleday Roget's Thesaurus* (1977), *Reader's Digest Family Word Finder* (1975), and *Webster's Collegiate Thesaurus* (1976) are preferable.

Original Roget's Thesaurus

Descriptive Information

Full Title: **The Original Roget's Thesaurus of English Words and Phrases.** *Editor:* Robert A. Dutch. *Publisher:* St. Martin's Press. Alternate title: *Roget's Thesaurus of English Words and Phrases. Edition Reviewed:* Third Edition, 1962.

Classification: Special-Purpose—Synonyms, Antonyms & Homonyms. *Pages:* 1488. *Physical Size:* 7 by 9½ in.; 25 cm. *LC:* 64-23442. *Lowest Retail Price:* $8.95.

Comments

This is not quite the "original" Roget's thesaurus but rather a revised, "modernized," and "Americanized" version which adheres to Roget's original arrangement (i.e., logical as opposed to alphabetical order). Many American slang terms and colloquialisms have been added, along with numerous foreign words and phrases. The index, which is well over 700 pages in length, accounts for half the book. At present, *Roget's International Thesaurus* (Fourth Edition, 1977), which also retains the original format, is recommended over *The Original Roget's Thesaurus* simply on the basis of recency.

Other Critical Opinions

American Reference Books Annual 1971 (review by Lawrence E. Spellman), p. 424.

Random House Dictionary of Synonyms and Antonyms

Descriptive Information

Full Title: **The Random House Dictionary of Synonyms and Antonyms.** *Editor:* Laurence Urdang. *Publisher:* Random House. *Edition Reviewed:* 1960.
Classification: Special-Purpose—Synonyms, Antonyms & Homonyms. *Pages:* 310. *Main Entries:* 5,000. *Physical Size:* 3 by 5½ in.; 14 cm. *LC:* 60-5553. *Lowest Retail Price:* $1.65 flexible covers.

Comments

The Random House Dictionary of Synonyms and Antonyms is a pocket-size list of undiscriminated synonyms and antonyms. According to the editor's introduction, "The numerical order of the synonym lists corresponds to that of the definitions in *The American College Dictionary*." For quick reference only.

Reader's Digest Family Word Finder

Descriptive Information

Full Title: **Reader's Digest Family Word Finder: A New Thesaurus of Synonyms and Antonyms in Dictionary Form.** *Editors:* Editors of *Reader's Digest* in association with Stuart B. Flexner. *Publisher:* Reader's Digest Association. *Distributor:* W. W. Norton & Co. Alternate title: *Family Word Finder.* *Edition Reviewed:* 1975.
Classification: Special-Purpose—Synonyms, Antonyms & Homonyms. *Pages:* 896. *Main Entries:* 10,000. *Physical Size:* 7¼ by 9½ in.; 24 cm. *LC:* 75-18006. *Lowest Retail Price:* $13.95.

Comments

The *Reader's Digest Family Word Finder* is an up-to-date synonym dictionary which includes about 200,000 individual words within its 10,000 main entries. Synonymic words are discriminated with sample sentences provided when necessary to clarify shades of meaning. Unlike most other synonym dictionaries, the book includes helpful usage notes, brief etymological commentaries, and pronunciation tips. A carefully prepared work which compares favorably with such similar works as *The Doubleday Roget's Thesaurus*, *Webster's Collegiate Thesaurus*, and *Webster's New World Thesaurus*.

Other Critical Opinions

American Reference Books Annual 1977 (review by Frances Neel Cheney), p. 524.
Booklist, July 15, 1976, pp. 1625–1626.
Library Journal, February 1, 1976, p. 518.

Roget's International Thesaurus

Descriptive Information

Full Title: **Roget's International Thesaurus.** *Editor:* Robert L. Chapman. *Publisher:* T. Y. Crowell Co. *Edition Reviewed:* Fourth Edition, 1977.
Classification: Special-Purpose—Synonyms, Antonyms & Homonyms. *Pages:* 1455. *Total Entries:* 250,000. *Physical Size:* 6¼ by 9¼ in.; 24 cm. *ISBN:* 0-690-00010-3 (plain); 0-690-00011-1 (thumb-indexed). *Lowest Retail Price:* $10.50.

Comments

The publisher claims this latest revision of *Roget's International Thesaurus* is the "newest, largest, and most useful thesaurus in print." The work, last issued in 1962 (Third Edition), has been thoroughly revised and updated. It includes many words and phrases which have recently entered the language, including slang, technical terms, and idiomatic expressions. The work is arranged in topical (rather than alphabetical) fashion, adhering to the general principles established by Peter Mark Roget in the original edition (1852) of his *Thesaurus of English Words and Phrases*, although C. O. Sylvester Mawson did add some new categories in 1922 when the first edition of *Roget's International Thesaurus* appeared. Preferable to Dutch's *Original Roget's Thesaurus* (Third Edition, 1962), which is now considerably dated.

Roget's Pocket Thesaurus

Descriptive Information

Full Title: **Roget's Pocket Thesaurus: Based on Roget's International Thesaurus of English Words and Phrases.** *Editors:* C. O. Sylvester Mawson; Assisted by Katharine Aldrich Whiting. *Publisher:* Pocket Books. *Edition Reviewed:* 1946.

Classification: Special-Purpose—Synonyms, Antonyms & Homonyms. *Pages:* xxviii, 484. *Physical Size:* 4¼ by 7 in.; 18 cm. *ISBN:* 0-671-80001-9. *Lowest Retail Price:* $1.50 paper.

Consumer Note

This is actually a modest revision of the earliest edition (1922) of *Roget's International Thesaurus* (now in its Fourth Edition, 1977). The book is sadly out-of-date and should be avoided by consumers.

Roget's Thesaurus of Synonyms and Antonyms

Descriptive Information

Full Title: **Roget's Thesaurus of Synonyms and Antonyms.** *Editors:* Peter Mark Roget; Enlarged by John Lewis Roget; Revised and Enlarged by Samuel Romilly Roget. *Publishers:* Dennison Manufacturing Co.; also Pathmark Books. *Edition Reviewed:* New Edition Revised and Enlarged, 1925.

Classification: Special-Purpose—Synonyms, Antonyms & Homonyms. *Pages:* 201. *Physical Size:* 5¼ by 7½ in.; 20 cm. *Lowest Retail Price:* $2.25 paper.

Comments

Peter Mark Roget first published his *Thesaurus of English Words and Phrases* in 1852. In 1879, John L. Roget, the author's son, revised the work, materially improving it by adding an extensive alphabetical index. Some 45 years later, in 1925, Samuel Romilly Roget, grandson of the original author, issued a major revision. Although the paperback editions sold by Dennison (blue covers) and Pathmark (red covers) have changed the 1925 title (from *Thesaurus of Words and Phrases* to *Thesaurus of Synonyms and Antonyms*), include some American phrases circa World War II, and carry a 1972 copyright by Ottenheimer Press, they are hardly distinguishable from the old and now very dated 1925 revision. Consumers are advised to avoid *Roget's Thesaurus of Synonyms and Antonyms* published by Dennison and Pathmark (both copyrighted by Ottenheimer Press).

Roget's Thesaurus of Words and Phrases

Descriptive Information

Full Title: **Roget's Thesaurus of Words and Phrases.** *Editors:* Peter Mark Roget; Enlarged by John L. Roget; Revised and Enlarged by Samuel Romilly Roget; American Edition Revised and Edited by Willard Jerome Heggen. *Publisher:* Grosset & Dunlap. Alternate title: *Thesaurus of Words and Phrases.* *Edition Reviewed:* Revised and Authorized American Edition, 1941.

Classification: Special-Purpose—Synonyms, Antonyms & Homonyms. *Pages:* xxix, 705. *Physical Size:* 5½ by 8½ in.; 22 cm. *ISBN:* 0-448-01607-9. *Lowest Retail Price:* $5.95.

Comments

This *Roget* is an Americanized version of the 1925 edition of the *Thesaurus of English Words and Phrases* prepared by Samuel Romilly Roget, grandson of Peter Mark Roget, the originator of the thesaurus. A page-by-page comparison of the American Edition (1941) with the 1925 Edition reveals only relatively minor changes, meaning that the Grosset & Dunlap American Edition of *Roget* is dreadfully out-of-date (e.g., current terms like *détente* are not included). Though it costs a few dollars more ($10.95 as opposed to $5.95), *Roget's International Thesaurus* (Fourth Edition, 1977) is a much better buy for those who want a true thesaurus based on Roget's principles.

Roget's University Thesaurus

Descriptive Information

Full Title: **Roget's University Thesaurus.** *Editor:* C. O. Sylvester Mawson. *Publisher:* T. Y. Crowell Co. (Apollo Editions). Original title: *Roget's International Thesaurus of English Words and Phrases. Edition Reviewed:* Apollo Edition, 1963.

Classification: Special-Purpose—Synonyms, Antonyms & Homonyms. *Pages:* xxiv, 904. *Physical Size:* 5½ by 8 in.; 21 cm. *LC:* 63-13469. *ISBN:* 0-8152-0062-5. *Lowest Retail Price:* $3.49 paper.

Consumer Note

Roget's University Thesaurus is a reprint of Mawson's 1922 edition of *Roget's International Thesaurus.* The latter is now available in an up-to-date Fourth Edition (1977) and the older and now very dated earlier edition should be avoided by consumers.

Sisson's Synonyms

Descriptive Information

Full Title: **Sisson's Synonyms: An Unabridged Synonym and Related-Terms Locater.** *Editor:* A. F. Sisson. *Publisher:* Parker Publishing Co. *Distributor:* Prentice-Hall. *Edition Reviewed:* 1969.

Classification: Special-Purpose—Synonyms, Antonyms & Homonyms. *Pages:* xi, 691. *Main Entries:* 19,000. *Physical Size:* 6½ by 9½ in.; 24 cm. *LC:* 74-77314. *ISBN:* 0-13-810630-4. *Lowest Retail Price:* $12.95.

Comments

Sisson's Synonyms, which includes 324,500 related words under 19,000 alphabetical main entries, covers "applicable foreign words and expressions, acceptable slang, short words, long words, simple words, abstruse words, and technical, legal, medical and other scientific nomenclature suited to the subject involved." Sisson notes in his introduction, for instance, that 465 synonyms are entered under *bad,* 64 under *evil,* and 111 under *cruel.* Unfortunately, there is no comprehensive index of all 324,500 words and expressions. Moreover, the synonyms are merely listed, not discriminated in any manner. A useful source for those who have sufficient mastery of the language to handle an extensive list of undiscriminated synonyms.

Other Critical Opinions

American Reference Books Annual 1972 (review by Marjorie P. Holt), p. 470.

Sisson's Word and Expression Locater

Descriptive Information

Full Title: **Sisson's Word and Expression Locater.** *Editor:* A. F. Sisson. *Publisher:* Parker Publishing Co. *Distributor:* Prentice-Hall. *Edition Reviewed:* 1966.
Classification: Special-Purpose—Synonyms, Antonyms & Homonyms. *Pages:* xi, 371. *Main Entries:* 7,500. *Physical Size:* 6 by 9¼ in.; 24 cm. (paper). *LC:* 66-10390. *ISBN:* 0-13-810663-0 (paper). *Lowest Retail Price:* $10.95; also $3.95 paper.

Comments

Similar in arrangement to *Sisson's Synonyms* (1969), this earlier compilation by Sisson emphasizes "the more obscure and unusual words and phrases useful in English construction." Among the 100,000 words and expressions entered under the 7,500 main entries are such terms as *misoneism, misoneist, xenophobia,* and *xenophobic.* Another example: under the word *nest* the user finds the definitional phrase *"leaving shortly after hatching"* followed by the word *nidifugous.* An informative complement to such standard synonym works as *Doubleday Roget's Thesaurus, Funk & Wagnalls Modern Guide to Synonyms, Roget's International Thesaurus, Webster's Collegiate Thesaurus,* and *Webster's New Dictionary of Synonyms.*

Synonym Finder

Descriptive Information

Full Title: **The Synonym Finder.** *Editors:* J. I. Rodale, Editor in Chief; Edward J. Fluck, Associate Editor. *Publisher:* Rodale Books, Inc. *Edition Reviewed:* 1961.
Classification: Special-Purpose—Synonyms, Antonyms & Homonyms. *Pages:* 1388. *Main Entries:* 20,000. *Physical Size:* 6¾ by 9½ in.; 24 cm. *Lowest Retail Price:* $16.95.

Comments

The Synonym Finder, though now somewhat out-of-date, is a useful compilation which contains approximately 300,000 synonymic words and expressions under 20,000 main entries. The synonyms are not discriminated although words with more than one connotation group the synonyms by broad definitions with the most common sense first and so on. Example: The entry *flowing* has three synonymic groupings: (1) "Moving in a stream, running, gushing, gliding, issuing, fluvial, meandering, flexuous, streamy, tidal, fluid, liquid, effluent"; (2) "Proceeding smoothly and easily, gracefully continuous throughout the length, cursive, fluent, easy, glib, facile, graceful, round, full, harmonious, voluble, abundant, copious"; and (3) "Falling at full length, hanging loosely." There is no comprehensive index listing all terms in the book. Complements the standard sources.

Synonyms, Antonyms and Related Words

Descriptive Information

Full Title: **Synonyms, Antonyms and Related Words: An Easy to Use Alphabetized Word Finder for Writers, Teachers and Students.** *Editor:* Stuart Reid. *Publisher:* Exposition Press. *Edition Reviewed:* 1972.

Classification: Special-Purpose—Synonyms, Antonyms & Homonyms. *Pages:* 55. *Main Entries:* 500. *ISBN:* 0-682-47309-X. *Lowest Retail Price:* $3.00.

Comments

Reid's little book provides synonyms and antonyms for only some 500 common words and is quite superficial when compared with such standard works as the *Doubleday Roget's Thesaurus* (also arranged alphabetically), *Webster's Collegiate Thesaurus,* and *Webster's New Dictionary of Synonyms.* Not recommended.

Other Critical Opinions

American Reference Books Annual 1973 (review by Barbara Marconi), p. 455.

Webster's Collegiate Thesaurus

Descriptive Information

Full Title: **Webster's Collegiate Thesaurus.** *Editor:* Mairé Weir Kay. *Publisher:* G. & C. Merriam Co. *Edition Reviewed:* 1976.

Classification: Special-Purpose—Synonyms, Antonyms & Homonyms. *Pages:* 32a, 944. *Main Entries:* 20,000. *Physical Size:* 7 by 10 in.; 25 cm. *LC:* 75-45167. *ISBN:* 0-87779-069-8. *Lowest Retail Price:* $9.95.

Comments

Webster's Collegiate Thesaurus, an entirely new work issued in 1976, provides over 100,000 synonyms, related words, idioms, contrasted words, and antonyms among its 20,000 main entries. The book is alphabetical in arrangement and hence more like the *Doubleday Roget's Thesaurus, Reader's Digest Family Word Finder*, and *Webster's New World Thesaurus* than Roget's original thesaurus which lists similar words by concept rather than alphabetically. Main entries include a brief definition (called a "meaning core"), a list of words considered to be strictly synonymous, then a list of related (as opposed to synonymous) terms, and finally a list of contrasted terms and antonyms. When, in the opinion of the editors, an entry requires further explanation, an illustrative sentence is included. *Webster's Collegiate Thesaurus* is up-to-date, authoritative, easy to use, attractively produced, and reasonably effective as a source of synonyms and antonyms. Words are not discriminated as fully as they are in, say, *Funk & Wagnalls Modern Guide to Synonyms* or *Webster's New Dictionary of Synonyms*. On the other hand *Webster's Collegiate Thesaurus* is much more than a simple list of synonyms and antonyms.

Other Critical Opinions

American Reference Books Annual 1977 (review by D. Bernard Theall), pp. 524–525.
Booklist, July 1, 1977, pp. 1671–1672.
Library Journal (review by B. Hunter Smeaton), July 1976, p. 1515.
Wilson Library Bulletin (review by Charles A. Bunge), September 1976, p. 91.

Webster's New Dictionary of Synonyms

Descriptive Information

Full Title: **Webster's New Dictionary of Synonyms: A Dictionary of Discriminated Synonyms with Antonyms and Analogous and Contrasted Words.** *Editor:* Philip B. Gove. *Publisher:* G. & C. Merriam Co. Former title: *Webster's Dictionary of Synonyms* (1942). *Edition Reviewed:* 1973.

Classification: Special-Purpose—Synonyms, Antonyms & Homonyms. *Pages:* 31a, 909. *Main Entries:* 7,500. *Physical Size:* 7 by 10 in.; 25 cm. *ISBN:* 0-87779-141-4. *Lowest Retail Price:* $8.95.

Comments

Originally published in 1942 as *Webster's Dictionary of Synonyms* and thoroughly revised and retitled in 1968, *Webster's New Dictionary of Synonyms* has long been considered a model of what a good synonym dictionary should be. Like *Funk & Wagnalls Modern Guide to Synonyms*, it carefully discriminates groups of similar words, e.g., *exculpate, absolve, exonerate, acquit,* and *vindicate*. Illustrative quotations, drawn from Merriam-Webster's large citation file, are liberally provided, serving to explain or clarify subtle connotations and discriminate shades of meaning. A list of the authors quoted appears in the back of the dictionary. The work is alphabetically arranged and contains numerous cross-references. Complements the publisher's newer *Webster's Collegiate Thesaurus* (1976).

Other Critical Opinions

Katz, William A. *Basic Information Sources*. Vol. 1 of *Introduction to Reference Work*, 2nd ed. (New York: McGraw-Hill, 1974), pp. 278–279.

Webster's New World Thesaurus

Descriptive Information

Full Title: **Webster's New World Thesaurus.** *Editor:* Charlton Laird. *Publishers:* Collins+World (hardcover); New American Library (paper); Popular Library (paper). *Edition Reviewed:* 1971.

Classification: Special-Purpose—Synonyms, Antonyms & Homonyms. *Pages:* ix, 678. *Main Entries:* 30,000. *Physical Size:* 6½ by 9¼ in.; 24 cm. (hardcover). *LC:* 79-137340. *ISBN:* 0-529-05186-9 (plain, hardcover); 0-529-05187-7 (thumb-indexed, hardcover); 0-445-08385-125 (paper, Popular Library). *Lowest Retail Price:* $6.95; also $3.95 paper (New American Library); $1.50 paper (Popular Library).

Comments

Webster's New World Thesaurus is similar in scope and arrangement to *The Doubleday Roget's Thesaurus, Reader's Digest Family Word Finder*, and Rodale's *Synonym Finder*. The 30,000 alphabetical main entries are defined concisely (e.g., *ignominy* is "offensive behavior"), then followed by lists of undiscriminated synonyms. Many idiomatic expressions are included, but antonyms are seldom indicated. The Popular Library paperback edition (issued in 1974), which includes several pages of discriminated synonyms in the back, is sold as part of the "Desk Top Reference Set," a six-volume paperback library of wordbooks which sells for $9.45 and includes *Webster's New World Dictionary* (Pocket-size Edition) as well as the thesaurus and several other useful titles.

Other Critical Opinions

American Reference Books Annual 1976 (review by Francis J. Witty), p. 547.

Webster's Synonyms, Antonyms & Homonyms

Descriptive Information

Full Title: **Webster's Synonyms, Antonyms & Homonyms.** *Editor:* None listed. *Publisher:* Barnes & Noble. Alternate title: *Webster's Vest-Pocket Synonyms, Antonyms and Homonyms* (also titled *Dennison Synonyms, Antonyms and Homonyms*). *Edition Reviewed:* 1962.

Classification: Special-Purpose—Synonyms, Antonyms & Homonyms. *Pages:* 256. *Main Entries:* 2,500. *Physical Size:* 3½ by 5 in.; 13 cm. *Lowest Retail Price:* $1.95 paper (with vinyl jacket).

Comments

Published by Barnes & Noble but copyrighted by Ottenheimer Publishers (1953 and 1962), this little dictionary is simply a list of undiscriminated synonyms and antonyms. Homonyms are listed separately in the back. Note that this work has exactly the same text as *Webster's Vest-Pocket Synonyms, Antonyms and Homonyms* (also known as *Dennison Synonyms, Antonyms and Homonyms*). Whatever title it goes by, this dictionary is not recommended. The Barnes & Noble edition is especially overpriced.

Webster's Vest-Pocket Synonyms, Antonyms and Homonyms

Descriptive Information

Full Title: **Webster's Vest-Pocket Synonyms, Antonyms and Homonyms.**
Editor: None listed. *Publisher:* Dennison Manufacturing Co. Alternate title:
Dennison Synonyms, Antonyms and Homonyms (on cover); *Webster's
Synonyms, Antonyms and Homonyms* (published by Barnes & Noble).
Edition Reviewed: 1962.
Classification: Special-Purpose—Synonyms, Antonyms & Homonyms.
Pages: 192. *Main Entries:* 2,500. *Physical Size:* 2¾ by 5½ in.; 14 cm. *Lowest
Retail Price:* $1.25 paper.

Consumer Note

This little pocket-size dictionary of undiscriminated synonyms and
antonyms is a verbatim reprint of *Webster's Synonyms, Antonyms and
Homonyms.* (See the profile immediately preceding for additional information.) The work has minimal reference value and is not recommended.

The Word Finder

Descriptive Information

Full Title: **The Word Finder.** *Editor:* J. I. Rodale. *Publisher:* Rodale Books,
Inc. Alternate title: *The Phrase Finder* (1953). *Edition Reviewed:* 1947.
Classification: Special-Purpose—Synonyms, Antonyms & Homonyms.
Pages: xxv, 1317. *Main Entries;* 10,000. *Physical Size:* 6¼ by 9¼ in.; 24 cm.
Lowest Retail Price: $14.95.

Comments

The Word Finder, which has also appeared under the title *Phrase Finder*
(Garden City Books, 1953; out of print), is a unique sort of synonym dictionary. It is designed, according to the editor, "not merely [to] yield a substitute
word but [to produce] an augmentative word, one to embellish and add to the
idea." For instance, under the main entry *face* (the noun) there are nearly five
columns of adjectives which might be used to describe the face, e.g., *absorbed,
accusing, aggrieved, adored, aged, aghast, agitated, agonized,* and *alert.*
When appropriate, subentries are categorized by part of speech (verbs, nouns,
adjectives, etc.) under the main entry. Under *face,* for example, there are
about 40 verbs, including *animate, contort, flush, furrow, pinch, pucker up,*
and *scrutinize.* A useful aid to writers looking for different words and phrases
to liven up their prose. Complemented by Rodale's *Synonym Finder.*

Writer's Book of Synonyms and Antonyms

Descriptive Information

Full Title: **The Writer's Book of Synonyms and Antonyms.** *Editor:* None
listed. *Publisher:* The Writer, Inc. Original title: *The Pitman Book of
Synonyms and Antonyms. Edition Reviewed:* 1960.

Classification: Special-Purpose—Synonyms, Antonyms & Homonyms. *Pages:* vi, 110. *Main Entries:* 5,000. *Physical Size:* 5 by 7½ in.; 19 cm. *LC:* 60-3290. *ISBN:* 0-87116-058-7. *Lowest Retail Price:* $2.95.

Comments

The Writer's Book of Synonyms and Antonyms was initially published in Great Britain as *The Pitman Book of Synonyms and Antonyms*. The first American edition (1960) has been reprinted several times but the book has never been revised. It consists of some 5,000 main entries which merely list undiscriminated synonyms, usually followed by an antonym or two. British spellings have been retained (e.g., *honour*) and many standard words, particularly those of American origin and usage, are not included. This work is too slight and too dated to be of more than incidental reference value.

CROSSWORD PUZZLES AND WORD GAMES

Apollo Crossword Puzzle Dictionary

Descriptive Information

Full Title: **Apollo Crossword Puzzle Dictionary.** *Compiler:* Andrew Swanfeldt. *Publisher:* T. Y. Crowell Co. (Apollo Editions). Original title: *Crossword Puzzle Dictionary* (1944). *Edition Reviewed:* Apollo Edition, 1971.

Classification: Special-Purpose—Crossword Puzzles & Word Games. *Pages:* 568. *Total Words:* 200,000. *Physical Size:* 6 by 9 in.; 23 cm. *LC:* 67-23679. *ISBN:* 0-8152-0303-9. *Lowest Retail Price:* $5.95 paper.

Consumer Note

In actuality the *Apollo Crossword Puzzle Dictionary* is a reprint of the Second Edition of Swanfeldt's *Crossword Puzzle Dictionary* (1944). In view of the fact that the dictionary is now in its Fourth Edition (1977), the Apollo Edition should either be updated or withdrawn from the market. For further information, see the profile of Swanfeldt's *Crossword Puzzle Dictionary* which follows in this section of the *Buying Guide*.

Other Critical Opinions

American Reference Books Annual 1973, p. 457.

Bell's Acrostic Dictionary

Descriptive Information

Full Title: **Bell's Acrostic Dictionary.** *Compiler:* W. M. Baker. *Publisher:* Gale Research Co. *Edition Reviewed:* 1927; reprinted 1971.

Classification: Special-Purpose—Crossword Puzzles & Word Games. *Pages:* 277. *Total Words:* 40,000. *LC:* 77-141772. *Lowest Retail Price:* $10.00.

Comments

Bell's Acrostic Dictionary, originally published in England in 1927 by G. Bell & Sons and reprinted some years ago by Gale Research, arranges the first and last letters of approximately 40,000 answer words in alphabetical order. Example: Under the heading "A–C" the user finds *abc, abietic, academic,* and so on. Obviously dated but still of supplementary value to puzzle fanatics. Most people, however, will turn first to the larger and more current *Funk & Wagnalls Crossword Puzzle Word Finder* (1974) for a by-the-letters approach.

Other Critical Opinions

American Reference Books Annual 1973 (review by Mary Jean Nottveit), p. 457.

Collins Gem Dictionary for Crossword Puzzles

Descriptive Information

Full Title: **Collins Gem Dictionary for Crossword Puzzles.** *Compiler:* J. A. MacAuslane. *Publisher:* Collins+World. *Edition Reviewed:* 1971.
Classification: Special-Purpose—Crossword Puzzles & Word Games. *Pages:* vii, 504. *Total Words:* 47,500. *Physical Size:* 3¼ by 4½ in.; 12 cm. *ISBN:* 0-00-458707-3. *Lowest Retail Price:* $2.45 paper (Leatheroid).

Comments

The *Collins Gem Dictionary for Crossword Puzzles* is a handy pocket work which groups over 47,000 words in nine main categories (e.g., "The Arts," "Living Creatures," "Measurement," and "Science and Technology") which are in turn subdivided (e.g., "The Arts" is broken down into such areas as "Architecture," "Art," "Education," "Literature," and "Music"). There is no comprehensive A–Z list of all words included in the dictionary. Useful for the traveler but by no means competitive with the larger dictionaries like Swanfeldt's *Crossword Puzzle Dictionary, Funk & Wagnalls Crossword Puzzle Word Finder,* and *The New York Times Crossword Puzzle Dictionary.*

Complete Scrabble Dictionary

Descriptive Information

Full Title: **The Complete Scrabble Dictionary.** *Compilers:* Tom Pulliam and Gorton Carruth. *Publisher:* McGraw-Hill. *Edition Reviewed:* 1977.
Classification: Special-Purpose—Crossword Puzzles & Word Games. *Pages:* 640. *Total Words:* 220,000. *ISBN:* 0-07-050914-X (plain); 0-07-050915-8 (thumb-indexed). *Lowest Retail Price:* $12.50.

Comments

New in 1977, *The Complete Scrabble Dictionary* is so trendy that it even includes vulgarisms among its 220,000 total word stock. Pulliam also compiled the popular *New York Times Crossword Puzzle Dictionary*. Both works are reliable, up-to-date, and can be recommended without hesitation to all word game addicts.

Crossword Puzzle Dictionary

Descriptive Information

Full Title: **Crossword Puzzle Dictionary.** *Compiler:* Andrew Swanfeldt. *Publisher:* T. Y. Crowell Co. Alternate title: *The Famous Andrew Swanfeldt Crossword Puzzle Dictionary* (used in advertisements). *Edition Reviewed:* Fourth Edition, 1977.

Classification: Special-Purpose—Crossword Puzzles & Word Games. *Total Words:* 330,000. *ISBN:* 0-690-00426-5 (plain); 0-690-01198-9 (thumb-indexed). *Lowest Retail Price:* $9.95.

Comments

Swanfeldt's dictionary is one of the oldest and largest such works currently available. It first appeared in 1940 and was subsequently revised in 1944, 1967, and 1977. Based on studies of actual puzzles, each edition has grown larger, e.g., the 1944 Second Edition included some 200,000 answer words whereas the most recent revision claims well over 300,000 words. The new Fourth Edition has been completely reset in clear type on a larger page. *The Crossword Puzzle Dictionary*, which is authoritative, easy to use, and up-to-date, compares favorably with the other major word puzzle dictionaries, namely, *Funk & Wagnalls Crossword Puzzle Word Finder*, *The New York Times Crossword Puzzle Dictionary*, and *Webster's New World Crossword Puzzle Dictionary*.

Expert's Crossword Puzzle Dictionary

Descriptive Information

Full Title: **The Expert's Crossword Puzzle Dictionary.** *Compiler:* Herbert M. Baus. *Publisher:* Doubleday & Co. *Edition Reviewed:* 1973.

Classification: Special-Purpose—Crossword Puzzles & Word Games. *Pages:* 585. *Total Words:* 200,000. *LC:* 72-84960. *ISBN:* 0-385-04788-6. *Lowest Retail Price:* $2.95 paper.

Comments

Baus has conscientiously gone through crossword puzzles noting every clue word (i.e., word in the question section of the puzzles). Altogether he provides some 60,000 clue words and 140,000 answer words, including many recent terms as well as "a liberal sprinkling of archaic and obsolete terms." *The Expert's Crossword Puzzle Dictionary*, which has an elaborate system of cross-referencing designed to reduce repetition of answer words, is a useful compilation in a convenient paperbound format. Not as comprehensive, however, as works like Swanfeldt's *Crossword Puzzle Dictionary* and Pulliam's *New York Times Crossword Puzzle Dictionary*.

Other Critical Opinions

American Reference Books Annual 1974 (review by Barbara Marconi), p. 459.

Funk & Wagnalls Crossword Puzzle Word Finder

Descriptive Information

Full Title: **Funk & Wagnalls Crossword Puzzle Word Finder.** *Compilers:* Edmund I. Schwartz and Leon F. Landovitz. *Publisher:* Funk & Wagnalls Publishing Co. *Distributor:* T. Y. Crowell Co. *Edition Reviewed:* 1974.

Classification: Special-Purpose—Crossword Puzzles & Word Games. *Pages:* xiv, 754. *Total Words:* 300,000. *Physical Size:* 5½ by 8½ in.; 22 cm. *LC:* 74-22450. *ISBN:* 0-308-10126-X. *Lowest Retail Price:* $8.95.

Comments

Funk & Wagnalls Crossword Puzzle Word Finder "is designed to help you solve crossword puzzle sticklers solely through letters you already filled in." That is, if you have a five-letter word, for instance, but only two letters filled in, you can find various five-letter word combinations in this book which might solve the puzzle. Example: You need a five-letter word beginning with *s* and ending with *o*. By looking under *s . . . o* in the book, you will find *sacro, salvo, sambo, sapro, sarco, sarto, sauro,* and 24 more possibilities. The *Word Finder* covers from two- to-six-letter word combinations, all conveniently arranged in alphabetical sequence within each numbered group. The book was developed with the help of a computer and, because definitions are not given, the compilers suggest using *Funk & Wagnalls Crossword Puzzle Word Finder* in combination with *Funk & Wagnalls Standard College Dictionary*. An effective source for puzzle fans which nicely complements such standard items as Swanfeldt's *Crossword Puzzle Dictionary, The New York Times Crossword Puzzle Dictionary,* and *Webster's New World Crossword Puzzle Dictionary*.

Other Critical Opinions

Booklist, June 15, 1975, pp. 1092–1093.

New American Crossword Puzzle Dictionary

Descriptive Information

Full Title: **New American Crossword Puzzle Dictionary.** *Editors:* Albert Morehead and Loy Morehead. *Publisher:* New American Library. *Edition Reviewed:* 1967.

Classification: Special-Purpose—Crossword Puzzles & Word Games. *Pages:* 512. *Total Words:* 125,000. *Physical Size:* 4¼ by 7 in.; 18 cm. *Lowest Retail Price:* $1.50 paper.

Comments

The Moreheads' little book is something of a hodgepodge. Section I comprises about 100 pages of alphabetically listed clue words with answers frequently used in puzzles, e.g., the clue word *chair* is followed by *kago, rocker, seat, sedan, speaker,* and *stool.* Section II provides answer words grouped by categories, e.g., under "Famous Bridges" the user finds such words as *Elsa, Forth, Meric,* and *Rialto.* And Section III is a word locater for two- to four-letter words, similar to (though much less thorough than) *Funk & Wagnalls Crossword Puzzle Word Finder.*

New Comprehensive A–Z Crossword Dictionary

Descriptive Information

Full Title: **The New Comprehensive A–Z Crossword Dictionary.** *Compilers:* Redentor Ma. Tuazon and Edy Garcia Schaffer. *Publisher:* Grosset & Dunlap. *Edition Reviewed:* 1973.

Classification: Special-Purpose—Crossword Puzzles & Word Games. *Pages:* 542. *Total Words:* 250,000. *Physical Size:* 7¼ by 10¼ in.; 26 cm. *LC:* 72-79971. *ISBN:* 0-448-01525-0. *Lowest Retail Price:* $6.95.

Comments

Tuazon and Schaffer's dictionary includes some 75,000 clue words and 175,000 answer words. Example: After the clue word *government* (in boldface type), the user finds CONTROL, RULE, DIRECTION, STATE, REGIME(N), and POLITY (in capitals). There are also various subentries of *government,* such as *by gods* (THEARCHY), *by men* (PATRIARCHY), *declaration* (MANIFESTO), *mob's* (OCHLOCRACY), *report* (WHITE PAPER and BLUE BOOK), and *women's* (GYNARCHY and GYNECOCRACY). A good source for unusual word puzzle answers, including variant spellings, idioms, slogans, and archaic terms, but not as comprehensive as Swanfeldt's *Crossword Puzzle Dictionary* and *The New York Times Crossword Puzzle Dictionary.* Tuazon and Schaffer's dictionary, though larger, is quite similar in design to Newman's *New Practical Dictionary for Crossword Puzzles.*

Other Critical Opinions

Booklist, February 1, 1974, p. 566.

New Practical Dictionary for Crossword Puzzles

Descriptive Information

Full Title: **New Practical Dictionary for Crossword Puzzles.** *Compiler:* Frank Eaton Newman. *Publisher:* Doubleday & Co. Alternate title: *The Pocket Crossword Puzzle Dictionary.* Former title: *The Perma Cross Word*

Puzzle and Word Game Dictionary (1955). *Edition Reviewed:* Completely Revised and Updated Edition, 1975.

Classification: Special-Purpose—Crossword Puzzles & Word Games. *Pages:* viii, 320. *Total Words:* 100,000. *Physical Size:* 5¾ by 8¼ in.; 22 cm. *LC:* 74-5608. *ISBN:* 0-385-05280-4. *Lowest Retail Price:* $3.95.

Comments

Newman's work first appeared in 1942 and has been revised a number of times since, most recently in 1975. The book appeared under the title *Perma Cross Word Puzzle and Word Game Dictionary* in 1955 (now out of print) and later as *The Pocket Crossword Puzzle Dictionary* (still in print). The 1975 version has some 25,000 main entries and 75,000 answer words. The work is reasonably up-to-date and emphasizes difficult words (e.g., the answer words for *moonstone* are *feldspar* and *hecatolite*), but it is not as comprehensive or as useful as Swanfeldt's *Crossword Puzzle Dictionary* and *The New York Times Crossword Puzzle Dictionary*. It most resembles Tuazon and Schaffer's *New Comprehensive A–Z Crossword Dictionary*.

New Webster's Crossword Puzzle Dictionary

Descriptive Information

Full Title: **New Webster's Crossword Puzzle Dictionary.** *Compiler:* Bettye M. Melnicove. *Publishers:* Crown (coil binding); Fawcett World (paper). *Edition Reviewed:* 1976.

Classification: Special-Purpose—Crossword Puzzles & Word Games. *Lowest Retail Price:* $1.95 (coil binding); also $1.50 paper.

Comments

The *New Webster's Crossword Puzzle Dictionary* is a handy, easy-to-use little item. Although it cannot compare in size or quality with the more substantial puzzle dictionaries (e.g., Swanfeldt's *Crossword Puzzle Dictionary* and Pulliam's *New York Times Crossword Puzzle Dictionary*), it might comfort the traveler who is a word-puzzle freak. Comparable to Norman Hill's *Webster's Red Seal Crossword Dictionary*.

New York Times Crossword Puzzle Dictionary

Descriptive Information

Full Title: **The New York Times Crossword Puzzle Dictionary.** *Compilers:* Thomas Pulliam and Clare Grundman. *Publishers:* Quadrangle (hardcover); Warner Books (paper). *Edition Reviewed:* 1974.

Classification: Special-Purpose—Crossword Puzzles & Word Games. *Pages:* vi, 685. *Total Words:* 500,000. *Physical Size:* 6½ by 9½ in.; 24 cm. (hardcover). *LC:* 73-79912. *ISBN:* 0-8129-0382-X (hardcover). *Lowest Retail Price:* $12.50; also $5.95 paper.

Comments

The compilers claim in their preface that this dictionary "exceeds in completeness and scope all other puzzle dictionaries. No useful word has been omitted. Not only have puzzles themselves been combed for synonyms that are used over and over, but also a word-for-word reading of major unabridged dictionaries, both current and old, produced a thoroughly complete and extensive checklist." There is no question that *The New York Times Crossword Puzzle Dictionary*, which bears the distinctive "Hudson Group Book" logo, is the largest such work on the market. It includes some 40,000 alphabetically arranged main entries with over 500,000 answer words. Essentially a dictionary of undiscriminated synonyms, it is up-to-date and easy to use. There are also many terms associated with various countries of the world and U.S. states. Example: The entry for *Iowa* is set off in a gray box and provides answer words for the state's capital, colleges, lakes, major towns, etc. Along with Swanfeldt's *Crossword Puzzle Dictionary, Funk & Wagnalls Crossword Puzzle Word Finder*, and *Webster's New World Crossword Puzzle Dictionary*, Pulliam and Grundman's dictionary is among the most useful works of its kind.

Other Critical Opinions

American Reference Books Annual 1976 (review by Robert Parslow), p. 547.
Booklist, March 15, 1976, p. 1071.

Pocket Crossword Puzzle Dictionary

Descriptive Information

Full Title: **The Pocket Crossword Puzzle Dictionary.** *Compiler:* Frank Eaton Newman. *Publisher:* Pocket Books. Original title: *New Practical Dictionary for Crossword Puzzles. Edition Reviewed:* Newly Revised and Enlarged Edition, 1966.

Classification: Special-Purpose—Crossword Puzzles & Word Games. *Pages:* xxi, 362. *Total Words:* 80,000. *Physical Size;* 4¼ by 7 in.; 18 cm. *ISBN:* 0-671-80219-4. *Lowest Retail Price:* $1.75 paper.

Consumer Note

The Pocket Crossword Puzzle Dictionary is a paper edition of Newman's 1964 *New Practical Dictionary for Crossword Puzzles.* The latter has now been replaced by the 1975 edition, a thorough revision which, according to the compiler, has brought the book "into tune with the language of the 1970s" and added many new words throughout. Consumers are therefore advised to wait for the new revision of *The Pocket Crossword Puzzle Dictionary* based on the 1975 edition of the *New Practical Dictionary for Crossword Puzzles.* No publication date for this edition has yet been announced. See the comments on the *New Practical Dictionary for Crossword Puzzles* in this section of the *Buying Guide* for further information about the contents of the dictionary.

Unabridged Crossword Puzzle Dictionary

Descriptive Information

Full Title: **The Unabridged Crossword Puzzle Dictionary.** *Compiler:* A. F. Sisson. *Publisher:* Doubleday & Co. Original title: *The Unabridged Crossword Puzzle Word Finder. Edition Reviewed:* 1963.

Classification: Special-Purpose—Crossword Puzzles & Word Games. *Pages:* 526. *Total Words:* 200,000. *Physical Size:* 5¾ by 8½ in.; 22 cm. *LC:* 62-15910. *ISBN:* 0-385-02843-1 (plain); 0-385-01350-7 (thumb-indexed). *Lowest Retail Price:* $5.95.

Comments

A. F. Sisson's name is well known in synonym circles. In addition to *The Unabridged Crossword Puzzle Dictionary*, he has also produced *Sisson's Word and Expression Locater* (1966) and *Sisson's Synonyms* (1969). *The Unabridged Crossword Puzzle Dictionary*, at one time the largest word puzzle dictionary available, is alphabetically arranged with main entries followed by answer words in small capitals. Example: The entry *hit* includes 22 synonyms, such as SMASH, BOP, SLOG, BUFFET, FIND, BUNT, SINGLE, FLICK, STRIKE, LAM, AGREE, KNOCK, SWAT, and SMITE. At the present time, the dictionary is beginning to show its age. Though still useful, it cannot successfully compete with more recent and larger works like *The New York Times Crossword Puzzle Dictionary* (1974) and Swanfeldt's *Crossword Puzzle Dictionary* (Fourth Edition, 1977).

Webster's New World Crossword Puzzle Dictionary

Descriptive Information

Full Title: **Webster's New World Crossword Puzzle Dictionary.** *Compiler:* Jane Shaw Whitfield. *Publisher:* Collins+World (hardcover); Pocket Books (paper). *Edition Reviewed:* 1975.

Classification: Special-Purpose—Crossword Puzzles & Word Games. *Pages:* 656. *Total Words:* 300,000. *Physical Size:* 6 by 9¼ in.; 24 cm. *LC:* 75-926. *ISBN:* 0-529-05176-1 (plain); 0-529-05278-4 (thumb-indexed). *Lowest Retail Price:* $6.95; also $1.95 paper.

Comments

Webster's New World Crossword Puzzle Dictionary, a new work in 1975, contains approximately 35,000 main entries and 265,000 answer words. Many main entries have subentries pertaining to the term. Example: Subentries of *life* include "after death" (the answer word is *Olam-haba*), "god of" (answer word is *Faunus*), and "lifelike" (answer words are *alike, vital, biotic, realistic*). A convenient feature of the dictionary is that letter counts are given immediately preceding the answer words, e.g., the answer words for *excise* are "3. *tax* 4. *toll* 6. *impost*." Entries for countries of the world and the U.S. states provide many geographical and other related terms, e.g., under *China* are found names of cities, mountains, etc. *The New York Times Crossword*

Puzzle Dictionary has some of the same features. Both dictionaries are authoritative, up-to-date, and reasonably comprehensive. Along with Swanfeldt's *Crossword Puzzle Dictionary* and *Funk & Wagnalls Crossword Puzzle Word Finder*, they are the most useful word-puzzle sources currently in print.

Other Critical Opinions

Booklist, March 15, 1976, p. 1071.

Webster's Red Seal Crossword Dictionary

Descriptive Information

Full Title: **Webster's Red Seal Crossword Dictionary.** *Compiler:* Norman Hill. *Publisher:* Popular Library. *Edition Reviewed:* 1971.

Classification: Special-Purpose—Crossword Puzzles & Word Games. *Pages:* 271. *Total Words:* 100,000. *Physical Size:* 4¼ by 7 in.; 18 cm. *ISBN:* 0-445-08299-150. *Lowest Retail Price:* $1.50 paper.

Comments

This little pocket-size crossword puzzle dictionary contains approximately 25,000 clue words (main entries) and 75,000 answer words. The work concentrates on the standard puzzle vocabulary, e.g., the entry *former Russian ruler* lists TZAR and CZAR as the answers. Easy to use and helpful for simple word puzzles.

Other Critical Opinions

American Reference Books Annual 1972, p. 474.

RHYMES

Poetic geniuses rarely if ever need dictionaries of rhymes. The T. S. Eliots and Robert Frosts of the world hardly require such aids. On the other hand, the amateur rhymester (a poet and don't know it), the writer of advertising jingles or popular songs, and the puzzle contestant often make good use of rhyming dictionaries. Rhyming dictionaries usually organize their vocabulary by vowel sounds and number of rhyming syllables, the most elementary entries being rhyming monosyllables (e.g., *bit/flit/kit/skit*) and polysyllabic words with final rhyming syllables (e.g., *peptic/sceptic/septic/antiseptic*). The larger dictionaries include two-syllable rhymes (e.g., *nation/abdication/ abnegation/accumulation*) and three-syllable rhymes (e.g., *botony/bottony/ cottony/monotony*). Most of the rhyming dictionaries currently on the market have been around for years. For instance, the earliest edition of Walker's unique *Rhyming Dictionary of the English Language* dates back to 1775 and the most comprehensive such dictionary available, *Wood's Unabridged Rhyming Dictionary*, appeared in 1943.

Capricorn Rhyming Dictionary

Descriptive Information

Full Title: **Capricorn Rhyming Dictionary (Aid to Rhyme).** *Editor:* Bessie G. Redfield. *Publisher:* Putnam (Capricorn Books). Original title: *Aid to Rhyme. Edition Reviewed:* Capricorn Books Edition, 1965.

Classification: Special-Purpose—Rhymes. *Pages:* 315. *Physical Size:* 4¼ by 7 in.; 18 cm. *ISBN:* 0-399-50200-9. *Lowest Retail Price:* $1.95 paper.

Comments

The Capricorn Rhyming Dictionary, originally published in 1938 as *Aid to Rhyme* and unrevised since that time, is arranged alphabetically by vowel sounds (A, E, I, O, U). Usually only one- and two-syllable rhymes are given. Example: Under "E Sounds" the user finds such entries as "EAGE" (*acreage/lineage/mileage*), "EAK" (*beak/bespeak/bleak/creak/freak/*etc.), and "EAL" (*anneal/appeal/armorial seal/cochineal/* etc.). Easy to use but far from complete. Similar to the little *Random House Rhyming Dictionary*.

Complete Rhyming Dictionary

Descriptive Information

Full Title: **The Complete Rhyming Dictionary and Poet's Craft Book.** *Editor:* Clement Wood. *Publisher:* Doubleday & Co. *Edition Reviewed:* 1936.

Classification: Special-Purpose—Rhymes. *Pages:* xii, 607. *Physical Size:* 5¾ by 8½ in.; 22 cm. *Lowest Retail Price:* $5.95.

Comments

The first 105 pages of this work deal with prosody (the study of versification) and types of poetry (the sonnet, lyric, limerick, etc.). The remainder constitutes the rhyming dictionary, which is arranged in three parts: single, double, and triple rhymes. In addition to standard vocabulary, the dictionary includes familiar first names for men and women, rhyming geographical names, and common family names (e.g., *Payne*). Though now dated, *The Complete Rhyming Dictionary* is still useful for versifiers. However, *Wood's Unabridged Rhyming Dictionary*, which is more detailed, is preferable for serious writers.

New Rhyming Dictionary and Poets' Handbook

Descriptive Information

Full Title: **New Rhyming Dictionary and Poets' Handbook.** *Editor:* Burges Johnson. *Publisher:* Harper & Row. *Edition Reviewed:* Revised Edition, 1957.

Classification: Special-Purpose—Rhymes. *Pages:* x, 464. *Physical Size:* 6 by 8½ in.; 22 cm. *LC:* 57-9585. *Lowest Retail Price:* $9.95.

Comments

This work begins with 60 some pages of information about the study of versification and concludes with a one- , two- , and three-syllable dictionary of rhymes. A standard work for the "eager versifier," Johnson's dictionary is similar in scope to Clement Wood's *Complete Rhyming Dictionary* and Stillman's *Poet's Manual and Rhyming Dictionary.*

New Rhyming Dictionary of One and Two Syllable Rhymes

Descriptive Information

Full Title: **New Rhyming Dictionary of One and Two Syllable Rhymes.** *Editor:* None listed. *Publisher:* Barnes & Noble. *Edition Reviewed:* 1963. *Classification:* Special-Purpose—Rhymes. *Pages:* vii, 246. *Physical Size:* 3¼ by 5 in.; 13 cm. *Lowest Retail Price:* $1.75 paper (with vinyl jacket).

Comments

Published by Barnes & Noble (a division of Harper & Row) by arrangement with Ottenheimer Publishers (Baltimore, Md.), this little dictionary of rhymes is overpriced and poorly printed. *The Random House Rhyming Dictionary* and *Capricorn Rhyming Dictionary*, both simple rhyming dictionaries available in paperback, are preferable.

Poet's Manual and Rhyming Dictionary

Descriptive Information

Full Title: **The Poet's Manual and Rhyming Dictionary: Based on the Improved Rhyming Dictionary by Jane Shaw Whitfield.** *Compiler:* Frances Stillman. *Publisher:* T. Y. Crowell Co. *Edition Reviewed:* 1965. *Classification:* Special-Purpose—Rhymes. *Pages:* xviii, 387. *Physical Size:* 6¼ by 9¼ in.; 24 cm. *LC:* 65-11650. *ISBN:* 0-690-64572-4. *Lowest Retail Price:* $9.95.

Comments

Approximately one-third of the book (123 pages) comprises "The Poet's Manual," which explains the techniques of versification and various poetic forms. The dictionary section, based on Whitfield's *Improved Rhyming Dictionary*, provides single, double, and triple rhymes grouped according to key vowel sounds, e.g., $\overline{oo}$ as in *good*. Many colloquial and foreign terms are included among the 115,000 rhyming words. Stillman's work is similar in purpose and scope to Wood's *Complete Rhyming Dictionary* and Johnson's *New Rhyming Dictionary and Poets' Handbook*. Note that the dictionary portion of this book is also published as the *Songwriters' Rhyming Dictionary* and *Whitfield's University Rhyming Dictionary*. The original *Improved Rhyming Dictionary* is out of print.

Random House Rhyming Dictionary

Descriptive Information

Full Title: **The Random House Rhyming Dictionary.** *Editor:* Jess Stein. *Publisher:* Random House. *Edition Reviewed:* 1960.
Classification: Special-Purpose—Rhymes. *Pages:* 239. *Physical Size:* 3 by 5½ in.; 14 cm. *LC:* 60-5551. *Lowest Retail Price:* $1.65 flexible covers.

Comments

The Random House Rhyming Dictionary is a small pocket-size work of one- and two-syllable rhymes. There is also a concise glossary of poetic terms in the back of the book. Though now somewhat dated, the dictionary remains a useful source for simple rhymes. Preferable to either the *Capricorn Rhyming Dictionary* or the *New Rhyming Dictionary of One and Two Syllable Rhymes*, two other paperback items on the market.

Rhyming Dictionary

Descriptive Information

Full Title: **Rhyming Dictionary.** *Author:* Thomas McGee. *Publisher:* Vantage Press. *Edition Reviewed:* 1974.
Classification: Special-Purpose—Rhymes. *Pages:* 422. *Physical Size:* 5½ by 8¼ in.; 21 cm. *ISBN:* 0-533-00736-4. *Lowest Retail Price:* $9.95.

Comments

Rhyming Dictionary is not a rhyming dictionary in the ordinary sense. Rather, it consists of a series of rhyming couplets arranged alphabetically by keyword, which is italicized. Example: The following couplet is found under "C." "All the committee members have *cooperated;*/ Thus, a successful outing is anticipated." Example: Under "M" one finds: "When a person is caught in a lie,/ It will profoundly *mortify.*" Imagine over 400 pages of such couplets. Note that, as the *Buying Guide* was going to press, the *Rhyming Dictionary* was reported out of print.

Rhyming Dictionary of the English Language

Descriptive Information

Full Title: **The Rhyming Dictionary of the English Language: In Which the Whole Language Is Arranged According to Its Terminations; With an Index of Allowable Rhymes.** *Compiler:* John Walker; Revised and Enlarged by Lawrence H. Dawson. *Publisher:* E. P. Dutton & Co. *Edition Reviewed:* Revised and Enlarged Edition, 1936.
Classification: Special-Purpose—Rhymes. *Pages:* vii, 549. *Physical Size:* 5¾ by 8 in.; 20 cm. *ISBN:* 0-525-19128-3. *Lowest Retail Price:* $9.95.

Comments

Walker's *Rhyming Dictionary of the English Language* first appeared in 1775 and since that time has undergone a number of revisions by different people, including Lawrence Dawson's Revised and Enlarged Edition, published in Great Britain in 1924 and the United States in 1936. The work's arrangement of entries is unique. As Dawson explains in his preface, "the words are grouped, not phonetically, but strictly alphabetically in accordance with the *reversed* spelling of the word; i.e. it is not the words *beginning* with A, B, C, etc., that will be found under those letters but those *ending* with them." Thus, the user looks up the word *dictionary* not under "d" but under "y." Immediately following *dictionary* are the words *functionary, concretionary, discretionary, traditionary, expeditionary, transitionary*, and so on. In addition, the words are briefly defined. There is also a cursory index of "allowable" rhymes in the back which lists all possible rhyming combinations. Obviously the vocabulary included in the dictionary is not up-to-date but, as Dawson rightly points out, Walker's *Rhyming Dictionary* "has been for over a hundred and fifty years a standard work of reference and has been a friend in need to generations of poets and rhymesters from Byron downwards."

Songwriters' Rhyming Dictionary

Descriptive Information

Full Title: **Songwriters' Rhyming Dictionary.** *Editor:* Jane Shaw Whitfield. *Compiler:* Frances Stillman. *Publisher:* Wilshire Book Co. Original title: *The Improved Rhyming Dictionary.* Alternate titles: *The Poet's Manual and Rhyming Dictionary* (1965); *Whitfield's University Rhyming Dictionary* (1951). *Edition Reviewed:* 1975.

Classification: Special-Purpose—Rhymes. *Pages:* xx, 283. *Physical Size:* 5¼ by 8¼ in.; 21 cm. *ISBN:* 0-87980-293-6. *Lowest Retail Price:* $4.00 paper.

Consumer Note

This is a reprint of Whitfield's *Improved Rhyming Dictionary* (now out of print) as edited by Stillman and published by T. Y. Crowell as part of *The Poet's Manual and Rhyming Dictionary* (1965). The rhyming vocabulary is therefore well over two decades old and perhaps a bit antique for contemporary songwriters. Exactly the same work is also available under the title *Whitfield's University Rhyming Dictionary* (1951) in a paperback edition. Overall, however, the Whitfield/Stillman dictionary is a satisfactory source for standard rhymes. See the profile of *The Poet's Manual and Rhyming Dictionary* in this section of the *Buying Guide* for further information about the contents of *Songwriters' Rhyming Dictionary*.

Other Critical Opinions

American Reference Books Annual 1976, p. 548.

Whitfield's University Rhyming Dictionary

Descriptive Information

Full Title: **Whitfield's University Rhyming Dictionary.** *Editor:* Jane Shaw Whitfield. *Compiler:* Frances Stillman. *Publisher:* T. Y. Crowell Co. (Apollo Editions). Original title: *The Improved Rhyming Dictionary.* Alternate titles: *The Poet's Manual and Rhyming Dictionary* (1965); *Songwriters' Rhyming Dictionary* (1975). *Edition Reviewed:* Apollo Edition, 1964.

Classification: Special-Purpose—Rhymes. *Pages:* xx, 283. *Physical Size:* 5 by 7¾ in.; 20 cm. *ISBN:* 0-8152-0080-3. *Lowest Retail Price:* $3.95 paper.

Consumer Note

This work is a revision of Whitfield's *The Improved Rhyming Dictionary,* published in 1951 and now out of print. The dictionary has also been reprinted as the *Songwriters' Rhyming Dictionary* and appears as part of *The Poet's Manual and Rhyming Dictionary.* (See comments under the latter title in this section of the *Buying Guide* for additional information.)

Wood's Unabridged Rhyming Dictionary

Descriptive Information

Full Title: **Wood's Unabridged Rhyming Dictionary.** *Editor:* Clement Wood. *Publisher:* Collins+World. Alternate title: *Wood's New World Unabridged Rhyming Dictionary* (on spine and jacket cover). *Edition Reviewed:* 1943.

Classification: Special-Purpose—Rhymes. *Pages:* xv, 1040. *Physical Size:* 5½ by 8½ in.; 22 cm. *ISBN:* 0-529-03390-9. *Lowest Retail Price:* $12.95.

Comments

Wood's Unabridged Rhyming Dictionary is the most extensive and complicated dictionary of its kind available today. Single, double, and triple rhymes are grouped by consonantal openings and vowel sounds. The arrangement of rhymes is by phonetic sound rather than spelling. The dictionary also includes composite (or mosaic) rhymes, e.g., *Pocono/smoke? O, no.* In addition, there is much information about the techniques and types of prosody. Among the good rhyming dictionaries on the market (which include Wood's earlier *Complete Rhyming Dictionary,* Burges Johnson's *New Rhyming Dictionary,* and Frances Stillman's *Poet's Manual and Rhyming Dictionary*), *Wood's Unabridged Rhyming Dictionary* is the most accurate, scientific, and comprehensive.

Writer's Rhyming Dictionary

Descriptive Information

Full Title: **The Writer's Rhyming Dictionary.** *Editor:* Langford Reed. *Publisher:* The Writer, Inc. *Edition Reviewed:* 1961.

Classification: Special-Purpose—Rhymes. *Pages:* xii, 244. *Physical Size:* 5 by 8½ in.; 20 cm. *LC:* 61-16086. *ISBN:* 0-87116-044-7. *Lowest Retail Price:* $4.95.

Comments

The Writer's Rhyming Dictionary is a simple one- and two-rhyme dictionary of some 25,000 rhyming combinations, e.g., *cradle/ladle.* Curiously, the book lacks a table of contents which makes it difficult to use. Good for beginners but serious versifiers will want a more substantial work such as Johnson's *New Rhyming Dictionary* or *Wood's Unabridged Rhyming Dictionary.*

SPELLING AND SYLLABICATION

Bad Speller's Dictionary

Descriptive Information

Full Title: **The Bad Speller's Dictionary.** *Compilers:* Joseph Krevisky and Jordon L. Linfield. *Publisher:* Random House. *Edition Reviewed:* 1967.

Classification: Special-Purpose—Spelling & Syllabication. *Pages:* vi, 186. *Total Entries:* 10,000. *Physical Size:* 3 by 5½ in.; 14 cm. *LC:* 67-14465. *ISBN:* 0-394-49199-8. *Lowest Retail Price:* $1.65 flexible covers.

Comments

The Bad Speller's Dictionary, first published in 1963 and revised in 1967, is published by Random House although Innovation Press holds the copyright. It lists approximately 10,000 frequently misspelled words, arranged alphabetically by misspelled words, followed by the correct spelling. Example: *abbandon/abandon; abbolition/abolition; abcess/abscess.* This approach is helpful if you know how to say but not spell a particular word. For instance, if you do not know how to spell *aardvark,* you would naturally look under *ard-.* In a general dictionary you would not find the word but in *The Bad Speller's Dictionary* it is under *ardvark* (labeled "incorrect") followed by *aardvark.* Lists of "Look-Alikes" (*adapt/adept/adopt*) and "Sound-Alikes" (*cereal/serial*) are provided. Included is an A–Z list of all words covered in the dictionary by their correct spellings. Comparable to the Norbacks' *Misspeller's Dictionary* and *Elliott's foe-né-tic Spelling Dictionary.*

Collins Gem Word Speller & Divider

Descriptive Information

Full Title: **Collins Gem Word Speller & Divider.** *Compiler:* None listed. *Publisher:* Collins+World. *Based on: Collins Gem Dictionary of Spelling & Word Division. Edition Reviewed:* 1973.

Classification: Special-Purpose—Spelling & Syllabication. *Pages:* xi, 499. *Total Entries:* 50,000. *Physical Size:* 3 by 4½ in.; 12 cm. *ISBN:* 0-00-458734-0. *Lowest Retail Price:* $2.45 paper (Leatheroid).

Comments

This dictionary, part of the publisher's "Gem Reference Library," aims "to give a guide to all permissible places where a word may be split on the basis of etymology and word structure." An effort has been made to include "all words likely to cause difficulty in normal correspondence and everyday printed matter." The book also includes basic spelling rules, a list of one- and two-syllable words (e.g., *ache, afar, banned*) which are normally not divided, and a selection of foreign words and phrases commonly used in English. Similar in design and scope to the *Follett Vest-Pocket 50,000 Words* and Ellis's *The Word Book.*

Comparative Study of Spelling

Descriptive Information

Full Title: **A Comparative Study of Spelling in Four Major Collegiate Dictionaries.** *Compiler:* Lee C. Deighton. *Publisher:* Hardscrabble Press. *Distributor:* Van Nostrand Reinhold Co. *Edition Reviewed:* 1972.

Classification: Special-Purpose—Spelling & Syllabication. *Pages:* 144. *Total Entries:* 2,000. *Physical Size:* 6¼ by 9¼ in., 24 cm. *LC:* 72-94070. *Lowest Retail Price:* $5.95.

Comments

Deighton combed four major college (semi-unabridged) dictionaries—*The American Heritage Dictionary* (1969); *The Random House College Dictionary* (1969); *Webster's New World Dictionary* (Second College Edition, 1970); and *Webster's Seventh New Collegiate Dictionary* (1969)—for alternate spellings of relatively common words. He found more than 2,000 such variants. "For a dismaying portion of these words," says Deighton in his foreword, "the dictionaries offer no indication of preference or frequency of occurrence and indicate that one spelling is as acceptable as another. The reader is left without guidance. Even more disconcerting, for about 1,770 words, the dictionaries are in disagreement as to spelling." Deighton lists the words alphabetically in tabular form, indicating how the four dictionaries spelled each word. He also provides preferred spellings (in boldface type) based on a consensus among the four dictionaries. Hence, one can consult *A Comparative Study of Spelling* and find that, for example, *epilogue* is preferred over *epilog, highhanded* over *high-handed,* and *pantsuit* over *pant suit or pants suit.* Compare with Emery's *Variant Spellings in Modern American Dictionaries,* a similar study involving five major college dictionaries.

Dictionary of Correct Spelling

Descriptive Information

Full Title: **Dictionary of Correct Spelling: A Handy Reference Guide.**
Compiler: Norman Lewis. *Publisher:* Funk & Wagnalls Publishing Co.
Distributor: T. Y. Crowell Co. *Edition Reviewed:* 1962.

Classification: Special-Purpose—Spelling & Syllabication. *Pages:* xi, 206.
Total Entries: 5,000. *Physical Size:* 4¼ by 7 in.; 18 cm. *LC:* 62-9901. *Lowest Retail Price:* $1.25 paper.

Comments

Lewis's dictionary covers over 5,000 commonly misspelled words. Most entries are briefly annotated with notes on preferred spellings, spelling tips, and general orthographic comments. Example: The entry *good-by, good-bye* informs that both spellings are "Equally correct, the former more common. The modern trend is to write these words solid, especially in informal writing (*goodby, goodbye*)." Spelling rules (about 130 of them) are also covered. A note in the front of the book indicates that "The author has used as his final authority on correct spelling, preferable forms, and hyphenated or unhyphenated compounds his favorite reference work—*Webster's New World Dictionary of the American Language—College Edition.*"

Elliott's foe-né-tic Spelling Dictionary

Descriptive Information

Full Title: **Elliott's foe-né-tic Spelling Dictionary.** *Compiler:* William Thatcher Elliott. *Publisher:* William Thatcher Elliott. *Distributor:* Hancock House. *Edition Reviewed:* 1975.

Classification: Special-Purpose—Spelling & Syllabication. *Pages:* vi, 329.
Total Entries: 35,000. *Physical Size:* 5½ by 8½ in.; 22 cm. *LC:* 75-28864.
Lowest Retail Price: $5.95 paper.

Comments

In this unique and rather idiosyncratic dictionary, "words are found by the way they sound!" The sounds are based on Elliott's "foe-né-tic" alphabet, which must be mastered in order to use the dictionary effectively. For instance, to find the spelling of *postpone*, the user looks under *poest-poen* (the "foe-né-tic" spelling). Likewise, *phone* is found under *foen, pneumonia* under *noo-moen'yu*, and *cyclone* under *sie'cloen*. There is an index key to the "foe-né-tic" alphabet which facilitates matters somewhat, but it takes a bit of getting used to. *The Bad Speller's Dictionary* and *The Misspeller's Dictionary* also organize their vocabularies based on how words are pronounced, not spelled. The latter two dictionaries are easier to use and hence preferable to Elliott's dictionary.

Follett Vest-Pocket 50,000 Words

Descriptive Information

Full Title: **Follett Vest-Pocket 50,000 Words.** *Compiler:* Harry Sharp. *Publisher:* Follett Publishing Co. Former title: *Vest-Pocket Word Divider.* *Edition Reviewed:* 1964.
Classification: Special-Purpose—Spelling & Syllabication. *Pages:* xiv, 466. *Total Entries:* 50,000. *Physical Size:* 3 by 5¼ in.; 14 cm. *LC:* 64-10914. *ISBN:* 0-695-89110-3. *Lowest Retail Price:* $2.25 paper.

Comments

According to the compiler's preface, "The *Follett Vest-Pocket 50,000 Words* was initiated as an attempt to provide a handy reference to the most common [word] division points currently in use." Sharp's primary authority for syllabication is the unabridged *Webster's Third New International Dictionary*, but some 3,400 variant word divisions found in *Webster's New International Dictionary* (Second Edition) and *Funk & Wagnalls New Standard Dictionary* are denoted. The word list includes many proper names. A useful pocket-size aid, though now somewhat dated. Comparable in size and purpose to *Collins Gem Word Speller & Divider.*

Grosset & Dunlap Wordfinder

Descriptive Information

Full Title: **The Grosset & Dunlap Wordfinder.** *Publisher:* Grosset & Dunlap. *Edition Reviewed:* 1977.
Classification: Special-Purpose—Spelling & Syllabication. *Pages:* 128. *Total Entries:* 20,000. *Physical Size:* 4½ by 6½ in.; 17 cm. *ISBN:* 0-448-14334-8. *Lowest Retail Price:* $1.95 paper.

Comments

The Grosset & Dunlap Wordfinder is a handy, up-to-date list of approximately 20,000 "commonly encountered words." The words are spelled, syllabified, and simply pronounced via stress marks. The book also includes basic rules for syllabication. It compares favorably with spelling dictionaries of similar size, e.g., the *Instant Spelling Dictionary*, Louis Leslie's *20,000 Words*, *Webster's New World 20,000 Word Book*, Kahn and Mulkerne's *Word Book*, and the *Word Finder* (Prentice-Hall).

Handbook of American English Spelling

Descriptive Information

Full Title: **Handbook of American English Spelling.** *Compiler:* Lee C. Deighton. *Publishers:* Van Nostrand Reinhold Co. (Trade Edition); Harcourt Brace Jovanovich (Text Edition). *Edition Reviewed:* Trade Edition, 1973.

290 Spelling and Syllabication

Classification: Special-Purpose—Spelling & Syllabication. *Pages:* vi, 258. *Total Entries:* 20,000. *Physical Size:* 5¾ by 8½ in.; 22 cm. *LC:* 73-13811. *ISBN:* 0-442-22075-8 (trade); 0-15-320202-5 (text). *Lowest Retail Price:* $5.95.

Comments

Deighton, an authority on spelling (see his *Comparative Study of Spellings in Four Major Collegiate Dictionaries* profiled in this section of the *Buying Guide*), spells and syllabifies some 20,000 "potentially troublesome" common words. Note that proper names are excluded. Only one spelling is given—the one Deighton has determined as preferred based on his extensive research. The trade edition includes information about American spelling patterns in the back of the book, whereas the text edition (published in 1977) places similar material in the front and comes with student lesson books. The *Handbook of American English Spelling* is reasonably up-to-date and unquestionably authoritative. It compares favorably with the best lists of similar size: *The Grosset & Dunlap Wordfinder*, Louis Leslie's *20,000 Words*, and *Webster's New World 20,000 Word Book*. But unlike the others, Deighton's dictionary attempts to standardize spelling where variants exist.

Other Critical Opinions

American Reference Books Annual 1974, p. 459.

Instant Spelling Dictionary

Descriptive Information

Full Title: **Instant Spelling Dictionary.** *Compilers:* Margaret M. Dougherty, Julia H. Fitzgerald, and Donald O. Bolander. *Publisher:* Career Institute. *Distributor:* Franklin Watts, Inc. *Edition Reviewed:* New Third Edition, 1967.

Classification: Special-Purpose—Spelling & Syllabication. *Pages:* 320. *Total Entries:* 25,000. *Physical Size:* 4¼ by 6¼ in.; 16 cm. *LC:* 67-11788. *ISBN:* 0-911744-01-0. *Lowest Retail Price:* $2.95.

Comments

"The main purpose of this *Instant Spelling Dictionary* is to provide a quick, easy way to determine the *correct spelling*, the *correct division*, and the *correct accent* of 25,000 English words" (Introduction). In addition, the back matter includes basic spelling rules, guides for correct punctuation and capitalization, abbreviations, forms of address for business correspondence, and proofreaders' marks. First published in 1960 and revised in 1964 and then 1967, *Instant Spelling Dictionary* is a handy guide, similar in purpose and scope to Deighton's *Handbook of American English Spelling*. Both provide only one spelling—the preferred one—when variants exist. The basic difference between the two is that we know how Deighton decided which spelling is preferred whereas the editors of the *Instant Spelling Dictionary* give no clue.

Misspeller's Dictionary

Descriptive Information

Full Title: **The Misspeller's Dictionary.** *Compilers:* Peter Norback and Craig Norback. *Publisher:* Quadrangle. *Edition Reviewed:* 1974.

Classification: Special-Purpose—Spelling & Syllabication. *Total Entries:* 20,000. *Physical Size:* 6 by 8½ in.; 22 cm. *LC:* 72-90464. *Lowest Retail Price:* $6.95.

Comments

The Misspeller's Dictionary includes "over 20,000 words with incorrect spellings in red . . . designed for people who spell the way they hear." Both correct and incorrect spellings are interfiled in one A–Z sequence. As indicated, red type denotes an incorrect spelling (e.g., *preverbial*); correct spellings are in black type. Similar in concept and purpose to *The Bad Speller's Dictionary* and *Elliott's foe-né-tic Spelling Dictionary.*

Other Critical Opinions

Booklist, December 15, 1974, p. 431.
Wilson Library Bulletin (review by Charles A. Bunge), June 1974, p. 854.

38,000 Words

Descriptive Information

Full Title: **38,000 Words: Spelling & Division; A Word Directory.** *Compiler:* Adele Christoffers. *Publisher:* Hippocrene Books. *Edition Reviewed:* 1957.

Classification: Special-Purpose—Spelling & Syllabication. *Pages:* 192. *Total Entries:* 38,000. *Physical Size:* 5¼ by 8¼ in.; 21 cm. *LC:* 56-7464. *ISBN:* 0-88254-025-4. *Lowest Retail Price:* $2.95 paper.

Comments

Originally published in 1957 by Exposition Press and reissued (but not revised) in 1972 in a paperback edition by Hippocrene, *38,000 Words* is limited strictly to spelling and syllabication information. Only common words are included, except for a list of nationalities on the last page. Words which have entered the language over the past two decades are, of course, not found in the dictionary, nor are variant spellings (e.g., *sizable/sizeable*). How Christoffers decided which variant (*sizable* or *sizeable*) to list is not explained. Several other dictionaries of similar size are available which are more up-to-date and authoritative than Christoffers', for instance, *Webster's Instant Word Guide, Webster's New World 33,000 Word Book,* and Ellis's *Word Book.*

20,000 Words

Descriptive Information

Full Title: **20,000 Words: A Dictionary of Essential Words Spelled and Divided for Quick Reference.** *Compiler:* Louis A. Leslie. *Publisher:* McGraw-Hill. *Edition Reviewed:* Seventh Edition, 1977.

Classification: Special-Purpose—Spelling & Syllabication. *Pages:* 288. *Total Entries:* 20,000. *LC:* 77-71178. *ISBN:* 0-07-037302-2. *Lowest Retail Price:* $4.95.

Comments

Leslie's *20,000 Words* is a well-selected, up-to-date list of frequently encountered words. Published in handy pocket-size, the dictionary is revised every six years or so (the Sixth Edition appeared in 1971, the Fifth in 1965). The current (Seventh) edition has added a number of new words, plus a section on antonyms. Over the years, *20,000 Words* has achieved a reputation as a carefully compiled little list which accurately spells and syllabifies basic words, including variants. It compares favorably with such other works of similar scope as *The Grosset & Dunlap Wordfinder*, *Webster's New World 20,000 Word Book*, and Kahn and Mulkerne's *Word Book*.

Other Critical Opinions

American Reference Books Annual 1973 (review by Helen W. Fair), p. 457. (Review is of Sixth Edition, 1971.)

Variant Spellings in Modern American Dictionaries

Descriptive Information

Full Title: **Variant Spellings in Modern American Dictionaries.** *Compiler:* Donald W. Emery. *Publisher:* National Council of Teachers of English (NCTE). *Edition Reviewed:* Revised Edition, 1973.

Classification: Special-Purpose—Spelling & Syllabication. *Pages:* 130. *Total Entries:* 2,400. *LC:* 73-83843. *ISBN:* 0-8141-5170-3. *Lowest Retail Price:* $4.95 paper; $3.35 to NCTE members.

Comments

This valuable study, sponsored by the Washington State Council of Teachers of English and published by the National Council (NCTE), aims "to provide a list including those fairly common words assumed to be in the active vocabulary of most adults, which the dictionaries offer as variants or secondary spellings, and which, consequently, could lead to questions in the mind of student or teacher concerning the propriety of an authority for certain spellings." Emery, an English professor at the University of Washington, limited his dictionary research to those five college (semi-unabridged) dictionaries "that are accepted, I believe, as the most reputable and that are used most commonly," namely, *The American Heritage Dictionary* (1973), *Funk & Wagnalls Standard College Dictionary* (1968), *The*

Random House College Dictionary (1972), *Webster's New Collegiate Dictionary* (1973), and *Webster's New World Dictionary* (1970). Like Lee Deighton's *Comparative Study of Spelling in Four Major Collegiate Dictionaries*, which is quite similar to Emery's work both in terms of methodology and findings, *Variant Spellings in Modern American Dictionaries* identifies spelling variants and shows precisely how our major college dictionaries treat them. A smaller (43 pages) first edition of *Variant Spellings* appeared in 1958.

Other Critical Opinions

American Reference Books Annual 1974, pp. 459–460.
Booklist, December 1, 1974, p. 390.

Webster's Instant Word Guide

Descriptive Information

Full Title: **Webster's Instant Word Guide.** *Compiler:* Merriam-Webster Staff. *Publisher:* G. & C. Merriam Co. *Edition Reviewed:* 1972.

Classification: Special-Purpose—Spelling & Syllabication. *Pages:* viii, 369. *Total Entries:* 35,000. *Physical Size:* 4¼ by 5¾ in.; 15 cm. *LC:* 72-1947. *ISBN:* 0-87779-173-2. *Lowest Retail Price:* $2.95.

Comments

Webster's Instant Word Guide spells and syllabifies approximately 35,000 words drawn from the semi-unabridged *Webster's Seventh New Collegiate Dictionary* (which was replaced in 1973 by *Webster's New Collegiate Dictionary*—Eighth Edition). Variant spellings are given, e.g., *labeled/labelled*. In addition, there are brief notes on look-alikes, e.g., *excess* is followed by the one-word definition "surplus" and a *see* reference to *access*. Abbreviations, proofreaders' symbols, pronunciation rules, and weights and measures are appended. Bound in sturdy hardcovers, this convenient pocket-size book is a standard reference for secretaries, typists, stenographers, et al. It is preferable to Christoffers' *38,000 Words* and compares favorably with *Webster's New World 33,000 Word Book* and Ellis's *Word Book*.

Other Critical Opinions

American Reference Books Annual 1973 (review by Helen W. Fair), p. 457.

Webster's New World 33,000 Word Book

Descriptive Information

Full Title: **Webster's New World 33,000 Word Book.** *Compiler:* Shirley M. Miller. *Publisher:* Collins+World. *Edition Reviewed:* Revised Edition, 1971.

Classification: Special-Purpose—Spelling & Syllabication. *Pages:* xiii, 338. *Total Entries:* 33,000. *Physical Size:* 4 by 5½ in.; 15 cm. *LC:* 71-

164001. *ISBN:* 0-529-03960-5. *Lowest Retail Price:* $2.95 paper (with vinyl jacket).

Comments

Based on *Webster's New World Dictionary* (Second College Edition), an outstanding semi-unabridged dictionary, *Webster's New World 33,000 Word Book* is an authoritative, reasonably up-to-date list which spells and syllabifies "the 33,000 most used words." Irregular verb forms (e.g., *ride/ rode/ridden/riding*) and irregular plurals (*goose/geese*) are given, as well as common spelling variants (e.g., *sizable/sizeable*). Seven pages on punctuation rules conclude the book. Comparable in coverage and quality to *Webster's Instant Word Guide* and Ellis's *Word Book*.

Webster's New World 20,000 Word Book

Descriptive Information

Full Title: **Webster's New World 20,000 Word Book.** *Compiler:* Thomas Layman. *Publisher:* Collins+World. *Edition Reviewed:* 1974.

Classification: Special-Purpose—Spelling & Syllabication. *Pages:* vi, 184. *Total Entries:* 20,000. *Physical Size:* 2½ by 5½ in.; 14 cm. *LC:* 74-13509. *ISBN:* 0-529-05090-0. *Lowest Retail Price:* $1.00 paper.

Comments

Constructed like a note pad (the book is bound at the top), *Webster's New World 20,000 Word Book* is an abridgment of *Webster's New World 33,000 Word Book*. Both dictionaries merely spell and syllabify commonly encountered words. Similar in size and content to *The Grosset & Dunlap Wordfinder*, Leslie's *20,000 Words*, and Kahn and Mulkerne's *Word Book*.

The Word Book (Glencoe Press)

Descriptive Information

Full Title: **The Word Book.** *Compilers:* Gilbert Kahn and Donald J. D. Mulkerne. *Publisher:* Glencoe Press. *Distributor:* Macmillan Publishing Co. *Edition Reviewed:* 1975.

Classification: Special-Purpose—Spelling & Syllabication. *Pages:* xiii, 240. *Total Entries:* 23,000. *Physical Size:* 4¾ by 5¾ in.; 15 cm. *LC:* 74-10137. *ISBN:* 0-02-474780-7. *Lowest Retail Price:* $2.95.

Comments

The Word Book by the late Gilbert Kahn and Donald Mulkerne, both professors of business education, is a hardcover, pocket-size dictionary which spells and syllabifies some 23,000 common words frequently misspelled. Standard spelling variants are given. The compilers have used *Webster's New Collegiate Dictionary* (Eighth Edition) as their final lexical authority. The back matter includes a simple gazetteer, common abbreviations, a table of metric equivalents, and proofreaders' marks. Comparable in size and quality to *The Grosset & Dunlap Wordfinder*, Leslie's *20,000 Words*, and *Webster's New World 20,000 Word Book.*

Other Critical Opinions

American Reference Books Annual 1976, pp. 546–547.

The Word Book (Houghton Mifflin)

Descriptive Information

Full Title: **The Word Book: Based on The American Heritage Dictionary.** *Compiler:* Kaethe Ellis. *Publisher:* Houghton Mifflin. *Edition Reviewed:* 1976.

Classification: Special-Purpose—Spelling & Syllabication. *Pages:* 384. *Total Entries:* 40,000. *Physical Size:* 4¼ by 5¾ in.; 15 cm. *LC:* 76-698. *ISBN:* 0-395-24521-4. *Lowest Retail Price:* $2.95.

Comments

The Word Book by Ellis spells and syllabifies over 40,000 words drawn from *The American Heritage Dictionary*, an authoritative semi-unabridged dictionary. Common spelling variants are given, e.g., *labeled/labelled.* There are 30 pages of appended reference matter, including a pronunciation chart to help poor spellers, a list of abbreviations, rules governing spelling, and tables of weights and measures. Compares well with other lists of similar scope, i.e., Christoffers' *38,000 Words, Webster's Instant Word Guide,* and *Webster's New World 33,000 Word Book.*

Other Critical Opinions

Booklist, January 15, 1977, p. 748.

Word Division Manual

Descriptive Information

Full Title: **Word Division Manual: The Fifteen Thousand Most-Used Words in Business Communication.** *Compilers:* J. E. Silverthorn and Devern J. Perry. *Publisher:* South-Western Publishing Co. *Edition Reviewed:* Second Edition, 1970.

Classification: Special-Purpose—Spelling & Syllabication. *Pages:* 151. *Total Entries:* 15,000. *LC:* 77-106912. *Lowest Retail Price:* $3.36 paper.

Comments

Word Division Manual spells and syllabifies about 15,000 commonly used words. The vocabulary was selected by means of a word frequency count involving over 4,000 representative business letters, memoranda, etc. Note that individual, company, and brand names are deliberately omitted from the vocabulary. Not as extensive or as useful as such works of similar size as *The*

Grosset & Dunlap Wordfinder, Leslie's *20,000 Words*, *Webster's New World 20,000 Word Book*, and Anderson's *Word Finder*.

Other Critical Opinions

American Reference Books Annual 1971 (review by Christine L. Wynar), p. 425.

Word Finder

Descriptive Information

Full Title: **Word Finder: The Spelling, Accent, and Division of the Words Most Commonly Referred to by Students, Writers, Secretaries, Printers, and Proofreaders.** *Compilers:* Ruth I. Anderson, Lura Lynn Straub, and E. Dana Gibson. *Publisher:* Prentice-Hall. *Edition Reviewed:* Fourth Edition, 1974.

Classification: Special-Purpose—Spelling & Syllabication. *Pages:* 250. *Total Entries:* 15,000. *Physical Size:* 4 by 5½ in.; 14 cm. *ISBN:* 0-13-963330-8. *Lowest Retail Price:* $3.95.

Comments

The Word Finder, first published in 1960 and revised several times since, includes many proper nouns and adjectives (e.g., *Calvinism, Canadian, Caribbean*) but fails to list spelling variants. The compilers note in their introduction that "Only the first choices for spelling and pronunciation are given," but there is no indication how the "first choice" was determined. In the back of the book are rules concerning word division, spelling, and forming possessives; a list of often misconstrued words like *affect* and *effect;* and information about numbers, capitalization, and punctuation. This handy authoritative spelling dictionary is comparable in scope to such works as Leslie's *20,000 Words* and *Webster's New World 20,000 Word Book*, but consumers should be aware that it does not include spelling variants.

PRONUNCIATION

How do you pronounce *redolent?* Or *ebullient, exigencies, controversial, lozenge?* Not only are these words difficult to pronounce—and English has thousands more like them—but each has more than one generally accepted pronunciation. Moreover, there are many relatively simple words like *depot, route, root, roof, creek, laboratory*, and *schedule* which are pronounced differently in different geographical areas of the country or the English-speaking world.

Ordinarily, the larger general adult dictionaries provide sufficient pronunciation information, including common regional and national variations. In the past, such information usually reflected the lexicographer's informed opinion about which pronunciations were preferred or "correct" and which were not. More recently, however, some dictionary-makers have become less authoritarian about pronunciations, basing their judgments on current regional and national usage rather than some artificial standard of what is proper or correct. For instance, Merriam-Webster, the largest and most influential American maker of dictionaries, bases its pronunciations strictly on usage among educated speakers. One of the firm's full-time editors responsible for pronunciations remarked recently that Merriam-Webster's "aim isn't to stigmatize people's pronunciation. People prefer their own pronunciation, and if they don't hear it the way they say it, they think the other person is wrong. If a person sees one pronunciation listed first in the dictionary, he thinks that is the preferred way. It isn't. It just *happens* to be listed first." (Quoted from Stuart Norwood's article "Watching Webster's Wordmen at Work" in the *Valley Advocate*, Springfield, Mass., edition, October 8, 1975, pp. 8–9.)

Because the larger general dictionaries normally provide sufficient pronunciation information to meet most people's needs, few specialized pronunciation dictionaries have been developed. Those that are available tend to emphasize words that are difficult to pronounce, words with regional or national variants, and proper names (e.g., *Grand Teton, Pavlova*) not always included in general dictionaries. Significantly, most pronunciation dictionaries provide recommended or preferred pronunciations.

Concise Pronouncing Dictionary of British and American English

Descriptive Information

Full Title: **A Concise Pronouncing Dictionary of British and American English.** *Editor:* J. Windsor Lewis. *Publisher:* Oxford University Press. *Edition Reviewed:* 1972.

Classification: Special-Purpose—Pronunciation. *Pages:* xx, 233. *Total Entries:* 24,000. *Physical Size:* 5½ by 8¾ in.; 22 cm. *ISBN:* 0-19-431123-6. *Lowest Retail Price:* $7.50.

Comments

Lewis's dictionary is "planned solely for the benefit of users of English as a foreign or second language," though native speakers from both countries might use it with good results. Only one pronunciation is given for each word, except when American and British pronunciations differ; in such cases two recommended pronunciations (one American, one British) are given. Pronunciation recommendations are based on major American authorities (particularly the unabridged *Webster's Third New International Dictionary*) and Lewis's study of British news announcers' preferences. The phonetic transcription "is fully in accordance with the principles of the International Phonetic Association and makes use of only their authorized symbols." Unfortunately, most Americans are not familiar with IPA symbols, although they are not terribly difficult to master. Obviously, foreign students studying English will benefit most from this work.

Other Critical Opinions

American Reference Books Annual 1973 (review by Francis J. Witty), p. 447.
Booklist, March 1, 1973, p. 610.
Library Journal (review by B. Hunter Smeaton), January 15, 1973, p. 152.
Wilson Library Bulletin, February 1973, p. 521.

Dictionary of Pronunciation (*Lass*)

Descriptive Information

Full Title: **Dictionary of Pronunciation.** *Editors:* Abraham Lass and Betty Lass. *Publisher:* Quadrangle. *Edition Reviewed:* 1976.

Classification: Special-Purpose—Pronunciation. *Pages:* 334. *Total Entries:* 8,000. *Physical Size:* 6¼ by 9½ in.; 24 cm. *LC:* 75-36252. *ISBN:* 0-8129-0614-4. *Lowest Retail Price:* $12.50.

Comments

The Lasses' *Dictionary of Pronunciation* covers some 8,000 commonly mispronounced words, e.g., *columnist, euphony, impotence, literature, oath, shish kebab,* and *vehement.* The words were checked in four leading college dictionaries (*American Heritage Dictionary, Random House College Dictionary, Webster's New Collegiate Dictionary,* and *Webster's New World Dictionary*) and every pronunciation found therein is recorded in the *Dictionary of Pronunciation.* Moreover, as the Lasses explain, "all the dictionaries . . . do not list the same number of acceptable pronunciations. So we compiled a 'box score' for each acceptable pronunciation of each word, and next to each pronunciation we placed a figure that tells you how many of our four desk dictionaries record that specific pronunciation. For example, the figure 4 at the right of the pronunciation tells you that all of the four desk dictionaries recognize this pronunciation as heard among educated speakers, and hence record it as acceptable." Also, the Lasses add their own admittedly subjective pronunciation recommendations (indicated by an asterisk). The pronunciation key, an adapted version of the precise system used in *Webster's New World Dictionary* (Second College Edition), appears at the bottom of every right-hand page. This work, quite different in purpose and scope from Samuel Noory's dictionary of the same title, is a unique and authoritative albeit limited (only 8,000 entries) pronunciation guide.

Other Critical Opinions

American Reference Books Annual 1977 (review by L. Zgusta), pp. 525–526.
Library Journal, December 1, 1976, p. 2470.
Wilson Library Bulletin (review by Charles A. Bunge), January 1977, p. 439.

Dictionary of Pronunciation (*Noory*)

Descriptive Information

Full Title: **Dictionary of Pronunciation.** *Editor:* Samuel Noory. *Publisher:* A. S. Barnes & Co. *Edition Reviewed:* Second Edition, 1971.

Classification: Special-Purpose—Pronunciation. *Pages:* xliii, 525. *Total Entries:* 58,000. *Physical Size:* 6½ by 9½ in.; 24 cm. *LC:* 76-151120. *ISBN:* 0-498-07917-1. *Lowest Retail Price:* $12.00.

Comments

Noory's *Dictionary of Pronunciation* provides recommended pronunciations for "45,000 terms and 13,000 names of persons and places, and names from the Bible, literature and legend, comprising in total a coverage of all but rare words and names in English." Usually only one pronunciation is given for each word. Pronunciation recommendations derive from Noory's own research and "consultation of all available authority on pronunciation," a vague statement which is nowhere further explained. An important feature of the dictionary is Noory's simple pronouncing alphabet, a phonetic system "patterned after the reading and writing habits of English speakers" which comprises 40 sounds and is easier to comprehend—but less precise—than the widely used International Phonetic Alphabet. The dictionary also briefly defines about 10,000 "frequently misused" terms, e.g., *southpaw* ("left-hander"), and identifies homonyms, e.g., *sonny/sunny.* Unfortunately, Noory's *Dictionary of Pronunciation* completely ignores variant regional and national pronunciations. Moreover, the dictionary's authority is questionable and although Noory's phonetic pronouncing alphabet is easy to use, it lacks precision. This work has been called "flawed." That is an accurate description. A better dictionary of similar purpose (though older and less extensive) is the *NBC Handbook of Pronunciation.* Also, Noory's *Dictionary of Pronunciation* should not be confused with the Lasses' work of the same title. They are almost exact opposites in terms of purpose, treatment, and scope.

Other Critical Opinions

American Reference Books Annual 1972 (review by Ann J. Harwell), p. 472. *Wilson Library Bulletin*, May 1972, p. 845.

NBC Handbook of Pronunciation

Descriptive Information

Full Title: **NBC Handbook of Pronunciation.** *Editors:* Originally Compiled by James F. Bender for the National Broadcasting Co.; Revised by Thomas Lee Crowell, Jr. *Publisher:* T. Y. Crowell Co. *Edition Reviewed:* Third Edition, 1964.

Classification: Special-Purpose—Pronunciation. *Pages:* xii, 418. *Total Entries:* 20,000. *Physical Size:* 6¼ by 9¼ in.; 24 cm. *LC:* 63-9205. *ISBN:* 0-690-752-X. *Lowest Retail Price:* $9.95.

Comments

Long a standard reference, the *NBC Handbook of Pronunciation* first appeared in 1943 and most recently in 1964. The more than 20,000 entries are listed in three tabular columns. The first column spells the word, the second pronounces it via simplified phonetic respelling (e.g., *Jamaica = juh MAY kuh*), and the third pronounces the word using the authoritative but more complex International Phonetic Alphabet. Entries cover words frequently mispronounced or difficult to pronounce (e.g., *literature, lucre, luxuriance*), as well as numerous geographical and personal names (e.g., *Hiroshima, Ho Chi Minh, Hohenzollern*). Only one pronunciation is given. Like Noory's *Dictionary of Pronunciation*, regional and national variants are excluded. The 1964 edition added a section in the back called "Names in the News" which covers people like Joan Baez, Theodore Idzumbuir, and Norodom Sihanouk, but it is now much out-of-date. Obviously, the *NBC Handbook of Pronunciation* is in need of revision. On the other hand, it is more authoritative and precise than Noory's *Dictionary of Pronunciation*, more current and easier to use than Kenyon and Knott's *Pronouncing Dictionary of American English*, and much more inclusive than the Lasses' *Dictionary of Pronunciation*.

Pronouncing Dictionary of American English

Descriptive Information

Full Title: **A Pronouncing Dictionary of American English.** *Editors:* John Samuel Kenyon and Thomas Albert Knott. *Publisher:* G. & C. Merriam Co. *Edition Reviewed:* 1953.

Classification: Special-Purpose—Pronunciation. *Pages:* lvi, 484. *Total Entries:* 45,000. *Physical Size:* 5¾ by 8½ in.; 22 cm. *ISBN:* 0-87779-047-7. *Lowest Retail Price:* $5.95.

Comments

Kenyon and Knott's *Pronouncing Dictionary of American English* appeared initially in 1943 and has been revised several times, most recently in 1953. The dictionary covers "the great body of common words in use in America," as well as selected proper names. The International Phonetic Alphabet is used to give the pronunciations, which represent "colloquial English of the everyday unconscious speech of cultivated people." Frequently two or three or even more pronunciations are given, with regional variants noted. With the exception of Noory's idiosyncratic *Dictionary of Pronunciation* (58,000 entries), *A Pronouncing Dictionary of American English* (45,000 entries) is the largest such work currently available. Moreover, it is authoritative, often cited as the American counterpart to Daniel Jones's *English Pronouncing Dictionary*, a standard British reference which has appeared in numerous editions (but is now out of print in the U.S., perhaps only temporarily). Of course, the dictionary's greatest limitation is its age. The many words which have entered the language over the past quarter of a century are not included. In addition, although the editors thoroughly explain the system, some users will find the International Phonetic Alphabet difficult to understand.

ABBREVIATIONS AND ACRONYMS

Several years ago Ellen T. Crowley, editor of the *Acronyms, Initialisms, & Abbreviations Dictionary*, wrote in a letter to *Library Journal* (October 1, 1973) that "The acronym world seems to be a long way from ZPG and apparently doesn't believe in the PILL (Process To Impede Letter Language)!" Indeed, sprawling government and bureaucracy, big science and technology, and proliferating organizations and committees breed abbreviations and acronyms like rabbits. For instance, Crowley's dictionary contained 12,000 entries when it first appeared in 1960; the current Fifth Edition (1976) claims over 130,000 entries and is growing everyday.

General dictionaries normally include some standard abbreviations and acronyms (e.g., *HEW* and *SEATO*), either in the main A–Z section or in a separate list in the back. But general dictionaries cannot be expected to keep up with such diverse though oft encountered items as *a.k.a.* (also known as), *M.V.P.* (Most Valuable Player), and *S.R.O.* (Standing Room Only). Hence, in recent years a number of new or revised and greatly expanded dictionaries devoted to abbreviations, acronyms, and the like have been compiled, Crowley's being the best and the biggest. Bear in mind, however, that no such dictionary is all-inclusive.

Abbreviations: A Reverse Guide

Descriptive Information

Full Title: **Abbreviations: A Reverse Guide to Standard and Generally Accepted Abbreviated Forms.** *Compiler:* Stephen A. Rybicki. *Publisher:* Pierian Press. *Edition Reviewed:* 1971.

Classification: Special-Purpose—Abbreviations & Acronyms. *Pages:* 334. *Total Entries:* 18,000. *LC:* 74-143239. *ISBN:* 0-87650-010-6. *Lowest Retail Price:* $12.95.

Comments

Rybicki's reverse abbreviations dictionary is arranged alphabetically by the term the abbreviation represents, not (as is usual) alphabetically by the abbreviation itself. For instance, in the typical abbreviations dictionary the order of entries would be: *mah* (mahogany), *MARC* (Machine-Readable Cataloging), and *mc* (magnetic console). In the reverse dictionary, however, the entry order is: *MARC* (Machine-Readable Cataloging), *mc* (*magnetic* console), and *mah* (*mahogany*). Rybicki's dictionary has been effectively superseded by Crowley's more current and more inclusive *Reverse Acronyms, Initialisms, & Abbreviations Dictionary* (Fifth Edition, 1976).

Other Critical Opinions

American Reference Books Annual 1972, pp. 71–72.
Library Journal, December 1, 1971, p. 3990.
RQ, Spring 1972, pp. 279–280.
Wilson Library Bulletin, November 1971, p. 277.

Abbreviations Dictionary

Descriptive Information

Full Title: **Abbreviations Dictionary: Abbreviations, Acronyms, Anonyms, Contractions, Initials and Nicknames, Short Forms and Slang Shortcuts, Signs and Symbols.** *Compiler:* Ralph De Sola. *Publisher:* American Elsevier Publishing Co. *Distributor:* Elsevier North-Holland. *Edition Reviewed:* New International Fourth Edition, 1974.

Classification: Special-Purpose—Abbreviations & Acronyms. *Pages:* xiii, 428. *Total Entries:* 40,000. *Physical Size:* 6¼ by 9¼ in.; 24 cm. *LC:* 73-7687. *ISBN:* 0-444-00139-5. *Lowest Retail Price:* $25.00.

Comments

As the subtitle indicates, De Sola's *Abbreviations Dictionary* ranges far and wide, from *GT & EA* (Georgia Teachers and Education Association), *GTL* (Glass Technology Laboratories), and *Guadal* (Guadalajara) to *gth* (go to hell), *gtT* (gone to Texas, one jump ahead of the sheriff), and *gywp* (gee you're wonderful, professor). Among the missing, however, are such commonly encountered items as *AAP* (Association of American Publishers), *byo* (bring your own), *CETA* (Comprehensive Employment and Training Act), and *CREEP* (Committee to Re-Elect the President). De Sola's dictionary, first published in 1958 and revised and enlarged several times since, is relatively current and certainly broad in scope. It manages to cover most standard abbreviations, etc., but has a long way to go before it can challenge Crowley's *Acronyms, Initialisms, & Abbreviations Dictionary* (Fifth Edition, 1976), which contains over 130,000 entries as opposed to De Sola's 40,000. A new revised and enlarged edition of De Sola's dictionary is scheduled for publication in late 1977.

Other Critical Opinions

American Reference Books Annual 1975, p. 54.
Booklist, September 1, 1975, p. 65.

Acronyms, Initialisms, & Abbreviations Dictionary

Descriptive Information

Full Title: **Acronyms, Initialisms, & Abbreviations Dictionary: A Guide to Alphabetic Designations, Contractions, Acronyms, Initialisms, Abbreviations, and Similar Condensed Appellations;** Covering: Aerospace, Associations, Biochemistry, Business and Trade, Domestic and International Affairs, Education, Electronics, Genetics, Government, Labor, Medicine, Military, Pharmacy, Physiology, Politics, Religion, Science, Societies, Sports, Technical Drawings and Specifications, Transportation, and Other Fields. *Compiler:* Ellen T. Crowley. *Publisher:* Gale Research Co. *Edition Reviewed:* Fifth Edition, 1976.

Classification: Special-Purpose—Abbreviations & Acronyms. *Pages:* xiii,

757. *Total Entries:* 130,000. *Physical Size:* 8¾ by 11¼ in.; 29 cm. *LC:* 76-10036. *ISBN:* 0-8103-0502-X. *Lowest Retail Price:* $38.50

Comments

Crowley's *Acronyms, Initialisms, & Abbreviations Dictionary (AIAD)* first appeared in 1960, a modest work containing some 12,000 entries. Now in its Fifth Edition (1976), *AIAD* has ballooned to more than 130,000 entries, reflecting the dramatic and apparently ineluctable growth of acronyms and their ilk in recent years. As if to underscore this point, *AIAD* is supplemented by the paperbound *New Acronyms, Initialisms, & Abbreviations*. At present *NAIA* has appeared in a 1976 supplement (adding 12,618 new items) and 1977 supplement (some 10,000 more entries). In addition, *AIAD* is published in a different alphabetical sequence as *Reverse Acronyms, Initialisms, & Abbreviations Dictionary* (see profile following in this section of the *Buying Guide*). Unquestionably, *AIAD* and its companions lead the field, not only numerically but in terms of up-to-dateness, practical arrangement, and informational content. For instance, *AIAD* not only includes the slang *byo* (bring your own) but adds two parenthetical notes: "(Liquor)" and "(Party invitation notation)." Recent editions have greatly expanded standard and popular acronyms, foreign phrases, and historical abbreviations (e.g., the Roman *SPQR*). The outstanding abbreviations and acronyms dictionary.

Other Critical Opinions

American Reference Books Annual 1974 (review by Frances Neel Cheney), p. 38. (Review is of the Fourth Edition, 1973.)
Booklist, February 15, 1977, pp. 918–920.
Katz, William A. *Basic Information Sources.* Vol. 1 of *Introduction to Reference Work*, 2nd ed. (New York: McGraw-Hill, 1974), pp. 281–282.

Cassell's Dictionary of Abbreviations

Descriptive Information

Full Title: **Cassell's Dictionary of Abbreviations**. *Compilers:* J. W. Gurnett and C. H. J. Kyte. *Publisher:* Cassell & Co., Ltd. *Distributor:* International Publications Service. *Edition Reviewed:* Revised and Enlarged Edition, 1972.
Classification: Special-Purpose—Abbreviations & Acronyms. *Pages:* vi, 245. *Total Entries:* 23,000. *Physical Size:* 4½ by 7¼ in.; 19 cm. *ISBN:* 0-304-93879-3. *Lowest Retail Price:* $7.50.

Comments

Cassell's Dictionary of Abbreviations, originally published in 1966 with 21,000 entries and expanded in 1972 to its present 23,000 entries, is a British compilation which emphasizes "abbreviations that have gained some degree of general currency both nationally and internationally." Of marginal reference value in the U.S.

Complete Dictionary of Abbreviations

Descriptive Information

Full Title: **The Complete Dictionary of Abbreviations.** *Compiler:* Robert J. Schwartz. *Publisher:* T. Y. Crowell Co. *Edition Reviewed:* Enlarged-Type Edition, 1959.

Classification: Special-Purpose—Abbreviations & Acronyms. *Pages:* 211. *Total Entries:* 25,000. *Physical Size:* 6½ by 8¾ in.; 22 cm. *LC:* 55-5843. *ISBN:* 0-690-20620-8. *Lowest Retail Price:* $9.95.

Comments

First published in 1955 and reissued (but not revised) in 1959 in a larger type edition, *The Complete Dictionary of Abbreviations* is neither complete nor up-to-date. Of little practical reference value today.

Dictionary of Acronyms & Abbreviations

Descriptive Information

Full Title: **Dictionary of Acronyms & Abbreviations: Some Abbreviations in Management, Technology and Information Science.** *Compiler:* Eric Pugh. *Publishers:* Shoe String Press—Archon Books (hardcover); Gaylord Bros., Inc. (paper). *Edition Reviewed:* Second, Revised and Expanded Edition, 1970.

Classification: Special-Purpose—Abbreviations & Acronyms. *Pages:* 389. *Total Entries:* 10,000. *Physical Size:* 5¾ by 8¾ in.; 22 cm. (hardcover). *ISBN:* 0-208-00889-6 (hardcover); 0-015794-03-9 (paper). *Lowest Retail Price:* $15.00; also $8.95 paper.

Comments

Pugh, a British librarian, currently has three related abbreviation and acronym dictionaries on the market. The first (covered here) is the *Dictionary of Acronyms & Abbreviations*, published originally in Great Britain by Clive Bingley, Ltd. in 1968 with some 5,000 entries and expanded to 10,000 entries in 1970. The *Second Dictionary of Acronyms & Abbreviations* appeared in 1974 as a supplement to the first dictionary and contains another 10,000 entries. And in 1977 the *Third Dictionary of Acronyms & Abbreviations* added another 5,000 entries to the series. Note that Pugh's works are limited to the areas of management, technology, and information science. Moreover, although the dictionaries are international in scope, there is a distinct British emphasis. *Pugh I, II, and III* (as the series is informally called by the publishers) does include some entries not found in Crowley's *Acronyms, Initialisms, & Abbreviations Dictionary* (Fifth Edition, 1976), the largest such work available. But altogether the three Pugh volumes, which contain only a total of 25,000 items, cost as much as Crowley's dictionary which offers five times as many entries.

Other Critical Opinions

Booklist, January 15, 1971, p. 403.
RQ, Spring 1971, p. 277.

Everyman's Dictionary of Abbreviations

Descriptive Information

Full Title: **Everyman's Dictionary of Abbreviations.** *Compiler:* John Paxton. *Publisher:* J. M. Dent. *Distributor:* Rowman & Littlefield. Alternate title: *Dictionary of Abbreviations. Edition Reviewed:* 1974.

Classification: Special-Purpose—Abbreviations & Acronyms. *Pages:* xv, 384. *Total Entries:* 25,000. *Physical Size:* 5¾ by 8¾ in.; 22 cm. *LC:* 73-5881. *ISBN:* 0-460-07894-1. *Lowest Retail Price:* $11.50.

Comments

Everyman's Dictionary of Abbreviations—also available in the U.S. under the title *Dictionary of Abbreviations*—is a British production though its scope is international. The dictionary does an especially good job covering social, political, and scientific organizations of the world, particularly those in European and Commonwealth countries. There are, however, numerous omissions of abbreviations American users might expect to find in such a list, e.g., *AAP* (Association of American Publishers), *M.V.P.* (Most Valuable Player), and *OSHA* (Occupational Safety and Health Administration). Overall, not as useful as Ralph De Sola's *Abbreviations Dictionary* (Fourth Edition, 1974) and certainly not anywhere near Crowley's *Acronyms, Initialisms, & Abbreviations Dictionary* (Fifth Edition, 1976) in terms of coverage or currency. Note that, as the *Buying Guide* was going to press, *Everyman's Dictionary* was reported out of print in the United States.

Other Critical Opinions

American Reference Books Annual 1975 (review by Stephen A. Rybicki), pp. 54–55.
Booklist, October 1, 1974, p. 196.
Library Journal, July 1974, p. 1793.
Wilson Library Bulletin (review by Charles A. Bunge), September 1974, p. 93.

New Acronyms, Initialisms, & Abbreviations

Descriptive Information

Full Title: **New Acronyms, Initialisms, & Abbreviations: 1976 Supplement to Acronyms, Initialisms, & Abbreviations Dictionary, Fifth Edition.** *Compiler:* Ellen T. Crowley. *Publisher:* Gale Research Co. *Edition Reviewed:* 1976.

Classification: Special-Purpose—Abbreviations & Acronyms. *Pages:* xv, 108. *Total Entries:* 12,000. *Physical Size:* 8½ by 11 in.; 28 cm. *LC:* 76-10036.

ISBN: 0-8103-0501-1. *Lowest Retail Price:* $35.00 paper (price includes 1977 Supplement).

Comments

New Acronyms, Initialisms, & Abbreviations (*NAIA*), described by the publisher as volume 2 of *Acronyms, Initialisms, & Abbreviations Dictionary* (*AIAD*), is an annual supplement to *AIAD.* Two paperbound volumes have appeared covering the years 1976 and 1977. Presumably, supplements will continue to be published annually until there is a new (Sixth) edition of *AIAD.* For further information, see the profile of *AIAD* in this section.

Other Critical Opinions

American Reference Books Annual 1976 (review by Richard A. Gray), pp. 74–75.

Reverse Acronyms, Initialisms, & Abbreviations Dictionary

Descriptive Information

Full Title: **Reverse Acronyms, Initialisms, & Abbreviations Dictionary: A Companion Volume to Acronyms, Initialisms, & Abbreviations Dictionary, with Terms Arranged Alphabetically by Meaning of Acronym, Initialism, or Abbreviation.** *Compiler:* Ellen T. Crowley. *Publisher:* Gale Research Co. *Edition Reviewed:* Fifth Edition, 1976.

Classification: Special-Purpose—Abbreviations & Acronyms. *Pages:* x, 754. *Total Entries:* 130,000. *Physical Size:* 8¾ by 11¼ in.; 29 cm. *LC:* 76-25734. *ISBN:* 0-8103-0515-1. *Lowest Retail Price:* $45.00

Comments

As the title and subtitle explain, this is a "reverse" dictionary which arranges the terms (e.g., *Machine-Readable Cataloging; magnetic console; mahogany*) in alphabetical order, *not* the abbreviations or acronyms (e.g., *MARC; mc; mah*) as is usually done in such dictionaries. Actually, *Reverse Acronyms, Initialisms, & Abbreviations Dictionary* (*RAIAD*) is simply a rearrangement of all the entries included in *Acronyms, Initialisms, & Abbreviations Dictionary* (Fifth Edition, 1976); the publisher describes *RAIAD* as volume 3 of *AIAD.* Some critics (Katz; Cheney) have questioned the need for a "reverse" approach to *AIAD.* Indeed, the Reference & Subscription Books Review Committee of the American Library Association belatedly said *RAIAD* "fills no perceptible need." Apparently such critics have never been asked to track down all accepted abbreviations of a term like *booklet, edition, follow, intestine, nurse,* or *retarded*—or been asked to locate the abbreviation for *European Industrial Space Study Group* (*EUROSPACE*), or for *strikeout* (*K*).

Other Critical Opinions

American Reference Books Annual 1973 (review by Frances Neel Cheney), p. 110.
Booklist, March 1, 1977, p. 1039.

Katz, William A. *Basic Information Sources*. Vol. 1 of *Introduction to Reference Work*, 2nd ed. (New York: McGraw-Hill, 1974), pp. 281–282.
Wilson Library Bulletin (review by Frances Neel Cheney), October 1972, pp. 199–200.

Second Dictionary of Acronyms & Abbreviations

Descriptive Information

Full Title: **Second Dictionary of Acronyms & Abbreviations: More Abbreviations in Management, Technology and Information Science.** *Compiler:* Eric Pugh. *Publisher:* Clive Bingley, Ltd. *Distributors:* Shoe String Press—Archon Books (hardcover); Gaylord Bros., Inc. (paper). *Edition Reviewed:* 1974.

Classification: Special-Purpose—Abbreviations & Acronyms. *Pages:* 410. *Total Entries:* 10,000. *Physical Size:* 5½ by 8¾ in.; 22 cm. (hardcover). *ISBN:* 0-85157-172-7 (hardcover); 0-915794-04-7 (paper). *Lowest Retail Price:* $16.50; also $9.95 paper.

Comments

This is the second of Pugh's three abbreviations dictionaries, all of which are limited to the subject areas stated in the subtitle and have a somewhat British orientation. Altogether, *Pugh I–III* cover some 25,000 abbreviations and acronyms. See the profile of the *Dictionary of Acronyms & Abbreviations* for further information.

Other Critical Opinions

American Reference Books Annual 1975, p. 55
Booklist, February 1, 1975, p. 582.
Wilson Library Bulletin (review by Charles A. Bunge), December 1974, p. 318.

Third Dictionary of Acronyms & Abbreviations

Descriptive Information

Full Title: **Third Dictionary of Acronyms & Abbreviations: More Abbreviations in Management, Technology and Information Science.** *Compiler:* Eric Pugh. *Publisher:* Clive Bingley, Ltd. *Distributors:* Shoe String Press—Archon Books (hardcover); Gaylord Bros., Inc. (paper). *Edition Reviewed:* 1977.

Classification: Special-Purpose—Abbreviations & Acronyms. *Pages:* 208. *Total Entries:* 5,000. *Physical Size:* 5½ by 8¾ in.; 22 cm. *ISBN:* 0-208-01535-3. *Lowest Retail Price:* $12.00; $9.95 paper.

Comments

The third in Pugh's continuing series of related dictionaries covering abbreviations in the areas of business and science. The scope is international (with a British orientation) and the books are designed to complement, not supersede, one another. For instance, *OPEC* (Organization of Petroleum Exporting Countries) is listed in the first volume, *A Dictionary of Acronyms & Abbreviations*, and is not repeated in the *Second Dictionary* or the *Third Dictionary*. For more information about *Pugh I–III* (as the publishers call the set), see the profile of *A Dictionary of Acronyms & Abbreviations* in this section of the *Buying Guide*.

World Guide to Abbreviations

Descriptive Information

Full Title: **World Guide to Abbreviations.** *Compiler:* Paul Spillner. *Publisher:* Verlag Dokumentation. *Distributor:* R. R. Bowker Co. *Edition Reviewed:* Second Edition, 1970–1973.

Classification: Special-Purpose—Abbreviations & Acronyms. *Volumes:* 3. *Pages:* 1295. *Total Entries:* 50,000. *LC:* 79-134637. *ISBN:* 3-7940-1198-8 (vol. 1); 3-7940-1098-1 (vol. 2); 3-7940-1298-4 (vol. 3). *Lowest Retail Price:* $20.00 per volume; $60.00 the set.

Comments

World Guide to Abbreviations, a three-volume work, contains over 50,000 abbreviations of organizations, societies, political groups, academic institutions, and government agencies of national or international character in some 120 countries. Information for each entry includes the full name of the association or agency, when it was founded, and where its headquarters are located. Spillner's list, which combines the characteristics of an abbreviations dictionary and a directory, is the largest single source available for abbreviations of foreign groups. Crowley's huge (130,000 entries) *Acronyms, Initialisms, & Abbreviations Dictionary* contains the most extensive coverage of domestic associations, organizations, agencies, etc. In addition, Buttress's *World Guide to Abbreviations of Organizations*, while not as large as Spillner's *World Guide to Abbreviations* (18,000 entries vs. 50,000), provides strong coverage of European, British, and American groups.

Other Critical Opinions

American Reference Books Annual 1974 (review by Bohdan S. Wynar), pp. 38–39.
RQ, Summer 1971, p. 363.
Wilson Library Bulletin, June 1971, p. 992.

World Guide to Abbreviations of Organizations

Descriptive Information

Full Title: **World Guide to Abbreviations of Organizations.** *Compiler:* F. A. Buttress. *Publisher:* Leonard Hill Books. *Distributor:* Gale Research Co. *Edition Reviewed:* Fifth Edition, 1974.

Classification: Special-Purpose—Abbreviations & Acronyms. *Pages:* 473. *Total Entries:* 18,000. *Physical Size:* 7½ by 10 in.; 25 cm. *LC:* 74-13530. *ISBN:* 0-8103-2015-0. *Lowest Retail Price:* $24.00.

Comments

Buttress's *World Guide to Abbreviations of Organizations* is a standard British reference work first published in 1954 and now in its fifth edition (1974). Considerably expanded over the previous edition (Fourth Edition, 1971) which contained 12,000 entries, the current edition alphabetically lists abbreviations for over 18,000 national and international agencies, organizations, associations, companies, etc. Many of the new entries cover European groups. Buttress explains in his introduction, "In view of our [British] entry into the Common Market, European entries now amount to over 5,000 exclusive of British and international bodies." Buttress's guide, while not as extensive as Spillner's three-volume *World Guide to Abbreviations*, provides comparable coverage of British and European organizations. It is also a useful complement to Crowley's indispensable *Acronyms, Initialisms, & Abbreviations Dictionary* (Fifth Edition, 1976).

Other Critical Opinions

American Reference Books Annual 1976, p. 74.
Library Journal, August 1975, p. 1404.

SIGNS AND SYMBOLS

Dictionary of American Sign Language

Descriptive Information

Full Title: **A Dictionary of American Sign Language on Linguistic Principles.** *Editors:* William C. Stokoe, Dorothy C. Casterline, and Carl G. Croneberg. *Publisher:* Linstok Press. *Edition Reviewed:* New Edition, 1976.

Classification: Special-Purpose—Signs & Symbols. *Pages:* xxxiii, 346. *Physical Size:* 5¼ by 8½ in.; 22 cm. *LC:* 65-28740. *Lowest Retail Price:* $7.95 paper.

Comments

This invaluable dictionary aims "to describe not only the vocabulary but also the transmission system (phonology) and the syntax (grammatical system) of American Sign Language." Unfortunately, the New Edition (1976) is simply a reissue of the original 1965 edition with a new preface and updated bibliography. Stokoe, in his preface to the New Edition, laments the cost of a thorough revision or entirely new work which, if undertaken, would "by conservative estimate [entail] thrice the number of signs and an indeterminate time to complete." American Sign Language (ASL) is the language of more than 300,000 Americans. *A Dictionary of American Sign Language on Linguistic Principles* is their "Webster."

Dictionary of Gestures

Descriptive Information

Full Title: **A Dictionary of Gestures.** *Compilers:* Betty J. Bäuml and Franz H. Bäuml. *Publisher:* Scarecrow Press. *Edition Reviewed:* 1975.

Classification: Special-Purpose—Signs & Symbols. *Pages:* xxxv, 249. *Physical Size:* 5¾ by 8¾ in.; 22 cm. *LC:* 75-23144. *ISBN:* 0-8108-0863-3. *Lowest Retail Price:* $11.00.

Comments

The introduction states "This dictionary contains primarily non-codified, non-arbitrary, culturally transmitted (semiotic) gestures. It does not include sign languages, gestures used in narrative dances, military gestures, or such fragmentary sign languages as the occupationally determined gestures of truck drivers, railroad men, or monks, nor is it primarily concerned with autistic gestures." Entries appear alphabetically by part(s) of the body. For instance, one page includes these main entries: "Buttocks"; "Buttocks, hand"; "Buttocks, hand, tongue"; "Cheek"; "Cheek, eye"; "Cheek, eye, hand"; "Cheek, eye, mouth." Under each main entry, there are various "significances," such as *affection, anger, cunning, sorrow, warning,* and *welcome.* Each gesture is described and a documented source is cited, giving full bibliographic information, including page references. The user can also approach the gestures through the alphabetical index of significances in the back. A fascinating catalog of common and uncommon gestures used throughout the world, ranging from the familiar "Finger, Neck" gesture for *death* ("Drawing the index, or index and middle fingers, representing a knife, quickly across the throat") to the exotic "Finger, Tooth" gesture for *apology* ("Biting middle joint of right index with heel of hand pointing forward, hand closed"), a folk gesture indigenous to Saudi Arabia.

Other Critical Opinions

Booklist, September 1, 1976, p. 54.
RQ (review by V. Hale Starr), Summer 1976, pp. 348–349.

Handtalk

Descriptive Information

Full Title: **Handtalk: An ABC of Finger Spelling & Sign Language.** *Compilers:* Remy Charlip and Mary Beth Miller. *Photographer:* George Ancona. *Publisher:* Parents' Magazine Press. *Edition Reviewed:* 1974.

Classification: Special-Purpose—Signs & Symbols. *Pages:* 48. *Physical Size:* 7½ by 10¼ in.; 26 cm. *LC:* 73-10199. *ISBN:* 0-8193-0705-X. *Lowest Retail Price:* $5.95.

Comments

Handtalk "is the first book of its kind for young people on two ways that deaf people talk: *finger spelling,* forming words letter by letter with the fingers of one hand, and *signing*, making a picture or sign with one or two hands for each word or idea." Illustrated with full-page color photographs, *Handtalk* takes the reader through the alphabet, providing simple examples of both finger spelling and signing for each letter. Obviously the book is introductory in nature. As the compilers note in their preface, "This is only a beginning. There are over 5,000 signs in the language of the deaf. It is a rich and beautiful language used by hundreds of thousands in the United States alone." Serious students will graduate to *A Dictionary of American Sign Language on Linguistic Principles.*

Shepherd's Glossary of Graphic Signs and Symbols

Descriptive Information

Full Title: **Shepherd's Glossary of Graphic Signs and Symbols.** *Compiler:* Walter Shepherd. *Publisher:* J. M. Dent. *Distributor:* Dover Publications. *Edition Reviewed:* 1971.

Classification: Special-Purpose—Signs & Symbols. *Pages:* 597. *Total Entries:* 5,000. *LC:* 74-153895. *ISBN:* 0-486-20700-5. *Lowest Retail Price:* $15.00.

Comments

Shepherd's Glossary of Graphic Signs and Symbols, like Dreyfuss's *Symbol Sourcebook,* is an effort to bring some order to the many and varied signs and symbols people use in all walks of life. *Shepherd's* emphasis is on technical signs, but the book also covers alphabets, accents, insignias, internationally agreed upon signs, and the like. There are various helpful classifications, appendixes, and indexes.

Other Critical Opinions

American Reference Books Annual 1973 (review by Paul H. Spence), pp. 359–360.

Symbol Sourcebook

Descriptive Information

Full Title: **Symbol Sourcebook: An Authoritative Guide to International Graphic Symbols.** *Compiler:* Henry Dreyfuss. *Publisher:* McGraw-Hill. *Edition Reviewed:* 1972.

Classification: Special-Purpose—Signs & Symbols. *Pages:* 288. *Total Entries:* 8,000. *Physical Size:* 8½ by 11¼ in.; 29 cm. *LC:* 71-172261. *ISBN:* 0-07-017837-2. *Lowest Retail Price:* $34.95.

Comments

Henry Dreyfuss's *Symbol Sourcebook,* based on an ongoing data bank of more than 20,000 symbols, attempts to codify graphic symbols used in business, industry, science and technology, safety and traffic, home economics, etc. throughout the world. The symbols are classified by subject (e.g., Accommodations and Travel; Agriculture; Architecture; Astronomy; Biology; Chemistry; Engineering; Folklore) and graphic forms. The contents appear in 18 languages, but the subject index is only in English. More comprehensive than *Shepherd's Glossary of Graphic Signs and Symbols*, a work of similar purpose. *Symbol Sourcebook* and *Shepherd's* each contain material not found in the other and thus are complementary sources.

Other Critical Opinions

American Reference Books Annual 1973 (review by Paul A. Winckler), pp. 359–360.
Booklist, June 1, 1972, p. 832.
Library Journal, March 15, 1972, p. 1002.

FOREIGN WORDS AND PHRASES COMMONLY USED IN ENGLISH

Dictionary of Foreign Phrases and Abbreviations

Descriptive Information

Full Title: **Dictionary of Foreign Phrases and Abbreviations.** *Editor:* Kevin Guinagh. *Publisher:* H. W. Wilson Co. *Edition Reviewed:* Second Edition, 1972.

Classification: Special-Purpose—Foreign Words & Phrases. *Pages:* xiv, 352. *Total Entries:* 4,500. *Physical Size:* 5¼ by 7½ in.; 19 cm. *LC:* 72-149383. *ISBN:* 0-8242-0460-3. *Lowest Retail Price:* $12.00.

Comments

First published in 1965 and substantially revised in 1972, Guinagh's *Dictionary of Foreign Phrases and Abbreviations* comprises over 4,500 entries, of which about 2,000 are Latin phrases and abbreviations. The entries are arranged alphabetically, regardless of the language, but there is a "List of Phrases Arranged by Languages" in the back. Sources of phrases are given when possible, e.g., "*Cogito, ergo sum.* L—I think; hence I exist. Advanced by Descartes as *a priori* proof of one's existence.—*Descartes, Discourse on Method, IV.*" The word *phrase* in the title "is to be understood in the recognized and not uncommon meaning of a pithy, quotable expression, such as a proverb, motto, or maxim." Items "longer than a couplet" have been excluded and in most instances single words are not covered. Hence, Guinagh's dictionary complements rather than duplicates such similar works as Mawson and Berlitz's *Dictionary of Foreign Terms* and Pei and Ramondino's *Dictionary of Foreign Terms.*

Other Critical Opinions

American Reference Books Annual 1973 (review by Marjorie P. Holt), p. 458.

Dictionary of Foreign Terms (Carroll)

Descriptive Information

Full Title: **The Dictionary of Foreign Terms in the English Language.**
Editor: David Carroll. *Publisher:* Hawthorn. *Edition Reviewed:* 1973.
Classification: Special-Purpose—Foreign Words & Phrases. *Pages:* 212.
Total Entries: 7,000. *LC:* 70-39281. *Lowest Retail Price:* $10.95.

Comments

The 7,000 foreign terms represent some 30 different languages, with Latin
and French accounting for the largest percentage of entries. English loanwords are also included, e.g., *Nisei; Weltanschauung.* Each term is defined or
translated, whichever seems most informative. Illustrative sentences are
sometimes provided for definitional clarity. Standard abbreviations of
foreign terms are listed separately in the back. Compares well with other
works in this category, e.g., Guinagh's *Dictionary of Foreign Phrases and
Abbreviations.*

Other Critical Opinions

American Reference Books Annual 1974, p. 450.
Booklist, December 1, 1973, p. 351.
Library Journal (review by B. Hunter Smeaton), March 15, 1973, p. 857.
Wilson Library Bulletin, October 1973, p. 163.

Dictionary of Foreign Terms (Mawson/Berlitz)

Descriptive Information

Full Title: **Dictionary of Foreign Terms.** *Editors:* C. O. Sylvester Mawson;
Revised and Updated by Charles Berlitz. *Publisher:* T. Y. Crowell Co.
Former title: *Dictionary of Foreign Terms Found in English and American
Writings of Yesterday and Today* (1934). *Edition Reviewed:* Second Edition,
1975.
Classification: Special-Purpose—Foreign Words & Phrases. *Pages:* x, 368.
Total Entries: 15,000. *Physical Size:* 5¾ by 8¼ in.; 21 cm. *LC:* 74-12492.
ISBN: 0-690-00171-1 (hardcover); 0-8152-0402-7 (paper). *Lowest Retail
Price:* $9.95; also $4.95 paper.

Comments

This revision of Mawson's dictionary which first appeared in 1934 includes
foreign words, phrases, and quotations (but no abbreviations) from approximately 50 languages, including French Canadian, Swahili, American Indian,
ancient Greek, and modern Russian. The terms are spelled, identified as to
language, and very briefly defined or translated, but not pronounced. In some
cases sources are cited, but only by author. Example: *"hunc tu, Romane,
caveto* [L.], of him, Roman, do thou beware: *Horace."* Also, when appropriate, regional labels are affixed. Example: *"presidio* [Sp.], garrison town;
army post; also, Spanish penal settlement: *Sp. Am. & southwestern U.S."*

Likewise, subject labels are used to indicate *cookery, law, music*, and so forth. The *Dictionary of Foreign Terms*, as revised by Charles Berlitz in 1975, is authoritative, up-to-date, and broad in coverage. As such it compares very favorably with such similar titles as Guinagh's *Dictionary of Foreign Phrases and Abbreviations* and Carroll's *Dictionary of Foreign Terms*.

Other Critical Opinions

American Reference Books Annual 1976 (review by Stanley Joe McCord), p. 540.
Booklist, January 15, 1975, p. 476; also June 15, 1975, p. 1092.
Library Journal, April 15, 1975, p. 748.
Wilson Library Bulletin (review by Charles A. Bunge), June 1975, p. 753.

Dictionary of Foreign Terms (Pei)

Descriptive Information

Full Title: **Dictionary of Foreign Terms.** *Editors:* Mario Pei and Salvatore Ramondino in collaboration with Laura Torbet. *Publishers:* Delacorte (hardcover); Dell Publishing Co. (paper). *Edition Reviewed:* 1974.

Classification: Special-Purpose—Foreign Words & Phrases. *Pages:* 366. *Total Entries:* 7,000. *Physical Size:* 4¼ by 7 in.; 18 cm. (paper). *LC:* 74-34091. *ISBN:* 0-440-01779-3 (hardcover). *Lowest Retail Price:* $8.95; also $1.95 paper.

Comments

Pei and Ramondino's *Dictionary of Foreign Terms* consists mainly of words and phrases from Latin, French, Italian, German, and Spanish, although once in a while a Zulu or Tagalog term appears. The dictionary is only about half the size of Mawson and Berlitz's *Dictionary of Foreign Terms* but it provides simple pronunciations and etymologies which the larger work lacks. The pronunciations, however, are not always reliable (e.g., *placebo* is pronounced *"plah-KEH-boh"* but should be *plah-SEE-boh*). Moreover, some quite standard foreign phrases are not covered (e.g., *in excelsis*). The definitions are brief but usually accurate and informative. Pei and Ramondino's *Dictionary of Foreign Terms*, though not as extensive as the Mawson/Berlitz work of the same title, does offer some terms not included in the larger dictionary. Hence, the two books complement one another. The same is true of Guinagh's *Dictionary of Foreign Phrases and Abbreviations* and Carroll's *Dictionary of Foreign Terms*, which is about the same size as Pei and Ramondino's dictionary.

Other Critical Opinions

American Reference Books Annual 1976 (review by Robert Parslow), pp. 540–541.
Booklist, October 15, 1975, p. 326.
Library Journal, June 15, 1975, p. 1203.
Wilson Library Bulletin (review by Charles A. Bunge), June 1975, pp. 753–754.

Dictionary of Foreign Words and Phrases

Descriptive Information

Full Title: **Dictionary of Foreign Words and Phrases:** Compiled from English Sources and Containing Foreign Words, Phrases, Mottos, Proverbs, Place Names, Titles, Allusions and Abbreviations from the Latin, Greek, French, Italian, Spanish, German, Russian, Hebrew and Other Foreign Languages. *Editor:* Maxim Newmark. *Publisher:* Greenwood Press. *Edition Reviewed:* 1957.

Classification: Special-Purpose—Foreign Words & Phrases. *Pages:* 245. *Total Entries:* 12,000. *Lowest Retail Price:* $14.50.

Comments

Newmark's *Dictionary of Foreign Words and Phrases* contained 10,000 entries when it initially appeared in 1950. The 1957 revision added 2,000 words and phrases. Each entry indicates the language of origin and provides a brief definition or translation. The Newmark dictionary is a standard reference work prepared in Great Britain and, despite its present age, the dictionary remains useful because of its wide-ranging scope. Most users, however, will find the other dictionaries in this category to be preferable, largely because they are more up-to-date, e.g., Mawson and Berlitz's *Dictionary of Foreign Terms* and Guinagh's *Dictionary of Foreign Phrases and Abbreviations.*

APPENDIX A

RECENTLY DISCONTINUED DICTIONARIES

The dictionaries briefly noted in this section of the *Buying Guide* have been reported out of print. Consumers might, however, encounter any of these titles in secondhand bookstores or in discount stores as remainder items. Bear in mind that a few of these dictionaries, while currently not available through normal trade channels, are undergoing revision and will most likely reappear in the near future, either under the original title or a new one. Only general adult and school and children's dictionaries are included here. Note also that previous editions of dictionaries currently in print are not included. Former titles of dictionaries currently in print are indicated, however, in the profiles in Part II and can be located through the index. For instance, *Webster's International Dictionary of the English Language* (Second Edition, 1934), replaced in 1961 by *Webster's Third New International Dictionary of the English Language*, is not covered here but is discussed in the profile of *Webster's Third*.

American Family Reference Dictionary

A semi-unabridged dictionary (1,663 pages) of indifferent quality, the *American Family Reference Dictionary* was published by the McCall Corporation in 1964 and reported out of print several years later.

Avon Webster English Dictionary and Encyclopedia

This inconsequential pocket item comprised 628 pages and 30,000 simple definitions. Published in 1958 by Avon Books in a paperback edition for 75¢, it went out of print in 1967.

Cassell's English Dictionary

A British work of substance, *Cassell's English Dictionary* was initially published in 1891 and revised most recently in 1962. It contained 130,000 entries (1,348 pages), emphasized British usage, included some vocabulary peculiar to the Commonwealth and South Africa, and was authoritatively edited by Arthur L. Hayward and John L. Sparkes. Funk & Wagnalls published *Cassell's* in the U.S. in 1964 but it is no longer available. It remains in print in England, however, published by Cassell & Co., Ltd. Prior to its 1962 revision, *Cassell's* was known as the *New English Dictionary*.

Century Dictionary and Cyclopedia

The *Century Dictionary and Cyclopedia*, first published between 1889 and 1891 in six volumes by the now defunct Century Company (New York) and later revised and expanded to 12 volumes in 1911, is generally recognized as one of the greatest dictionaries ever produced in the U.S. Some critics speak of it in the same breath as the incomparable *Oxford English Dictionary*. Now out of print for some time, *Century* is, of course, quite dated but it retains some current reference value, particularly for lexicographers, etymologists, and historians. In its final revision, the unabridged *Century* contained over 200,000 main entries and 500,000 definitions augmented by numerous well-selected illustrative quotations. Although the dictionary's scope encompassed the whole of American English, scientific and technical terms were emphasized. As the title indicates, *Century* provided not only lexical but much encyclopedic information. The final two volumes were a "Cyclopedia of Names" and an atlas. (In 1954, the volume on names was revised, retitled, and republished in three volumes as *The New Century Cyclopedia of Names*, a set which is still available from Appleton-Century-Crofts for $79.95.) An outstanding example of an encyclopedic dictionary.

Everyman's English Dictionary

A small (50,000 entries) British-produced dictionary compiled by D. C. Browning, *Everyman's English Dictionary* was published by J. M. Dent (London) in 1956 and distributed in the U.S. by E. P. Dutton & Company. A 1964 reissue incorporated a section on new words.

Funk & Wagnalls Concise Standard Dictionary

First published in 1914, *Funk & Wagnalls Concise Standard Dictionary* contained 38,000 entries and 780 pictorial illustrations. This pocket dictionary last appeared in 1964.

Funk & Wagnalls Encyclopedic College Dictionary

High-priced at $19.95, this dictionary comprised the contents of *Funk & Wagnalls Standard College Dictionary* (a good semi-unabridged dictionary of 150,000 entries) and several hundred pages of reference supplements. It went out of print in 1975.

Funk & Wagnalls New Comprehensive Standard Dictionary

Another small desk dictionary from Funk & Wagnalls, this one originally appeared in 1937 and disappeared in 1965. It included some 50,000 entries and 1,800 line drawings in 1,024 pages.

Funk & Wagnalls New Practical Standard Dictionary

This semi-unabridged work contained 150,000 entries in 1,592 pages. First published in 1922, it went out of print in 1965. There were two editions, a one-volume format which sold for $12.50 and a two-volume set at $25.00.

Funk & Wagnalls Standard High School Dictionary

Exactly the same work as *Funk & Wagnalls New Comprehensive Standard Dictionary*. Both titles were withdrawn from the market in 1965.

Funk & Wagnalls Standard Junior School Dictionary

A 39,000-entry dictionary for upper elementary and middle school students, *Funk & Wagnalls Standard Junior School Dictionary* was distinguished by clear, simple definitions and its "Word Quiz" feature. Like the other titles in Funk & Wagnalls now defunct school series, this one was discontinued in 1965.

Funk & Wagnalls Student's Standard Dictionary

A sizable dictionary of 140,000 entries and 2,500 drawings in 1,357 pages, *Funk & Wagnalls Student's Standard Dictionary* aimed to serve high school students as well as freshmen and sophomores in college. It included about 15,000 proper names, some synonyms and antonyms, and a useful section on grammar and spelling. Out of print in 1965.

Giant Picture Dictionary for Boys and Girls

Published by Garden City Publishing Company in 1949, this picture dictionary was similar to Wendell Wright's *Rainbow Dictionary for Young Readers*, now also out of print. *The Giant Picture Dictionary*, prepared by Alice Howard Scott, contained 3,600 entries with meanings indicated by sample sentences and colorful drawings. The book went out of print in 1977.

Golden Picture Dictionary

The *Golden Picture Dictionary*, edited by Lucille Ogle, was published in 1954. It contains only 800 entries in 77 pages. Not to be confused with a much newer (1976) and larger (2,500 entries) work of the same title also published by Western Publishing Company.

Grosset-Webster Dictionary

First published in 1947 as *Words: The New Dictionary* and retitled *The Grosset-Webster Dictionary* in 1960, this 75,000-entry dictionary was designed for junior and senior high school students. It was edited by Charles P. Chadsey and William Morris and contained only basic information concerning spelling, pronunciation, syllabication, and word meanings. The dictionary was never revised and Grosset & Dunlap, the publisher, withdrew it from the market several years ago.

Holt Basic Dictionary of American English

A dictionary for elementary school students first published in 1962 as the *Basic Dictionary of American English* (*Holt* was added in 1966), this work contained approximately 25,000 entries and 1,250 black-and-white line drawings in 858 pages. Published by Holt, Rinehart & Winston, the dictionary was well regarded but became out of date and was discontinued in the mid-

1970s. It also appeared in paperback under the title *Scholastic Dictionary of American English*, which is likewise out of print.

Macmillan Modern Dictionary

The *Macmillan Modern Dictionary*, first published in the 1930s and revised frequently until 1951, was noted for its excellent format and clear definitions. Designed for high school students, it contained 140,000 entries in 1,509 pages. Replaced by the equally fine *Macmillan Dictionary* (1973), also published by the Macmillan Publishing Company.

Modern American Dictionary

A paperback edition of *The Modern Library Dictionary* (see below), *The Modern American Dictionary* first appeared in 1957 published by Dell Publishing Company. It was reported out of print in the mid-1970s. See the next entry for more information.

Modern Library Dictionary

Based on the once outstanding *American College Dictionary*, this 60,000-entry general adult dictionary (636 pages) was published by Random House in 1957 and reissued with corrections in 1961. Never revised, it went out of print in the mid-1970s. Note that *The Modern Library Dictionary* has the same contents as *The Modern American Dictionary* and is very similar to *The Random House American Everyday Dictionary* (also known as *The American Everyday Dictionary* and *The American Dollar Dictionary*), which remains in print and is profiled in the *Buying Guide*. See "Abridged Dictionaries" in Part II.

My Picture Dictionary

My Picture Dictionary, published in 1963 by Ginn & Company, was part of the publisher's "Elementary English Series." The dictionary contained nearly 600 words, all selected from the compositions of first grade students. The book was prepared by Hale C. Reid and Helen W. Crane. Reported out of print in 1977.

New American Webster Dictionary

This small, inconsequential dictionary of 25,000 entries is an abridgment of *The New American Webster Handy College Dictionary*, a pocket item which remains in print and is reviewed in Part II of the *Buying Guide* (see "Pocket Dictionaries"). Both dictionaries are in paperback format and published by New American Library. *The New American Webster Dictionary*, first published in 1951 and last reprinted in 1961, was reported out of print in the late 1960s.

New Century Dictionary

A revision of the justly famous twelve-volume *Century Dictionary and Cyclopedia* (also out of print; see above), *The New Century Dictionary of the English Language* originally appeared in three volumes in 1927 and was reissued several years later in a two-volume edition. It comprised nearly 200,000 entries and 4,000 pictorial illustrations in 2,840 pages. The definitions, though based on research done for the *Century Dictionary and Cyclopedia*, were entirely rewritten and new illustrative quotations added. Edited by H. G. Emery and K. G. Brewster, the dictionary remains noteworthy for the fullness of its definitions and the high quality of its etymological material. Though revised a number of times over the years, the dictionary's text remained essentially that of the 1927 work and in the early 1970s the publisher, Appleton-Century-Crofts, allowed *New Century* to go out of print.

New Handy Webster Dictionary

A small pocket dictionary of 385 pages with 23,000 entries, the *New Handy Webster Dictionary* was published by the World Publishing Company (now Collins+World) for 39¢. It went out of print in 1966.

New Webster Dictionary

Published in 1964 in a two-volume format by Consolidated Book Publishers (Chicago), the *New Webster Dictionary* was an inferior and overpriced, semi-unabridged work of 140,000 entries in 1,400 pages. The second volume contained ten supplements covering such material as quotations, synonyms and antonyms, biographies, and foreign expressions. It is possible that *The Living Webster Encyclopedic Dictionary* (see profile under "Semi-Unabridged Dictionaries" in Part II of the *Buying Guide*) derives at least in part from the *New Webster Dictionary*. Note also that *Living Webster* is published in an illustrated edition under the title *New Webster's Dictionary* (see note under "Semi-Unabridged Dictionaries" in Part II). Virginia S. Thatcher is listed as the chief editor of the *New Webster Dictionary* whereas Dana K. Kellerman is the editor of *New Webster's Dictionary* and *Living Webster*. In any event, all three dictionaries are of poor quality and should be avoided by consumers.

Rainbow Dictionary

The Rainbow Dictionary for Young Readers, a longtime favorite picture dictionary, contained 2,300 words culled from standard word lists. First published in 1947 and very slightly revised twice thereafter, the dictionary was prepared by Dr. Wendell W. Wright with color illustrations (over a thousand) by Joseph Low. In 1977, the publisher, Collins+World, reported *The Rainbow Dictionary* out of print. Note, however, that the text (but not the illustrations) found in *The Charlie Brown Dictionary* is based on *Rainbow*. (See the profile of *The Charlie Brown Dictionary* under "Elementary School Dictionaries" in Part II of the *Buying Guide*.) *The Rainbow Dictionary* was especially noted for its clear, instructive definitions and carefully chosen sample sentences. As the *Buying Guide* went to press, the publisher announced a revised edition, updated by the editorial staff of *Webster's New World Dictionary*. The revision reportedly contains the same number of words (2,300) and illustrations (1,100).

Rand McNally Picture-Book Dictionary

Subtitled *A Thousand Words to See and Say*, this 96-page picture dictionary was published by Rand McNally in 1971 and reported out of print in 1977. It was compiled by Robert L. Hillerich and others, with illustrations by Dan Siculan. The thousand entries derived from word frequency lists for children from three to eight.

Reader's Digest Great Encyclopedic Dictionary

A potpourri of lexical information, *The Reader's Digest Great Encyclopedic Dictionary* contained over 150,000 dictionary entries, 1,060 black-and-white line drawings, and 18 supplements covering such items as concise foreign-language dictionaries, essays on etymology and English-language history, guides to correct usage and grammar, sections on spelling and punctuation, and lists of specialized terms in such areas as space, medicine, slang, and signs and symbols—all in 2,112 pages. The main dictionary and major portion of the *Great Encyclopedic Dictionary* was *Funk & Wagnalls Standard College Dictionary* (1963), a respectable semi-unabridged dictionary which remains in print (see the profile in Part II of the *Buying Guide*). Published by the Reader's Digest Association, Inc. in Pleasantville (N.Y.) in 1966, the *Great Encyclopedic Dictionary* was poorly received by knowledgeable critics. For instance, one remarked that "the danger of the encyclopedic dictionary is that it might fall between two stools and serve satisfactorily neither as dictionary nor as encyclopedia. *The Reader's Digest Great Encyclopedic Dictionary* . . . is an effective example of the genre." Quoted from Kenneth Whittaker's *Dictionaries* (Philosophical Library, 1966, p. 14). The *Buying Guide* is informed that a new edition of the *Great Encyclopedic Dictionary* is in progress. The 1966 edition was reported out of print in 1977.

Thorndike-Barnhart Comprehensive Desk Dictionary

When it first appeared in 1951, all reputable critics acknowledged the *Thorndike-Barnhart Comprehensive Desk Dictionary* as a first-rate abridged dictionary. Published by Doubleday (trade edition) and Scott, Foresman (text edition), it included some 80,000 entries, among which were many abbreviations, slang expressions, and biographical and geographical entries. Doubleday informed the *Buying Guide* in 1977 that the dictionary was out of print. Note, however, that an abridgment—the 36,000-entry *Thorndike-Barnhart Handy Pocket Dictionary*—remains in print (see the profile under "Pocket Dictionaries" in Part II of the *Buying Guide*).

Thorndike-Barnhart Concise Dictionary

This abridged adult dictionary of 70,000 entries and 600 pictorial illustrations in 544 pages is a slightly reduced version of the *Thorndike-Barnhart Comprehensive Desk Dictionary* (see above). The *Concise* was published by Doubleday in 1956 and never thoroughly revised thereafter. Available in an inexpensive hardcover edition, the dictionary was widely used in offices.

Webster's Approved Dictionary

Originally published in 1940 as the *New Illustrated Webster's Approved Dictionary*, this undistinguished but good-sized (1,278 pages) adult dictionary appeared under the imprint of the World Publishing Company (now Collins+World). *Webster's Approved Dictionary* was last issued in 1956 and went out of print in the mid-1960s.

Webster's Dictionary

Designated as a "Handi-Thumb Index Book," this small pocket dictionary of approximately 30,000 entries was published by Crown Publishers. In a coil binding, it sold for $1.95 and was frequently marketed in drugstores, discount houses, and the like. Though declared out of print in 1977, the *Buying Guide* has had reports that it is still being sold in various areas of the country. Crown's *Webster's Dictionary*, like all pocket dictionaries, has minimal reference value and will satisfy only the simplest vocabulary needs.

Webster's Home University Dictionary

Webster's Home University Dictionary was a large type edition of *Webster's New American Dictionary*, also now out of print (see below). The dictionaries contained approximately 66,000 entries, 1,000 black-and-white line illustrations, a few color plates, and a 16-page atlas in 1,300 pages. Both works were published by an outfit called Books, Inc. (New York), a subsidiary of the Publishers Company, Inc. (now the Publishers Agency, Inc.). *Webster's Home University Dictionary*, edited by Edward N. Teall, usually sold for $19.95 in a brown or white deluxe binding with gold stamping. Although it carried a 1965 copyright, its contents were essentially the same as those of *Webster's New American Dictionary*, published in 1939 and never thoroughly revised. *Webster's Home University Dictionary* was an overpriced, out-of-date work of inferior quality. Although the dictionary is out of print, it might be encountered in some dark corner of the book world. Avoid it.

Webster's Illustrated Dictionary

A mediocre pocket-size dictionary of 40,000 entries in 832 pages, *Webster's Illustrated Dictionary* was published by the Publishers Company, Inc. (now the Publishers Agency, Inc.) and distributed by Books, Inc. (New York), a subsidiary. It was available in several cheap, poorly printed editions.

Webster's New American Dictionary

Originally published in 1939 and never revised in any significant way, *Webster's New American Dictionary* has a complicated, checkered history. An abridged dictionary of 66,000 entries and 1,000 black-and-white illustrations in 1,300 pages, it also appeared in a so-called deluxe edition under the title *Webster's Home University Dictionary* (also out of print; see above). It was also issued as the *World University Dictionary*, the *World Universal Dictionary*, and as the dictionary portion of a now defunct conglomeration entitled *Webster's Unified Dictionary and Encyclopedia*. *Webster's New American Dictionary* was published by the Publishers Company, Inc. (now called the Publishers Agency, Inc.), a firm noted for producing and merchandising outdated, inferior reference works. Another publisher, Wehman Brothers, Inc., was known to distribute *Webster's New American Dictionary*. The *Buying Guide* believes this dictionary (and all its aliases) to be out of print, but it is possible that it might surface again at any time and under any title. *Caveat emptor.*

Webster's New Handy Dictionary

A small pocket dictionary of 257 pages, *Webster's New Handy Dictionary* was based on *Webster's International Dictionary of the English Language* (Second Edition, 1934), Merriam-Webster's unabridged work which was superseded by *Webster's Third New International Dictionary* in 1961. It was published by the American Book Company (by arrangement with the G. & C. Merriam Company). A useful abridgment when first issued in 1955, *Webster's New Handy Dictionary* eventually became dated and went out of print in the late 1960s or early 1970s.

Webster's New Handy Pocket Dictionary

Webster's New Handy Pocket Dictionary, published by the Publishers Company, Inc. (now the Publishers Agency, Inc.), contained about 20,000 entries in 371 pages. It appeared in paperback and had little practical reference value. Not to be confused with *Webster's New World Handy Pocket Dictionary*, a small 30,000-entry dictionary published by Collins+World (see profile under "Pocket Dictionaries" in Part II of the *Buying Guide*).

Webster's New Handy Vest Pocket Dictionary

A cheaply produced book of 256 pages, this dictionary had practically the same contents as *Webster's New Handy Pocket Dictionary* (see above), also published by the Publishers Company, Inc. Both works were inferior to other pocket dictionaries on the market.

Webster's New Illustrated Dictionary

This dictionary was an abridgment of *Webster's New American Dictionary* (see above), a work of inferior quality. Both dictionaries were published by the Publishers Company, Inc.

Webster's New Peerless Dictionary

A work of indifferent quality, *Webster's New Peerless Dictionary* contained approximately 100,000 entries along with routine line drawings. It was published by the World Publishing Company (now Collins+World) prior to the introduction of the excellent "Webster's New World" line of dictionaries.

Webster's New Practical School Dictionary

Designed chiefly for junior and senior high school students, *Webster's New Practical School Dictionary* included 45,000 carefully selected terms, about 800 drab illustrations, and a valuable 50-page introduction to dictionary use in 975 pages. It was published by the G. & C. Merriam Company and drew upon the firm's extensive citation files. Published in 1964, the dictionary originally appeared five years earlier as *Webster's New Secondary School Dictionary*. Replaced by *Webster's New Students Dictionary* (for high school pupils) and *Webster's Intermediate Dictionary* (for junior high pupils). The latter two titles are currently in print and are profiled under "School Dictionaries" in Part II of the *Buying Guide*.

Webster's New School and Office Dictionary

A fairly useful abridged dictionary of some 52,000 words in 896 pages, *Webster's New School and Office Dictionary* was initially published in 1943 and occasionally revised by inserting new words and deleting a like number of old ones. An inexpensive hardcover edition appeared under the imprint of the World Publishing Company (now Collins+World) and Fawcett Books offered the book in paperback.

Webster's New Secondary School Dictionary

Published between 1959 and 1964, this Merriam-Webster dictionary was geared to students from the seventh grade through the early high school years. In 1964, its title was changed to *Webster's New Practical School Dictionary*, now also out of print (see above).

Webster's New World Dictionary (Encyclopedic Edition)

This two-volume dictionary of 142,000 entries in a total of 1,814 pages was the forerunner of the excellent semi-unabridged *Webster's New World Dictionary* (Second College Edition), reviewed in Part II of the *Buying Guide*. The Encyclopedic Edition first appeared in 1951 and was revised two years later at which time it was also issued as the one-volume College Edition (without the encyclopedic material). Sold in a high-priced ($29.50) binding, the Encyclopedic Edition remained in print throughout the 1960s. Note that David Guralnik, currently editor of all dictionaries in the Webster's New World line, started with the Encyclopedic Edition.

Webster's New World Dictionary (Everyday Encyclopedic Edition)

A combination of *Webster's New World Dictionary* (Concise Edition) and 310 pages of reference supplements, the Everyday Encyclopedic Edition was distributed by the Southwestern Company (Nashville, Tenn.) in cooperation with the World Publishing Company (now Collins+World). At the present time, the Concise Edition (105,000 entries) is available but the supplemented Everyday Encyclopedic Edition went out of print several years ago. For more information, see the profile of *Webster's New World Dictionary* (Second Concise Edition) under "Abridged Dictionaries" in Part II of the *Buying Guide*.

Webster's Tower Dictionary

One of several undistinguished small dictionaries published by the World Publishing Company prior to the vastly superior Webster's New World series, *Webster's Tower Dictionary* comprises only 25,000 entries in 382 pages.

Webster's Unified Dictionary and Encyclopedia

In 1953, H. S. Stuttman & Company issued this bizarre item which re-arranged the entries in two very different reference works—the *New American Encyclopedia* (1938) and *Webster's New American Dictionary* (1939)—into a single alphabet. The result was quite ludicrous but *Webster's Unified Dictionary and Encyclopedia* remained in print for 15 years, sold in a hardcover edition at the exorbitant price of $25.00 and in weekly parts in supermarkets for a total of $15.00 or so. For additional information, see the description of *Webster's New American Dictionary* above.

Winston Dictionary (Advanced Edition)

At one time, there was a whole line of Winston dictionaries for both adults and school use. Published by the old John C. Winston Company of Phila-delphia (now part of Holt, Rinehart & Winston), all Winston dictionaries are currently out of print, except for *The Winston Dictionary for Schools*, which will surely expire soon (see the note under "Middle School Dictionaries" in Part II of the *Buying Guide*). All of the various editions of *The Winston Dictionary* (Advanced, College, Encyclopedic, and Senior) derive from the same lexical base developed by the firm in 1936. All of these editions contain approximately 100,000 entries and were once considered works of some substance.

Winston Dictionary (College Edition)

This 100,000-entry dictionary (1,280 pages) included about 3,000 pictorial illustrations, a 16-page color atlas, and a number of appendixes. Its contents are exactly the same as those of the Encyclopedic Edition (see below) except for the omission of the encyclopedic material.

Winston Dictionary (Encyclopedic Edition)

The Encyclopedic Edition of *The Winston Dictionary* (1,566 pages) con-tained some 100,000 entries, 3,000 line drawings, and much appended material, including a list of British expressions, a Scottish glossary, a detailed section on grammar, a chronological table of historical events, and a gazetteer of nearly 10,000 place-names. The dictionary's contents are the same as those of the College Edition (see above) except for the many encyclo-pedic supplements. The Encyclopedic Edition also appeared for a time under the title of the *Winston Universal Reference Library*.

Winston Dictionary (Senior Edition)

A somewhat abridged version of the College and Encyclopedic editions (see above), this work dropped some of the more difficult vocabulary terms.

Winston Dictionary for Children

The Winston Dictionary for Children was a smaller version of *The New Winston Dictionary for Young People* (eventually revised and retitled *The Winston Dictionary for Schools*). Whereas *The New Winston Dictionary for Young People* defined 46,000 terms, the children's abridgment included only 30,000 entries. Also, some entries were simplified.

Winston Home, School and Office Dictionary

Initially published in 1919 and revised as recently as 1956, *The Winston Home, School and Office Dictionary* (1,024 pages) covered over 60,000 terms. The definitions were quite brief and there were a number of useful appendixes, e.g., a section on business forms and law. The dictionary was also published in a slightly larger edition (1,280 pages) entitled *The New Secretary's Desk Book* (also out of print).

World University Dictionary

World University Dictionary—also *World Universal Dictionary*—are alternate titles for *Webster's New American Dictionary*, an inferior work of 66,000 entries which is also out of print (see above).

APPENDIX B

DICTIONARY BIBLIOGRAPHY

Additional Sources for Dictionary Evaluations

American Reference Books Annual. (ARBA). Littleton, Colo.: Libraries Unlimited, Inc., 1970– . *ARBA* is subtitled a "Comprehensive annual reviewing service for reference books published in the United States." The chief value of the service is the quantity, not quality, of coverage. The signed reviews, which tend to be brief and critical, vary from competent to mediocre or worse, depending on the caliber of the particular reviewer. Unfortunately, over the years the dictionary reviews have too often fallen into the latter category. The reviewers, almost all librarians, contribute their opinions gratis.

Booklist. Chicago: American Library Association, 1905– . Semi-monthly. This periodical includes unsigned reviews by the ALA Reference and Subscription Books Review Committee (RSBRC), a group of 50 librarians who volunteer their time and comments. The Committee, established in 1930, at one time produced from 35 to 50 carefully considered reviews each year and was widely regarded as the last word in reference book criticism. In recent times, however, while the number of RSBRC reviews has increased greatly, the quality of the criticism has noticeably deteriorated. The reviews are quite uneven in treatment and style, frequently appear ludicrously late, often lack vital comparisons with analogous publications, and tend to belabor superficial features of the work under review while ignoring matters of substance. The dictionary reviews are especially unreliable. For instance, the January 15, 1975 review of *Funk & Wagnalls Comprehensive Standard International Dictionary* (Bicentennial Edition, 1973) is so slipshod that it neglected to mention that the dictionary's main text is almost identical to that of *Funk & Wagnalls Standard Dictionary* (International Edition), a two-volume work first published in 1958 and not significantly revised since that time. The Bicentennial Edition, which costs $49.95, was "recommended." Under no circumstances should RSBRC reviews, especially those of recent vintage, be used as the sole authority for the purchase of a dictionary.

Cheney, Frances Neel. *Fundamental Reference Sources.* Chicago: American Library Association, 1971. Chapter 4, called "Sources on Words," includes a brief but knowledgeable review of major English-language dictionaries and wordbooks.

Choice. Middletown, Conn.: Association of College and Research Libraries, a division of the American Library Association, 1964– . Monthly. This book review journal, a selection aid for academic librarians, provides unsigned reviews which are concise and generally thought to be reliable. The reviewers, usually junior level faculty members at American colleges and universities, evaluate some 6,000 titles annually. New dictionaries and major revisions of older titles are sometimes covered, sometimes not.

Katz, William A. *Basic Information Sources* (vol. 1 of *Introduction to Reference Work*), 2nd ed. New York: McGraw-Hill, 1974. Bill Katz's comments on dictionaries are succinct, readable, and informative. See Chapter 10 entitled "Dictionaries" for an overview of the most important or noteworthy titles.

Library Journal. (*LJ*). New York: R. R. Bowker Company, 1876– . Semimonthly (monthly in July and August). *LJ* reviews are short, generally bland, and often more descriptive than critical. The reviewers, who work for a by-line and a copy of the book, are mostly recruited from public libraries around the country. For a number of years, one reviewer—B. Hunter Smeaton of the Linguistics Department of the University of Calgary (Canada)—has evaluated the major dictionary sources for *LJ*. His opinions are sound and hence the *Buying Guide* includes citations to *LJ*'s dictionary reviews.

RQ. Chicago: Reference and Adult Services Division of the American Library Association, 1960– . Quarterly. *RQ* (which stands for *Reference Quarterly*) includes a section devoted to reference book reviews. The signed reviews are by librarians, usually from the academic field. Though often fairly lengthy (half a page to a page), the reviews vary greatly in quality. Over the years, the number and type of reference works covered in *RQ* have fluctuated from editor to editor. General English-language dictionaries have never been systematically covered, though wordbooks are occasionally reviewed.

Sheehy, Eugene P., comp. *Guide to Reference Books*, 9th ed. Chicago: American Library Association, 1976. This essential list, formerly prepared by Constance M. Winchell, includes brief notes on selected dictionaries and wordbooks of all types. The annotations normally contain only descriptive information.

Wilson Library Bulletin. New York: H. W. Wilson Company, 1914– Monthly (except July and August). Succinct reviews of reference books appear in Charles A. Bunge's column "Current Reference Books" in the back of the magazine. Dr. Bunge's critical comments are usually informed, incisive, and reliable. New English-language dictionaries and wordbooks from major publishers are covered.

Other Informative Books and Articles about Dictionaries

Bailey, Richard W. "Research Dictionaries," *American Speech*, Fall 1969, pp. 166–172. Originally a paper delivered at a lexicography meeting of the Modern Language Association, Bailey's article knowledgeably assesses the problems encountered in making a scholarly dictionary.

Barnhart, Clarence L. "General Dictionaries," *American Speech*, Fall 1969, pp. 173–178. A companion article to Bailey's (see above), this is an instructive view of commercial lexicography by America's premier lexicographer.

Brewer, Annie M., comp. *Dictionaries, Encyclopedias, and Other Word-Related Books, 1966–1974*. Detroit: Gale Research Company, 1975. Library of Congress catalog cards for dictionaries, encyclopedias, concordances, glossaries, gazetteers, thesauri, and the like published between 1966 and 1974 are arranged by LC classification order and reprinted here, 18 cards to the page. Both general and specialized works are included. Useful for bibliographic information.

Collison, Robert L. "Dictionaries before 1800," in *Encyclopedia of Library and Information Science*, vol. 7. Edited by Allen Kent and Harold Lancour. New York: Marcel Dekker, Inc., 1972, pp. 170–191. An erudite overview of the development of English-language dictionaries up to 1800.

Collison, Robert L. *Dictionaries of English and Foreign Language: A Bibliographical Guide to Both General and Technical Dictionaries with Historical and Explanatory Notes and References*, 2nd ed. New York: Hafner, 1971. A revision and enlargement of Collison's *Dictionaries of Foreign Languages* (1955). Useful for historical and bibliographic information about dictionaries around the world.

Douglas, George H. "What's Happened to the Thesaurus?" *RQ*, Winter 1976, pp. 149–155. An English professor speculates about the future of synonym dictionaries and particularly Roget's *Thesaurus*.

Evans, Bergen. "'dik-shə-ner-ēs 'ōld & 'n(y)ü," *Today's Education*, February 1970, pp. 24–27. Evans highlights major English-language dictionary developments from Cawdrey's *Table Alphabeticall* to *The American Heritage Dictionary*. Along the way he asserts that dictionaries have no business attempting to dictate proper usage. (See also "More about 'dik-shə-ner-ēs" in the March 1970, *Today's Education* in which Morris Bishop, Theodore Bernstein, and the late Wilson Follett reply to Evans.)

Guralnik, David B. "The Making of a Dictionary," *The Bulletin of the Cleveland Medical Library*," January 1977, pp. 5–23. In this informative article, one of the country's most experienced and successful lexicographers recounts how Webster's New World dictionary series evolved.

Hoss, Norman. "Words," *Penthouse*, January 1974, pp. 36–37. The managing editor of *The American Heritage Dictionary* discusses the "dirty words" issue in this amusing piece subtitled "Lexicography in America, or Why Texans Don't Shit."

Hulbert, James R. *Dictionaries: British and American*, rev. ed. London: Deutsch, 1968. First published in 1955, this small book does not evaluate individual titles but provides general information on the history, production, and uses of dictionaries. The revised edition (prepared by S. Potter and E. Partridge) has added material about etymology and slang.

Kučera, Henry. "Computers in Language Analysis and in Lexicography," in *The American Heritage Dictionary*. Edited by William Morris. Boston: Houghton Mifflin, New College Edition, 1976, pp. xxxviii–xl. A readable, authoritative discussion of the application of computers to dictionary-making.

Landau, Sidney I. "Little Boy and Little Girl," *American Speech*, Fall/ Winter 1970, pp. 195–204. The editor of the Funk & Wagnalls dictionaries and the recent *Doubleday Dictionary* discourses on compound words and bias in lexicography.

Landau, Sidney I. "The Numbers' Game: Dictionary Entry Count," *RQ*, September 1964, pp. 6, 13–15. Landau says the entry count "can be a useful guide in estimating a dictionary's comparative size and comprehensiveness"—if it is understood what an entry is and how they are counted.

Read, Allen Walker. "Approaches to Lexicography and Semantics," in *Current Trends in Linguistics*, vol. 10. The Hague, Netherlands: Mouton & Company, 1972, pp. 145–205. An excellent, informative review of modern lexicographical developments and concerns. The article contains an especially good bibliography.

Read, Allen Walker. "Dictionary," in *Encyclopaedia Britannica—Macropaedia*, vol. 5. Chicago: Encyclopaedia Britannica, Inc., 1977, pp. 713–722. The most thorough and up-to-date encyclopedia article on dictionaries.

Rogers, Byron. "Eric Partridge and the Underworld of Language," *Horizon*, Winter 1976, pp. 49–53. An affectionate look at the "Godfather of slang."

Sledd, James, and Ebbitt, Wilma, R. *Dictionaries and That Dictionary*. Chicago: Scott, Foresman & Company, 1962. Pro and con articles and reviews about the unabridged *Webster's Third New International Dictionary*, which was labeled permissive by its critics when it appeared in 1961. Repercussions of this intense debate are still felt today in dictionary circles.

Stubbs, K. L. "Dictionaries after 1800," in *Encyclopedia of Library and Information Science*, vol. 7. Edited by Allen Kent and Harold Lancour. New York: Marcel Dekker, Inc., 1972, pp. 191–207. A companion piece to Collison's "Dictionaries before 1800" (see above).

U.S. General Services Administration. Federal Supply Service. *Federal Specification: Dictionaries, English*. Washington, D.C.: Government Printing Office, June 28, 1974. (Superintendent of Documents Number: GS 2.8: G-D-331D.) This eight-page document details specifications for U.S. government purchase of general English-language dictionaries. The specifications are described at some length in the section "Choosing the Right Dictionary" in Part I of the *Buying Guide*.

Wells, Ronald A. *Dictionaries and the Authoritarian Tradition: A Study in English Usage and Lexicography*. The Hague, Netherlands: Mouton & Company, 1973. A scholarly monograph of 129 pages that "examines the tradition which has associated conservative or authoritarian attitudes with dictionaries of English, and which has perpetuated the fiction that the dictionary establishes the standard of usage for the language" (preface). Extensive bibliography.

Whittaker, Kenneth. *Dictionaries*. New York: Philosophical Library, 1966. The author, a senior lecturer at Manchester Polytechnic (England), briefly covers what dictionaries intend to do, how to use them effectively, their historical development, the various types, and criteria for selection. The final sections survey individual titles, though in no great depth. Recently, Whittaker himself described the book as "rather slight and now somewhat dated" (*RQ*, Fall 1972, p. 51).

Recent General-Interest Books on Language

Chomsky, Noam. *Reflections on Language*. New York: Pantheon, 1976. A collection of essays and lectures which elucidates Professor Chomsky's conviction that the human linguistic capability is innate and that a common grammatical structure underlies the world's many and varied languages.

Dillard, Joey Lee. *American Talk: Where Our Words Came From*. New York: Random House, 1976. Dillard argues that American English is widely influenced by black, Latino, Jewish, and other ethnic cultures.

Dillard, Joey Lee. *Black English: Its History and Usage in the U.S.* New York: Random House, 1972. A readable study of the contributions of black English to American English. Dillard's other books on the subject are *All-American English* (Random House, 1975) and *Lexicon of Black English: The Words the Slaves Made* (New York: Seabury, 1977). Note that the latter book is not a dictionary despite the word *lexicon* in the title.

Hartmann, R. R. K., and Stork, F. C. *Dictionary of Language and Linguistics*. New York: Halsted (a division of John Wiley), 1972. This specialized dictionary contains some 2,600 entries covering all branches of language and linguistic study. The best work of its kind available.

Katzner, Kenneth. *The Languages of the World*. New York: Funk & Wagnalls, 1975. A useful survey which lists, groups, and describes 500 of the world's living languages, including English.

Laird, Charlton Grant. *Language in America*. New York: World Publishing Company, 1970. Professor Laird, who believes that linguistic development and cultural achievement are interrelated, examines American English and its effect on our attitudes and institutions.

Miller, Casey, and Swift, Kate. *Words and Women: New Language in New Times*. New York: Anchor/Doubleday, 1976. Miller and Swift document pervasive sexism in the English language and offer practical suggestions for its elimination.

Newman, Edwin. *A Civil Tongue*. New York: Bobbs-Merrill, 1976. A sequel to *Strictly Speaking* (see below).

Newman, Edwin. *Strictly Speaking: Will America Be the Death of English?* New York: Bobbs-Merrill, 1974. Newman, an NBC news commentator, bemoans the lack of standards regarding language usage, the corruption of English by bureaucrats and others, and the introduction of such words as *optimize*, *prioritize*, and *studenthood*. Written in an entertaining, popular style.

Pei, Mario. *Words in Sheep's Clothing*. New York: Hawthorn, 1969. A breezy look at various words which have changed their meaning in recent times due to political, racial, or economic developments.

Shipley, Joseph T. *In Praise of English: The Growth and Use of Language*. New York: Times Books, 1977. A popularly written history of the English language, this book covers such topics as slang, vulgarisms, puns, synonyms, and the use of words in advertising, politics, propaganda, and psychology.

Smitherman, Geneva. *Talkin and Testifyin: the Language of Black America*. Boston: Houghton Mifflin, 1977. The author, a Wayne State University professor, contends that black English is a valid language and should be treated as an independent dialect, not as slang or a corruption of American English.

Stoller, Paul, ed. *Black American English: Its History and Its Usage in the Schools and in Literature*. New York: Dell, 1975. An original paperback, this collection of essays complements Smitherman's *Talkin and Testifyin* (see above).

APPENDIX C

DIRECTORY OF U.S. PUBLISHERS AND DISTRIBUTORS

Airmont Publishing Co., Inc.
Distributed by Associated Booksellers
147 McKinley Ave.
Bridgeport, Conn. 06606
203-366-5494
Webster's Scholastic Dictionary

American Book Co. (by arrangement with the G. & C. Merriam Co.)
450 W. 33 St.
New York, N.Y. 10001
212-594-8660
Webster's Intermediate Dictionary (Text Edition)
Webster's New Elementary Dictionary (Text Edition)
Webster's New Students Dictionary (Text Edition)

American Elsevier Publishing Co., Inc.
See Elsevier North-Holland, Inc.

American Heritage Publishing Co., Inc.
See Houghton Mifflin Co.

Arno Press, Inc.
3 Park Ave.
New York, N.Y. 10016
212-725-2050
Name into Word

Atheneum Publishers
122 E. 42 St.
New York, N.Y. 10017
212-661-4500
The Careful Writer
Watch Your Language

Banner Press
See Hippocrene Books, Inc.

Bantam Books, Inc.
666 Fifth Ave.
New York, N.Y. 10019

212-765-6500
Dictionary of English Synonyms
How to Speak Southern
Thorndike-Barnhart Handy Pocket Dictionary

A. S. Barnes & Co., Inc.
Forsgate Dr.
Cranbury, N.J. 08512
609-655-0190
Dictionary of Pronunciation (Noory)

Barnes & Noble, Inc. (a division of Harper & Row, Publishers, Inc.)
10 E. 53 St.
New York, N.Y. 10022
212-593-7000
Allen's Synonyms and Antonyms (paper)
New Rhyming Dictionary of One and Two Syllable Rhymes
Webster's Dictionary (pocket)
Webster's Dictionary for Everyday Use
Webster's Synonyms, Antonyms and Homonyms

Barnhart/Harper & Row, Publishers
See Harper & Row, Publishers, Inc.

Barron's Educational Series, Inc.
113 Crossways Park Dr.
Woodbury, N.Y. 11797
516-921-8750
Dictionary of American Idioms

Beginner Books (a division of Random House, Inc.)
201 E. 50 St.
New York, N.Y. 10022
212-751-2600
Cat in the Hat Beginner Book Dictionary

Berkley Publishing Corp. (an affiliate
of G. P. Putnam's Sons, Inc.)
200 Madison Ave.
New York, N.Y. 10016
212-883-5500
New Roget's Thesaurus (paper)

Bobbs-Merrill Co., Inc.
4 W. 58 St.
New York, N.Y. 10019
212-688-6350
Jazz Talk

Books for Libraries Press, Inc.
See Arno Press, Inc.

R. R. Bowker Co. (a Xerox Publishing
Company)
1180 Ave. of the Americas
New York, N.Y. 10036
212-764-5100
World Guide to Abbreviations

British Book Centre, Inc. (a division of
Pergamon Press)
153 E. 78 St.
New York, N.Y. 10021
212-879-6577
Children's Dictionary
Usage and Abusage

Cambridge University Press
32 E. 57 St.
New York, N.Y. 10022
212-688-8885
Preparation of Manuscripts

Career Institute, Inc.
See Franklin Watts, Inc.

Carroll Book Service, Inc.
Box 1776
North Tarrytown, N.Y. 10591
914-631-1776
International Visual Dictionary

Childrens Press
1224 W. Van Buren St.
Chicago, Ill. 60607
312-666-4200
Dictionary of Basic Words
Picture Book Dictionary

Chilton Book Co.
201 King of Prussia Rd.
Radnor, Pa. 19089

215-687-8200
Human Words
Truck Talk

Citadel Press
See Lyle Stuart, Inc.

Clute International Institute
See Carroll Book Service, Inc.

**William Collins+World Publishing Co.,
Inc.**
2080 W. 117 St.
Cleveland, Ohio 44111
216-941-6930
American Words
*Collins Gem Dictionary of American
Usage*
*Collins Gem Dictionary for Cross-
word Puzzles*
*Collins Gem Dictionary of Synonyms
& Antonyms*
Collins Gem Word Speller & Divider
English Gem Dictionary
*Rainbow Dictionary for Young
Readers*
*Webster's New Twentieth Century
Dictionary*
*Webster's New World Crossword Puz-
zle Dictionary*
*Webster's New World Dictionary
(Second College Edition)*
*Webster's New World Dictionary
(Compact School & Office Edition)*
*Webster's New World Dictionary
(Second Concise Edition)*
*Webster's New World Dictionary
(Modern Desk Edition)*
*Webster's New World Dictionary for
Young Readers*
*Webster's New World Handy Pocket
Dictionary*
*Webster's New World Quick Refer-
ence Dictionary*
Webster's New World Thesaurus
*Webster's New World 33,000 Word
Book*
*Webster's New World 20,000 Word
Book*
*Webster's New World Vest Pocket
Dictionary*
*Wood's Unabridged Rhyming Dictio-
nary*

Commonwealth Books, Inc.
See Dennison Manufacturing Co.

Commonwealth Press, Inc.
Box 3547
First St. Sta.
Radford, Va. 24141
703-639-2475
Mountain-ese

Consolidated Book Publishers (a division of Processing and Books, Inc.)
420 Lexington Ave.
New York, N.Y. 10017
212-867-2255
Living Webster Encyclopedic Dictionary
New Webster's Dictionary

Thomas Y. Crowell Co., Inc. (a subsidiary of Harper & Row, Publishers, Inc.)
10 E. 53 St.
New York, N.Y. 10022
212-489-2200
Apollo Crossword Puzzle Dictionary (Apollo Edition)
Complete Dictionary of Abbreviations
Complete University Word Hunter (Apollo Edition)
Crossword Puzzle Dictionary
Current American Usage
Dictionary of American Slang
Dictionary of Correct Spelling
Dictionary of Foreign Terms (Mawson/Berlitz)
Funk & Wagnalls Comprehensive Standard International Dictionary
Funk & Wagnalls Crossword Puzzle Word Finder
Funk & Wagnalls Modern Guide to Synonyms
Funk & Wagnalls New Standard Dictionary
Funk & Wagnalls Standard College Dictionary
Funk & Wagnalls Standard Desk Dictionary
Funk & Wagnalls Standard Handbook of Synonyms
NBC Handbook of Pronunciation
Poet's Manual and Rhyming Dictionary
Roget's International Thesaurus
Roget's University Thesaurus (Apollo Edition)
Whitfield's University Rhyming Dictionary (Apollo Edition)

Crown Publishers, Inc.
419 Park Ave. S.
New York, N.Y. 10016
212-532-9200
New Webster's Crossword Puzzle Dictionary

Dabco Industries
Webster Division, Dept. F 11
1701 W. Lake St.
Glenview, Ill. 60025
Living Webster Encyclopedic Dictionary

Delacorte Press
One Dag Hammarskjold Plaza
245 E. 47 St.
New York, N.Y. 10017
212-832-7300
Dictionary of Foreign Terms (Pei)

Dell Publishing Co., Inc.
One Dag Hammarskjold Plaza
245 E. 47 St.
New York, N.Y. 10017
212-832-7300
American Heritage Dictionary (Paperback Edition)
Dictionary of Foreign Terms (Pei)

Dennison Manufacturing Co.
Framingham, Mass. 01701
617-879-0511
New Webster's Vest Pocket Dictionary
Roget's Thesaurus of Synonyms and Antonyms
Webster's Dictionary (pocket)
Webster's Vest-Pocket Synonyms, Antonyms and Homonyms

Dome, Inc.
1169 Logan Ave.
Elgin, Ill. 60120
312-695-6661
Living Word Vocabulary

Doubleday & Co., Inc.
245 Park Ave
New York, N.Y. 10017
212-953-4561
Complete Rhyming Dictionary
Doubleday Dictionary
Doubleday Roget's Thesaurus
Expert's Crossword Puzzle Dictionary
New Practical Dictionary for Cross-Word Puzzles

Scott, Foresman Beginning Dictionary (Trade Edition)
Thorndike-Barnhart Advanced Dictionary (Trade Edition)
Thorndike-Barnhart Advanced Junior Dictionary (Trade Edition)
Thorndike-Barnhart Beginning Dictionary (Trade Edition)
Thorndike-Barnhart Handy Pocket Dictionary (dist. by Bantam Books, Inc.)
Thorndike-Barnhart Intermediate Dictionary (Trade Edition)
Unabridged Crossword Puzzle Dictionary

Dover Publications, Inc.
180 Varick St.
New York, N.Y. 10014
212-255-3755
Etymological Dictionary of Modern English
Phrase and Word Origins
Shepherd's Glossary of Graphic Signs and Symbols

Down East Magazine
Bayview St.
Camden, Maine 04843
207-236-4354
Maine Lingo

E. P. Dutton & Co., Inc.
201 Park Ave. S.
New York, N.Y. 10003
212-674-5900
Rhyming Dictionary of the English Language

Wm. Thatcher Elliott, publisher
See Hancock House Publishers, Inc.

Elsevier North-Holland, Inc.
52 Vanderbilt Ave.
New York, N.Y. 10017
212-686-5277
Abbreviations Dictionary
Comprehensive Etymological Dictionary

Elsevier Publishing Co.
See Elsevier North-Holland, Inc.

English Language Institute of America
332 S. Michigan Ave.
Suite 963
Chicago, Ill. 60604
312-663-0880

Dictionary of Contemporary and Colloquial Usage
Living Webster Encyclopedic Dictionary (dist. by Consolidated Book Publishers)
The Third Ear

Exposition Press, Inc.
900 S. Oyster Bay Rd.
Hicksville, N.Y. 11801
516-822-5700
Synonyms, Antonyms and Related Words

Farrar, Straus & Giroux, Inc.
19 Union Sq. W.
New York, N.Y. 10003
212-741-6900
Miss Thistlebottom's Hobgoblins

Fawcett World Library
1515 Broadway
New York, N.Y. 10036
212-869-3000
New Webster's Crossword Puzzle Dictionary

J. G. Ferguson Publishing Co. (a subsidiary of Doubleday & Co., Inc.)
111 E. Wacker St.
Chicago, Ill. 60601
312-782-8284
Funk & Wagnalls Comprehensive Standard International Dictionary (dist. by T. Y. Crowell Co., Inc.)
Funk & Wagnalls Standard Dictionary (International Edition)
Funk & Wagnalls Standard Encyclopedic Dictionary

Field Enterprises Educational Corp.
510 Merchandise Mart Plaza
Chicago, Ill. 60654
312-341-2424
Living Word Vocabulary (dist. by Dome, Inc.)
World Book Dictionary

Follett Publishing Co.
1010 W. Washington Blvd.
Chicago, Ill. 60607
312-666-5858
Follett Beginning-to-Read Picture Dictionary
Follett Vest-Pocket 50,000 Words
Follett Vest-Pocket Secretary's Handbook

Follett Vest-Pocket Webster Dictionary

Funk & Wagnalls, Inc. (a subsidiary of Dun & Bradstreet Inc.)
666 Fifth Ave.
New York, N.Y. 10019
212-581-3122
Current American Usage (dist. by T. Y. Crowell Co., Inc.)
Dictionary of Correct Spelling (dist. by T. Y. Crowell Co., Inc.)
Funk & Wagnalls Crossword Puzzle Word Finder (dist. by T. Y. Crowell Co., Inc.)
Funk & Wagnalls Modern Guide to Synonyms (dist. by T. Y. Crowell Co., Inc.)
Funk & Wagnalls New Standard Dictionary (dist. by T. Y. Crowell Co., Inc.)
Funk & Wagnalls Standard College Dictionary (dist. by T. Y. Crowell Co., Inc.)
Funk & Wagnalls Standard Desk Dictionary (dist. by T. Y. Crowell Co., Inc.)
Funk & Wagnalls Standard Handbook of Synonyms (dist. by T. Y. Crowell Co., Inc.)

Funk & Wagnalls Publishing Co., Inc.
See Funk & Wagnalls, Inc.

Gale Research Co.
Book Tower
Detroit, Mich. 48226
313-961-2242
Acronyms, Initialisms, & Abbreviations Dictionary
Bell's Acrostic Dictionary
Dictionary of Collective Nouns
Eponyms Dictionaries Index
New Acronyms, Initialisms, & Abbreviations
Reverse Acronyms, Initialisms, & Abbreviations Dictionary
World Guide to Abbreviations of Organizations

Gaylord Bros., Inc.
Box 61
Syracuse, N.Y. 13201
315-457-5070
Dictionary of Acronyms & Abbreviations (paper)

Second Dictionary of Acronyms & Abbreviations (paper)

Ginn & Co. (a Xerox Publishing Company)
191 Spring St.
Lexington, Mass. 02173
617-861-1670
Ginn Beginning Dictionary
Ginn Intermediate Dictionary

Glencoe Press
See Macmillan Publishing Co., Inc.

Golden Press
See Western Publishing Co., Inc.

Greenwood Press
51 Riverside Ave.
Westport, Conn. 06880
203-226-3571
Concise Usage and Abusage
Dictionary of Foreign Words and Phrases
Dictionary of Word Origins

Grosset & Dunlap, Inc.
51 Madison Ave.
New York, N.Y. 10010
212-689-9200
Clear and Simple Thesaurus Dictionary
Grosset & Dunlap Word Finder
Grosset Starter Picture Dictionary
Len Buckwalter's CB Channel Dictionary (Grosset & Dunlap/Today Press)
My First Dictionary
New American Roget's College Thesaurus
New Comprehensive A–Z Crossword Dictionary
Picture Dictionary for Children
Roget's Thesaurus of Words and Phrases
Weekly Reader Beginning Dictionary
Xerox Intermediate Dictionary (Xerox Family Education Services)

G. K. Hall & Co.
70 Lincoln St.
Boston, Mass. 02111
617-423-3990
Merriam-Webster Dictionary for Large Print Users

Halsted Press (a division of John Wiley & Sons, Inc.)
605 Third Ave.
New York, N.Y. 10016
212-867-9800
Concept Dictionary of English

Hancock House Publishers, Inc.
12008 First Ave. S.
Seattle, Wash. 98168
206-243-1500
Elliott's foe-né-tic Spelling Dictionary

Harcourt Brace Jovanovich, Inc.
757 Third Ave.
New York, N.Y. 10017
212-754-3100
Handbook of American English Spelling (Text Edition)
Harcourt Brace Intermediate Dictionary
HBJ School Dictionary

Hardscrabble Press
See Van Nostrand Reinhold Co.

Harper & Row, Publishers, Inc.
10 E. 53 St.
New York, N.Y. 10022
212-593-7000
Allen's Synonyms and Antonyms
Barnhart Dictionary of New English since 1963 (Barnhart/Harper & Row)
Brewer's Dictionary of Phrase and Fable
Dictionary of Word and Phrase Origins
Harper Dictionary of Contemporary Usage
Heavens to Betsy!
Hog on Ice
Horsefeathers
Look It Up
New Rhyming Dictionary and Poets' Handbook
Successful Secretary's Handbook
Thereby Hangs a Tale
What's the Difference? A British/ American Dictionary
Wordpower

Hawthorn Books, Inc.
260 Madison Ave.
New York, N.Y. 10016
212-725-7740
Dictionary of Foreign Terms (Carroll)

Hill & Wang (a division of Farrar, Straus & Giroux, Inc.)
19 Union Sq. W.
New York, N.Y. 10003
212-741-6900
Modern American Usage

Hippocrene Books, Inc.
171 Madison Ave.
New York, N.Y. 10016
212-685-4371
Langenscheidt Lilliput Webster English Dictionary
Langenscheidt Universal Webster Dictionary
38,000 Words
Webster's Dictionary (abridged)

Holt, Rinehart and Winston (a subsidiary of CBS, Inc.)
383 Madison Ave.
New York, N.Y. 10017
212-688-9100
Holt Intermediate Dictionary
Winston Dictionary for Schools
Word Wonder Dictionary

Houghton Mifflin Co.
One Beacon St.
Boston, Mass. 02107
617-725-5000
American Heritage Dictionary (New College Edition)
American Heritage Dictionary (Standard or Larger Format Edition)
American Heritage School Dictionary
American Heritage Word Frequency Book
Concise Heritage Dictionary
Illustrated Heritage Dictionary and Information Book
The Word Book

Indiana University Press
Tenth & Morton Sts.
Bloomington, Ind. 47401
812-337-4203
Style Manual for Authors

International Publications Service
114 E. 32 St.
New York, N.Y. 10016
212-685-9351
Cassell's Dictionary of Abbreviations

International Publishers Co., Inc.
381 Park Ave. S.
New York, N.Y. 10016
212-MU5-2864
Dictionary of Afro-American Slang

Alfred A. Knopf, Inc.
201 E. 50 St.
New York, N.Y. 10022
212-751-2600
The American Language

Larousse & Co., Inc.
572 Fifth Ave.
New York, N.Y. 10036
212-575-9515
English Larousse
Larousse Illustrated International Encyclopedia and Dictionary (World Publishing Co.)
Strawberry Picture Dictionary

Linstok Press
9306 Mintwood St.
Silver Springs, Md. 20901
Dictionary of American Sign Language

Littlefield, Adams & Co.
81 Adams Dr.
Totowa, N.J. 07512
201-256-8600
Chambers' English Dictionary
Chambers Etymological English Dictionary
Chambers Twentieth Century Dictionary
Dictionary of English Word-Roots
Dictionary of Word Origins
Hugo Pocket Dictionary: English

Longman, Inc.
19 W. 44 St.
New York, N.Y. 10036
212-354-3166
International Reader's Dictionary

Lothrop, Lee & Shepard Co. (a division of William Morrow & Co., Inc.)
105 Madison Ave.
New York, N.Y. 10016
212-889-3050
In Other Words I: A Beginning Thesaurus (Library Edition)
In Other Words II: A Junior Thesaurus (Library Edition)

My First Picture Dictionary (Library Edition)
My Pictionary (Library Edition)
My Second Picture Dictionary (Library Edition)

Macdonald-Raintree, Inc.
205 W. Highland Ave.
Milwaukee, Wis. 53203
414-276-3430
Oxford Universal Dictionary Illustrated
Two Thousand Plus Index & Glossary

McGraw-Hill Book Co.
1221 Ave. of the Americas
New York, N.Y. 10020
212-997-1221
Complete Scrabble Dictionary
Dictionary of Do's and Don'ts
Dictionary of Problem Words and Expressions
Larousse Illustrated International Dictionary
Larousse Illustrated International Encyclopedia and Dictionary
Standard Handbook for Secretaries
Symbol Sourcebook
20,000 Words
Washington Post Deskbook on Style

David McKay Co., Inc.
750 Third Ave.
New York, N.Y. 10017
212-661-1700
Word Watcher's Handbook

Macmillan Publishing Co., Inc.
866 Third Ave.
New York, N.Y. 10022
212-935-2000
British Self-Taught: With Comments in American
Dictionary of Clichés
Dictionary of Slang and Unconventional English
Dictionary of the Underworld, British and American
The Elements of Style
Macmillan Beginning Dictionary
Macmillan Dictionary
Macmillan Dictionary for Children
Macmillan Dictionary of Historical Slang
Macmillan School Dictionary

New Standard Reference for Secre-
taries
Origins
The Secretary's Handbook
The Word Book (Glencoe Press)

Louis J. Martin Associates
95 Madison Ave.
New York, N.Y. 10016
212-725-2157
'Official' CB Slanguage Language
Dictionary

G. & C. Merriam Co. (a subsidiary of
Encyclopaedia Britannica, Inc.)
47 Federal St.
Springfield, Mass. 01101
413-734-3134
Pronouncing Dictionary of American
English
6,000 Words
Webster's Collegiate Thesaurus
Webster's Concise Family Dictionary
Webster's Instant Word Guide
Webster's Intermediate Dictionary
(Trade Edition)
Webster's New Collegiate Dictionary
(Eighth Edition)
Webster's New Dictionary of Syno-
nyms
Webster's New Elementary Dictionary
(Trade Edition)
Webster's New Ideal Dictionary
Webster's New Students Dictionary
(Trade Edition)
Webster's Secretarial Handbook
Webster's Seventh New Collegiate Dic-
tionary (Large Format Edition)
Webster's Third New International
Dictionary

William Morrow & Co., Inc.
105 Madison Ave.
New York, N.Y. 10016
212-889-3050
Reference Handbook of Grammar &
Usage

National Council of Teachers of En-
glish
1111 Kenyon Rd.
Urbana, Ill. 61801
217-328-3870
Variant Spellings in Modern American
Dictionaries

The New American Library, Inc. (a sub-
sidiary of The Times Mirror Co.,
Inc.)
1301 Ave. of the Americas
New York, N.Y. 10019
212-956-3800
Dictionary of American-English Us-
age
Dictionary of Difficult Words
New American Crossword Puzzle Dic-
tionary
New American Roget's College The-
saurus (paper)
New American Webster Handy Col-
lege Dictionary
New Horizon Ladder Dictionary
Webster's New World Dictionary
(100,000 Entry Edition)
Webster's New World Thesaurus (pa-
per)

Newhouse Press
Box 24282 Westwood
Los Angeles, Calif. 90024
Encyclopedia of Homonyms

W. W. Norton & Co., Inc.
500 Fifth Ave.
New York, N.Y. 10036
212-354-5500
Reader's Digest Family Word Finder

Ottenheimer Publishers, Inc.
1632 Reisterstown Rd.
Baltimore, Md. 21208
301-484-2100
Webster's Encyclopedia of Dictio-
naries

Oxford University Press, Inc.
200 Madison Ave.
New York, N.Y. 10016
212-679-7300
Concise Etymological Dictionary
Concise Oxford Dictionary
Concise Pronouncing Dictionary of
British and American English
Dictionary of Modern American Us-
age
Dictionary of Modern English Usage
English-Reader's Dictionary
Etymological Dictionary of the En-
glish Language
The King's English
Little Oxford Dictionary

Oxford Advanced Learner's Dictionary
Oxford Children's Dictionary in Colour
Oxford Dictionary of Current Idiomatic English
Oxford Dictionary of English Etymology
Oxford English Dictionary (with Supplements)
Oxford Illustrated Dictionary
Oxford School Dictionary
Oxford Universal Dictionary Illustrated (dist. by Macdonald-Raintree)
Pocket Oxford Dictionary
Progressive English Dictionary
Shorter Oxford English Dictionary

Parents' Magazine Press
52 Vanderbilt Ave.
New York, N.Y. 10017
212-685-4400
Handtalk

Parker Publishing Co.
See Prentice-Hall, Inc.

Pathmark Books, Inc.
1238 Chestnut St.
Box 115
Newton Upper Falls, Mass. 02164
617-964-2300
Roget's Thesaurus of Synonyms and Antonyms
Webster's Dictionary (abridged)

Pierian Press
Box 1808
Ann Arbor, Mich. 48106
313-434-5530
Abbreviations: A Reverse Guide
Words and Phrases Index

Playboy Press (a division of Playboy Enterprises, Inc.)
919 N. Michigan Ave.
Chicago, Ill. 60611
312-751-8000
Playboy's Book of Forbidden Words

Pocket Books, Inc. (a division of Simon & Schuster, Inc.)
630 Fifth Ave.
New York, N.Y. 10020

212-245-6400
Merriam-Webster Book of Word Histories
Merriam-Webster Dictionary
Merriam-Webster Pocket Dictionary of Synonyms
Pocket Crossword Puzzle Dictionary
Pocket Dictionary of American Slang
Roget's Pocket Thesaurus
Webster's New World Crossword Puzzle Dictionary

Popular Library, Inc. (a division of CBS, Inc.)
600 Third Ave.
New York, N.Y. 10016
212-975-4321
Desk Top Reference Library
Dictionary of Synonyms and Antonyms
Webster's New World Dictionary (Pocket-size Edition)
Webster's New World Thesaurus (paper)
Webster's Red Seal Crossword Dictionary

Prentice-Hall, Inc.
Englewood Cliffs, N.J. 07632
201-592-2440
Complete Secretary's Handbook
Encyclopedic Dictionary of English Usage
Modern Secretary's Guide (Parker Publishing Co.)
Sisson's Synonyms (Parker Publishing Co.)
Sisson's Word and Expression Locater (Parker Publishing Co.)
Webster's New World Dictionary (Special School Printing)
Word Finder
Words into Type

G. P. Putnam's Sons, Inc.
200 Madison Ave.
New York, N.Y. 10016
212-576-8900
Capricorn Rhyming Dictionary
New Roget's Thesaurus

Pyramid Communications, Inc.
See Pyramid Publishers, Inc.

Pyramid Publishers, Inc.
9 Garden St.
Moonachie, N.J. 07074
201-641-3311
 Chambers Etymological English Dictionary
 Webster's Dictionary (dist. by Hippocrene Books, Inc.)

Quadrangle/The New York Times Book Co., Inc. (now **Times Books**)
3 Park Ave.
New York, N.Y. 10016
212-725-2050
 Bernstein's Reverse Dictionary
 Dictionary of Pronunciation (Lass)
 Do's, Don'ts and Maybes of English Usage
 Misspeller's Dictionary
 New York Times Crossword Puzzle Dictionary
 New York Times Everyday Reader's Dictionary
 New York Times Manual of Style and Usage

Raintree Publishers, Ltd.
See Macdonald-Raintree, Inc.

Random House, Inc. (a subsidiary of the RCA Corp.)
201 E. 50 St.
New York, N.Y. 10022
212-751-2600
 American College Dictionary
 Bad Speller's Dictionary
 Cat in the Hat Beginner Book Dictionary (Beginner Books)
 Charlie Brown Dictionary
 Dictionary of Contemporary American Usage
 Random House American Dictionary
 Random House American Everyday Dictionary
 Random House College Dictionary
 Random House Dictionary (School Edition)
 Random House Dictionary (Unabridged Edition)
 Random House Dictionary of Synonyms and Antonyms
 Random House Rhyming Dictionary

The Reader's Digest Association
Pleasantville, N.Y. 10570
914-769-7000

 Reader's Digest Family Word Finder (dist. by W. W. Norton & Co., Inc.)

Rodale Books, Inc.
33 E. Minor St.
Emmaus, Pa. 18049
215-967-5171
 Synonym Finder
 Word Finder

Routledge & Kegan Paul, Ltd.
9 Park St.
Boston, Mass. 02108
617-742-5863
 Dictionary of Rhyming Slang
 Slang To-day and Yesterday
 Smaller Slang Dictionary

Rowman & Littlefield, Inc. (a division of Littlefield, Adams & Co.)
81 Adams Dr.
Totowa, N.J. 07512
201-256-8600
 Everyman's Dictionary of Abbreviations
 General Basic English Dictionary

St. Martin's Press, Inc.
175 Fifth Ave.
New York, N.Y. 10010
212-674-5151
 Original Roget's Thesaurus

Scarecrow Press, Inc. (a subsidiary of Grolier Educational Corp.)
52 Liberty St.
Box 656
Metuchen, N.J. 08840
201-548-8600
 Dictionary of Gestures

Scholastic Paperbacks
906 Sylvan Ave.
Englewood Cliffs, N.J. 07632
 Charlie Brown Dictionary (paper)

Scott, Foresman & Co. (in association with Doubleday & Co., Inc.)
1900 E. Lake Ave.
Glenview, Ill. 60025
312-729-3000
 In Other Words I: A Beginning Thesaurus (Text Edition)
 In Other Words II: A Junior Thesaurus (Text Edition)
 My First Picture Dictionary (Text Edition)

My Pictionary (Text Edition)
My Second Picture Dictionary (Text Edition)
Scott, Foresman Beginning Dictionary (Text Edition)
Thorndike-Barnhart Advanced Dictionary (Text Edition)
Thorndike-Barnhart Advanced Junior Dictionary (Text Edition)
Thorndike-Barnhart Beginning Dictionary (Text Edition)
Thorndike-Barnhart Intermediate Dictionary (Text Edition)

Charles Scribner's Sons
597 Fifth Ave.
New York, N.Y. 10017
212-486-2700
Scribner-Bantam English Dictionary

Shoe String Press, Inc.
995 Sherman Ave.
Hamden, Conn. 06514
203-248-6307
Dictionary of Acronyms & Abbreviations
Second Dictionary of Acronyms & Abbreviations
Third Dictionary of Acronyms & Abbreviations

Simon & Schuster, Inc.
630 Fifth Ave.
New York, N.Y. 10020
212-245-6400
The Underground Dictionary

South-Western Publishing Co.
5101 Madison Rd.
Cincinnati, Ohio 45227
513-271-8811
Word Division Manual

Standard Educational Corp.
130 N. Wells St.
Chicago, Ill. 60606
312-346-7440
Words to Know

Straight Arrow Books
825 Third St.
San Francisco, Calif. 94107
415-362-4730
The Queens' Vernacular

Strawberry Books
See Larousse & Co., Inc.

Lyle Stuart, Inc.
120 Enterprise Ave.
Secaucus, N.J. 07094
201-866-0490
Book of Synonyms
Mrs. Byrne's Dictionary

Teachers College Press
Columbia Univ.
1234 Amsterdam Ave.
New York, N.Y. 10027
212-870-4078
Dictionary of American Homophones and Homographs
Teachers' Word Book of Thirty Thousand Words

Times Books
See Quadrangle/The New York Times Book Co., Inc.

Today Press
See Grosset & Dunlap, Inc.

Troll Associates
320 Route 17
Mahwah, N.J. 07430
201-529-4000
Troll Talking Picture Dictionary

Two Continents Publishing Group, Ltd.
30 E. 42 St.
New York, N.Y. 10017
212-661-7520
Chambers Twentieth Century Dictionary
Dixie-Doodle Dictionary

Frederick Ungar Publishing Co., Inc.
250 Park Ave. S.
New York, N.Y. 10003
212-GR3-7885
English Language in America

U.S. Government Printing Office
Superintendent of Documents
Washington, D.C. 20401
202-275-2051
Style Manual

University Books, Inc.
See Lyle Stuart, Inc.

University of Chicago Press
5801 Ellis Ave.
Chicago, Ill. 60637
312-753-3344
Americanisms

Dictionary of American English
Dictionary of Americanisms
A Manual for Writers
A Manual of Style
Student's Guide for Writing College Papers

University of Texas Press
Box 7819
University Sta.
Austin, Tex. 78712
512-471-7233
Boontling

Van Nostrand Reinhold Co. (a division of Litton Educational Publishing, Inc., Litton Industries)
450 W. 33 St.
New York, N.Y. 10001
212-594-8660
Comparative Study of Spelling (Hardscrabble Press)
Handbook of American English Spelling (Trade Edition)
I Hear America Talking

Vantage Press
516 W. 34 St.
New York, N.Y. 10001
212-736-1767
Rhyming Dictionary

Warner Books, Inc.
75 Rockefeller Plaza
New York, N.Y. 10019
212-484-8630
Heavens to Betsy! (paper)
Modern American Usage (paper)
New York Times Crossword Puzzle Dictionary (paper)
Thereby Hangs a Tale (paper)

Franklin Watts, Inc. (a subsidiary of Grolier, Inc.)
845 Third Ave.
New York, N.Y. 10022
212-757-4050
Instant Spelling Dictionary (Career Institute)
Instant Synonyms and Antonyms (Career Institute)

The Webster's Dictionary Co.
1775 Broadway
New York, N.Y. 10019

Living Webster Encyclopedic Dictionary

Western Publishing Co., Inc.
850 Third Ave.
New York, N.Y. 10022
212-753-8500
Courtis-Watters Illustrated Golden Dictionary
Golden Picture Dictionary
Little Golden Picture Dictionary
My First Golden Dictionary
New Golden Dictionary
Storybook Dictionary

Wilshire Book Co.
12015 Sherman Rd.
North Hollywood, Calif. 91605
213-875-1711
Songwriters' Rhyming Dictionary

H. W. Wilson Co.
950 University Ave.
Bronx, N.Y. 10452
212-588-8400
Dictionary of Foreign Phrases and Abbreviations

World Book-Childcraft International, Inc.
See Field Enterprises Educational Corp.

World Publishing Co.
See Larousse & Co., Inc.

The Writer, Inc.
8 Arlington St.
Boston, Mass. 02116
617-536-7420
Concise Dictionary of English Idioms
Concise Dictionary of English Slang
Preparing the Manuscript
Writer's Book of Synonyms and Antonyms
Writer's Rhyming Dictionary

Xerox Family Education Services
See Grosset & Dunlap, Inc.

Zondervan Publishing House
1415 Lake Dr., S.E.
Grand Rapids, Mich. 49506
616-459-6900
Zondervan Manual of Style

TITLE-AUTHOR-SUBJECT INDEX

Dictionaries and wordbooks profiled in the *Buying Guide* are set in **boldface** type. Chief dictionary editors, compilers, and authors are cited in the index, along with all authorities quoted in the *Buying Guide*.